SMASHMOUTH

SMASHMOUTH

*Two Years in the Gutter with Al Gore
and George W. Bush—Notes from the
2000 Campaign Trail*

DANA MILBANK

BASIC
BOOKS

A Member of the Perseus Book Group

Published by Basic Books
A Member of the Perseus Books Group

Chapters of the manuscript have been adapted from articles previously
published in *The New Republic* and *The Washington Post*.

A Cataloging-in-Publication record is available from the Library of Congress.
ISBN 0-465-04590-1

01 02 03 04 / 10 9 8 7 6 5 4 3 2 1

Contents

Preface

I write this from a dreary hotel room in the Tallahassee Radisson. This is not how the 2000 presidential election was supposed to end. I was to be in Argentina by now, exploring the wilds of Patagonia and strolling the boulevards of Buenos Aires.

Instead, I have become a war correspondent. "Coup d'etat," is how New York Democratic Rep. Greg Meeks describes the situation here. "A theft in progress," is House GOP Whip Tom DeLay's description. New York Democratic Rep. Jerry Nadler smells a "whiff of fascism" in the air, while Republican bon vivant Bill Bennett decries Democratic "thug tactics." No wonder Charlie Rangel, would-be Ways and Means Committee chairman if the Democrats took control of the House, jokes that he might get a gun.

Al Gore himself complains of "organized intimidation" of Miami elections officials, while his spokesman savages the duly elected secretary of state of Florida as a "commissar" and a "lackey." The Bush side disparages Florida's highest court and accuses Gore of declaring war on the military. All that's left is for George W. Bush to lead a squadron of the Texas Air National Guard into town.

This is all cause of much consternation for the good-government types, who wonder if the presidency is forever sullied and debased. But they are wrong. Americans, for once, are engaged in—and fascinated by—politics. To me, this is a fitting climax to a campaign that celebrated the virtue of tough, nasty, smashmouth politics.

This is a treatise on political toilet humor. These pages contain an exclusive account of Muffie, the dog who soiled Al Gore's pant leg in New Hampshire, and the story of how Gore introduced frozen bull semen to the Iowa electorate. You'll learn why Gore slept around with public school teachers, why he wore tight underwear during his announcement speech and why he fired a pollster who kept his bathroom messy. You'll meet the Gore adviser who snored loudest, and you'll spend time alone in a closet with Gore's second-born daughter.

a hotel in Beverly Hills, where Larry Flynt attends a party to tease the candidacy of Warren Beatty, described at the event by Roseanne as a "nice piece of ass."

See? I can't keep my mind out of the gutter. And this is as it should be. For the purpose of this book is to celebrate the virtues of good, solid, in-the-gutter campaigning. Such nasty, smashmouth politics are said by the goody-goodies to be destroying our democracy, alienating the electorate and suppressing voter participation. I believe the opposite is true: that nasty is nice on the campaign trail, that it's cool to be cruel.

Contrary to everything you hear and read, presidential campaigns are not getting more negative or nastier. Even if they were, there's evidence that negativity doesn't necessarily hurt turnout or increase cynicism, as the righteous have claimed. There's even reason to believe that tough, negative campaigning helps strengthen our leaders, boost creativity in policy-making and bring reform to government.

Time after time during the 2000 campaign, the candidates did their best, and attracted the most public enthusiasm, when they were sounding their toughest attacks: Gore knocking off Bradley in contentious debates, Bush turning back McCain in a nasty South Carolina fight, Gore gaining ground by staging a tough-talking convention after Bush's soft-and-fuzzy show in Philadelphia, and Bush regaining his footing by making an issue of Gore's character. For both men, periods of soft-focus themes and gauzy photo-ops tended to end with plummeting poll numbers.

Our problem is not negative campaigning but an increasingly puritanical press that often makes no distinction between negative comparisons (which are common and useful) and gratuitous personal attacks (which are harmful but rare). The result is that journalists are the ones poisoning public opinion and injecting cynicism into the electorate by making people think politics is much uglier than it is.

Implicit in the media coverage is an assumption that we've turned our backs on some golden era of high-minded campaigning. But when, precisely, was that age? Was it before Thomas Jefferson's opponents called him "a mean-spirited low-lived fellow, the son of a half-breed Indian squaw"? Or was it after the pols called Abe Lincoln (who engaged in many nasty attacks against Stephen Douglas during the 1858 Senate campaign debates) "the original gorilla" and mocked his "hideous apelike form"?

It is time for us to admit that negative can be positive for the body politic. A study by academics from Rutgers and George Washington universities turned on its head the conventional wisdom that negative ads depress turnout. "We uncovered little evidence to warrant the fears," the researchers reported. Of course, shrill attacks and utterly baseless charges of the liar-liar-pants-on-fire variety can turn off voters. But at the same time, campaigns heavy with substantive criticism can increase enthusiasm.

The 2000 campaign benefited from the employment of two smash-mouth specialists, Gore adviser Bob Shrum and Republican Alex Castellanos, who made the party's ads in support of Bush. "Politics without conflict," Castellanos says, "is the politics of the amoeba." And Shrum? "I agree with him."

Why? First, political campaigns are high-stakes, zero-sum games. This isn't Madison Avenue, where a growing market helps all competitors. Politics isn't about getting another point or two of market share; it's winner take all. Presidents govern not just the people who voted for them, but those who didn't, too.

Second, tough and negative campaigns allow candidates to demonstrate and build leadership qualities. Governing is full of choices between clashing, sometimes irreconcilable ideas. Negotiating with Congress, not to mention dealing with China or Iraq, requires tough stuff. What's wrong with testing a candidate in the election process to see if he or she has what it takes?

Third, tough and negative campaigns can actually increase voter interest and participation. Conflict, after all, is part of human nature; more people watch wrestling than ballet. If Americans don't see the true differences between candidates, some voters won't feel a personal stake in the election, and they won't go to the polls.

It's time to stop equating the negative with the bad. There's a huge difference between purposeful comparisons and frivolous attacks. What matters is not whether a campaign claim is positive or negative, but whether the claim is relevant. Let the candidates fight it out. Candidates who cross the line tend to be punished. Voters are smart enough to distinguish between fair criticism and unfair abuse.

Republicans like to distribute a 1991 Gore quote that says a presidential candidate should "rip the lungs out of anybody else who's in the race." They want us to disapprove of Gore as a master of the negative. But one person who won't criticize Democrat Gore for that statement is the GOP's Castellanos. "I don't have a problem with that," he says. Neither should we.

Uh-oh. This sounds like heavy stuff. But fear not: this is no political science textbook. It is a tour through the 2000 presidential campaign, from its early days in the fall of 1998 to its climactic end, two years later, on November 7. But it is not about the stuff you read in the news columns. It's about the human comedy that unfolds behind the news. I watched the campaign from a perspective rarely allowed reporters because of deadline and editorial constraints. On primary night in New Hampshire, I was in John McCain's private hotel suite, sipping a bourbon and watching him celebrate victory with friends and family. I was with Bill Bradley early in the campaign at Notre Dame when he put the school's president emeritus, Father Theodore Hesburgh, to sleep with his lecture; 18 months later, I was with Bradley during his collapse, when he wondered if he'd have to rob a bank to get attention.

When Bill Daley, just named Gore campaign chairman, attempted a Full Ginsburg—appearances on all five Sunday talk shows—I was there when the Fox security guard wouldn't let him in the building because he'd forgotten his I.D. I stalked House Minority Leader Tom DeLay on a golf course during the Republican National Convention, and I watched Tipper Gore surf in the aisle of a NASA jet during takeoff. I saw fisticuffs between Gore and Bradley supporters, listened to Gore perform a rap, and successfully predicted the naming of Dick Cheney and Joe Lieberman as vice presidential candidates. (OK, so my veep predictions about John Travolta and Strom Thurmond were less accurate.)

You will find, in addition to the smashmouth theme, various subthemes that are as frivolous as they are irrelevant. One is the recurring attention to food on the campaign trail: the Gore aide who puts zucchinis in his colleagues' luggage, a food fight between McCain staff and reporters in a South Carolina restaurant, Gary Bauer's unfortunate tumble during a New Hampshire pancake flip and Ralph Nader's presence at a vegan fundraiser. I predicted the results of the GOP's straw poll in Ames, Iowa, by measuring the pounds of barbecue served by each candidate; to gauge general-election results, I reviewed the press food on both the Bush and Gore campaigns.

Another recurring irrelevancy contained herein is transportation. I explored the logistics of Gore's 29-vehicle motorcade making a stop at a Dairy Queen in Iowa. I joined Orrin Hatch driving through a blizzard in a vain attempt to galvanize the chiropractic vote. I risked life and limb to travel on Bush's charter plane, *Miami Air*, which treated passengers to bad landings, broken equipment and a fire on board. Far preferable was Donald Trump's 727, and the subsequent bus ride in which a Yorkshire terrier named Pee Wee got loose. Speaking of terriers, there's also the obligatory tour of George W.'s adventures in language, which caused tariffs and barriers to become terriers and bariffs, missile launches to become mential losses, Slovenia to become Slovakia, and mysterious Grecians, Kosovians and East Timorians to appear without warning.

Perhaps the most pervasive subtheme, though, is the prevalence of odd characters: a presidential candidate who levitates, one who dresses up as a lobster, and a fellow running on the ticket of Mike's Party. Bob Jones gets a mention, of course, but more compelling is the uprising of one Reverend

Garlic at a Bush event in New Jersey. There's also the Forbes campaign adviser who models his strategy on Hamas, and investors who buy and sell candidates on a political futures market. But the strangest of all are the candidates themselves. Would McCain have won New Hampshire if voters had known he carried with him a lucky compass, lucky feather, lucky pen, lucky rock, lucky shoes and lucky imaginary reptile known as the Spring Hill Lizard?

These are the tough questions. Fortunately, I have not been alone in my quest for the answers. I'm grateful to the capable Vanessa Mobley of Basic Books for getting this project done, and to Tim Bartlett for getting it started. The wily Rafe Sagalyn came up with the title and favored me with his wry insight. I'm in debt to Marty Peretz and Chuck Lane for bringing me to the *New Republic*, and to my editors and colleagues at the magazine for helping me to craft the "Campaign Journal," which launched this book. At the *Washington Post*, which I joined at the beginning of 2000, Steve Reiss, Maralee Schwartz and Steve Luxenberg skillfully edited the stories that form the backbone of this book. I'm also grateful to Gene Robinson, Deborah Heard, Bill Hamilton, Jackson Diehl and Liz Spayd for allowing me to make the *Post* my home.

Friends and family tolerated (or perhaps enjoyed) my frequent absences. In particular, I owe much to the influence of my grandfather and mentor, Howard Schulman; though he died before I began this project, he had much to do with its completion. Finally, not a word of my election coverage could have been written without the help of my wife, Donna DePasquale, to whom this book is dedicated. She is not only my dearest friend but my toughest and most trusted editor. Many a night over the past two years, I protested when she directed me to strike a beloved phrase. In every case, she was right.

SMASHMOUTH

Part I

★ ☆ ★

THE FALL OF MR. NICE GUY
AL GORE

1

★ ☆ ★

JugGoreNaut

Al Gore is about seven miles above the desert of the Southwest, in the brand-new Boeing 757 that serves as Air Force Two. It's an impressive machine, with televisions plotting the jet's progress, business-class leather chairs for everybody, an office and bed for Al and Tipper, and a steady stream of food and drink served on china. Wherever it lands, it commands a motorcade and a swarm of dignitaries and press.

It's a week before the midterm elections in October 1998, and Gore is flying at least as high as his new machine. All signs point to an unprecedented gain of seats for the Democrats, and Gore is returning from a California trip during which he raised money for the party and collected chits from the state's Democrat hierarchy. His own race for the presidency will start in a couple of months, and from the way it looks now, he might not even have an opponent for the Democratic nomination. The JugGoreNaut, as I call it, cannot be stopped. And Gore is feeling mighty pleased with himself.

"I see you're talking to my brain," he tells me as he strolls the aisle of Air Force Two. I stand to greet him but he waves me back into my seat. "Sorry to interrupt," he says, and continues on. The situation is absurd; like every other reporter, I've come on the trip for just such a moment with Gore, but instead I wind up with a bald strategist from Dorchester known to Gore as the Brain.

Not that I'm complaining. The Brain is a chain-smoking, foul-mouthed, street-smart Democratic operative named Michael Whouley, who helped to get John Kerry into the U.S. Senate and Bill Clinton into the White House. Right now he's about to start on his newest project, the election of the still-undeclared Democratic candidate for president. And he's offered to map out Gore's primary strategy for me on the back of a piece of letterhead from his consulting firm, the Dewey Square group.

At the top of the page Whouley scribbles "*Feb '99*," the start of the campaign, and after that the goal: "*Nomination*." The trick, he says, is simple: "To win it quick enough that it's worth having." Next, down the left side of the page, the Brain lists the campaign components: "*Message*," "*Organization*," and "*$*." Down the right side of the page, he creates a second column, titled "*X-Factors*." Here there are two: "*Economy*" and a catch-all category called "*Fuckup*," one at which Gore can be particularly adept. The idea is to get the message, organization, and money strong enough that the campaign can withstand even a barrage of X-factors.

Whouley lists message first, which seems obvious. It's hard to run a campaign without a message. Yet, at least for now, Gore is basically doing just that. Though his policy shop is stirring a message brew to be sampled later, Gore's campaign theme, at the moment, is essentially a show of force. The machine is the message. The JugGoreNaut, with its overwhelming domination of Democratic fund-raising, strategists, party officials, and activists, makes any primary assault on Gore seem foolhardy.

Ominously, there are signs of complacency among Gore's top advisers. Bob Squier, his old friend and media expert, tells me, surprisingly, that Gore needn't introduce any specific proposals. "It's enough to say, 'Here's what I do already,'" he says. But that's a dangerous way to think.

But Michael Whouley is the one guy determined not to let such complacency take hold. He's already talking about how to cope with a loss in Iowa or New Hampshire. "If we lose at first, it becomes World War I, a delegate race, winning through attrition," he says. "If we lose in New Hampshire, we regroup in California and then go south to Florida and Texas and we're recovered." But this much is clear, at least to the Brain: "We've got to be prepared to fight in the long run. . . . We can muddle through and still win the nomination, but we'll be bloodied." And bloody is no way to face George W. Bush, who led Gore by 55.7 percent to 34.3 percent in a recent Zogby International poll.

Whouley's—and Gore's—first task is to get rid of Whouley's old mentor, Massachusetts Senator John Kerry. The man is potentially Gore's toughest rival for the Democratic nomination. Nebraska Senator Bob Kerrey, one potential challenger, has already decided against a run after a typical bout of indecision. Dick Gephardt has been telling confidants he won't run and has been doing little of the necessary homework to launch a campaign; he wants to be Speaker of the House.

Kerry worries Gore the most. He's a Vietnam hero, smart, good-looking, a favorite son in New Hampshire—and he could use his wife Teresa Heinz's fortune for a presidential race. Kerry also has the ability to take from Gore the Clintonian moderates who favor reform. Already, he has staked a controversial claim as an education reformer, much as Clinton did with welfare in 1992. In twin speeches delivered recently in Boston and Washington, Kerry ostentatiously defied the teachers' unions, his long-time friends, declaring that "we must end teacher tenure as we know it" and proposing "to make every public school in this country essentially a charter school."

But while Kerry has the money and a reform agenda that trumps Gore's, he lacks anything near the infrastructure and name recognition of the front-runner. Kerry also doesn't have Whouley, who was Kerry's field director in his 1982 lieutenant governor's race. As Kerry begins to con-template a presidential run, Whouley visits his old boss to tell him that he was going with Gore. Not long after, Kerry decides against a challenge to Gore. And the man from Dorchester has at least something to do with it. "I would not have enjoyed running against Whouley," Kerry says. "I definitely want him in my foxhole."

At the moment, it's feeling fairly secure in Gore's foxhole. With his most formidable competitors out of the race, he's faced with challenges from Minnesota Senator Paul Wellstone, who doesn't have much more than the short professor vote, and former Senator Bill Bradley, whom the Gore campaign does not fear, at least not yet. A December NBC News/Wall Street Journal poll showed Gore leading Bradley 49 percent to 12 percent.

★ ☆ ★

Sure, I had been warned: a Bill Bradley speech could be something less than electrifying. Still, I am not quite prepared for what happens when the aspiring presidential candidate takes the podium at the University of Notre Dame one night late in the fall of 1998.

His lecture is titled "Meaning in American Politics," but it might have been better titled "Dreaming in American Politics," for it proves a power-ful soporific. As Bradley stands with his glasses low on his nose, a red neck-tie not quite covering his lengthy torso, he reads straight from his prepared text in a slow drone. After ten minutes, many of his three hundred listeners begin to rest their heads in their hands; after twenty minutes, several are slouching in their seats. After half an hour, a guy in front of me in a Notre Dame jacket falls asleep, his head hitting his chest, bouncing up, and hitting his chest again. I look down the row and find several others in various states of repose. The university's venerable president emeritus, Father Hesburgh, who is sitting next to me, emits what sounds very much like a snore.

Oblivious, Bradley drones on, about how "capital follows knowledge" and how "we can reclaim the public sector as a venue for the source of our fulfillment." Bradley roams from religion to income inequality, from Edmund Burke to Virginia Woolfe. After forty-five minutes, it begins to sound like a filibuster. Bradley waves his right hand in a continuous circle. Is it a hypnoic gesture? Is there enough oxygen in the room? I am growing sleepy. Sleepy. Sleepy. Fortunately, Father Hesburgh snores again, breaking the spell.

"I was listening to everything he said—when I was awake," admits Tim Casale, the fellow in the Notre Dame jacket, when I confront him after the speech. Casale, a junior, is from New Jersey, and he wanted to see whether Bradley really sounded like the kind of guy who could challenge the vice president in 2000. "You look at the Democratic Party and you see Al Gore getting the nomination," Casale says. He's more convinced of that than ever after Bradley's talk. "He made a lot of interesting points, but nothing huge," Casale says. "It seemed there was something missing, like a spark."

That question, whether Bradley has the spark, is the central issue facing the candidate as he prepares for a presidential run. He has the resume, the policies and the instinct to mount a challenge to Gore, but does he have the fortitude? Can he bring himself down from his lofty heights to engage in a tough and nasty fight with Gore? Can he play smashmouth politics?

Bradley is again flirting with a presidential run, just as he flirted in '88, '92 and '96. This time, it appears, he's actually planning on doing it. With Gephardt declining to run, he's arguably the only Democratic candidate with a national stature that could rival Gore's. His famous resume can be recited by nearly everyone: basketball All-American at Princeton, captain of the 1964 Olympic basketball team, Rhodes Scholar, Hall-of-Famer who led the Knicks to two NBA championships before getting himself elected to the U.S. Senate on his first run for office in 1978. His attraction now is he's the un-Clinton: straight as an arrow, earnestly bookish, squeaky clean.

And boring. Bradley has developed a reputation for being one of the most cerebral and remote figures in American politics, a man not of the people, but above the people. Americans will indeed be looking for an honest man like Bradley to replace the shifty Clinton. But when they get a glimpse of the clean and good Bradley on the campaign trail, they may decide a rascal like Clinton isn't such a bad thing, after all. Ideologically, Bradley is little different from the Democrats' standard-bearer, Gore; stylistically, he is even more plodding. Bradley stands a chance if Gore stumbles in a campaign finance scandal or an economic downturn. But after Clinton's resurgence in November's midterm elections, Gore, as the heir-apparent to a popular president, appears invincible.

"People always said I would pick the time when it was hardest to do," Bradley told an audience recently. "We may be approaching that time."

All signs are that Bradley wants to run. Officially, he says he will decide by January whether he and his wife "want to jump off a 50-story building," as he puts it. But Bradley is being less coy than usual, and his friends and advisers are putting out the word that he'll do it. "It certainly seems like it," says Marcia Aronoff, his staff chief for 12 years in the Senate. "He's serious about it," says Ed Turlington, who runs Bradley's three-person office now.

The ever-cosmic Bradley himself, in an interview, says he is searching to see whether his "ability matches the moment." Gore's commanding lead, he insists, has nothing to do with his decision. "The only given in politics is whatever you think will happen won't happen," he says. "You don't make this kind of life decision on a tactical basis. It's an internal issue not related to external dynamics." In a sense, that seems absurd: How can a man prepare to run for the presidency without considering "external dynamics" such as whether or not he actually has a chance? But in another sense, this is genuine Bradley—and it explains much about his candidacies and noncandidacies. He is listening to an inner voice, and he will do whatever that inner voice tells him to do, no matter what anybody else thinks.

The inner voice told him not to run in '88 and '92 when everybody was begging him to run; now it seems to be telling him to run at a time when nobody is asking him to. This is the politics of self-absorption: the candidacy is about Bill Bradley, not about America. A presidential run is the only missing credential on an otherwise perfect resume. "Ever write your own eulogy, the perfect eulogy you'd like your friend to read at your funeral, to see if you're living up to it?" Bradley asks during his Notre Dame speech. Then he offers a favorite quotation: "The tragedy is to die with commitments undefined, convictions undeclared and service unfulfilled." The next day, I ask Bradley whether that quotation represents a bit of self-reflection for him. "It certainly resonates with me," he tells me. "The commitment and the convictions are there. The question is whether the service is fulfilled."

It's also not clear whether Bradley can muster the mechanics of a presidential run. The only real threat to Gore is a big bank account, and Bradley doesn't have one. He hasn't raised any serious money since 1990, and it was widely reported that he was having trouble raising funds for his '96 reelection to the Senate. His PAC (political action committee), called Time Future, handed out $81,000 this year through mid-October; Gore's PAC, by contrast, contributed nearly $1.3 million to Democratic candidates this year. Bradley, to his credit, is a fierce advocate of campaign finance reform, but this could limit his ability to raise the $10 to $25 million in funds he needs to run.

Bradley doesn't exactly dazzle on the campaign trail. He seems to take some pride in his public-speaking troubles. In his 1996 memoir, *Time Present, Time Past,* he cited a description of his 1992 Democratic convention speech as "by far, the most wooden speech of the evening. . . . The expressions of his face were clownishly inappropriate, as if someone else, not he, were controlling them." After six years of speeches, little has changed. At the Notre Dame speech, he appears alternately dyspeptic and tongue-tied, stumbling twice on the phrase "pretty penny pincher," making a phony spitting sound, then trying the phrase again. But Bradley's problem is not strictly oral; he has a way of showing disdain for voters' concerns if they don't match his own. In 1990, he almost lost his reelection bid when he refused to say what he thought of Governor Jim Florio's tax increase, even though voters were demanding his opinion. Bradley came across as arrogant and evasive, and barely beat the then-unknown Christine Todd Whitman. "I got the message," Bradley declared in a news conference after the election. But even then he refused to answer the question.

While many question Bradley's viability as a candidate, few doubt he's a man of conviction and substance. He spent thankless years in the Senate devoting himself to arcane issues such as strategic petroleum reserves and tax reform. He also made himself an expert on Russia and trade policy. He is perhaps the party's best spokesman on race, in part an outgrowth of his basketball experience, and he has also been a leading voice in the civil-society movement, which encourages nongovernmental groups to assume a greater role. In many matters he aligns himself with the reform-minded, New Democratic wing of the party; he favors a muscular foreign policy and free trade. And when it comes to personal behavior, the man is clearly no Clinton: Bradley would never have an "inappropriate relationship" with his interns; he probably wouldn't be able to pick them out of a lineup.

But for all his depth and decency, Bradley will be hard pressed to convince people that his ideas are somehow different from Gore's. The vice president long ago established himself as the party expert in technology, the environment and the New Economy—ideas upon which any Bradley campaign would be based. Also, Bradley's record in the Senate was deliberative to the point of squishiness. In the 1980s, he campaigned against aid to the Nicaraguan Contras, then decided to support it, then changed his mind again. In 1990, despite his hawkish reputation on foreign policy, he publicly criticized President George Bush for giving up too soon on sanctions against Iraq, and he later voted against authorizing military action against Iraq. Even Bradley loyalists say there's not much room between his philosophy and Gore's. "In terms of issues, most people would think they're pretty much the same," says Rick Wright, a businessman and longtime friend who played basketball with Bradley at Princeton.

What, then, is the message? Bradley acknowledges his policies are similar to Gore's. "A lot of time it isn't what you say but how it's received," he says. In other words, it's less about the message than the messenger. Already, Bradley has been aiming for the high ground in 2000 by knocking Clinton, something Gore can't do. "The presidency is only a potential," he says at Notre Dame. "It can be grand . . . or it can be less grand, as it has been from time to time," he adds with a smirk. "Could the presidency ever be the same after this? Absolutely. Every president can fill the office. It's fluid and open for whoever is next."

Another angle Bradley may try against Gore is that of outsider. Bradley, since leaving the Senate, has spent the last two years in a number of strategic positions: a teaching job at Stanford (where he courted Silicon Valley), an advisory position at J. P. Morgan & Co. (where he wooed Wall Street), a stint as commentator for CBS News (which maintained his visibility) and now a teaching job at Notre Dame (from which he can collect Chicago money). It wasn't long ago that Bradley, announcing his departure from the Senate, famously declared that "politics is broken." Politics is still broken, but Bradley now sees himself as fixer. "To say the system is broken without trying to change it is irresponsible," he says. Politics "is not beyond being able to fix. It starts with a politician who is true to his convictions." Hmmm, wonder who that might be.

Bradley has often said he set four criteria for himself when deciding on the 1988 race. He required a deep, "novelistic" sense of the country, a foreign policy not learned from briefing books, a team that could win and govern, and an ability to communicate with voters. "I looked in the mirror and said I wasn't there, so I didn't do it," Bradley says now. In 1992, "I was ready but something in me said don't do it." In that case, he was lucky: his wife developed breast cancer that year. Now, his wife is well and his daughter has gone off to college, and this time, he says, "the four criteria are met." Still, he tells me he now has a fifth consideration, deciding whether he can "most effectively lead the country at this moment."

His decision-making has a mysterious, almost mystical quality. "It's a kind of subconscious pattern," says Wright, who likens it to the philosopher Kierkegaard's leap of faith. Why didn't Bradley run before? "I don't think even he knows," Wright says. Bradley is inarguably the only presidential candidate who makes decisions like a nineteenth-century philosopher.

But if his decision-making is other worldly, Bradley's preparations for 2000 have been conventional. First is the obligatory campaign book. Bradley once resisted using his basketball superstar status in politics, but now he consciously links the two. The book, *Values of the Game*, has a basketball on the front, a photo of young Bradley in uniform on the back, and a foreword by coach Phil Jackson. No longer Senator Tax Policy, he's once again Dollar Bill, drawing an unbroken line between himself and Michael Jordan, Magic Johnson, even bad boy Dennis Rodman.

The book is about life lessons drawn from sports, and about the author's successful use of such lessons. "In the U.S. Senate, along the campaign trail, or in any number of projects I became involved with after Princeton, it was the same story," he writes. "I was determined that no one would outwork me." Even in retirement, Bradley continues an almost manic work ethic. At a book signing in South Bend, the manager in the Barnes & Noble wants him to sign a few stock copies, but Bradley, beckoning to a pile of a couple hundred books, declares to the surprised workers, "Let's get 'em all done." It was a bit like a free-throw practice; the bookstore staff would open and pass the books in an assembly line, and Bradley would sign. "We're a team!" he cheered.

Bradley is using his current role as a lecturer at Notre Dame, like his earlier gig at Stanford, to polish a presidential message. His syllabus for the seminar he's teaching at Notre Dame requires "a four-page paper for Senator Bradley which addresses . . . what they believe a presidential candidate in the year 2000 should address both as candidate and president." "He's testing the waters with us for a possible presidential run," says Mary Beth Lasseter, a student in the seminar. "He wants to see how it plays with the youth, or so we've been told."

Bradley's reception in South Bend hasn't been altogether presidential. Anti-abortion activists have protested his presence at the Catholic school, even flying a banner over a Notre Dame football game urging "Drop Senator Bradley." The protests have caused Bradley to move about campus with a plainclothes policeman and to keep his whereabouts confidential. Nor is everybody lining up to see the six-foot-five superstar. At the Barnes & Noble book signing, only about fifty people come, an unusually low turnout for the store. "I guess noon is not a good time," Bradley says when the crowd disappears before his one-hour signing is over.

Bradley gets a much better reception in his home base of northern New Jersey, where I also follow him around for a day. If New Jersey were America, President Bradley could start planning his inaugural. When he arrives at a breakfast in West Orange, he gets spontaneous applause when he walks in the door and a standing ovation after he speaks. He is introduced by State Senate Minority Leader Richard Codey, who in the past called him "Abe Lincoln with a jump shot," and who this time declares that Bradley is "warming up" for a presidential run. The Essex County Democratic chairman, Thomas Giblin, is showing off a "Bill Bradley for

President 2000" button, which he made himself. "I appreciate that," Bradley says to Giblin. "I really do." The reception is much the same for Bradley later in the morning at a festival in Cliffside Park, where a local sheriff candidate calls Bradley "the next president of the United States" and someone else greets him as "Mr. President."

But, of course, northern New Jersey is not America. And even in Jersey there is the occasional reminder that reality will likely intrude on Bradley's presidential ambitions. Doug Bern, a candidate for Bergen County freeholder and one of the Democrats for whom Bradley is campaigning in Cliffise Park, lets it slip that he "wouldn't be a Bradley man" in 2000. "I don't know if he has the fortitude to do it," says Bern, noting that Bradley "left us in the lurch" when he fled politics in 1996. "He missed his wave," Bern says, as Bradley works the crowd. "Sure, he's Mr. Clean. He's a good man. But Americans care about job performance, not character, and that's how it should be. Guys like Gore and Gephardt stayed in there and did the heavy lifting. I'd go with somebody who stayed in there, like Gore."

That question, about Bradley's willingness to mix it up in the rough-and-tumble world of presidential politics, will be his greatest obstacle on the campaign trail. "He's the Meg Greenfield, *Lehrer Newshour* choice," says one Democratic operative. "He doesn't want to get his hands dirty." *Time* magazine quoted a former Bradley aide as saying, "Bill wants very much to be president. But he doesn't particularly want to run for president." I ask Bradley about that line. "Whoever said that hasn't seen me campaign," he protests. "Campaigning is like playing basketball. It's full of joy, it's unscripted, it's unknown, it's invogorating." And if the campaign lowers him to the gutter, so be it. "You have to go with your convictions, and if your convictions put you in the pit that's where you have to be."

Bradley says he's ready to descend into the pit; whether or not that's true will take some time to learn.

Back in the JugGoreNaut, there are few worries about Bradley. The campaign begins in earnest minutes after the polls close on November 3, 1998. The phones have begun to ring in New Hampshire; it's the vice president on the line, and he wants to talk to New Hampshire Democrats. All of them. He calls state Senator Sylvia Larson, who at first thinks it's a practical joke. "He knew my husband's name and the names of both of my children," she marvels. He calls Democrats elected to the state House. "One person took out the tape on her answering machine so she could keep playing it back to her grandchildren," reports Anita Freedman, the Portsmouth Democratic chairwoman. Gore speaks to about two-hundred people in 24 hours, and he leaves answering-machine messages for hundreds more. Then, he asks his weary staff for more phone numbers. "We were going to give him the New Hampshire phone book," says one aide, Michael Feldman.

Gore dials on. He rings the number for Greg Martin of Keene, congratulating him on his reelection to the county commission. "Having the vice president of the United States call me at home the day after my election to a part-time job, I'd say he's pretty aggressive," says Martin, who, with a horde of other New Hampshire Democrats, also is on the list for an invitation to a Christmas party at Gore's official residence. "It emphasized how important this is for him." Gore, of course, isn't dialing for fun; he figures the phone calls and the party invitations will win him the crucial support of Democratic activists like Martin in New Hampshire's first-in-the-nation primary a year from now. And he's probably right. "They've made me more of a Gore person," says Martin, who backed Gephardt in '88 but now pledges his support to the vice president. "I'd be very surprised if anybody could really give him a run for his money."

That's the picture emerging at the start of Gore's 2000 presidential campaign. Gore, who formally begins his quest on New Year's Eve, has an overwhelming advantage in his pursuit of his party's nomination. Using the trappings of his office and the power of incumbency, he has established himself as the heir to a president who, even in impeachment, remains hugely popular among Democratic primary voters.

Even the front-loaded 2000 primary calendar favors the JugGore-Naut. In 2000, the two giants, New York and California, will come immediately on the heels of Iowa and New Hampshire, which means, as one Gore adviser put it, "You've got to be on New York and California TV before you know if you've won New Hampshire." This obviously benefits Gore, who aims to raise $35 million by December 1999. Democratic donors are few enough that a second candidate is unlikely to reach the limit; Bradley, by contrast, told me he thinks he could do a campaign on $10 million to $12 million. If he's serious about spending so little, the whole race could be over after the first week of March.

There is, however, a danger in the JugGoreNaut strategy. By trying to nail down support from such a broad spectrum of Democratic constituencies, Gore could spread himself too thin and allow himself to drift ideologically to the left, making him a less promising general-election candidate. Similar problems hurt Walter Mondale in '84 and George Bush in '88, when complacency about their front-runner status and the lack of a clear message made them vulnerable to challenges from Gary Hart and Pat

Robertson, respectively. Now, some Democrats worry that Gore is repeating that mistake by pandering to labor, black groups, feminists, and environmentalists. "He tells them exactly what they want to hear," says one Democrat from the Democratic Leadership Council, the party's centrist caucus. Clinton in '92 defied some interest groups, taking on teachers' unions for opposing testing and making an issue of a black rap artist's divisive remarks. But Gore has been all caution—putting him in danger of falling into the Mondale trap.

The message of Gore 2000, its architects say, will be Clinton II—which points to both the central strength and weakness of the campaign. He is, for better or worse, establishing himself as the incumbent. "The question is not how he's going to track an entirely new course," says Marla Romash, a Gore communications consultant. "It's how I've made a difference in your life, and how the Clinton administration has made a difference in your life." Now, that message seems right. With Clinton's popularity and the economy booming, and the machinery of incumbency on his side, Gore seems invincible. But, while Gore can ride the JugGoreNaut all the way to the Democratic convention in 2000, he eventually will need something more than a mighty machine to make it to the White House.

For now, though, campaign apparatus is what matters. And in that sense, at least, Gore seems unlikely to repeat the mistakes of Bush and Mondale. Taking nothing for granted, he's campaigning as fiercely as if he were the underdog. "It's going to be a dogfight," says one top Gore adviser. In '98, the vice president went to more than 200 campaign events in 38 states, including appearances in 41 of the 57 competitive House races and 14 of the 15 competitive gubernatorial races. And, judging by the JugGoreNaut's preparations in the four most important primary states— Iowa, New Hampshire, New York, and California—Gore doesn't suffer from front-runner complacency.

In Iowa, Gore became the first presidential candidate to take credit for moving pork *away* from the state. As Gore traveled from Washington to Iowa this fall, aides on Air Force Two passed out a new announcement Gore would make on the ground. The Clinton administration, just hours earlier, had reached an agreement with Argentina to open up its market to U.S. pork, meaning millions of dollars in sales for Iowa's 20,000 hog farmers. Gore had pushed the negotiations along for two weeks, and trade officials were furiously negotiating the night before the Iowa trip so Gore could announce a deal. Such is the power of incumbency. "He certainly opens up a lot of doors that way," said Norman Schmitt, head of the Iowa Pork Producers Association, after meeting Gore in Iowa.

A couple of years ago, David Yepsen, the *Des Moines Register*'s political reporter, wrote a story about whether Gore would repeat Bush's '88 mistakes: allowing himself to be swallowed by his security bubble, failing to keep up contacts, and taking Iowa for granted. After the piece ran, Yepsen got a call from Gore's spokeswoman, who said Gore had read it. "They understand what Bush did wrong in this state, and they're correcting it," Yepsen says. "They're not going to let a Democratic Pat Robertson sneak up on them."

In New Hampshire, Gore has methodically courted the state's party leaders. Larson, the state senator, figures she has spoken to the vice president twenty times already. He raised money for the Democratic candidates for the state legislature this year, and she attended Gore's Christmas party in Washington. Now, she's for Gore. "I don't think there's been as dominant a situation as this," Larson says. "Mondale had the ability to do it, but he didn't have the same network of people. There's a lot more human-contact feeling from Gore."

Of the two hundred or so key Democratic activists in New Hampshire, Gore aides claim they have commitments from more than half, even more than the incumbent Clinton had gathered at this stage in the '96 campaign. Karen Brown, news director at ABC affiliate WMUR in Manchester, the state's most powerful media outlet, doesn't argue with the Gore claim: "They've done a great job of getting in here early and getting those commitments. It's going to be tough for a Bill Bradley or a John Kerry to come up with enough Democratic activists." And Brown has been wooed herself: she had three extensive interviews with the vice president in 1998.

In New York, Gore recently entertained top Wall Street fund-raisers for two hours at the Sheraton Hotel in Manhattan. On another occasion, Gore did a fund-raiser for Chuck Schumer at the home of Jamie Dimon. Along the way, says Michael Schlein, an investment banker and Democratic fund-raiser, "they've really lined up a who's who of New York fund-raisers." Among the Wall Street Democrats for Gore are Dimon, Loews's Jonathan Tisch, Lazard Freres's Steven Rattner, hedge-fund investor Orin Kramer, Goldman Sachs boss Jon Corzine, and Cravath, Swaine & Moore partner Bob Joffe.

In Manhattan, Herman "Denny" Farrell, the Democratic leader for 19 years, committed to Gore when the vice president came to New York after the November election. Gore had worked hard for the endorsement, meeting with Farrell three times this past fall and inviting him to a party in Washington. "I feel like I've moved in next to him," says Farrell.

And California? Gore has been there 44 times since he became vice president, a dozen times last year alone. On a trip just before the election, for example, he announced that California would get $129 million as part of the new budget, allowing the state to hire 3,322 new teachers, a Clinton priority. This fall, Gore campaigned for candidates for U.S. Senate, House, governor, lieutenant governor, attorney general, treasurer, and the state legislature. Then, there's Hollywood. Gore is close to Disney Executive Vice President John Cook, and, at DreamWorks, "we will certainly be there with the vice president," says Corporate Affairs Chief Andy Spahn. Gore tries to compensate for his lack of celebrity friendships by talking policy. This fall, he helped Rob Reiner pass an early childhood development ballot initiative in California. Though Bradley and Kerry have ties to Hollywood, Reiner says Gore is "clearly in first position by a long shot, and I don't think anybody's even competing."

The JugGoreNaut's commanding presence extends nationwide. The mayors, for example, are already on board. Gore backers include Detroit's Dennis Archer, Chicago's Richard Daley, Kansas City's Emanuel Cleaver, Atlanta's Bill Campbell, Philadelphia's Edward Rendell, and Boston's Thomas Menino. Gore's campaign has also lined up the elite Democratic strategists, many of them Clinton veterans. Craig Smith, the outgoing White House political director, will manage the campaign; Peter Knight, who ran Clinton's '96 campaign, will direct Gore's fund-raising. Bob Squier, a longtime Gore backer, will oversee Gore's television campaign, while top Democratic operatives Whouley and Theresa Vilmain will plan strategy in New Hampshire and Iowa, respectively. The president's pollster, Mark Penn, is also tied to the vice president. Two Cabinet members, Housing Secretary Andrew Cuomo and Commerce Secretary William Daley, will also help.

Perhaps nowhere is the JugGoreNaut as dominant as in fund-raising. There are only so many big-time donors, and, if Gore wins them early, there won't be any funds left for Bradley et al. (This is less of a concern for John Kerry, who can spend his wife's fortune.) Democratic strategists figure there are about 31,000 Americans who give the maximum $1,000 to a Democratic candidate in a primary. "We're relatively confident we'll get twenty-five or twenty-six thousand of them," says one Gore money man. Gore aides hope to raise the maximum $35 million by December 1999. Gore fund-raisers plan to have the bulk of their work done in 90 days—the earliest ever for a presidential campaign and three to six months earlier than Clinton's in '96.

So what pitfalls—X-factors, as Whouley calls them—lie ahead? Gore was relatively free of mistakes in '98. True, he confused Michael Jordan with Michael Jackson and told a Minnesota crowd how the local Democrats would do the state of Missouri proud. But there was nothing of the magnitude of "no controlling legal authority" in '98—and Gore's campaign finance exposure, thanks to Janet Reno, is now slight. As for Clinton's impeachment, it might hurt in a general election, but during the primaries it can help. Clinton remains tremendously popular among Democrats, and core Democratic primary voters have made saving Clinton a favorite cause.

The X-factors will hit the campaign even harder if Gore were to come up empty on broad themes. And that's where the all-important Gore message comes in. If Gore can't convince Americans that he has big new ideas, he will be more vulnerable to the X-factors.

And, as anybody who has studied Gore's past knows, the X-factors are sure to come.

2

★ ☆ ★

The Wonk

Let us suppose you are driving to Dairy Queen for a chocolate sundae. The procedure is simple enough: you park your car, place your order, and eat your ice cream. But now let us suppose you are Al Gore. Here is how you procure the dessert:

You direct your 29-vehicle motorcade—two armored limousines, six vans, seven sedans, a dozen motorcycles, an ambulance, and a helicopter—to take you to the Dairy Queen. All 85 members of your entourage, including a bomb-sniffing dog and the man who carries the codes to launch nuclear missiles, descend on the ice cream shop. Police stop traffic, and security agents scurry about, speaking into microphones in their sleeves. As four photographers vie for position, you stroll to the counter to order your Chocolate Rock. Then you sit down to eat the confection and pretend not to notice that everybody in the place is staring at you.

That, at any rate, is what happens while I am traveling with the vice president in Des Moines, Iowa. Like his boss, Gore lives in a security bubble, isolated from the daily human interactions the rest of us have on the subway, at the mall or in a bar. Gore hasn't seen a hotel lobby in six years; he's whisked through kitchens, freight elevators, and windowless corridors leading to trash compactors. With luck, he's allowed to drive once a year, when he picks up the family Christmas tree.

This is no small matter for Gore. After too many macarena jokes—wanna see it again?—and gags about termites and stiffness, Gore has managed to, er, solidify his image as a wooden drone. As he struggles to find his voice on policy for the 2000 campaign and to step out of Clinton's shadow, he's hamstrung by the perception that he lacks anything resembling charisma. Even his attempts to get out of his shell are methodical and contrived.

To pierce his isolation, the vice president has assembled a group of what his advisers call his "real people," a collection of several dozen normal Americans he visits regularly just to chew the fat. The group is Gore's Joe Average board of advisers, a council of the common man—the equivalent, you might say, of Phil Gramm's Joe Average. He meets with these people when he travels, brings them to Washington, and calls them on the phone, sometimes retelling their stories on the stump.

To some, this may seem artificial coming from a man who lived in a bubble long before the Secret Service required him to—a man who, unlike his boss, lacks an innate feel for the common man. (As a senator's son, Gore was reared in a luxury hotel and a prep school far from the masses.) On the other hand, at least his motives seem genuine. The real people are not a focus group (there is nothing representative about them), and they don't exist primarily for p.r. value (the sessions are private). Gore says his real-people sessions are a revival of the three thousand town meetings he hosted in Tennessee when he was in Congress, "often in small general stores in remote crossroads communities." Gore, in his quest for what he calls "the human dimension," has abandoned the general-store spontaneity for closed-door meetings and scripted public forums, but with the same purpose. "It's one of the best parts of my job," Gore says.

I sat in on a real-people session in the veep's West Wing office a couple of weeks ago. There were eight specimens assembled in wingback chairs and couches, most of them real people Gore had met at school safety forums around the country. Gore, dipping a tea bag into a cup of hot water, had no particular agenda. They talked about Tipper's running injury, complained about the "gruesome" fare on cable television, reminisced about the Mickey Mouse Club, and lamented the decline of after-school activities. Gore recalled his time in the Glee Club and his fondness for his art teacher. He only wished, he told them, that he'd learned to play a musical instrument when he had been young. Gore held a serious pose, chin in hand, occasionally leaning forward in his chair and arching his eyebrows or narrowing his eyes to slits and unleashing a toothy smile.

Gore's foreign affairs adviser and other top staffers were waiting outside the room, and the vice president's secretary kept buzzing him. But Gore let the conversation ramble on for three-quarters of an hour. Affairs of state could wait; Gore seemed to be genuinely savoring the small talk. "You ever watch the Power Rangers?" he asked a fidgety young boy seated with his parents. But the boy wouldn't be distracted from his hand-held video game. When Gore finally ended the meeting, one of the real people rose to deliver an impromptu testimonial. "You're not plastic," she said, sounding a bit surprised at her discovery.

The real people come from all walks of life. One of the regulars is Joann Crowder, a former welfare recipient in Detroit who is now a supervisor in a car parts company. She describes Gore, whom she has met three times, as "my old friend Al." He met her in 1996 and mentioned her in a debate. He visited her again on a Detroit trip in 1997 and this spring invited her to another meeting in Detroit. They talk about everything from Red Wings hockey to her children's health insurance. Crowder is smitten. "You can tell he's a down-home country boy," she says. That is a distinction shared by very few former members of the St. Albans Glee Club.

Gore uses his real people not just to overcome his isolation but to put to rest any lingering concerns about his wooden image as he prepares for the 2000 campaign. In that sense, the real people are part of a broader effort to turn Analytical Al into Gregarious Gore, giving him real-life anecdotes to liven his speeches. Another source of these stories for Gore is something his staff calls the "reverse town-hall meeting." Invented last year, this format has become a staple of the Gore road show. Instead of a free-wheeling, Clinton-style town meeting, Gore does most of the talking, working with a stack of note cards referring him to various people who have been planted in the audience.

The meetings are essentially infomercials, but local TV stations carry them live; and they provide Gore with a constantly replenished source of real-people stories. Last week in Davenport, Iowa, for example, Gore hosted a forum on school modernization during which a principal talked about the rope-and pulley system needed to get equipment to the old school's sixth floor. Gore called aside the janitor after the session to elaborate. That afternoon, in Cedar Rapids, Gore told the story about the rope and pulley, adding a new part about the janitor's complaints of back pain. At the next stop, Gore again talked about the janitor with the bad back— this time adding that the janitor wanted a Democratic Congress so he could get a higher minimum wage. I half-expected to learn at the next speech that the janitor had been denied treatment by his HMO.

The reverse town-hall meetings, like the real-people sessions, are a bit unnatural. Throughout the meetings, Gore checks his note cards, then asks, "I wonder if there's anybody here . . ." Just such a person invariably rises. Last week in Davenport, the vice president was briefly flummoxed when one of the plants in the audience was slow to respond to his cue. "I was beginning to get worried," Gore said after the man rose. "Nobody was standing up."

The vice president still sometimes has trouble escaping his caste. Gore opened a recent union-hall rally in Illinois by saying: "Within three to four years we are going to have completed the Human Genome Project." More than once I've heard him plunge into a discussion of Moore's Law before a crowd that didn't seem to want to hear about it.

But Gore is developing more of a common touch—the main reason behind his improved performance on the stump this fall. Stories collected from his town-hall forums and real-people meetings form the core of his campaign speech. He inevitably recounts what aides call "The Dead Man Story," about a man who was resuscitated after his heart had stopped but whose HMO wouldn't pay the bill, saying it wasn't an emergency. "The man was dead," Gore bellows, as the crowd roars.

Is Prince Albert becoming a commoner? Don't count on it, but he sure sounded convincing in East Los Angeles recently at a get-out-the-vote rally of Latino union members. Gore was pumping his fists in the air, chanting "Sí se puede" ("Yes we can") without looking self-conscious. Finding a number of waiters and waitresses in the crowd, he shouted, "People don't realize the same hands serving their food will also pick the next governor of California!" There was no talk of Moore's Law that afternoon, no mention of the genome, nothing about reinventing government. It was just Ordinary Al.

Now, it seems the vice president, in his zeal to be real, is going a bit over the top. Gore, who emerged as the Democrats' top campaigner in this fall's off-year elections while Clinton hid in the White House, has at times been turning himself into a veritable hip-hop artist. Each speech of late has a section that his aides call "the rap," performed with ever-improving cadence:

> *We say, "Legislate"; the Republicans say, "Investigate."*
> *We say, "Educate"; they say, "Instigate."*
> *We say, "Illuminate"; they say, "Interrogate."*
> *We say, "Protect our children"; they launch more inquisitions.*
> *We say, "Make the decisions"; they take depositions.*
> *We know our future is nearing; they hold more hearings.*
> *We say, "Heal our nation"; they just say, "Investigation."*

Like any rap artist, Gore massages his rhymes in between performances. Noticing that the line about "children" and "inquisitions" doesn't quite work, he substitutes new raps at subsequent performances:

> *We say, "Unify"; they say, "Vilify."*
> *We want to help the sick; they're playing partisan tricks.*

"He's the chemist," one of his aides says. "The Al-chemist." Grandmaster Al even ordered his rap translated into Spanish for a concert he's giving in the Bronx: *"Ellos dicen, 'Investigacion'; nosotros decimos, 'Inspiracion.'"*

When I got a moment with Fresh Prince Albert recently, I suggested that he do his entire speech in rap. Here's what I have in mind:

> *We say, "No more gay attacks"; Lott says, "Kleptomaniacs."*
> *We save Social Security; they plot right-wing conspiracy.*
> *We fix Medicare's trouble; they lock up poor Webb Hubbell.*

For reasons unclear, Gore has yet to take my advice. The danger, I suppose, is that the rap could take over Gore's life. One pictures him returning from a hard day on the campaign trail and sitting down at the family table to pronounce: "I say, 'I'm a winner'; Tipper says, 'Eat your dinner.'"

Is this what the Apocalypse looks like? It's a September morning in 1998, and Americans are waking up this morning to all manner of disaster, natural and man-made. A Swissair jumbo jet has crashed in the Atlantic. Hurricane Earl is attacking Florida. The Dow Jones Industrial Average has fallen again, and Russia is imploding. The Justice Department is renewing its investigation of Clinton over campaign finance violations, and more damning details about the president's sexual escapades are dribbling out.

But, as the vice president takes his seat in his cabin on Air Force Two for a flight from Andrews Air Force Base to Pittsburgh, he has another matter on his mind. There on his desk, alongside a basket of grapes, the daily press clippings await his review. Curiously, the story at the top of the pile concerns neither death at sea nor scandal at home. No, the vice president's top story this morning is about the ravages of . . . urban sprawl. "Gore calls for 'smart' growth," reads the headline of the brief story, pulled from the obscurity of the *Washington Post*'s page A17, which it shares with a Macy's ad and the findings of a U.N. population report.

Gore's office had billed the sprawl talk as a "major speech," and, in the vice president's largely cerebral world, it was indeed a big deal—a plan to slow the suburban housing developments that are gradually destroying American farmland, cities and neighborhoods. Alas, Americans' concerns have been a bit more immediate of late: the possibility that their fortunes would be wiped out in a day on Wall Street, or that Osama Bin Ladin would drop some nerve gas on the Washington Monument. Still, Gore plodded on stubbornly with his treatise on "livability." Some aides wondered if Gore would be wiser to wait, but he didn't entertain a delay. "If you wait for a quiet time, you'll be waiting forever," a top adviser says.

It's easy to see why Gore feels that way these days, given that the return of old demons—Bimbroglio and the campaign finance probe—and the debut of a new one—the shaky stock market—threaten to hobble the Democrats' front-runner for 2000. But, as Gore begins crisscrossing the country in the formal campaign season for this fall's races, he's working hard not to flinch. Some of this is simply whistling past the graveyard. Gore also wants to prove, as one adviser puts it, that "he can take a punch" better than he did in early 1997, when, accused of campaign finance abuses, he assumed the fetal position. In the long run, though, Gore's fascination with unconventional issues like livability is part of his plan to defeat a bigger threat to his candidacy than scandal or economic distress: the perception that, after two terms of Clinton-Gore, the vice president has run out of big ideas.

On the truly big ideas—say, the unprecedented economic expansion—he seems to be invisible. And no matter what he seems to do, people can't help but view the guy as a stiff old bore.

At this early stage in the campaign, Gore lacks any clear sense of the enemy, and therefore any clear sense of purpose. Without an obvious opponent for the Democratic nomination, he's following his own rhythm, trying to create his own big issues, and seeming oddly detached from the issues of the day. Clinton popularized the "third way" between the historically liberal and conservative approaches to problems, and Gore is feebly trying to campaign on that same idea, calling himself at one point a "pragmatic idealist." That phrase lasted about five minutes. Gore doesn't seem to feel threatened, and he's unable to get up the fight that he needs. But it's not hard to see that he'll need to find some spunk soon.

Early on, it seemed Clinton's scandal might help Gore—a man of Clintonian ideas without Clintonian appetites. But now it appears the whole administration will limp through the final quarter. Gore, though no doubt personally appalled, hasn't even discussed his thoughts with his closest aides, and he isn't allowing any cracks in his famous loyalty to Clinton. Before Clinton's televised confession, Gore, in Hawaii, rewrote and strengthened a statement supporting Clinton that his aides had drafted. That morning, as Clinton testified, Gore had called his senior staffers with orders not to appear disloyal to the president, "under penalty of death," as one top aide puts it.

The campaign finance probe, which Janet Reno has just renewed over evidence Gore misled investigators, is no less scary for the vice president, but he's trying not to show it. With Monica, Janet Reno and recessionary rumbles, Gore has plenty to worry about. But he behaves almost ostrich-like, finding shelter and comfort in his world of policy detail. The livability theme, with its tranquil and pastoral overtones, may be just the thing to beat the independent-counsel, global-meltdown blahs.

At the speech on livability at Brookings, Gore unveiled such headline-grabbers as $100 million worth of "location-efficient mortgages" from Fannie Mae to encourage home buying near mass transit. Early next month, he will release a thick, interagency report on the topic. With luck, say his advisers, the notion of livable communities might evolve into the sort of "family first" issue that worked so well for Clinton. It will also allow Gore to develop his own story. In the Brookings speech, he talked about his hometown of Carthage, Tennessee, "a place where people know about it when you're born and care about it when you die."

Many, of course, will see this as a diversion—and an eye-glazing one at that. While discussing with another journalist what questions to ask the vice president when he visited us on the flight to Pittsburgh (Reno? Lewinsky? Yeltsin?), I mentioned I wanted to ask about livability. "Please don't ask him," my colleague implored. If I did, Gore surely would spout endlessly about the Farmland Protection Program and the National Spatial Data Infrastructure, thus avoiding the tough questions. I held my tongue.

Besides, we'd already heard enough. The day before at Brookings, Gore obsessed earnestly about his latest foray into arcane matters of policy. The meeting began with the unwelcome announcement that "the vice president's office has prepared a short videotape." The tape's audio failed, and the audience was left to see a series of meaningless pictures—cows, skyscrapers, tractor, housing development—punctuated by painful bursts of feedback. A few minutes later, with the vice president in the room, the tape played again, with the same result: silent cows and skyscrapers.

Gore, in his element, seemed not to mind a bit. He proceeded excitedly through his lengthy speech. For a moment, I forgot about Dan Burton, the stock market, and Monica's book contract. By the speech's end, Gore was almost singing. "This land is your land," he said. "From California to the New York island / From the redwood forests to the Gulf Stream waters / This land was made for you and me." Any day now, the vice president will pull out a harmonica and strip off his dress shirt to reveal the tie-dye beneath, ready to roam and ramble across this nation of subdivisions. And all around him, a voice will be saying, this issue was made for wonks like me.

While Gore plods on with the esoteric and the offbeat, he is having trouble finding traction in the most crucial policy areas, particularly the economy. So far, he's getting little credit for the central achievement of the administration, the historic economic expansion. This is the one issue he must have on his side to win in 2000.

Flying to the Motor City earlier this year for a speech to the Economic Club of Detroit, the vice president could have been forgiven for thinking the economic gods were against him. For six years, Al Gore had toiled in

the vineyards of economic policy, pruning bureaucracy and weeding reg-
ulations—while President Clinton grabbed all the glory for the nation's
prosperity. Business leaders, sore about Gore's energy tax and his call for
the demise of the internal combustion engine, still didn't trust him.

And here he was, about to set everything right in his most important
economic speech in years—and what happens? Chrysler goes and messes
everything up by selling itself to the Germans. The mega-merger,
announced the day before his speech, was sure to overshadow Gore's economic coming-out in Detroit. "I don't know who does your scheduling,"
Gene Sperling, the president's economic policy adviser, joked to the vice
president. Sure enough, the only substantial coverage was a *Washington
Post* story that noted the businessmen's predictable skepticism and rubbed
it in by observing that industrialists are more suspicious of the vice president than of his boss.

But the little-noted speech was an important event in the shaping of
Gore's 2000 presidential run, for it offered a blueprint of what will soon
become Goronomics. Gore, who in 1992 famously called for "completely
eliminating the internal combustion engine," appeared to spout the same
old claptrap that got him into trouble with business in the first place. "No
car company will be able to thrive in the twenty-first century if it relies
solely on internal combustion engines," he said. Only this time there was
a difference: the words were not his, Gore told them, but those of
then–General Motors Chairman John Smith. The implication: being pro-
environment is no longer inconsistent with being pro-business.

The vice president, Gore-watchers say, is entering a new phase. Early
on we saw the arms-control Gore, then the information-superhighway
Gore. Later came the Earth-in-the-balance Gore and the reinventing-
government Gore. Now econo-Gore has come to the fore, and he's talking about it everywhere, turning himself into an amateur economist.

Gore's economic coming-out is part of a broader plan to define a vice
president who, despite universal recognition, remains curiously undefined.
Gore's friends and strategists are looking for a strong identity for him that
will stick in voters' minds—lest he end up like George Bush, whose lack of
definition got him tagged as a "wimp." But so far, says HUD Secretary
Andrew Cuomo, "I don't have it down to a bumper sticker."

He'd better hurry. It's hard to paste an economics speech to a
bumper.

3

★ ☆ ★

What's the Big Idea?

When last we visited the Gore 2000 machine, it was busy convincing prospective Democratic opponents that any challenge to the mighty JugGoreNaut was futile. Alas for the vice president, the strategy has worked too well. Yes, it spooked Dick Gephardt, the most serious rival, thus avoiding a primary bloodbath. But it also knocked out the second-tier candidates, whom Gore strategists were counting on to carve up the anti-Gore vote. Senators Bob Kerrey and Paul Wellstone called it quits. Last week, Senator John Kerry folded, saying he didn't want to be a spoiler. That leaves only Bill Bradley, a man who was to have been a sideshow but who now will be a more formidable challenger—if solely because he is the only one left.

The reaction in the vice president's camp? "Oops," says one Gore strategist.

Gore, as a result, has dropped the invincibility routine. Now he wants to lower expectations by letting everybody know just how vulnerable he is. "For a long time we were pushing how strong we were," says one Gore adviser. "We wanted to thin out the field. We were so successful at that we have to race in the other direction."

Bradley aides, who have taken to mocking Air Force Two as the "State of Inevitability," can hardly contain their glee. "I hear they're backpedaling wildly," Bradley tactician Anita Dunn says. "In December, their line was 'the more the merrier.' Now it's 'we're helped by a two-man race.' The problem with the inevitability strategy is it only works if you're the only candidate."

Last year, Gore aides were hoping that, if their man had to face a primary battle, it would be without Gephardt but with a gaggle of dwarves chasing Gore. Instead, they got only one dwarf, who turns out to be six-foot-five. Gore aides aren't thrilled with a two-man race. "It makes it more precarious," concedes one. "Bradley's got all of the 'anything but' crowd." Or, as a top adviser puts it: "If Al Gore were running against five people, he'd get 60 percent and everybody else would get 8. Now he'll get 60 and the other guy will get 40."

The vice president's team worries that, because of high expectations surrounding Gore, every gain by Bradley will be seen as Gore slippage. Bradley can also, as the sole challenger, better publicize Gore's weaknesses, particularly campaign finance and his environment-related trouble with business. If there's one bit of good news for Gore in his looming slide, it's that the same thing will happen to George W., who now leads Gore by wide margins. A Fox News poll in February 1999 puts Bush at 55 percent support to Gore's 34 percent. Asked on National Public Radio last week about the polls showing him lagging Bush, the vice president declared: "I've never put much stock in polls." That was about as honest a declaration as Gary Bauer saying, "I've never put much stock in Jesus." But this much is true: those who like to turn politics into a horse race will inevitably make the high-flying Gore vulnerable to Bradley. Just as certainly, they will make the high-flying Bush vulnerable to Gore.

Fly up to New Hampshire, and you can immediately see the crumbling JugGoreNaut. Just look at the press coverage. When I arrive at Andrews Air Force Base for Gore's flight north, I'm surprised to find that I'm the only journalist on the flight. An exclusive!

OK, so there are a few local reporters waiting when we land. Still, the light coverage is a sign of the times for Gore. This morning, as Gore travels to New Hampshire for the fourth time this year, a fresh poll by Pew Research Center finds his favorability rating plunging to 47 percent from 58 percent last year. Yesterday, a *USA Today* poll finds Bill Bradley with better-than-expected 34 percent support to Gore's 54 percent.

What press Gore gets has been about his miscues: how Senator Gore invented the Internet and how as a child denizen of Washington's Fairfax Hotel he was actually a farmhand. All over the country, people have been complaining about him—that he's the Democrats' Bob Dole, that he's condescending, or that he doesn't "connect."

I came on this flight to answer a perplexing question: What's Al Gore's deal? Divining the answer is complicated by the fact that those who follow Gore the closest—the media—tend to like him the most. In this regard, he is the exact opposite of Clinton. Though the masses love the president, the closer one gets to Clinton, the more phony and repellent the chief becomes. Gore, on the other hand, is a personable fellow who has trouble convincing the masses of it. "When the curtain's drawn, Gore's a likable guy," says a *New York Times* reporter who follows the vice president closely. "He says cuss words. He jokes. He's a guy you can sit and have a beer with. Then he goes out and gives this screeching speech. It sounds like somebody's stepping on his foot. You can't believe it's the same guy."

In New Hampshire, I find both drinking buddy and screecher. When Gore stops at the studio of Manchester's all-important WMUR-TV for a live interview, his performance is lifeless. He walks into the studio in a gray suit and a tie pulled tight. And he sits rod-straight in his chair, his jacket buttoned, his hands flat on his knees. He swallows frequently, reciting his lines in didactic, sing-song style. When he smiles, it seems more of a grimace. Out of the camera's view, his feet shift and his toes tap.

The performance is baffling, for I had seen an entirely different man just half an hour earlier in a living room in nearby Salem. There, Gore stood before eighty people, wearing a casual checked shirt, with neither note cards nor podium nor microphone. This time he spoke with emotion and apparent pleasure. He brought the audience into the conversation, and he timed his jokes well. Instead of lecturing, he spoke in a normal cadence. He rose to grand themes, promising "truly revolutionary change in our public schools," demanding universal preschool for every child and vowing "to restore the American spirit to our body politic." After his talk, he worked the crowd on the front lawn as if he were the guy from down the street with something to celebrate.

The trouble with such "house party" meetings is that, if Gore wants to reach all voters with these hour-long appearances, he must visit eight million living rooms before Election Day, his aides calculate. Even if he cut that down to two million living rooms by targeting the most likely voters, the process would take him 228 years, assuming he went without sleep.

Why can't Gore make his private side public? His friends offer an explanation at once simple and peculiar: the vice president of the United States, they say, is a shy man, able to open up in a small setting but not on a large stage. "He is probably the shyest man who has ever risen this high in American public life," says Gore's friend Bob Squier. "He has difficulty sharing himself with strangers." A better, but related, explanation suggests that Gore's problem is a fairly ordinary one. He connects when he's genuinely talking with people but finds it awkward to inject emotion into a speech in the abstract, like an actress who must weep in each performance. "He can't affect emotion," a senior Gore aide says. "He needs to interact with another person to show emotion."

Of course, Gore is bound to take a beating regardless these days, because he's fighting a primary and general election all at once. Even as Bradley hammers away at him, a Republican group has been airing ads in California ridiculing Gore for his Internet paternity claim. Gore's predicament is startlingly like George Bush's in 1987. In April of that year, a head-to-head poll matching Bush and Bob Dole showed Bush with a 54–35 lead over Dole, an almost identical margin to Gore's lead over Bradley. At the time, the *New York Times* wrote about how Bush was "unable to garner support from rank-and-file Republicans," raised doubts about his "ability to lead" and went on to discuss his gaffes and the perception that he was "not a strong and decisive person."

Meanwhile, the candidate is busy crossing New Hampshire one living room at a time. "Hi, George, how are you?" he says to a fellow who reminded him of a similar meeting in 1988. "I remember it well," Gore replies, then: "Hi, Pat. Hi, Penny." He spends the next hour, hands in his pockets or folded on his chest, chatting easily about everything from his daughter's pregnancy to the economy. "When he gets in a crowd like this, he loosens up," said Randy Filiault, a Keene city councilor and bar owner. "It's unfortunate the rest of the country can't see what we do."

The rest of the country sees only a tense Gore on television these days reciting a script on Kosovo. Gore aides say the vice president, if discussing a military action on television, should wear a suit and tie. But it seems to me they're equating seriousness with stuffiness. Nobody thought the casually clad Gore was out of line, for example, when he spoke movingly at one of the house parties of a young girl in Kosovo driven from her home, or when he drew a parallel to the Holocaust using the Hebrew "Shoah." He was without suit, without notes and, for the moment, without condescension. It's a pity for Gore that only eighty people were there.

The contrast between the campaigns of Gore and Bradley in the early part of 1999 could hardly be greater. In one corner is a loose and surprisingly potent challenger presenting an expansive vision for the country. In the other is a tired champ, obsessed with the picayune and intent on self-immolation. The result is lopsided coverage in Bradley's favor these days, when everybody seems to be judging candidates on whether or not they think grand thoughts.

Here, roughly, is the handicapping so far:

Bill Bradley: Size XXL ideas

Al Gore: Itsy-bitsy ideas

George W. Bush: No ideas at all

None of these caricatures is quite right, though each has a grain of truth. So far, Bradley has presented lofty goals but no proposals. Gore has a profusion of proposals that obscure his big goals. And Bush, while endowed with a philosophy, is yet to present either goal or proposal. In the end, all three will have a mixture of big goals and small proposals to achieve them. But that doesn't stop the big-idea buzz.

Bradley started the comparison, criticizing the "postage-stamp proposals" of Clinton-Gore. While Bradley is off combating racism and giving health care to all, Gore is establishing a telephone line for traffic jams and a bill of rights for airline passengers. "It's not just the small things but the big challenges," Bradley likes to say. Lefty Senator Paul Wellstone picked up on the big thing when endorsing Bradley. "We Democrats are the party of big ideas," the diminutive Minnesotan proclaimed.

In truth, the really big ideas in this campaign are the bad ones: Gary Bauer's proposal to make all abortion illegal or Pat Buchanan's plan to close the borders. But, for mainstream candidates, the era of big ideas is over, as it should be. Failed gambles on massive programs are being replaced with goals and a multitude of experiments to achieve them—the "let a thousand flowers bloom" approach that worked so well with welfare reform. Candidates talk of the vision thing, but their proposals by necessity are small ones. The big idea is now a goal, not a prescription.

Gore and his allies are frustrated with Bradley's big-idea monopoly. David Axelrod, a consultant and Gore man, likens Bradley's big-ideas theme to a toy cannon. "He rolls the cannon out, lights the fuse, and the flag comes out and says, 'POP,'" Axelrod told the *Chicago Tribune* in a typical rendition. Privately, Gore has been using the same line himself, as he did recently with me. Bradley aides acknowledge big ideas are "shorthand for big priorities," not specific plans. Bradley talks of nurturing oaks rather than house plants, but even oaks begin as saplings.

Bradley's five big ideas—racial unity, universal health insurance, a fight against child poverty, a strong American role in the global economy, and campaign finance reform—are all noble. He has yet to say, however, how he would achieve these things. In his recent speech on race, he made clear that there wasn't much he could do as president other than use the bully pulpit and require federal agencies to hire minorities. But that doesn't get far beyond such banalities as Clinton's race initiative. Senator Bradley was known for solid but bite-size solutions to race problems—landing an empowerment zone in Camden, New Jersey, for example.

In a variety of areas, Bradley's legislation was Gore-like in scope, such as his delving into California water conservation and canned-mushroom tariffs. On health care, Bradley recently made a major proposal: means-testing Medicare. But his spokesman backtracked, declaring, "This is not a statement of policy." On his global big idea, Bradley has been fuzzy on specifics. Speaking to the United Auto Workers in Iowa about NAFTA, the free-trader declared: "We need to look at the agreement, see how it's working, and then make judgments."

Still, Bradley has begun to fill in some of his big ideas. He upstaged the timid Gore campaign with a strong anti-handgun proposal (large portions of which Gore copied in his own proposal), and Bradley will soon stand before the National Press Club to outdo the vice president with a specific proposal for campaign finance reform. Whether or not Bradley can beat Gore—and that still seems unlikely—a contested race might not leave either with enough money to compete against the $36 Million Man next spring.

George W., for his part, still lives in the cocoon of Austin, running but not yet campaigning. This allows him to criticize the administration without offering an alternative. "Clinton sounds like a superintendent of schools," says Karen Hughes, his spokeswoman. "Governor Bush will offer a vision." The operative word seems to be "will," for he is studiously avoiding any previews. The congressional Republican retreat into isolationism cries out for a strong rejoinder from Bush, but he offers little, calling the Kosovars "Kosovians" (and the Greeks "Grecians"). Similarly, after the Littleton tragedy, Bush said he supported a gun control measure that a Texas House committee had already killed, apparently without Bush's objection.

These blunders give the impression that Bush is an empty vessel. This isn't so, at least not entirely. Among the big ideas Bush has brought to Texas is a call for every child to read by the third grade. He also has big cultural goals, such as reducing teen pregnancy. His solutions for these big goals, not surprisingly, are small proposals—an end to social promotion here, a mentoring program there. "The times just don't call for major change," says one Bush adviser.

That leaves Gore, who has the opposite problem. He seems so full of proposals he loses the big picture. For example, while Bradley's race speech was full of platitudes, Gore struck back with a speech to the Detroit NAACP laden with numbing detail: $3.5 billion in minority business loans, 90,000 empowerment zone jobs, 2,000 community police officers, 1,300 drug counselors. The two rivals' views are largely the same—as, indeed, they are on many issues—but, while Bradley calls it a big idea, Gore rattles off line items.

Gore is trying to package his ideas more broadly. When asked at a gathering last month what a Gore presidency would be about, Gore ticked off several bigthink ideas: "truly revolutionary change in our public schools," universal preschool, a campaign against global warming, a prosperous transition to the Information Age. "I'd like to restore the American spirit to our body politic," Gore said, a concept as vaguely satisfying as any of Bradley's.

Gore also continues to alter the balance of his staff. Until now, he has surrounded himself with a Harvard-heavy gang of Washington whizzes, who are not necessarily the most streetwise or the type willing to speak bluntly to him. Now, Gore has brought a couple of street fighters on board to join Craig Smith, an old Clinton operative. He persuaded Michael Whouley, the tough-talking adviser from Boston, to move to Washington. He also recruited as his political director Donna Brazile, a Southern black Catholic from LSU. She helped engineer the House Democrats' upset in '98 and now will offset Gore's Ivy League crowd. "We have a lot of advisers—we're saturated with advisers," she says. "I'm looking for the activists. We've got to return Al Gore to the streets."

Gore in the streets? Now *that's* a big idea.

First, however, Gore must stop bleeding from self-inflicted wounds. Or, more accurately, boss-inflicted wounds. I refer, of course, to Bill Clinton's recent flop in his debut as freelance press secretary. His now-infamous call to the *New York Times*'s Rick Berke, which supposedly was made to debunk doubts about the Gore campaign, instead wound up reinforcing them, as Clinton confided his deep worries about Gore to a million *Times* readers.

Now Washington is atwitter with theories about why the president would sabotage his understudy. Some blame it on Clinton's insatiable need for attention at a time when Gore hasn't mentioned his name on the trail. Others see it as a way to distance himself from Gore so that his legacy (such as it is) could remain intact (relatively speaking), even if Gore loses.

But I think a much simpler dynamic is at work here. The culprit was Clinton the pleaser, trying hard to be agreeable to everyone he meets. He may well have meant to tell Berke that he had no worries about Gore's campaign, but when he heard the reporter at the other end of the line, he didn't have the heart to do it. Sure I have doubts, he said. Your story is right on the money. It's the same Clintonian quality that prevented him from breaking with Monica Lewinsky, thus leading to impeachment. Or his reluctance to get tough with the gun lobby, thus sinking his gun control proposals. Or his uneasiness about pointing fingers at Hollywood, thus missing an opportunity to reduce violent entertainment. Or his hesitance to offend Russia and China by pursuing a ground war in Kosovo, thus dooming the effort to failure. The man just craves approval.

Gore is rightly furious at his boss for the blunder. Actually, the call to the *Times* only compounded the problem of all of Clinton's earlier calls to his friends blabbing about Gore's weaknesses—calls that prompted the article in the first place. The episode became an unwelcome distraction just as Gore was trying to recover from his spring of vulnerability. (Indeed, *Newsweek*, which had planned a relatively puffy cover piece on Tipper and Al, toughened the story after Clinton's unhelpful contribution made headlines.)

Gore finally acted to stem the criticism that his campaign is leaderless and listless. Advisers scrapped their earlier plan to hold off on policy announcements until the fall. In Iowa, Gore unveiled his education plan— a package of proposals to shift from the Industrial Age model of classrooms to an Information Age model of one-on-one education. He'll roll out other pieces of his agenda in coming weeks. In part, this is a response to the unexpected strength of Bill Bradley. But it has more to do with George W. Bush, who, because of his dominant position among Republicans, has been able to start a general-election-style campaign early. Gore is calculating that his early shift to the "ideas phase" will pressure Bush and Bradley to give specifics to their own vague pronouncements.

In the meantime, the Washington echo chamber continues to reverberate with tales of Gore's demise, albeit from many of the same prognosticators who prophesied Clinton's undoing early last year. It's worthwhile to note that one group doesn't share this view of Gore's downward spiral: Bush allies, who privately expect a very tight race in the general election. Bush advisers have been concerned about the unrealistically high expectations surrounding their candidate. Already, a *Newsweek* poll found Gore, who has badly lagged Bush in polls, down just nine percentage points in a hypothetical matchup. That suggests Gore just needs to wait out the storm. Maybe that's why his campaign chairman, Tony Coelho, in his first week on the job, flew off to Portugal.

4

★ ☆ ★

Tony the Tiger
Meets Bradley's Believers

Early in this spring of 1999, Tipper Gore hinted to reporters that the vice president of the United States, the man who is a heartbeat from the presidency, sleeps in the nude. Now, I'm no Michael Isikoff, but I think I've got a scoop of my own concerning the vice presidential undergarments.

My troubling discovery came as I followed Al Gore on his presidential announcement tour last week. In Carthage, Tennessee, the normally plodding Gore raced through his speech at such breakneck speed that seven dense pages flew by in just 25 minutes. He spoke with even more haste at stops in Iowa, New Hampshire, and New York City. I checked with Laura Quinn, Gore's communications director, to see how she explained this new urgency.

"We gave him really tight underwear," she replied.

There are other possible explanations. Another aide credited performance-enhancing substances: "He's highly caffeinated." Yet another suggested the candidate was made to drink large quantities of water before his appearance, forcing him to finish quickly. It is not an altogether pleasant image to picture the superhydrated, overcaffeinated candidate hurrying cross-legged through his speech, bolting for the men's room, and peeling off his constricting skivvies.

But I'm not complaining. Whatever the cause, boxers or briefs, Gore's newfound need for speed is a blessing for listeners. I hear a good number of Gore speeches, so it's likely the faster pace will save me days of cumulative waiting time before the campaign is over. The quickspeak will also make Gore sound less condescending than he invariably does when he slowly articulates every syllable, as if he were reading a storybook to children or perhaps encountering a new word for the first time. One hopes he will never again decry "pro-*tek*-shuns for *gun* man-you-*fact*-chur-urs" or vow to protect "*ow*-ur *chilled*-run."

Yes, there were a couple of lapses into the old ways on the announcement tour. In Iowa City, Gore, who shrewdly avoided reading a list of acknowledgments in Carthage, felt it necessary to thank a local fellow from 4-H. "I was in the 4-H Club and raised beef cattle," he began, creating a momentary worry that we would hear another yarn about his youth as a farmer on the fertile plains of Massachusetts Avenue. But, once into his stump speech in Iowa, Gore delivered one line with such rat-a-tat-tat speed ("If-you-do-not-want-somebody-committed-heart-and-soul-to-bring-revolutionary-change-to-our-public-schools-then-vote-for-somebody-else") that Tipper jolted her head back in mock whiplash. Gore, thankfully, has stopped playing the 45 rpm record at 33.

The big story of the Gore announcement tour has been the candidate's efforts to separate from his boss. He spoke of the "moral leadership" invested in the presidency and criticized Clinton's sexcapades. On the press plane, Tony Coelho, tried to soften the vice president's remarks, telling reporters they were "fixating" on the Clinton split and saying, "We're not going to give you a headline that says this." But neither did he mind the distinction being drawn. In the same breath, Coelho spoke about a Gore who is now "unshackled." (Actually, it was Coelho himself who seemed unshackled, if not unhinged; the man was dancing on the tarmac in Cedar Rapids after Air Force Two landed, to the strains of U2 and, curiously, the Fleetwood Mac tune "Little Lies.")

Gore began to show some distance from Clinton on the eve of his announcement tour. "I'm completely different from President Clinton," he said. "I have a different set of priorities, a different approach." Gore won't put it like this, but the message is simple: I can keep the economy humming, and I won't sleep with the interns.

Some Gore strategists, who clung to Clinton earlier this year, are coming to the conclusion that the president, though still popular, is a liability. Gore aides had argued that his poor showing in polls was similar to Vice President Bush's fix in '88 (and that W.'s weaknesses were similar to Dukakis's), but some now say the situation is worse. One adviser was flummoxed by a CNN poll this month showing 71 percent approval of Bush's job as president, double what he got when actually in office in 1992. The adviser said such a number can only be explained by a Clinton backlash. When I asked Gore about this Bush revival, he answered, "Maybe there's a hitherto hidden fondness for deep recessions."

The getaway vehicle for Gore's departure from Clinton is faith and family, a familiar Gore theme anyway. The key passage in his announcement speech, according to campaign strategy, was this: "When we in our generation are finished adding up our deeds, our possessions, all our material and scientific advances, I believe we will ultimately be judged by whether we have strengthened or weakened the families that are the hope and soul of America." One reporter who bothered to count told me Gore used the word "family" 27 times.

In Carthage, a façade of boosterism for the local-boy-made-good was in evidence. Or maybe it was just capitalism. Storefront signs urged locals to "be a part of history" at Gore's announcement. One Gore souvenir booth promised the "lowest price T-shirts in Carthage." Even the Bass Funeral Home got in on Gore's campaign kickoff, erecting a tent on its lawn labeled, disconcertingly, "First Aid Center."

But not everybody went by the script. Shortly into the Carthage speech, demonstrators seeking cheaper AIDS drugs began to blow whistles and disrupt the speech—until one fellow in the crowd punched a whistle-blower in the jaw, apparently knocking him to the ground. The next morning, in New Hampshire, a militant AIDS group, ACT UP, was at it again about AIDS drugs, this time managing to get four or five protesters in the front row, where they unfurled their banners and blew whistles until police removed them.

And so it was obvious what awaited us at Gore's next appearance, a Manhattan rally. Much of the audience, it seemed, had come to put on a carnival of civil disobedience. There were the whistling AIDS protesters, to be sure, but there was also a man dressed up as a sunflower, apparently to make some point about gardening policy. Another man appeared to be in costume as a pickle, or perhaps a cucumber. "A pea," the *Los Angeles Times'* Ron Brownstein corrected me. A fellow with a beard spent the whole time ranting about how "Al Gore is a phony environmentalist." Another man shouted about animal tests, and somebody else protested NAFTA. A large banner proclaimed: "Al Gore: American Psycho!"

It began to drizzle as Gore spoke, and it seemed that most of the crowd couldn't hear what he was saying. To me, the whole event seemed like an unmitigated disaster, the protests a crushing blow. And yet the Gore aides didn't seem displeased. Then it occurred to me: the rally had nothing to do with me or the thousands of others here. It was about getting a good television shot of Gore, with his family on the flag-bedecked stage, and a spirited crowd. The sound would come directly from his microphone. And millions of Americans that night would see and hear almost nothing of the AIDS activists, the vegetable man, or the human sunflower.

The kickoff of Bill Bradley's presidential campaign in his boyhood home of Crystal City, Missouri, was strictly amateur. A singer botched the words to the national anthem ("through the perilous flight"). The American flag got tangled as it was hoisted up a rusty pole. The sound system crackled and squealed with feedback. When Bradley spoke, he was too tall for the microphone, which caused those toward the back of the crowd to shout that they couldn't hear. On his closing line, Bradley stumbled; instead of "Come with me—let us walk toward that dream together," he declared, like a foreign student of English: "Let us come with me."

But Anita Dunn, Bradley's communications director, was so swept away by the moment that she didn't even seem to notice. "It's so beautiful," she gushed as Bradley reached his finale, "I love this part." I offered her my bow tie to dab her moist eyes. Absurd though it seemed to weep at a presidential announcement speech, I had no doubt Dunn's tears were real. They were another sign of a phenomenon I'd observed over the past few months: the passion of the Bradley people. While the Gore staff is a collection of cool professionals, the Bradley staffers are on a mission from God.

Part of this is a natural expression of the challenger mentality. The contrast between the energetic Forbes campaign and the play-it-safe Bush campaign is much the same. Both the Forbes and the Bradley campaigns have little to lose and a greater sense of mission than their competitors. The front-runners' aides, by contrast, tend to see their campaign work as a meal ticket (a newly hired Bush aide told me he was "going to the show"), and the campaigns take on a mercenary aspect. Gore, for example, is hampered by advisers (six pollsters and counting) who still work for other clients, both political and commercial.

The Bradley and Forbes campaigns are similar in another way: both are stocked with true believers who see themselves as part of a cause, not a campaign. "He's the ideological heir to the legacy that started with Barry Goldwater," says Forbes pollster John McLaughlin, whose firm only takes on conservative causes. "I like Steve Forbes, but the most important thing is we share conservative principles."

That sounds much like the sentiments of Doug Berman, Bradley's campaign chairman and a longtime crusader for campaign finance reform. "This is not about Bradley," he says. "Bradley's the derivative." If Forbes's staff seeks to revive conservatism, the Bradley staffers want to salvage liberalism. They call themselves "progressives" these days, but it doesn't matter. "There's been no change in my ideology," says Bradley campaign manager Gina Glantz.

Here's where Gore is at a natural disadvantage. He's running a campaign as a centrist, and there just aren't many raging moderates out there. Though many of his staffers are passionate about their beliefs, they don't have a unifying cause. In 1992, Clinton's team, though not a gang of liberal purists, had a cause: saving the Democratic Party. Forbes's cause is conservatism. Bradley's cause is liberalism. Gore's and Bush's cause, it seems to some people, is getting elected.

Regardless of whether you agree with their ideas (and often I don't), it's hard not to admire the fervor of Bradley's troops. Diane Feldman, Bradley's pollster, states her priorities proudly: more spending on schools, universal health care, and less spending on weapons. Will Robinson, Bradley's media consultant, sees the candidate as a vehicle for progressive issues that haven't been top priorities for Clinton. "The wing of the party I'm in has been ignored," he says. "Bradley reached out to me."

For each of the themes Bradley has championed—campaign finance reform, abortion rights, gun control, child poverty—there's a Bradley aide for whom that issue is a lifelong cause. Berman, who grew up in Usonia, Frank Lloyd Wright's cooperative community in Pleasantville, New York, thinks campaign finance reform is a way to reduce income inequality. Glantz, whose "ideology-based" consulting firm has represented abortion rights groups, says, "I have a personal passion for the issue." Eric Hauser, Bradley's goatee- and earring-sporting press secretary, started a p.r. firm that handles only "progressive causes" such as representing the Coalition to Stop Gun Violence. His pet issue: gun control. Dunn says she got a "very strong social conscience" from her mother, a Mississippi social worker who ran a refugee program and a food bank. Her top causes are race and poverty.

"I came to D.C. a very liberal person to change the world," says Hauser. Among Bradley's campaign staffers, several of whom have been with the senator a decade or more, Hauser has found kindred spirits. "We're all very passionate progressives," he says. Not a centrist New Democrat in the lot. And Bradley's most loyal supporters are much the same. The cars at his rallies are plastered with stickers supporting gay rights or unions and printed with battle cries such as "Against abortion? Then don't have one" and "Friends don't let friends vote Republican."

This may explain why Bradley, so far, has emphasized his liberal views and played down his more moderate ones. As a senator, Bradley, after all, was as much a centrist as Gore. But he realizes that the unreconstructed liberals are the Democratic Party's most energetic members, much as the right-wingers are for the Republicans. Bradley's voice for liberal policies has given him a standing that virtually nobody (myself included) thought possible. This may have less to do with Bradley himself than with revulsion for Bill Clinton. But whatever the reason, Bradley is now a contender. Two polls in New Hampshire, the *Boston Globe*'s and CNN's, put Bradley in a statistical dead heat with Gore. A Zogby poll in New York showed Bradley down only six points.

However, Bradley, if he prevails, will do so by moving the party left, allowing the GOP to become the majority party by speaking for the middle. Just as Bush and the Republicans have begun to understand the lesson of Clinton's shift to the center in 1992 (underscored by Pat Buchanan's recent talk of leaving the party), the Democrats seem to have forgotten it. The Republican National Committee is already sending out a barrage of press releases about Bradley's liberal stances on welfare, school vouchers and Al Sharpton. "He's running to the left to get a benefit in the Democratic primary, but he's going to pay a price for that if he gets to the general election," says the RNC's Cliff May.

In that case, the best moderates can hope for is that Bradley tacks aggressively back to the center and drops the Dukakis platform. But how? If he forsakes the passions of his staff and abandons their causes, he will lose the energy of the true believers who made him a contender in the first place.

Bradley shows no signs of abandoning his true believers. After his announcement in Crystal City, he leads "a caravan of supporters" (as his press release puts it) to Keokuk, Iowa, two hundred miles north on the Mississippi River. The directions are fairly simple: Bradley turns to the left—often.

That, at least, is the impression the former senator has been giving of late. When asked on an Iowa radio show how his positions differ from Al Gore's, he volunteered that he is much tougher on gun control, much stronger on campaign finance reform, and a more enthusiastic supporter of abortion rights. The interviewer concluded: "You are a clear, unabashed, liberal Democrat."

Bradley demurred, but his recent words do convey a sense that he's been hanging out a lot with Senator Paul Wellstone. He says he'll release a universal health care plan that will be "raw meat" for his critics. Asked in Iowa about the budget surplus, he said he'd spend it on health care, child poverty, debt reduction, and a "rainy day" fund. In other words, he wouldn't cut current taxes by a dime—which puts him at odds with most members of his own party. When another questioner criticized welfare reform, Bradley responded, "You and I are on the same wavelength. I was one of ten or twelve who voted against it."

His crowds, packed with liberal activists, eat it up. "He's hitting all my buttons," said Vernon Stone after listening to Bradley in Ames—a town Stone identified as "the most liberal spot in Iowa."

For better or worse, Bradley has decided to attack Gore from the left. Many in the Democratic base will view this as heroic and call Bradley the party's savior. Others will see it as a cynical tactic and call Bradley a spoiler. Both sides have a point.

It's not implausible to view Bradley as the purist who can save the Democrats from the scandalous Clinton administration. "Hundreds of people have come up to me and said, 'I'm an independent, or a Republican, I'd vote for you, I wouldn't vote for him,'" Bradley likes to say. He's right: I hear it all the time in Iowa, in New Hampshire, and elsewhere. On the other hand, Bradley's campaign could re-create the intraparty rift Democrats thought they'd avoided when Dick Gephardt backed out of a run and endorsed Gore. Bradley is, in a sense, giving liberals false hope that their agenda may still be possible. (Remember when Clinton and Gore tried universal health care in 1994?) His move to the left also makes him less electable were he to win the nomination. The most likely outcome is that he and Gore will spend each other into poverty. When summer 2000 rolls around, whoever winds up with the nomination could be outspent the way Clinton outspent Bob Dole in '96.

Bradley, in a brief interview, dismissed these worries. Is he moving left? "No. Some people will say I'm on the left, some people will say I'm on the right, and some people will say I'm in the center." Will he and Gore make each other too weak to win? "Whichever candidate emerges will be stronger because of the competition. You benefit from the rat-a-tat-tat." Gina Glantz says she doesn't worry about repeating Dole's spring money woes. "If you continually play the last election this time, it's almost a guarantee that you'll be wrong," she says.

Bradley and his advisers don't see themselves as spoilers. The Bradley aides are more passionate than Gore's staff, and they seem to hold a quasi-religious belief that, just this once, message will defeat method. Whereas one Gore adviser told me the nomination is more about tactics than message, Glantz says the reverse is true. Bradley himself tells audiences, "I'm trying to do this in a different way."

But there's a fine line between idealism and naivete. Bradley is filling liberal hearts with hope, which earns him more enthusiastic crowds than Gore. But, in the end, it's about who has the most votes, and Bradley's liberal supporters may not realize that. Sonja Roberts, a Des Moines community activist who hosted a Bradley visit, pronounced herself enchanted after his speech on her front porch. But when I asked whether she worried that Bradley and Gore would carve up the party, handing the White House to a Republican, she lost some of her spirit. "That's a really good question," she said after some thought, "because I can see it happening."

Indeed, Bradley has left Gore little choice. The vice president must abandon his vague, conflicted, above-it-all campaign and his emphasis on esoteric issues of interest to the moderates. He must now engage Bradley in a bitter fight for the heart of the Democratic Party, and it won't be pretty.

★ ☆ ★

The Gore operation, facing an unexpected Bradley threat, appears to be coming unglued. As Gore's announcement tour moved from Tennessee to Iowa, his campaign chairman decided to take a ride on the press plane to give us a piece of his mind. When I came across Tony Coelho, he was gesticulating wildly to a group of reporters, shouting in their faces and looking as if he might burst a blood vessel. "That man," David Plotz of *Slate* remarked, "is going to explode."

Coelho's friends worry about his health. He works 16-hour days after rising for a workout each morning; his beach house in Delaware goes unused. He takes phenobarbital for epilepsy, he tells me, but he's still a blur of motion. "The joke is what I would be like if I didn't take it," he says.

Some inside the Gore campaign, after working under Coelho's frantic management for two months, would like to increase his dosage. In his first day on the job, he made Al Haig-style calls to key Democrats to assert his control over the Gore 2000 apparatus. Since then, he's been hiring consultants who are rivals of Gore's existing consultants, causing internal strife in a campaign that, just a few months ago, bragged about its harmony. A micromanager, Coelho supervises his minions down to the last semicolon, even deciding what color suit Gore should wear, leaving staffers feeling powerless. He's also reputed to be a screamer, and his list of people to fire, the existence of which is officially denied but privately believed in by Gore's aides, has spread pervasive fear.

There's a notion that Coelho, a sort of start-up chairman, will tire himself out and turn over the reins to another, white-knight chairman after the primaries. But for now, Coelho's grip seems firm. His message to those who don't like his style: Get used to it. "The issue isn't whether people are happy or upset," Coelho says during an interview in his K Street campaign office. "This doesn't have anything to do with whether people think I'm treating them right or wrong. I'll do whatever I have to do to make sure Al wins. . . . It's not about me. It's not about any consultant or staffer. Who cares if they get along?" Got that, everybody?

Coelho seems to see those who question his style as disloyal to Gore. "You really have to understand why I'm here," he says. "I'm doing it pro bono. I'm committed 100 percent to Al getting elected. My commitment isn't for people to like me."

Coelho's attitude does make some sense. The Gore operation had been in need of a jolt when he came aboard; it needed some bold decision-making and risk-taking to relieve it from terminal caution. He's brought clarity and organization to a campaign that was, by some measures, drifting. And though Coelho's command-and-control style builds resentment and demoralizes the staff, the campaign is short enough that the long-term effects may never be felt. Coelho's allies say the griping is inevitable as Coelho goes about selecting a half-dozen loyal deputies, who will probably be different from Gore's current top aides. There's also inevitable tension as the center of Goreland shifts from the White House and a circle of high-powered friends to the campaign office.

But the 57-year-old Coelho is taking a huge risk. A demoralized staff that feels its own ideas don't matter won't show initiative. And Coelho's style leaves Gore's troops feeling insecure. Whatever the ultimate wisdom of Coelho's early moves, his tendency to make them secretly has undermined morale. As a result of the turmoil, the Gore campaign is in full meltdown mode. The latest is that Gore, tossing his anti-tobacco principles, hired ad man Carter Eskew, the mastermind of the tobacco industry's fight against the administration's anti-tobacco legislation. Not only does this damage Gore's ability to use tobacco as an issue, but it has injected further turmoil into the fractious Gore camp; Gore's existing ad man, Bob Squier, was Eskew's mentor—before they had a bitter falling-out. After Eskew came aboard the Gore campaign, Squier shared his hurt feelings on the front page of the *New York Times.*

The next shop due for some turmoil is Gore's polling operation. Already, the delicate balance of pollsters Mark Penn, Mark Mellman and Paul Maslin was upset by Coelho's hiring of yet another pollster, Celinda Lake. (This for a campaign that spent $228,644 on polling between April and June—one of the major reasons Gore has gone through a greater proportion of the money he's raised than either Bill Bradley or George W. Bush has.) Eskew's arrival diminishes the role of lead pollster Penn, and there's some gossip that Penn, who has stretched himself thin working for the president, the first lady, and Microsoft, may soon feel Coelho's wrath. If this happens, Coelho would find some support: Penn, who favors having Gore push a vast array of themes, is clashing with communications advisers, who think the candidate should focus on a few solid messages.

Coelho points out that fewer than 1 percent of voters know who he, Coelho, is, evidence that internal squabbles don't matter to the electorate. True, but a squabbling staff will be distracted from its task. And many of Gore's top lieutenants feel they have lost all power, while some of Gore's best workers obviously fear for their jobs. Though Coelho is a veteran strategist, his unchallenged judgment isn't always perfect. It was his decision to make Gore's official announcement of his candidacy in June, but the hoped-for bounce in the polls never happened. According to Gore consultants, Coelho brought in outsiders to do the advance work in Carthage, Tennessee, and the event was a debacle: faulty sound, posters between the TV cameras and the candidate's face, even AIDS protesters in the VIP section. Now the campaign has delayed formulating Gore's themes because Eskew won't be ready to roll the message machine until September.

The good news for Coelho is that his problem is largely a matter of style, not substance. With a smoother bedside manner, friends and opponents agree, he could probably get the job done. If he were to lighten up a bit and give his underlings more autonomy, he could quiet the complaints. Coelho seems to grasp this. "I think it should change," he says. "I believe in giving people authority." Coelho himself says the campaign's condition wasn't all that bad to start with. "These people here are very qualified, capable folks," he says. "I'm pleased with the organization. If I weren't, I'd be firing people." (In fact, though Coelho hasn't fired anybody, George W. Bush just sacked his highly regarded spokesman, David Beckwith.) But if Coelho really didn't believe the Gore operation was in crisis, why did he adopt crisis-style management?

Coelho tells his staff that his decision to hire warring advisers stemmed from his stewardship of the House Democrats' elections in 1986, when he brought in a variety of strong-willed advisers who often disagreed loudly. "By the force of Tony's personality and commitment, we all got along," says Tom Nides, a Coelho ally who worked at the Democratic Congressional Campaign Committee in '86. The Democrats won big that year, and Coelho clearly hopes for a repeat with the Gore staff. If Coelho can calm and motivate his underlings, Gore could recover, as Bush did in '88. But if Coelho can't stop the anxiety he's unleashed, the result may be a replay of Dole '96.

It is now a few months into Tony Coelho's reign at Gore 2000, and the man is gradually nudging the vice president toward presenting a compelling vision of why he should be president. But such trivialities can be dispensed with if Coelho fulfills what appears to be another of his goals: putting a majority of American voters on the campaign payroll.

The first method has obvious benefits, but the Gore campaign has, until now, shown more inclination to follow the second. When I asked one Gore man about why the candidate needed a sixth pollster and a similar number of message mavens, he explained wryly that the campaign was adopting the "full-employment strategy"—under the assumption that Americans will vote for a man who pays their salaries.

Similar thinking seems to be at work in the recent endorsement sweepstakes, the very essence of the Gore campaign's tactical thinking. A few weeks back, Coelho set the tone. "I believe in endorsements," he said. "I don't believe in anything else." I had no idea how serious he was until the Gore campaign began circulating names of every Tom, Dick and Harry for Gore. On September 21, the campaign, after announcing some endorsements from congressmen, sent out a press release declaring that "more than 100 Long Island leaders" endorsed Gore. Who are these leaders? Well, there's Steve Goldberg, Long Beach deputy zone leader, and Lynne Bizzarro, senior assistant attorney for some unspecified town. Bizzarro indeed.

Does it really make a difference whether Irvin Toliver, director of human services for the town of Huntington, is a Gore man? Or how about Dolores Otter, listed on Gore's press release without a title? You can practically hear the buzz sweeping the nation: "Well, if Dolores Otter is on board, count me in."

Next came word that "Gore scores again in New York as more top leaders join his team." This time it was a batch of endorsements that included Assembly Speaker Sheldon Silvers (never mind that he'd been a Gore man for a decade or so), and it was clearly an effort to show momentum. The announcement "comes only one day after the vice president picked up the support of ten members of Congress and more than 100 Long Island Democrats," the press release said.

Bill Bradley, for his part, had snagged the more important endorsement of Senator Pat Moynihan, but the challenger wasn't above the silliness. Bradley sent out a press release announcing endorsements from 24 officials from Strafford County, New Hampshire, including the all important Bob Watson (Rochester school board member) and Gerald McCarthy (Farmington selectman). The next day, Gore fired back with word that "hundreds of women from across America today endorsed Al Gore"—and then proceeded to list them, including various and sundry school board members throughout this great land. The mayors of Burnsville and Fitchburg got a mention, as did Rhonda Walters, former First Lady of Oklahoma. The mayors of Madison and Greenwich were so important they were listed twice. Bradley capped the volley the next day with a press release declaring that four private citizens in Iowa had switched from Gore to Bradley; the release even quoted one Paul Slappey of Cedar Rapids as saying, "I mean, wow, this guy was a Rhodes Scholar." The upshot: Gore may have sewed up Dolores Otter, but with Bradley, Slappey is happy.

The strangest part of the endorsement ritual is the fact that the commitments aren't worth a thing. Gore, as expected, will get the lion's share of supporters, and Bradley, if he scores early upsets, will cause them to change sides. Either way, they're useless. And that's why Gore needs to do less of this tactical positioning and more of the vision thing. Gore aides promise they're shifting away from the endorsement bazaar—though, as I write, a fresh batch of endorsements from Hawaii is crossing my screen.

No doubt, the above portrait of the Gore campaign will bring an angry rebuke from one Bob Somerby of Baltimore. Somerby, Gore's roommate when they were students at Harvard University, runs a website that lashes out at the media miscreants who dare to criticize the vice president's flawless campaign. In a recent dispatch, Somerby, employing a naughty word for equine feces, describes your correspondent's campaign coverage as "stomach-turning" and accuses me of making light of child molestation, having an obsession with naked presidential candidates and, worst of all, being too hard on Gore.

Now, the first two charges are fair enough, but Somerby's point about Gore demands rebuttal. True, the coverage of Gore's campaign has been excessively negative. But the Gore campaign has brought much of this on itself by being tactical and reactive rather than articulating a vision. For a year now, Gore loyalists have been waiting and wondering when the vice president will tell his story.

Fortunately for Gore, his new message gurus, Carter Eskew and Bob Shrum, have finally begun to paint the big picture. Over the past three weeks, Gore has begun to speak in broad themes, and he rolled out his overarching message at the Democrats' meeting on September 25. "Let us make change work for working families," he said at the beginning of his speech. Aides say this theme, unlike the short-lived "practical idealism," is here to stay. It gives Gore what he desperately needs: a message that allows him to connect the dots among the dozens of policy proposals he has rolled out. The change-that-works idea lets Gore to talk about shifts occurring, changes in the economy and the American way of life, and it poses a question: Do we go back to George W. and the old Republican policies (the elder Bush's recession), or back to Bradley and the old liberal favorites (President Dukakis), or do we try something new?

At the same time, Gore has moved to calm Coelho's fractious organization. He has wisely decided to move the campaign headquarters to Tennessee, out of the Washington echo chamber. Also, the well-liked Michael Whouley has taken charge of the Gore forces in New Hampshire and Iowa. Whouley, arguably the party's top operative, will run the campaign's field work, while Craig Smith, Gore's campaign manager and a former Clinton hand, is assigned to solidify labor and party support, and Donna Brazile, Smith's deputy, handles constituency groups. For the first time, Gore can stop worrying about who's running what and start talking about why he wants to run the country.

Gore's advisers complain that they're damned no matter what they do. They avoided flooding the market with endorsements so that they wouldn't look like Walter Mondale, and they were criticized because Bush had more endorsements and Bradley was winning a fair number. Now Gore is pouring out endorsements, and, sure enough, he looks like Mondale. If Gore speaks earnestly from the podium, he is stiff. If he acts loose and casual, he's faking it. "We can't catch a break," says one top Gore adviser.

It's true. At a Democratic gathering recently, Gore gave the best performance I've ever seen him give. He did everything he was supposed to do: he was conversational, not condescending; he had few notes; he even threw in a Dole stroll. He told a cohesive story about his mom's rise from poverty (hence his concern for women and the poor), his dad, Tennessee's first labor commissioner and the man who showed young Al the slave rings in his hometown (concern for labor and race), and his turn from Vietnam to journalism to politics. And yet the college Democrat seated next to me wasn't impressed. "He sounded so fake," she said.

After his speech, Gore worked the crowd as his campaign played the Gore theme song, which segued into an unusual choice, the British artist Fatboy Slim's hit "Praise You." The lyrics seemed to express the Gore campaign's old belief that Democrats must inevitably flock to their standard bearer:

> *We've come a long, long way together*
> *Through the hard times and the good.*
> *I have to celebrate you, baby.*
> *I have to praise you like I should.*

Part II

★ ☆ ★

The Fall of Mr. Nice Guy
George W. Bush

5

★ ☆ ★

Can We Talk?

Let's make one thing perfectly clear: Dana Milbank, senior editor at *The New Republic*, is no Sidney Blumenthal," the media critic Russ Smith, a.k.a. "the Mugger," wrote in early 1999 in his weekly newspaper, the *New York Press*. "No, Milbank's difficulty—one that's significant enough that it will most likely damage his career—is that he's Marty Peretz's handpicked cheerleader for Al Gore. Peretz, of course, is the owner of *TNR* and has pushed the Veep's candidacy for years. . . . Peretz, who was Gore's mentor at Harvard, prefers to spend time in Cambridge, ruminating in the magazine about Israeli politics, and peppers *The Gore Republic* with his own partisanship. Hence, the need for a butt-boy, and this year Milbank, who's worked at *TNR* since March of '98, drew the short straw."

Smith was just beginning. He found an anonymous journalist to pronounce, "He does whatever Marty Peretz wants him to do. Weak. Not bad, but weak." He went on for hundreds of words in this vein. And, it turns out, as Peretz's "butt-boy" and "handpicked cheerleader" for Gore, writing for *The Gore Republic*, I will become a regular feature in the Mugger's column. A few issues later, Smith writes that I am "Peretz's pet lapdog for the current Gore campaign" who "obediently yips and yaps at George W. Bush." Unclear whether Smith's opinion of me has improved. Is it better to be a lapdog than a butt-boy?

I can't pretend this comes as a total surprise. When I first talked to *TNR* editor Chuck Lane about a job in early 1998, the dangers were clear. Michael Kelly, Lane's predecessor, had been fired a few months earlier, reportedly over his attacks in the magazine on the vice president. When I came down for my job interview (I was working for the *Wall Street Journal* in Boston at the time), Lane sat across a table from me at Georgetown Seafood and asked what I thought about "the Marty problem."

I told Lane I figured the Gore liability could be an asset; if we were close to the inner workings of the Gore campaign, we could get stories before everybody else—while still taking our shots at Gore as warranted. Lane made it clear we were to play it straight, to be tough on Gore whenever we wished. The only thing we wouldn't do is take gratuitous potshots at the boss's pal. "We're not going to make fun of his bald spot," Lane said. I looked down at the story list I was planning to give to Lane, and reviewed the story I wanted to do about "Gore's bald spot: Expanding like the ozone hole?" I decided not to give Lane a copy of my story list, after all.

In fact, Marty Peretz, to his great credit, never once interfered with a word I had to say about Gore in the magazine. He spoke weekly with Gore, and even popped up at Gore events I was covering once or twice, but he never meddled with my work. *TNR* even got kudos from Howie Kurtz, the *Washington Post* media critic, for running "Peretz's In-House Heretics." "I'll keep playing it straight until I get the pink slip," Kurtz quoted me as saying.

But impressions are another story. Matt Cooper, who had been my predecessor at *TNR* before joining *Newsweek*, asked me at one Gore event, "When are you getting your staff pin?"

The most damaging impression of all is that of the Bush campaign, which quite clearly has no use for me or *TNR*. There is, perhaps, some reason for this. *TNR*'s Sid Blumenthal, during the 1992 campaign, made an unwarranted attack on the elder Bush's war record. Later, Steve Glass, the fiction writer masquerading as a *TNR* writer, wrote a mocking (and false) story about people worshiping at the Church of George Herbert Walker Bush. One reporter, who left the magazine to work elsewhere, tells me how the younger Bush carries a grudge against the magazine and glared at him throughout their entire meeting.

I suppose my own behavior hasn't helped matters. For rather than accepting ostracism from the Bush campaign, I have decided to mock the governor for ignoring me. So, in the summer of 1999, I find myself writing about my attempts to talk to the governor.

I begin with a confession: for six months now, I have been engaged in an intimate relationship with George W. Bush. It is an inappropriate relationship. In fact, it is wrong.

Now, do not misunderstand. I did not have sexual relations with that man, Mr. Bush. There is no sexual relationship. And it doesn't matter what the meaning of "is" is. But it must be said that Bush has been touching me in an improper way.

We have had three encounters now. He has touched me in a hotel room. He has touched me while we were surrounded by leather and chains. And he has touched me in the most intimate of places: yes, the kitchen.

And yet, he will not speak to me. Apparently I am good enough to be touched by him, but not good enough to interview him. He makes me feel cheap: he only likes me for my body.

Each time, I wait with dread as he approaches me and reaches right for my (this is embarrassing—do you mind if I say it with my eyes closed?) hand. Sure, some would call this a handshake. But to me, it is contact with the intent to arouse my desire for an interview—only so he can frustrate me by saying no.

When people have asked me about my relationship with Governor Bush, I have been evasive and misleading, although my answers were legally accurate. I did not volunteer information about Bush's obvious avoidance of me. I was motivated by many factors, including a desire to protect myself from embarrassment.

Now, this matter is between me, the two people I love most—John McCain and Elizabeth Dole—and our God.

Let us examine the evidence, as Ken Starr would. In the first encounter, the Governor meets Milbank on March 22 in an Austin hotel room. (Okay, so it was the ballroom, after a press conference.)

THE GOVERNOR: Who's this?

MILBANK: Hello, sir, Dana Milbank. (*They smile, and the governor touches Milbank on the hand.*)

KAREN HUGHES, COMMUNICATIONS DIRECTOR: From *The New Republic* . . .

THE GOVERNOR (*Smile disappears, becomes sarcastic*): Oh, beautiful.

HUGHES: . . . and before that, the *Wall Street Journal.*

But it is too late. The Governor has turned away.

Second encounter: the Governor meets Milbank in a firehouse in Bow, New Hampshire, in June. In the meantime, the Governor's staff has given Milbank many gifts, including a pack of trading cards. The Governor, greeting everybody in the firehouse, discovers Milbank in the kitchen, where he is trying to stay out of the way. Without Milbank's consent, the Governor grips his hand.

MILBANK: Hello, Governor.

THE GOVERNOR: Where're you from?

MILBANK: *The New Republic.*

THE GOVERNOR: Thanks for coming.

This is said without sarcasm, leading Milbank to believe the relationship will soon be consummated.

Third encounter: the two meet in August in a parking lot in Ames, Iowa, where Bush is greeting two hundred bikers, hence the leather and chains. The Governor notices Milbank and grabs his hand.

MILBANK: How are you, sir?

The Governor looks at Milbank's baseball cap, which the Teamsters had just given him, and smirks. He says nothing and stops touching Milbank.

The reason I have been pursuing Bush for an interview is that I am trying to determine whether he is, in fact, a man of substance or whether he merely hires smart people.

The truth is, there are many reasons for liberals to like some of Bush's ideas. The few policies Bush has detailed this summer confirm that suspicion. Consider his education plan, released September 2 in Los Angeles. His plan is actually to strengthen the Education Department by giving it control over Head Start—a policy sure to infuriate conservatives, who have sought to abolish the department. Yes, he contemplates vouchers, but with a rigorous system of accountability. This, in essence, is the New Democrats' plan, the sort of plan Senator John Kerry was flirting with before he decided not to join the presidential race. It's closer to the New Democrats' position than Al Gore's policy, which bends to the teachers' unions. "It's further evidence George Bush is running as a New Democrat rebranded as a compassionate conservative," says Will Marshall, who runs the Progressive Policy Institute, the New Democrats' think tank.

Earlier this summer, in Indiana, Bush spoke about his plan to help the poor. It was a nice bit of symbolism that his first major policy speech was about the poor, but it also was more than just symbolic. He offered a plan much like one some New Democrats, among them Senator Joe Lieberman of Connecticut, have been praising for some time: a tax credit to encourage more giving to charities that deal with the disadvantaged. Yes, the sum he would devote to the tax credit, $8 billion in his first year, is paltry. He'd have to do much better than that for the program to be useful. But it's a start. "It will be government that both knows its limits and shows its heart," he declared. "Government must be carefully limited—but strong and active and respected within those bounds." This kind of activist-government talk sounds Clintonian (in the good sense), and it enrages conservatives—a reason for everyone else to take Bush seriously.

But is Bush for real? Or is this simply what his advisers are feeding him at the moment? If he were elected, would these sensible advisers be shouldered aside by House Republican firebrands ? These questions show why it's so important for Bush to reveal more of himself. His reluctance to talk (or his staff's reluctance to put him in harm's way) raises doubts. A wide range of reporters have begun to grumble about their lack of access to Bush—even those from some of the mass-media outlets Bush needs. Why is he hiding?

Bush's aides never technically reject my requests for an interview. They just put them off. David Beckwith, Bush's spokesman, told me this spring that he would arrange an interview. Shortly thereafter, Beckwith was (coincidentally?) fired. To hasten the day when I exchange meaningful words with the governor, I have reduced my demands: no questions about youthful indiscretions and nothing on the record (lest Bush's profanity wind up in print).

Finally, the Bush people said they could squeeze me in for a few minutes, on September 7 in New Hampshire. But, four days before the big moment, an e-mail message from the Bush campaign popped up on my screen. "Scheduling informs me there is no time available on this campaign swing," it said. "Do you want me to try and squeeze you in on another swing?"

What a tease.

A few weeks later, the Bush campaign sends out an unusually informative bulletin. The governor has released the results of Bush's medical exam, conducted by one Kenneth H. Cooper, M.D., M.P.H. In these pages we learn, for the first time, that George W. Bush's body is 19.11 percent fat, his cholesterol count is 176, and his triglyceride level is 45. The campaign tells reporters "to schedule an appointment with Dr. Cooper" (Would my HMO pay for it?) for more information.

Don't get me wrong: I am happy for Bush that he has such an impressive lipid profile. But we need to know more about what's in his brain, not what's in his arteries. And when it comes to intellectual examinations, Bush is not so willing a patient.

In the weeks since my first dispatch on my fruitless six-month quest to plumb the depths—or shallows, if you ask his critics—of Bush's mind, readers have asked whether the governor has been shamed into being interviewed. But they underestimate his determination. "It's not going to happen between now and the end of the year," says Karen Hughes, Bush's communications director. Presumably, his schedule will open up in January, on the eve of the Iowa caucus.

But don't pity me. It's reasonable that Bush, with 1,500 interview requests pending, wouldn't bother with a liberal magazine that was hostile to his old man. Instead, save the pity for guys like Bill Minutaglio, of the *Dallas Morning News*, and Mickey Herskowitz, of the *Houston Chronicle*. Minutaglio wrote a sympathetic biography of Bush, yet Bush declined to be interviewed for the book. And Bush fired his campaign-book ghostwriter, sports columnist Herskowitz. The Bush folks say it's because Herskowitz was late; Herskowitz, though he considers Bush a friend, says he had trouble getting details. He told the *Chronicle* that when he asked for substance, he got a thousand Bush speeches, but "it was actually five speeches the governor has given 200 times." Now Hughes is writing the book; don't expect it to be a kiss-and-tell.

Though I didn't get an interview, I did garner empathy from others in the press—even the ones Bush talks to. "You don't want an interview, anyway," said a network hotshot, trying to cheer me up. "He doesn't say anything." An Arizona reporter told me his visit with Bush was so restricted that he was told what type of questions he could ask. Journalists, for the most part, have reached the conclusion that Bush, in a bubble, is unwilling to reveal what or how he thinks. Eric Stern, a young reporter for Iowa's *Waterloo Courier*, got a half-hour with Bush. "He was so charming I almost neglected to notice that he didn't answer any of my questions," Stern says.

Bush does seem happy to level with some people. At a primary school in Bakersfield, California, one child told Bush that she had "a poodle dog." Bush was ready: "I have a dog named Spot. We have three cats, too. One cat is named Cowboy, one cat is named Willie, and another cat is named Ernie." Bush told of how he rescued Ernie, a stray, and adopted him. "Ernie the Cat never gave up, and now he's running the governor's mansion," he said. It was a brilliant performance. Bush revealed nothing but connected perfectly.

Now, Bush's opponents are trying to make an issue of his silence. When GOP candidates meet for a debate on October 28, Bush won't be there. "'Don't ask, don't tell' is no way to run a presidential campaign," Steve Forbes chides. Gary Bauer's line is, "What are you afraid of, Governor?" The pressure has become sufficiently intense that Bush has agreed to a December debate in New Hampshire.

Bush's foes want him to talk more because they think he'll get into trouble no matter how he answers questions. In the controversy over Pat Buchanan's Hitler apologia, Bush tried to be inclusive, earning barbs that he's unprincipled. But when Bush showed principle by defending the working poor from congressional marauders, House Majority Whip Tom DeLay sniffed that "he obviously doesn't understand how Congress works."

Bush's latest move earned him dreaded comparisons to Clinton's triangulation. He trashed fellow Republicans for painting an "America

slouching toward Gomorrah" and for confusing "the need for limited government with a disdain for government itself." He's absolutely correct, of
course, but the right howled. "The more he speaks, the more troubled I
am becoming about his candidacy," Rush Limbaugh bellowed.

Strategically, Bush's caution makes perfect sense: When you're the
prohibitive favorite, why blow it by talking too much and risking a gaffe?
He took that risk with Tucker Carlson, a conservative writer he trusted.
But Carlson's piece in *Talk* magazine made Bush look foul-mouthed and
insensitive. Since then, Bush's staff has insisted that reporters focus their
queries more, but he gets burned. He unwisely discussed books with Maureen Dowd. "I've always liked John La Care, Le Carrier, or however you
pronounce his name," he said. He told the *San Francisco Chronicle* that the
feds shouldn't compensate states for funds spent on illegal immigrants.
Never mind that Bush supported a lawsuit by the states seeking just such
payments. A spokeswoman said he misunderstood the question.

But the shy silence causes many in the press to conclude that Bush isn't
ready for prime time. "Is Dubya Dumb?" *U.S. News & World Report* asked
in July. I still don't think so. He is not learned, to be sure, but he is smart
and savvy. Still, the empty-vessel question will remain as long as he stays
cloistered. His October 5 education speech was laudable; he called for a
strong federal role in education and for establishing something close to
national standards. But was this Bush talking, or was he reading lines? Hard
to say; "surrogates" took the questions.

I confess that my desire for a tête-à-tête with Bush has verged on
the desperate. I've considered contributing to his campaign in order to
get into a Bush reception, but even that might not work. At a New York
fund-raiser, I watched fat cats leave the room after each had a photo-
op with Bush. They seemed to get about ten seconds apiece with him,
which seemed reasonable, given how many of them there were. One fellow told me he had raised $5,000 to get into the reception. If it cost him
$5,000 to get ten seconds with Bush, a 15-minute interview would cost
me $450,000.

Instead, I must settle for "media availabilities," Bush's mini-press
conferences. Reporters, because of their limited access to the candidate,
tend to use the brief sessions either to test him or to trap him. It
shouldn't be long before reporters ask Bush to recite π to seven decimal
places or to name Asian prime ministers. At a recent session in New York,
Mark Halperin of ABC News attempted an essay question. He asked Bush
to talk about the four national elections this decade and how they shaped
the conservative image. It was a deliberate attempt to explore Bush's brain.
The results? "Well, '88 was great," Bush responded, "and '92 stunk."
Moments later, our brief glimpse into the mind of Bush was over.

I have begun to contemplate more drastic measures to gain an audience with Bush. I try out on my colleagues in the press the possibility of carrying a sign that says, "Governor Bush, Talk to Me." Kurtz, of the *Post*, offers to write about it if I do, and a producer from *Good Morning, America* offers to have me on the show. But the danger here is that I could become known permanently as a clown, a Michael Moore of the campaign trail. "I don't think that will do much to boost your reputation around here," says Mark McKinnon, Bush's media strategist. He's right, I suppose. I'll have to follow the Bush campaign from the outside looking in. Such is the lot of the *Gore Republic* butt-boy.

6

★ ☆ ★

Great Expectations

The 2000 campaign, the morning papers tell us, has begun in earnest. It is June 13, 1999, and George W. Bush, in the maiden swing of his presidential campaign, has hit the trail in those two early primary states, Greenwich and Kennebunkport. Oh, yes, he's stopping in Iowa and New Hampshire, too, but something in Bush's (blue) blood is making him visit both of these Yankee villages. In Greenwich, the Bush ancestral seat, he will hold a fund-raiser. And in Kennebunkport, he has stopped today at the family home, Walker's Point, for some fishing with Dad.

The day is somewhat less relaxing for the 150 of us journalists piling off tour buses at noon here at Walker's Point for a photo-op. A plump Bush aide stands before the herd and opens a foul mouth. "This isn't going to be all assholes and elbows," he barks. "This is going to go one way: my way." He then instructs us on how to walk up the driveway. "I'm going to take a slow pace because I'm tired," the stout fellow says. "If you walk in front of me, your credential gets pulled." Presently, the gentlemen and ladies of the press respond to him with various *moooo*'s and *baaaaah*'s. We are herded past the tennis court, the pond and the swimming pool. "Stop! Stop! Stop! Stop! Stop!" the large fellow shouts. "Correspondents, stay back!"

It's going to be a long campaign.

I missed the first day of Great Expectations, as the Bushies call their tour, and so I did not get my official T-shirt. But I have a good excuse: I was picked off by Al Gore, who held a series of meetings with journalists yesterday at his residence. It was an obvious ploy to reduce Bush's press contingent, and I fell for it. Given the choice of Bush's plane with 105 reporters or Gore's dining room with three others, I opted to watch Bush's Iowa jaunt on television.

In our meeting, Gore, who officially announces his candidacy this week, finally seemed to be approaching a cogent vision. "What I represent is continuity where our economy is concerned, but dramatic change as to our social programs," he said. "We faced an economic crisis in '92. That was the main theme of the last six and a half years. Unlike in '92, the central issue we face now is the crisis of the American family. Instead of a budget deficit, we have a care deficit." Clinton's 1992 theme was "Putting People First." Gore's 2000 mantra is "Putting Families First."

By laying out his themes now, along with a mind-numbing array of proposals, Gore and his aides hope to smoke out Bush: either the governor gives no specifics and looks like a lightweight or he is forced to offer specifics that alienate one side or the other. So far, Bush seems unfazed, still loading his stump speech with pleasant platitudes: "prosperity must have a purpose" and "leave no one behind" and "usher in the responsibility era." Indeed, the only thing Bush uttered in Iowa that could truly be called a concrete plan was a proposal to "teach our youngest children phonics." Now there's a winning theme. It's the phonics, stupid.

At every campaign stop, Bush delivers his "leave no one behind" line. Yet this morning, leaving Kennebunkport, Bush aides do just that—to me. I join the caravan this morning, but when two press buses get lost, a Bush aide asks me to go back and find them. I do as I'm told, only to discover upon my return that the Bush staff has abandoned me. Is that compassionate?

I arrive in New Castle, a bit late and irritated, at a location the Bush aides call the most scenic coastal spot in New Hampshire. We will have to take their word for it; all that's visible this morning is a blanket of fog, and foghorns compete with Bush as he delivers the latest rendition of the speech. "Prosperity has a purpose . . . Promote the peace . . . Usher in the responsibility era . . . Rally the armies of compassion . . . Nobody gets left behind." Well, almost nobody.

Bush is good on the trail, almost unbelievably so. I constantly get the impression I am watching one of those movies about a political campaign in which the events are far too perfect to be real. The improbably handsome candidate, emerging from the obnoxious media pack with his wholesome wife, is constantly greeted by singing children, waving flags and patriotic music.

With all the traps being laid for Bush on his maiden voyage, it's a wonder he hasn't yet fallen. The Democrats are running around with T-shirts comparing him to the *Titanic* and posters of question marks. Meanwhile, the press, his opponents, and even feisty locals are all looking for The Stumble. I thought we had it this afternoon, at the Bow firehouse, when a local asked if Bush would support full funding of the Land and Water Conservation Fund. Bush was stumped. "I don't know the answer," he said. "You may be surprised there are some things a presidential candidate doesn't know about." Actually, no. But the press consensus is that this is too obscure to be The Stumble. We don't know what the fund is, either.

The absence of The Stumble hasn't stopped rivals from carping. After Bush, courageously, says at a press conference this morning that he wouldn't have an abortion litmus test for Supreme Court justices, laughing-stock Senator Bob Smith pipes up that "there should not be one pro-life vote for a George W. Bush presidency." I don't share Smith's outrage. In fact, just the opposite: Bush had been making some troubling nods to the right on this tour. In Iowa, he spoke about cutting marginal tax rates and shifting some Social Security tax revenues into private accounts—both conservative boilerplate. Today, asked what his first two priorities would be as president, he says "restoration of the military budget" and "cut marginal rates." Really? Where's the child literacy plan? The huge charity tax credit? Expanding the earned income tax credit for the working poor? Isn't prosperity's purpose the first priority, or the armies of compassion?

The Democrats are doing their best right now to paint Bush as a wolf in sheep's clothing, a Tom DeLay in disguise. I doubt that. Bush is no wolf—but he runs the risk of becoming a sheep, and that's worrisome enough. His compassionate, communitarian intentions won't be of much use if DeLay dominates him once elected—and his bows to the right suggest it could happen.

After Bush's rally in New Castle, I overhear one of his local supporters, Bill Fortune, grousing about the twin evils of high taxes and feminists ("they're bitter and angry little people"). So I ask Fortune about Bush's soothing rhetoric. "He's got to sing that moderate tune because the voters are mostly Democrats and feminists," Fortune replies. What about his pitch for education? "He has to say that. The point is, he needs to get elected. If we get a Republican president in there with a Republican Congress, it doesn't matter who he is."

That is exactly what scares me. I ask Fortune, who is wearing a Bush sticker and looks as if he might hit me, whether there is even the tiniest possibility that Bush really is a moderate. "You've been talking to space aliens," he replies. Later, I find myself wondering: What if he's right?

 ★ ☆ ★

In case you've been living in a cave, here's the conventional wisdom on the campaign thus far: the presidential contest, eight months before the Iowa caucuses, is a two-man race. Bush and Gore themselves, judging from their stump speeches, seem to have bypassed the primaries and gone straight to the general election. Bush campaigns against the "if it feels good, do it" culture identified with Clinton and promises "a fresh start after a season of cynicism." Gore decries the "crumbs of compassion" and the stands Bush has taken on guns and abortion.

The two campaign operations, both obsessed with fund-raising and endorsements, are disturbingly alike. A couple of weeks back, I received an e-mail from the Gore camp announcing endorsements from lieutenant governors; moments later, I received a fax from Bush with his own list of lieutenant governor endorsements. On June 3, nothing could distract the front-runners from their show-of-support competition. Three releases came over the fax machine within 66 minutes. "Forbes warns no U.S. troops should be sent into Kosovo," read a Forbes release. A Dole release had a "statement by Elizabeth Dole on Kosovo peace agreement." And the Bush fax? "Columbus Mayor Lashutka endorses Governor Bush."

This above-the-fray, off-the-trail strategy is utterly maddening to the other candidates. Lamar Alexander, who had to lay off staff after funds dried up, lashed out at Bush by saying that "most voters in Iowa couldn't pick him out of a lineup." It was an interesting theory, so I had *TNR*'s consulting art director create just such a lineup: a piece of paper printed with the photos of three Bushes (George, George W., and Jeb), three standard-issue Republicans (Lamar, Tom DeLay, and Pennsylvania Governor Tom Ridge), and three men with high, patrician foreheads that resemble the Bush brow (Ohio Senator George Voinovich, New York Governor George Pataki, and Democratic Representative Marion Berry of Arkansas).

I then took the lineup with me to Iowa and New Hampshire. Though half the people I asked could pick out both George W. and Lamar without much trouble, my lineup did indeed baffle a number of citizens. "George W. Bush? Sure. It's him," said one fellow, pointing without hesitation to Ridge. "That's him," said a woman, pointing confidently to the elder Bush. Another fellow fingered President Bush and, when I reminded him I was looking for W., confessed: "I don't know the difference." Another man studied the photos intently and pointed to Jeb.

But Lamar shouldn't celebrate the outcome. A similar number of Iowans and New Hampshirites couldn't identify him, either, even though he has been living among them for the past five years. When I asked my subjects to find Lamar, one fellow studied the photos at length and ultimately settled on Berry. Another man pointed to Ridge. Still another seemed to think the photo of George W. Bush was Lamar.

Perhaps the most compelling evidence that the primaries are over and the general election has begun comes from the debut of the hecklers. The presence of the heckler is a vote of confidence in the candidate's stature, a calculation that the heckler can get maximum exposure from the disruption. In New Hampshire, Bush hears from a heckler shouting about the anti–flag-burning amendment Bush supports. That ultimate heckler, Pat Buchanan, is talked about as a possible Reform Party candidate, so he could heckle Bush all the way to Election Day. Bush is even being heckled on the Internet: a clever website parody, GWBush.com ("Bush turns himself in for past drug crimes in an attempt to 'usher in the responsibility era'"), apparently got under the candidate's skin so much that he declared at a press conference that "there ought to be limits to freedom." Only Bush could get away with a line like that.

The Texas governor is clearly getting the best of his Republican competitors, who are pounding the pavement but failing to make any dent in the overwhelming Bush machine, with its money, endorsements and commanding lead in opinion polls. If you have any doubt of that, take a trip up to the picturesque village of Amherst, New Hampshire, on Independence Day, 1999.

It's a week before home-state Senator Bob Smith is to quit the Republican Party to run for president as an independent. But the man has already abandoned ship. Literally.

Smith had been planning to march in Amherst's Fourth of July parade, using a nautical theme. His campaign has rented a boat on a trailer to serve as a float. His supporters have donned sailor caps and T-shirts printed with captain's wheels and Smith's campaign theme, "Chart the Right Course for America." In fact, the only thing missing is the skipper himself. Smith has decided not to march, after all.

His followers aren't sure what changed his mind, but my guess is that the answer can be found in one word—nay, one initial. W., the $36 Million Man, has decided to march, and he immediately attracts a throng numbering more than a hundred: a squad of cheerleaders, a clown on stilts, a man with a remote-controlled skunk, and a woman with a sign reading "We want magnets on your body when you are in the White House." A calliope on wheels plays carnival music. Bush aides hand out Bush baseball cards ("Position: Governor of 2nd Largest State," they read, and tout, "Reduced welfare rolls by more than 335,000," as if that were a slugging percentage.) Reporters chase Bush with microphones on long poles, like so many drum majors with batons.

Had Smith come, he would have been forgotten, much as Gary Bauer now finds himself as he watches the Bush scrum. A small gang of Bauer volunteers is trying to stir up enthusiasm for their man. One young woman holds a sign saying "Yo Quiero Bauer," for all those Spanish-speaking New Hampshire residents. Another Bauer sign proclaims "Bauer? Yeah, Baby."

(It's unclear how the refrain of the sex-crazed Austin Powers will help the torchbearer of the religious right.) Bauer and his minions, squeezed between Bush and a procession of local realtors marching with briefcases, can't even persuade some spectators to shake the candidate's hand and take his leaflets. "Who's this Bauer guy?" one woman asks. "Is he a Democrat?" another confused spectator inquires. "Who's that?" a girl asks her mother. "Daddy just told me who he is," the mother replies, "and he's not somebody we would ever vote for."

But if the parade is an annointed event for Bush, the scene is entirely different a few hours later in Hopkinton. Here, at a picnic held by an anti-tax group, Smith, Bauer and Pat Buchanan are the stars—and it's Bush who has stayed away. The 1,200 attendees, many wearing pro-life stickers and one displaying plastic fetuses, fill the place with boos whenever Bush's name and his $36 million war chest are mentioned. "Let me say to that guy, George, with all his money: you're not going to win," Smith bellows. Bauer declares, "We don't have kings here." And Buchanan, amid chants of "Go third party," shouts, "We're not into coronations up here." When the attendees cast their votes in a straw poll, Buchanan gets 58 percent to Bauer's 21 percent and Smith's 9 percent. Bush's support? One percent.

Conservatives never loved Bush nor, for that matter, his father. But his record level of fund-raising—that astonishing amount of $36 million in the first six months of the year—seems to have galvanized the right in opposition to him. Smith, on July 13, quit the GOP. Buchanan has flirted with a Reform Party run, and Bauer has made hostile noises. True, conservatives are famous for empty threats about third parties. But Richard Lessner, the former editorial voice of the *Manchester Union Leader*, tells me over a plate of beans and sausage in Hopkinton that he sees a "critical mass" of frustration. "The Bush phenomenon has really rocked the Republican right," Lessner says. "He's going to win without a single vote being cast." Most galling is the $480 average contribution to Bush—not exactly from Mom and Pop. "People here feel he's another guy bought and paid for by Goldman Sachs."

Those of us who don't carry around plastic fetuses should be encouraged by the right's loathing of Bush. If he's making those kinds of enemies, he's probably a sensible fellow. Still, the conservatives are right that there's something obscene about his record $36 million take. Gore would have been able to make an issue of it were it not for his own fund-raising controversies from 1996. Absurdly, the greatest voice now for the little guy is Steve Forbes, who will spend his personal millions to make sure the Republican primary is competitive.

Of course, there's still John McCain, champion of campaign finance reform. McCain sent supporters an editorial about Bush from the *Littleton*

(N.H.) *Courier.* "It appears once again that money can buy everything," the editors opined. "Money can buy public office, money can buy public policy, money can buy the public interest and all but disenfranchise those who don't have it." The *Courier*'s solution: "Imagine a presidential race between McCain and former Senator Bill Bradley."

That's quite a fantasy. But why stop there? Imagine a McCain-Bradley debate interrupted by the arrival of a large boat on a flatbed truck. On the deck of the boat stands a six-foot-six, pear-shaped figure, a pirate hat concealing his comb-over, a dagger in one hand, a hook on the other, and a black patch over his eye. "Ladies and gentlemen," the moderator intones, "the nominee of the U.S. Taxpayers Party, former Republican Bob Smith."

Back on Planet Earth, the Bush advisers can hardly believe the good fortune their campaign has had so far. On Bush's triumphant maiden campaign swing, I found myself discussing the candidate's luck with Karl Rove, one of his top strategists, at dinner one night. "The only thing we haven't done well," he said, "is to lower expectations."

7

★ ☆ ★

McCainiacs

There is something remarkably pleasant about covering a presidential candidate who is at 2 percent in the polls, as John McCain is now, in the spring of '99. He acts as if he's got nothing to lose.

I am riding in a van in Manchester, New Hampshire, with McCain, his national political director, John Weaver, his New Hampshire director, Mike Dennehy, and one other reporter, the *New Yorker*'s Joe Klein. Bush attracts 50 or 100 reporters, but it's far more enjoyable to have a little one-on-one time with the challenger.

Wearing his Ray-Ban sunglasses, McCain treats us to indiscreet comments about Trent Lott and Barbara Boxer. He mocks a question on the Portsmouth military base closings he just got from WMUR, the dominant TV outlet in the state. "Sure, I'm going to protect Portsmouth," he says, dripping with sarcasm. "Why don't we turn it into an ethanol plant and ship the corn out from Iowa." Thus does McCain embrace the two positions—base closings and ethanol opposition—that should doom him in Iowa and New Hampshire. "Don't do that to me," Weaver says, shaking his head.

McCain doesn't stop there. He praises Bob Dole (who publicly spoke of contributing to McCain, to the consternation of his wife's campaign) for refusing to take on Clinton over Bosnia policy in 1996 even though it would have been politically expedient. He shows a disdain for the rituals of politics, such as New Hampshire's effort to force candidates to skip the early Delaware primary. ("I can't even take an Amtrak train through that state," he complains.) Stopping at a Rotary meeting, he doesn't even feign interest while the locals blather on about their golf tournament, about the woman who sings the "Follow Your Rotary Dream" theme song and about a new granddaughter, graduations, field hockey news, SAT results, visits from relatives, and a raffle. He wears the look of a man with little patience for such nonsense.

Journalists love McCain for such things. He's a habitual straight-shooter who always speaks his mind—a trait that's likely to cause him some trouble. McCain likes to speak hard truths, and journalists respect him for it. But hard truths don't work too well with voters. Just ask Bob Kerrey or Bruce Babbitt. Bob Dole was more like McCain than Elizabeth on the campaign trail (perhaps that's why he talks of contributing to McCain now) and was also admired by opinion-makers for his sharp wit. Today, Bob Dole works for Pfizer. But McCain presses on in this admirable tradition. He tells Iowans he opposes their ethanol subsidies. He stands boldly (and against the polls) in favor of ground troops in Kosovo, saying, "No army has ever surrendered to an airplane."

Surprisingly, the people McCain meets in New Hampshire seem to be captivated by his message, even when they don't like what he says. When McCain takes the podium at the breakfast meeting of the Bow Rotary Club, outside Concord, he connects immediately. Introduced as a former prisoner of war and a father of seven, he speaks like an ordinary guy in a gravely, no-nonsense voice. He charmingly mocks Clinton's China policy ("Los Alamos is like the visitors center at the Grand Canyon") and then speaks about how campaign finance abuses are alienating young voters: "They think we're corrupt. You know what? They're right."

Then he switches to a story about a fellow Vietnam POW named Mike Christian, a poor Alabaman who sewed an American flag inside his shirt so that they all could say the Pledge of Allegiance each day. He describes how the flag was discovered and how Mike was beaten for two hours, after which time he returned to the cell and began to sew another flag. McCain's listeners sit in rapt attention. One man actually begins to cry. Rotarians file up to a McCain staffer to pledge support. Then, an hour later, McCain bounds up the steps of the auditorium stage at Manchester Central High School, where hundreds of children seem as moved by McCain's speech as the Rotarians had been. The kids jump to their feet to give the candidate a standing ovation.

The contrast could hardly be more stark between McCain and Elizabeth Dole, who is touring New Hampshire at the same time McCain is. (Bush has yet to put in an appearance in the state.) But while Dole is the leading challenger to Bush in the polls, McCain clearly has the potential to arouse more passion.

Dole is only a few minutes into her act at Londonderry High School, and already one wishes that one of those vaudevillian hooks would magically appear and put her out of her misery. She searches pitiably for a way to connect with a group of about a hundred students, whom she is addressing in front of the cameras. "Maybe some of you have read Tom Brokaw's book *The Greatest Generation*?" she ventures. (Blank looks.) She tries another one: "Dr. Jeane Kirkpatrick signed on to be my foreign policy advisory chairman." (Baffled silence.)

She then launches a discussion about America's failing schools, but she assures the topic's irrelevance when she tells the kids "this doesn't apply" to them and their school. As the youngsters fidget, some with chins in hands, others giggling, she points out, helpfully, that the Red Cross, under her leadership, spent 92 cents of every dollar on its programs. The school principal finally decides to end the agony and walks up to the podium.

"Is my time over?" Dole asks.

"We're about to have a bell ring," the principal says, even though the bell doesn't ring for another ten minutes.

The contrast is an important one, because Dole and McCain are the two presidential candidates fighting to be the mainstream choice of Republicans should Bush falter. If the matter were up to the press and the political elite, the contest would already be over: McCain by a mile. Opinion-makers just won't give the robotic Dole any respect, even though she's second only to Bush in the polls, which also show her trouncing Al Gore. She doesn't have the money to go the distance, handicappers say, and she's too canned to survive on the campaign trail. Her scripting has become such a cliché that it's now a *Doonesbury* gag.

That leads to the main reason not to write off Liddy Dole—at least not in New Hampshire. Dole, despite her inability to charm the opinion-makers, understands something that some rivals seem to have missed here: the deeply changed Republican electorate. The old stereotype of a blue-collar, conservative state, enamored of hunting rifles and hostile to anything resembling a tax, no longer applies. New Hampshire is far more prosperous than it was even four years ago, with an exploding technology industry. It has the highest concentration of software workers in the United States, at 8.4 percent of the workforce, according to the American Electronics Association.

Thus, many of Dole's supposedly suicidal stands—tough on guns, neutralish on abortion—will likely play well in the new New Hampshire. During her speech to workers at the Lockheed-Martin plant in Nashua, her remark on gun control ("I don't see why we need an Uzi or an AK-47 to go hunting") drew the loudest applause by far. She's defied GOP isolationists by calling for victory in Kosovo, whatever it takes. In Londonderry, she even praised Clinton's Americorps program, which Republicans have labored to kill.

Naturally Dole's staff does not boast of this strategy, for fear of alienating the GOP's conservative base. But with so many conservative candidates splitting the right-wing vote, it makes sense to play for the middle. This strategy has the added benefit of allowing Dole to cultivate the image of a McCain-style maverick, even as she tailors her stances to fit the increasingly moderate New Hampshire electorate. On the air at Nashua's WSMN radio during her visit, Dole made another strong push for gun control and safety locks: voters, she declared, "respect a person who doesn't look to the polls to see what your position's going to be."

Similarly, at the high school, Dole promised the kids, "I don't get my passions from polling." Yet this came moments after she declared that education was Americans' number-one concern, a fact that could have been established only by polling. Later, she boasted to the Lockheed workers that her fund-raising deficiencies would be overcome by—you guessed it— polls. She leads Gore by 12 percent, she said, has 92 percent name recognition, and has 72 to 80 percent favorable ratings. "That's worth fifteen million dollars right there," she said. Yes, Dole gets passion from polls, but so what? Here, in increasingly liberal New Hampshire, she's reading them right.

The question isn't the message but the messenger: Can she surrender enough of the staging to make herself seem human to the opinion-makers? The signs are not encouraging. At each stop, she climbs from her van with a fixed smile, as if masking some unseen source of pain. "How are ewe?" she asks. "Good to see ewe today. So wonderful to be with ewe. Thank ewe." Over and over, like a Tickle Me Elmo. As I waited for her to arrive in Londonderry that morning, the school principal remarked to me that Dole was due at 9:55 but added, "I'll believe it when I see it." Believe it, I told her. She's very precise. Sure enough, the van pulled up at 9:55. The candidate was so well prepped that she already seemed to know everybody there. "Thank ewe for the introduction," she said to one boy, who hadn't yet introduced her.

Even the celebrated Dole stroll, her attempt to show a casual side, seems mechanical. Following her footwork in front of the high school students, as I did, was like watching some kind of foxtrot. Left forward, right forward, right back, left back, cross, cross, cross, cross, cross, cross, cross, cross, left forward, right forward, right back, left back. Rest right hand on lectern, and repeat. Ready? Left forward, right forward . . .

That afternoon, at the Lockheed facility, Dole had the microphone clipped to her jacket for another free-range appearance. "I'm talking from behind the podium today because I'd like to deliver a statement I just put together in the last couple of minutes," she began. "I'd like you all to listen while I deliver this statement. Then I can be more informal and get out in the middle." After reading her statement, on Clinton and China, she continued. "Now, let me be a bit more informal here," she said, brushing her hair back with her left hand, as if she had said, "Let me slip into something more comfortable." Then she assumed a broad smile and plunged forth toward the crowd. Oddly, announcing her stage instructions seemed to undercut the whole point of the Dole stroll. She had announced that she was about to make a gesture that connotes informality, thereby making the gesture, by definition, a formal one. Left forward, right forward, right back . . .

The man chiefly responsible for heading off the W. ascension is John Weaver, a brooding strategist constantly lurking in McCain's shadow. Weaver knows well how a popular Texas politician with lots of dough and a huge organization can be beaten handily. He once worked for such a man.

Four years earlier, Weaver, then field director for Phil Gramm's disastrous presidential bid, sat in a bar in Iowa with fellow Gramm advisers, figuring out why their man bombed in that day's caucuses. They scribbled down a 15-point list of "Lessons Learned." Those conclusions—skip the straw polls, create a crusade, downplay organization and emphasize media—would in time become the blueprint for McCain's insurgency against Bush.

These days, Weaver seeks to vanquish the ghosts of the Gramm fiasco. The 40-year-old Texan aims to best his bitter personal rival Karl Rove, Bush's top strategist. (Weaver was once a friend of Rove's and rejected entreaties from a Bush loyalist to join the Texas governor's campaign.) And Weaver feels a sense of salvation. "In the past I've worked for a lot of guys who want us to tell them what to believe. It's just a chase for money. You feel dirty, like a hired gun." But no more, Weaver says. "I'm on the side of the angels in this one."

A newspaper article described Weaver as a "soft-spoken Texan with a calming presence," a description that caused chortling McCain staffers to spend the next day ribbing the reporter. Clearly, she had never had what staffers have dubbed the "W.O.W. moment": experiencing the Wrath of Weaver.

This is a man who has thrown at least two baseballs through office walls and regularly heaves a variety of consumer goods: pagers, a coffee table, even a television set. When he and his wife went to New Orleans for Mardi Gras, he threw a suitcase out the window during an argument. During this campaign alone, he has smashed three Nokia cell phones. One bit the dust while Weaver was screaming at a colleague on it in a parking lot. "I was actually hit by some of the shrapnel," reports Jim Merrill, the McCain aide who witnessed the call from Weaver's end.

"I'm a big thrower," Weaver allows. "Four years ago, I hit Kurt Warner with a football in a sports bar. I didn't know he'd be the Super Bowl MVP." During the Gramm campaign, he organized a "telephone toss" from guest rooms into a swimming pool.

Weaver uses his volatile temper to motivate his staff. If anybody is late for the morning meeting, he orders the next day's held a half-hour earlier. When something went wrong with a campaign mailing, Weaver called for the subordinate responsible and told the receptionist, "Tell him the Icy Hand of Death is on the phone." Could it be that Weaver's fury is mostly shtick? He's fired only one person on the McCain staff. Before a telephone tirade, he'll tell people around him to "watch this."

"There's a lot of tension," Weaver explains. "If somebody will blow his stack, we'll get over it and move on, rather than letting it scab over and dwelling on it." Some McCainites, now wise to the methods of Weaver's tantrums, try to induce them. Cindy McCain, the candidate's wife, had New Hampshire aides call Weaver to relate a tall tale of being roughed up by Bush supporters and then running into the ladies' room crying, in full view of the press. "I do it to keep him on his toes," she explains.

Weaver also uses his temper to keep another guy on his toes: John McCain, who is known to have a short fuse himself. "I'm the one guy who can tell John 'no,'" Weaver says.

Though his title is political director, Weaver is equal parts campaign manager, field director, strategist, media expert, traveling aide and bodyguard. He's also the guy who wakes McCain in the morning and brings him coffee.

McCain acknowledges that Weaver is the core of the campaign. "He's quite a remarkable man," he says. But McCain can't resist needling his strategist: "He is an offense to every sense of style and grace."

In New York, Weaver grew tired of McCain's complaints about a staffer. "I'm sick and tired of this," Weaver shouted at the candidate. "If you want to fire him, go ahead, but don't sit and bitch about him." Weaver folded his arms and refused to talk to McCain for the rest of the day.

McCain finally called him at 1 a.m. to apologize, and later bought Weaver, whom he has nicknamed Sunny, some ice cream.

Weaver aims to make McCain a viable contender with a fraction of the money and manpower of the other candidates. He has fewer staffers even than longshot Gary Bauer, and less than half Bush's payroll. Weaver learned to get this right from a man who got it wrong: Phil Gramm.

Weaver met the future senator at Texas A&M, where Weaver was a journalism student and Gramm a professor. Weaver, who grew up as a Democrat in rural western Texas and joined Young Americans for Freedom in college, was political director for Gramm's 1984 Senate campaign.

The strategist went on to become executive director of the Texas Republican Party, a post later held by George W. Bush adviser Karen Hughes, and he worked on both of the senior Bush's presidential campaigns and advised 11 senators, including Fred Thompson and Rick Santorum. The Gramm campaign of 1996, however, was a disaster.

Weaver used the "Lessons Learned," scribbled in the Iowa bar, to build a strategy for McCain. "There are lessons learned from Gramm that we took to our core being," he says. "That's why the money advantage for Bush never scared me." Among the lessons:

No. 3, "*Realize media is critical.*" Weaver predicted, accurately, that the media's constant access to McCain would compensate for a relative lack of funds.

No. 4, "*Organization . . . drains off media money and may not be there at the end.*" The people in the Bush campaign "talk about their firewalls and their precinct chairmen and their governors," Weaver says. "It's all malarkey."

No. 6, "*Placing a premium on straw polls in the off-year is a cash drain.*" Weaver won his gamble to skip the Iowa straw poll last August and the Iowa caucuses this year.

No. 15, "*Be big, establish the crusade.*" McCain's campaign has successfully portrayed him as a larger-than-life war hero and a maverick.

Many of the other decisions that have defined McCain's candidacy have also been Weaver's. He nagged McCain to run. "Weaver's the guy who stayed on top of him, who said, 'Not only should you run, but I have a plan to get you there,'" says Howard Opinsky, McCain's spokesman. He assembled McCain's top team, including Opinsky and strategist Mike Murphy ("I wouldn't be here if Weaver didn't trick me into it," he says), and he approved the hiring of campaign manager Rick Davis. "Weaver is captain of the pirate ship, and we sail into uncharted waters for each campaign," says Lanny Wiles, McCain's advance man.

Weaver devised McCain's town-hall-meeting-concept bus tour for New Hampshire, naming it "Straight Talk Express" over a bottle of Merlot. He has kept his staff, often by intimidation, from "handling" the candidate. "Let McCain be McCain" is his mantra, and he rules out most gimmicks and photo ops (though McCain's New Hampshire event with Bill Bradley was Weaver's creation). He advises the campaign on ads, insisting that it keep a "presidential tone." "John Weaver has really driven all the decisions," says Mike Dennehy, McCain's New Hampshire director. "If anyone on the campaign has John McCain's ear, it's John Weaver."

"What do I need to know, Johnny?" That's the line McCain invariably directs to Weaver before each event. The political director is usually slouched in a captain's chair at the front of the bus, a cell phone clamped to his ear. Weaver and his telephone are the campaign's moving command center; he is constantly barking orders to "the Pentagon"—that's McCain headquarters in Alexandria—and to aides on the bus.

Weaver, though a half-foot taller than his candidate and 23 years younger, is remarkably like McCain. They share the same gallows humor, droll delivery and fierce competitiveness. Weaver "is like an expectant father," says Wendy Poole, assistant to the candidate's wife. "He feels what McCain feels." Cindy McCain agrees: "Whenever these things are lobbed at my husband, he takes it just as if it were him."

Indeed, Weaver seems literally to feel McCain's pain. When McCain is on a cable TV show, Weaver watches from the audience, visibly hurt when the questions turned to McCain's relationships with lobbyists. When the host plays a clip of the candidate's description of his torture as a prisoner of war in North Vietnam, Weaver leans forward, elbows on knees, and then puts a hand in front of his eyes to cover the tears.

In McCain, Weaver sees a savior, both personally and professionally. McCain has allowed Weaver finally to emerge from the shadow of Karl Rove. The two Texas consultants both worked on the elder Bush's presidential campaigns and in a Texas gubernatorial campaign in the 1980s. They once talked of being business partners; they and their wives were close. But in '88, when Weaver ran the Bush campaign in Texas and Rove was a consultant, the two got into a billing dispute. Rove, Weaver loyalists say, made it difficult for Weaver to work in Texas and spread ugly rumors about him. "He nearly destroyed John emotionally," says Weaver's wife, Rhonda. Rove declines to comment, and Weaver says he's moved on.

McCain and his staff have become something of a surrogate family for Weaver, who left his wife and seven-year-old daughter in San Antonio last year with a plan to return home on weekends. It's more like once every few months.

"I learned very early on, his first love is politics, and I come in second," his wife says. When her health deteriorated—she has multiple sclerosis—and she became bedridden for a time, John offered to take a reduced role in the campaign so he could spend more time at home, but she wouldn't hear of it.

In McCain, Weaver sees an almost messianic figure. "John will change the party, but also the way we conduct campaigns," he says while waiting for his candidate to finish a speech. "Our leaders have completely lost their way," he says. "It's nothing but a big money chase. They have no more in common with rank-and-file Republicans than the people they rail against. It's all a big fat joke to them."

Weaver insists this is his last campaign. He and his wife bought a house in New Hampshire, where the cooler weather should be better for her health. "That's the least I could do," he says.

Like his boss, Weaver speaks freely of his failings. "He talks about himself being a flawed person who's doing the best he can," Weaver says. "That hits home with me. I've not been a good husband or a good father." Maybe so. But in McCain's candidacy, Weaver can prove once and for all his worth as a political strategist.

Weaver is at the hub of a loosely organized group of McCain advisers that tends to do things ad hoc. The McCain candidacy, after all, is about character, not issues. McCain formed most of his positions long ago, and he trusts his instincts more than his advisers. So what's a guy like McCain's policy director, John Raidt, to do? "When you find out, let me know," says Raidt, who prefers the title "policy coordinator." "John McCain is his own policy director."

Okay, so there's no policy director. How about a brain trust? Sorry. "There isn't one," Chris Koch, McCain's first Senate chief of staff, says with a laugh.

But surely McCain has some sort of formal decision-making process. Nope, says Mark Salter, his current chief of staff. "There is none."

That, in a nutshell, is how the McCain brain works—and, most likely, how a McCain White House would work. To critics, it's chaotic and impulsive. To friends, it's ad hoc and instinctive. It lacks the heft and order of George W. Bush's policy operation, but most of the time it gets the job done. McCain relies on a loose and informal network of longtime advisers, a few policy wonks whose work matches McCain's worldview, and several trusted friends who warn the candidate if his instincts fail him.

McCain's friends say a diagram of the Arizona senator's decision-making process would resemble an ink blot. Salter explains the McCain brain by describing his experience watching football on television with the senator. "He flips from game to game, never getting the sense of how one game is going because he's watching fourteen," Salter says. "His interests are scattered and he indulges them simultaneously. He's got almost a childish appetite for new things. For a guy who grew up in the military culture, he's not regimented."

Salter isn't being disloyal; McCain says the same thing himself. "There is no brain trust; it's the no-brain trust," he jokes, then adds, seriously: "Most of the stuff I don't need a lot of help on."

It's hard to imagine a greater contrast with the deliberate world of Texas Governor Bush, who has twice the policy staff and many more outside advisers, organized neatly into policy committees that meet regularly. Every time Bush returns to Austin, he spends a couple of hours getting updates from well-known policy gurus such as Condoleezza Rice, Lawrence Lindsey and Steve Goldsmith. Much of this is necessary: though Bush isn't the puppet of his advisers, as the stereotypes have it, he did need to form policies on a range of federal issues he hadn't contemplated before.

The McCain operation is low-budget by comparison. Kevin Hassett, McCain's adviser on taxes and economics, describes his operation as "me and my laptop and three English majors and some economist friends keeping at bay an aircraft carrier of Ph.D. economists that has been attacking us." McCain, unlike Bush, doesn't require his advisers to be exclusive, or even to support him.

McCain didn't have the luxury of a big brain trust. Most of the usual suspects had already been taken by Bush, Weber says, and McCain didn't have the money to launch a big policy effort. Beyond that, Weber says, the informality matched McCain's style.

But McCain's informal method of gathering information and advice has also proven to be a source of creativity and flexibility. McCain is a one-man polling operation and his own focus group leader, each day soliciting the opinions of dozens of people who don't even know they're advising him. "He hunts and pecks a lot," Murphy says. Adds Raidt: "McCain is a 24-hour-a-day sponge."

The role of "adviser" to the ad-hoc McCain is a misnomer. It's really just a collection of McCain's longtime friends who endeavor to nudge him—occasionally and delicately. Chief among these is Salter, who wrote McCain's memoir and is now a constant traveling companion on the campaign trail.

McCain hired Salter 11 years ago as a foreign policy adviser, even though "I wasn't particularly qualified for the job." McCain simply liked his style. Throughout his time with the senator, Salter has learned to obey, and gently guide, McCain's hunches.

"My role with John McCain is to encourage his best instincts," Salter says. "It's a pretty small responsibility." Perhaps, but that's life in the McCain brain trust. And it's about as far as one can get from the policy factory that George W. Bush has created in Austin.

8

★ ☆ ★

The Coronation

When talking with Karl Rove, during Bush's triumphant first trip, I suggested the campaign orchestrate a series of deliberate, small flubs. The gaffes would inoculate Bush or divert the press, each one knocking him down a peg without being serious enough to wreck his candidacy. I offered to supply a series of miscues the governor could attempt. But as it turns out, Bush has done just fine coming up with small goofs on his own.

It began when he dubbed the Kosovars "Kosovians" and the Greeks "Grecians." It continued when the East Timorese became "East Timorians" on Bush's tongue. Then he confessed his ignorance of the Land and Water Conservation Fund.

His next attempt at deflating expectations came when a reporter from Slovakia asked Bush to comment on that country. "The only thing I know about Slovakia is what I learned firsthand from your foreign minister that came to Texas, and I had a great visit with him," he replied. "It's an exciting country, it's a country that's flourishing, and it's a country that's doing well." Actually, the fellow who came to visit was the prime minister of Slovenia, the former Yugoslav state, not the foreign minister of Slovakia. Slovakia, far from flourishing, is the poor sibling of the Czech Republic.

But this was not the end of Bush's efforts to lower expectations. A couple of days later, he came out in favor of displaying the Ten Commandments in public buildings. But then, asked whether he preferred the Protestant, Catholic or Jewish wording of the Ten Commandments, he answered, mysteriously, that he favored "the standard version." Bush, slyly, was giving the impression he hadn't the foggiest notion that the three faiths used very different translations of the Ten Commandments.

By way of contrast, I gave Orrin Hatch a quick quiz on the Grecians, Kosovians, and East Timorians. "You'll find I've been to most of these places," he said. Needless to say, the former Mormon bishop also knew about the different versions of the Ten Commandments. "People say he's a quick study," Hatch said of Bush. "But, you know, it's a lot more complex than that. You can spend a lifetime on Medicare alone, and a lot of us have. It's a very tough league up here. The more experience a person has had, the less likely you are to make mistakes."

To his credit, Bush certainly seems to be aware of his predicament. "This is a big world, and I've got a lot to learn," W. said after his string of bloopers. This has been a sensitive issue for some time. There was the famous *New York Times* correction in March, following a story about a series of tutorials to help Bush get up to speed on the issues. "As published, the article included an opinionated sentence casting doubt on his mastery of those issues," the correction said. The part about the tutorials was true. The offending sentence, inserted by editors, was: "There may never have been a 'serious' candidate who needed it more."

You can almost picture George W. at a table in the governor's mansion in Austin with his tutor and a pile of flashcards.

TUTOR: Governor, shall we go over Slovenia and Slovakia again?

BUSH: No, I've got it now. Slovakia is a country that used to be part of Czechoslovakia . . .

TUTOR: Very good.

BUSH: . . . and its capital, Bratislava, is a short drive from Vienna, the capital of Australia. The Czech Republic, whose citizens are known as "Czechmates," is led by the playwright Handel.

TUTOR: Moving right along, sir, let's see how you're coming on Asia. Do you remember your policy if North Korea invades South Korea?

BUSH: Easy. We help the South Koreavars push the North Koreavars right off the Iberian Peninsula.

TUTOR: Only one minor quibble, sir. The Iberian Peninsula is, technically speaking, home to Spain and Portugal.

BUSH: Wait a minute. Aren't the Portugecians one of the most prosperous peoples in all of Africa, second only to the Vietnamians?

TUTOR: (*Pause.*) Maybe we should take a short break.

Bush tells us precious little about what he believes. When the Texas governor announced his presidential exploratory committee, he offered but small nuggets. "I want the twenty-first century to be prosperous, and

I don't want anybody being left behind," he vowed, thus distancing himself from all those presidential candidates who favor malaise and oppression. "America must be prosperous and strong to make sure the next century will be peaceful," he elaborated a few days later, gratuitously provoking the famine and bloodshed lobbies.

To get a clearer idea of what Bush is about, one must leave the governor's mansion and drive 20 minutes north to the improbably named Austin suburb of Jollyville. There you will find Mrs. Gutierrez's second-grade class in the middle of its weekly character-building lesson. A boy named Tray raises his hand to compliment Philip for "trying not to hurt people's feelings." Pint-sized Jessie pipes up to praise Pamela because "when I had no friends at recess she came over and played with me." But then a boy complains about some naughty behavior. "Is that responsible?" Mrs. Gutierrez asks. "No!" the class says in unison. "Is that compassionate?" "No!" "What should we be doing at all times?" the teacher asks. "Personal best," the tots respond. Thus do the happy children of Jollyville, under a public school program championed by Governor Bush, learn how to become "good citizens for Texas."

Still don't grasp George W.'s philosophy? Then drive north for another hour to Waco, the town David Koresh and his radically anti-government Branch Davidian sect put on the map. Here, in another public school program backed by Bush, a Baptist seminary student named Brandon Barnard is warning a group of sixth-graders at Midway Intermediate School about genital warts "the size of my fist." Such warts are tough to remove, he adds. "You do what you want," Barnard says, as the children squirm. "I don't want anybody cutting, burning, or freezing that part of my body." Barnard flashes a slide on the screen listing the consequences of premarital sex: cancer, AIDS, death, pain, emotional scars, infertility. Then he shows a slide listing the consequences of abstinence: self-control, self-respect, self-discipline. "Virginity is a gift," Barnard declares, holding up a package in purple wrapping paper. "I'm proud to be a virgin."

The two scenes, and hundreds like them playing out across Texas, encapsulate the Bush ideology. It is, at first glance, a conservative message, based on the notion that traditional values will help prevent poverty and other ills. But deeper down, Bush's approach, warts and all, should sound familiar—and possibly comfortable—to some liberals. He assumes that government can be a force for good and that it has a responsibility to help the weak. Bush's stances so far on national issues such as Kosovo and abortion have been full of ambiguity and obfuscation, seemingly dictated more by tactic than by principle. Still, beneath Bush's mush is some evidence that he's trying to introduce a government-friendly conservatism to a party often hijacked by harsh and selfish ideology.

Bush's own label for his philosophy, "compassionate conservatism," is a tired phrase and easy to ridicule. Bob Dole used it to great effect in his 1988 presidential campaign. But in Bush's case, it appears to imply a more activist style of conservative governance. Instead of demanding anti-abortion laws, he seeks alternatives, such as abstinence and adoption programs, which will reduce abortions. Instead of the usual Republican lock-'em-up-and-throw-away-the-key line on criminal justice, he has fostered a faith-based rehabilitation program for prisoners. He has demanded increases in education funding and opposed anti-immigration measures. Instead of a flat tax, he talks of modest cuts and reducing regressivity.

"What he understands about conservatism that many conservatives don't is that, at its core, it's caring about the poor, the underclass," says Al Hubbard, an old business-school classmate of Bush's who has helped him line up advisers. "The biggest problem facing our country is the underclass and the lack of opportunity for the underclass." And the answer, says Hubbard, "is not about saying, 'Lower taxes, reduce regulation, and everybody will be fine.'" It is, rather, about a host of government interventions that Bush and his advisers have proposed: mentoring programs, literacy programs, welfare-to-work programs in which church volunteers offer both skills training and Bible study, cuts in sales taxes that disproportionately affect the poor, tax incentives to aid poor neighborhoods and substantial increases in public education spending.

These ideas may sound more like Jesse Jackson than Ronald Reagan, but they are common in Bush circles. Typical is Mark McKinnon, who worked for Democrats (he still has photos of Bush's Democratic predecessor, Ann Richards, in his office at Paul Begala's old firm) before agreeing to be Bush's media strategist. "He's willing to step out on issues that have long been contrary to the interests of the Republican Party," McKinnon says. "He's figured out a way for Republicans to actually be for something." Several conservative Democrats in the Texas legislature, likewise, backed Bush's reelection. Even Texas Democratic Party spokeswoman Liz Chadderdon admits: "When you look at Bush's agenda, you could plug in Clinton's name and it would be the same."

But while Bush's philosophy may have a ring of familiarity to some Democrats, they would be mistaken to think he is one of them. "It sounds like liberalism because there's concern for the poor, but it doesn't come out of liberalism," says Marvin Olasky, a University of Texas professor who advises Bush. "He's a throwback to one of the conservative strains of the nineteenth century." Bush doesn't come from the economic conservative/social Darwinist school, but neither does he side with the fundamentalists/moralists.

So what is Bush? Some conservatives have argued that he is reunifying the Reagan coalition of fiscal conservatives and the religious right that fell apart under Bush's father. But those wishful thinkers will be disappointed. First, Bush isn't fleeing from his old man. Many of young Bush's top advisers—Larry Lindsey, Michael Boskin, John Taylor, Martin Feldstein, Al Hubbard, Paul Wolfowitz, Condolleezza Rice, Bob Kimmitt and Josh Bolten—also served in or gave advice to his father's administration.

More significantly, the coalition Bush is assembling is in some ways the opposite of Reaganism. Reagan's alliance was in large part libertarian, and young Bush's is communitarian. The communitarian movement, known also by its "civil society," "social capital" and "quality of life" buzzwords, is vaguely defined, but it's based on the idea that too much Hobbesian individualism has created an atomized, selfish and disconnected society. Government, by encouraging private and nonprofit efforts to restore community, and by tempering individual rights with responsibility to society, can help to restore the purpose.

But in truth, the philosophy's roots go much further back, to Aristotle, who believed that government could help to engineer an ideal society. It's the kind of conservatism championed by Edmund Burke, and it claims such historic figures as Disraeli and Bismarck, who were pioneers of the welfare state. A few modern conservatives, including Olasky and columnist George Will (whose 1983 book *Statecraft as Soulcraft* was an anti-individualist tract), have taken this view, but they were oddballs until now.

"It's a new coalition," Olasky says. "That's why some people on the right are so uncomfortable" with Bush. In Bush's way of thinking, the individual-rights champions on both sides—the civil libertarians on the left and the anti-government, leave-us-alone right-wingers—are on the outside. They'll be replaced by a mixture of incentive-based conservatives and good-government liberals. "He could bring a lot of communitarian Democrats with him," Olasky says. If liberals were willing to give up some federal control, Bush and like-minded conservatives would be content to spend more money on the poor and other government pursuits. "Let's throw away the budget cutters," Olasky says. "I see that coming with Bush. I see that as part of a governing alliance."

Some still suspect that Bush is a moderate, establishment Republican in his father's image. But they, too, are mistaken. President Bush, with a sense of noblesse oblige, saw himself as a duty-bound steward with little ideological passion. But his son, a baby-boomer and a product of the 1960s, is more activist than caretaker.

Bush aides, not surprisingly, bristle at the Clinton-Gore comparison, which they see as an attempt to make their candidate appear too liberal to Republican primary voters. "Sorry, Lanny," says Karen Hughes, Bush's press secretary. "Governor Bush is not on the same field. The Democrats are trying to make comparisons that will hurt him in the Republican primary. It's ridiculous, and they know it's not true." Hughes, for her part, calls her boss an "activist conservative." "He's not anti-government," she says. "He believes there is a role for government, but it should be limited."

Hughes, in many respects, is correct. Though their coalitions overlap and their philosophies intersect, there will still be plenty to separate Bush and Gore. Bush leans toward private-sector solutions, while Gore errs on the side of government intervention. Bush backed legislation allowing Texans to carry concealed firearms; Gore is a strong gun control advocate. Gore is famously green, while Bush, backed by business and oil men, has been advised by the Competitive Enterprise Institute's Fred Smith, who wants public land privatized and says that the Environmental Protection Agency is "a massive mistake." Their differences on abortion and organized labor are equally stark. The two men also will be forced to placate the hardcore interest groups in their parties: Gore labor, Bush fundamentalists. If they are nominated, the choice for many voters may come down not to the men but to their fellow travelers: Bush's Bob Barr or Gore's Ted Kennedy?

Virtually none of this Bush philosophy has emerged yet, and that's just fine with the governor's advisers. "He gains in the polls every week by doing nothing," says one. Even Bush has been marveling at his good fortune. "I held a press conference on the drought, and it rained the next day," he told the Texas Daily Newspaper Association at a recent luncheon. "Now my mother's calling up for tips on the lottery." The reception for Bush is, as always, adoring. The governor, after a round of handshakes, gets a fawning introduction and a standing ovation from the newspaper executives. His speech is full of progressive-sounding themes—research and development tax credits and references to his sales tax cut for diapers and over-the-counter medicines. He calls education "by far the most important thing a state does," vowing to hold schools accountable, a favorite theme of New Democrats.

After the session, the Texas press tries to trap Bush into stating positions. They pepper him with abortion questions ("I'm pro-life, and I've had a consistent position"), gay rights ("I believe we should never discriminate against anybody"), and hate-crime legislation ("All crime is hate"). Three times, Bush falls into a reporter's trap and begins to elaborate on his philosophy but then catches himself. "I've stated my position," he says. Then he returns to his preferred subjects: limited government, local control, strong families, personal responsibility. The governor chats with the reporters about his latest fishing trip in his familiar, locker-room manner. His banter is friendly, his intonation half Poppy Bush, half Ross Perot. The reporters are charmed. And when they return to their type-writers they will find, once again, that deft Governor Bush has told them nothing new.

★ ☆ ★

The Russian kitsch industry specializes in matryoshkas, hollow wooden figures of the country's leaders. Inside a Yeltsin shell is a Gor-bachev egg, which surrounds a Brezhnev egg right down to a solid Lenin core. If one were building such a toy to explain Bush's domestic policy, the first layer inside the Bush shell would be Indianapolis Mayor Steve Gold-smith. Inside Goldsmith would be Harvard Professor Robert Putnam.

Goldsmith, a Republican, is Bush's chief domestic policy adviser. He is by necessity a pragmatist, and he has been a pioneer in the civil-society movement also championed by the likes of New York Mayor Rudolph Giu-liani. His idiosyncratic policies in Indianapolis have a streak of concern for social justice running through them—and Bush's will, too. "I think the gov-ernor is articulating a new vision for the Republican Party," Goldsmith says. "You can't miss the idea that the marketplace operates unevenly. . . . Prosperity ought to have a purpose. We're talking about the poor in a very serious way." Among the proposals that civil-society conservatives favor is a large charity tax credit for those who volunteer to help the poor. "I do think he's seriously conservative," Goldsmith says of Bush, but he doesn't think conservatism should be "an excuse to ignore people who are without opportunity."

The mayor lists among the civil-society thinkers who influence him Harvard's Putnam, a left-leaning thinker who worked in the Carter ad-ministration. Putnam, whose "bowling alone" theory seeped into national political discourse, sees promise for the left in the direction Bush and Goldsmith are taking. "Civic reengagement is a fundamental prerequisite for a new progressive era," he says. Though Goldsmith and Putnam dis-agree on the role of government in such efforts, Goldsmith's community programs are just the kind Putnam favors. "That's what worries the far right about Bush," he says.

Bush often seems to be torn between progressive instincts and Repub-lican constituencies. In other words, he waffles. This year, for example, the Texas legislature has been debating a federally authorized expansion of health care to children living at 150 percent of the poverty line, or even 200 percent. In February, Bush said, "If you get up to one hundred and fifty percent, we are going to be covering a lot of children that aren't covered today," according to the *Austin American-Statesman*. But two weeks later he softened, and the same paper quoted him as saying, "I'll take a definite position at the appropriate time."

Bush's economic policy, like his social policy, has a peculiar (for Republicans) preoccupation with the poor and the working class. Bush's economics chief, Larry Lindsey, a former Federal Reserve Board governor, has strong supply-side credentials. But Lindsey says times have changed. "The country doesn't need another revolution," he told me. "In my view, we need to refine. One group that particularly needs conservative help are those with low and moderate income." That sounds like the old liberal complaint about income inequality. Lindsey, who has described himself as a populist, would cut taxes but keep the charitable contribution and mortgage interest deductions and the capital gains tax. To offset tax cuts that favor the wealthy, he would cut regressive taxes like the telephone excise tax or offer a higher percentage cut to those in lower brackets.

In international affairs, Bush comes closer to being his father's son. This shouldn't be surprising. He is a typical governor, meaning he hasn't had to worry about foreign events. And he grew up with a foreign-policy-obsessed father, so something was bound to rub off. Young Bush doesn't care as deeply about the international scene as did his father, who served as CIA chief and ambassador to the United Nations and China. He would, advisers say, follow the Clinton model of a domestic policy presidency. Bush is surrounding himself with a hawkish crowd: Wolfowitz, of the Johns Hopkins School of Advanced International Studies, Stanford Provost Rice and Dick Cheney. Others include Donald Rumsfeld, Kimmitt and Richard Perle, committed internationalists who have no patience for Buchanan's protectionist line. His foreign policy advisers say Bush would be determined to project a more muscular presence overseas and pursue an aggressive missile defense system at home.

A number of conservative ideologues are already pouncing on Bush for his prospective policies, foreign and domestic. Terry Jeffrey, the editor of *Human Events* and '96 campaign manager for Pat Buchanan, signals the nature of the barrage George W. is likely to face. Buchanan will beat him up over trading partners' labor abuses and abortion policies. Jeffrey also says Bush will have to answer for his father's "appeasement in Tiananmen." Jeffrey says the right will be no kinder to Bush on abortion ("There effectively isn't much difference from Bill Clinton's position") and taxes ("His tax program had seventy new types of taxes in it").

This, perhaps, is why the Republican mainstream hasn't demanded specifics from Bush. A recent meeting at the Capitol Hill Club illustrated the tendency. Six GOP members of Congress had come to endorse Bush, such a familiar sight these days that only four reporters bothered to attend.

Congresswoman Jennifer Dunn, a member of Bush's exploratory committee, led the group in speaking vaguely of Bush's "strong, secure, quiet personal faith," his "free and fair trade" policy and his status as a "tax cutter." But then the questions began, one about Bush's policy on a Palestinian state, one about free trade with China. "All good questions," Dunn said. "We haven't talked about those specific ones, but Governor Bush has a very strong foreign policy team." A reporter persisted in a question about China's efforts to get U.S. missile technology. "We'll see where he comes out on that," she said. "I don't like to answer for him."

Bush's carefully calibrated and planned philosophy, his above-the-fray campaign strategy, and his general disinclination to join the rough and tumble of politics makes him vulnerable to the kind of insurgent campaign being waged by McCain. Bush, because of his vast funding and support, is inevitably overrated and McCain inevitably underrated.

While Bush struggles with the names of foreign leaders and countries names, he is furthering the impression that he's not ready for prime time by ignoring the early presidential debates. As the fall of 1999 comes, so do the first debates of the presidential season. For the first two debates, at least, there is no sign of Dubya.

Senator McCain's mission in the first two Republican presidential debates is to look "presidential," as his advisers put it. Given the company, this does not prove terribly burdensome.

For one thing, McCain benefits from sharing the stage with Orrin Hatch and Gary Bauer, who rated support levels of 0 percent and 1 percent, respectively, in the latest New Hampshire poll, by the *Boston Herald.* Worse for these two gentlemen, the poll had a margin of error of five percentage points, raising the troubling metaphysical possibility that Hatch and Bauer had the backing of −5 percent and −4 percent of New Hampshire voters.

McCain also profits from the fact that the other Republican candidate who seems presidential is AWOL. True, George W. had promised to attend an award ceremony for his wife on the night of the second debate, but nobody seems to buy his excuse—particularly after Laura Bush, in a pre-debate interview on New Hampshire television, confesses that if Governor Bush had really needed to go to the debate, "I'd have said, 'Sure, we can work it out.'" When the governor, in the same interview, justifies his absence by declaring, "I love my wife," a ripple of laughter spreads among the journalists who have gathered in the press room before the debate.

Finally—and this one can't be overestimated—McCain is aided by what I'll call the Keyes Effect. This holds that anybody, even Linda Tripp or Donald Trump, would sound presidential debating Alan Keyes. Keyes attends both debates with two bodyguards, men who call themselves his "advance team" but who, I imagine, are responsible for making sure the excitable Keyes did not douse himself with gasoline and light a match. When Keyes speaks, you can sometimes catch McCain and Steve Forbes, as well as various audience members, stifling concerned smiles, as if a man had begun singing on their subway car. He seems harmless, but what if there are explosives strapped to his chest?

To measure the Keyes Effect on McCain, I watch the first big debate, in Durham, New Hampshire, on October 22, with members of the Arizona senator's campaign. Keyes seems to be struggling to stay in his chair, waving his arms frantically and opening his eyes wide, and McCain, the unlucky one seated next to him, appears to be trying to inch away. The acoustics are bad in the listening room, so I frequently have to ask the McCain aides what Keyes is saying. "He's speaking in tongues," one of them explains, then translates: "If only those voices in my head would stop!"

Whether it's the Keyes Effect, the Bush no-shows or the mere presence of Hatch and Bauer, things seem to be going McCain's way. He's gaining on Bush: polls in New Hampshire now show his support at nearly 30 percent. And some in the press believe Bush is heading for his "Gore moment," a time when he can do no right. Karl Rove, Bush's top strategist, argues that while it's historically inevitable that a front-runner in Bush's position wins the nomination, "almost as inevitably, there's a bump along the way. Where it will be, I don't know."

Bush, paradoxically, may catch the same bug that infected Gore: Clinton fatigue. "He's our Clinton," says a Bauer adviser. Bush is Clintonian in the best sense: he's got charm, he's a moderate, and he has run a state with success. But his opponents also see the darker side of Clintonism in Bush: cockiness, impulsiveness, evasiveness, Vietnam avoidance, and triangulation. "While Bush is out checking the latest tracking poll on which cardigan to wear, we're out changing America," says McCain strategist Mike Murphy. "After Clintonism, authentic candidates are going to be more attractive."

Rove calls such efforts to link Bush to Clinton "laughable," adding, "They've been trying to do it for a number of months, and our numbers continue to go up." But that doesn't stop them from trying. When Pat Buchanan quit the Republican Party, McCain issued a statement that said, "Too many of my party's leaders [read: Bush] made the mistake of trying to appease Buchanan. . . . Running for president should not simply be about polls and political calculation. That is Clintonism. Our party must stand on principle." Now Forbes is trying to tie Bush to Clinton through his tax record. A Bush ad claimed the governor reduced state-government spending, but Forbes made the case, supported by various news reports, that Bush increased spending by 36 percent, "greater than Bill Clinton's 21 percent increase over his first six years." Even Clinton, perhaps aware that he's become a pariah, tried to hurt Bush by likening the governor to himself, praising Bush's "good instincts."

Bush isn't the only one threatened by McCain's moment. In an unusual primary twist, McCain may actually hurt Bill Bradley. Some 37 percent of the New Hampshire electorate are registered independents, and both men are focusing on that group. Asked whether he's competing with Bradley for independent voters, McCain replied: "I think so. . . . I think there may be a kind of a second contest going." Both Bradley and McCain strolled with Granny D— Doris Haddock, a famed New Hampshire campaign finance reformer. McCain even needled Bradley about his reversal on ethanol subsidies. "He may have found himself on the road to Damascus— or the road to Des Moines," McCain said.

Bradley's advisers, though they acknowledge competing with McCain, say that few independents are genuinely free of party leanings. "It's way overblown," says Mark Longabaugh, Bradley's New Hampshire man. Bradley, when I asked him about vying for independents, replied, "I'm not segmenting the market."

For now, though, McCain is dealing with the Republicans. And in these debates, he finds so many divergent views on so many issues that it's hard to muster a sustained argument. Hatch is a disaster, shouting, rambling and at one point boasting, Gore-like, that he "created the modern generic drug industry." Forbes scores points as Bush's attacker. But it is Keyes who stole the show—or, rather, hijacked it. Asked about drugs, he appears to blame property rights and proliferating laws. He rails about the "rat hole of United Nations waste" and "the socialist income tax," which he would abolish. On taxes, he asks the audience how much the government should take; the audience, thinking the question rhetorical, doesn't respond. Keyes erupts: "How much? Answer it!" After the event, he storms into the press room, where he declared himself "deadly sick" of the coverage of his campaign.

Keyes is a good opening act for McCain, who speaks about attracting pro-choice voters, rebuilding the military, the need for service to country and the urgency of reform. After Keyes's press room tirade, McCain strolls in and declines reporters' invitations to swipe at Bush. "We'll let the voters of New Hampshire decide that," he demurs. He sounds downright presidential.

But McCain's pious remarks are a bit misleading. He has begun to form the outline of what could be a tough assault on Bush's credibility. He is beginning, subtly, to get nasty.

At a smart-aleck event on the day before the Hanover debate, McCain's campaign holds a press conference featuring some cornstalks, some sugarcane, and a rusty black oil barrel. (A *Bush for President* sticker was put on the barrel but removed before the event.) McCain then argues that the three industries' soft money contributions, $23.6 million over four years, produced $12.8 billion in government breaks. McCain proposes cutting the breaks and using the proceeds to fund a voucher program—a swipe at Bush, who would fund his vouchers with public school money. It's a two-fer: McCain at once appears more attractive to moderates than Bush and holier than Gore on soft money. It's a sign of things to come, and Bush, with his platitudes, debate no-shows and photo-ops, urgently needs a way to respond.

9

★ ☆ ★

Smelling Blood

Attention Presidential Candidates:
You need votes? I need a new roof. Re-roof my house and you have my vote for both the straw poll and caucus; aerate my yard this fall and you have my wife's vote too. Serious inquiries only. Call (515) 633–0684.

—A classified ad in the *Des Moines Register*, August 13

The African nation of Mozambique sent a delegation of eight officials to Iowa last week on a "study mission" to observe the Republican Party's straw poll. The purpose was to pick up a few pointers for their new democracy's coming elections. But after observing the straw poll myself, I wouldn't be surprised if the delegates returned home with the conclusion that, all in all, their old socialist regime wasn't such a bad form of government. For here is what they were exposed to in Iowa:

—U.S. Senator Ben Nighthorse Campbell, his hair in a ponytail and wearing bandanna, black leather vest, and skull-and-crossbones belt buckle, leading 250 similarly attired, Harley-riding toughs to the poll in support of Texas Governor George W. Bush.
—Candidate Gary Bauer, lion of the Christian right, marching in a state fair parade in downtown Des Moines with a ten-foot-tall elephant on wheels and supporters on inline skates singing songs about Bauer to the tune of the *Gilligan's Island* theme song.

—Senator Orrin Hatch, a late entrant, trying to boost his meager prospects by busing to Ames, Iowa, chiropractors who had attended an alumni meeting at a chiropractic college.

—Steve Forbes, the multimillionaire publisher, building a massive, air-conditioned tent and an inflated theme park, hiring Ronnie Milsap, and flying two blimps over his encampment—outdoing Bush and former Vice President Dan Quayle, whose dirigibles hovered nearby.

—Roger Staubach stumping for Bush, Karl Malone stumping for Orrin Hatch, and Al Franken recording it all for *George* magazine (Franken asked Bauer at a press conference if he was worried about a millennial apocalypse ruining the 2000 election).

—The one serious event, a debate, canceled because only three candidates—Hatch, Pat Buchanan and Lamar Alexander—agreed to participate.

—Large-scale vote-buying, with candidates paying a $25 admission fee for each of the 24,000 voters who came to Ames to vote in the straw poll.

But for all that, the Ames poll, dismissed as unscientific and a poor indicator of the desires of the electorate at large, turned out to be more democratic than anyone expected. Nearly 25,000 Iowans took part—a quarter of those who will vote in the actual caucus next winter. In that sense, the poll deserved the primary-like status the press accorded it. The contest generated the kind of enthusiasm for politics not usually seen until much later in an election: the *Des Moines Register* listed the daily whereabouts of candidates so readers could meet them. On the day before the poll, the event was such big news that it shared the top of the paper's front page with an "odor alert" declared because of a "foul smell" in the city (from animal by-products, apparently, not journalists).

Whatever its merits, the poll has reshaped the Republican race in a fundamental way. Bush, who placed first, was confirmed as the front-runner, but he wasn't the real winner. Yes, the Texan shattered the previous record for total votes, but his victory was never in doubt. With a showing of 50 percent or even 40 percent, Bush could have clinched the nomination, short-circuiting the primary process. But in the end, Bush got 31 percent of the vote, below his public opinion poll numbers. Suddenly, the primaries look competitive.

As the tally board at the straw poll, initially concealed by a blue cloth, was uncovered, Bill Dal Col, Forbes's campaign manager, watched anxiously behind sunglasses, holding a pad of paper. "Yeah! Thank God!" he declared on seeing the results. Greg Mueller, the campaign's communications director, turned to Dal Col. "I'll take that, brother," he said. Rick Segal, Forbes's Internet man, hugged Dal Col. Within seconds, the spin had begun. "It shows it's a two-man race," said Mueller. "For the first time, it's the establishment that's splintering," said Dal Col. "It's gonna be a rough night in Austin," said pollster John McLaughlin.

Next came the Dole spinners, who rushed to the coliseum floor to remind everybody that Dole had spent only $250,000 on the poll. Tony Fabrizio, Dole's top strategist, said he was "thrilled." Bush "won, but he didn't dominate this field." Finally, the Bush team joined the action on the floor with some counterspin. "The real winner is the Democratic process," said Karen Hughes, Bush's communications director. "We did this in sixty-three days," declared top strategist Karl Rove. One Bush man, told that journalists were viewing the vote as a Bush setback, responded with the sort of expletive that recently got Bush himself into trouble.

But the Forbes campaign got the best of the spin session. The candidate emerged for a victory lap, drawing a scrum of a couple hundred. "We're going to win the nomination," he declared. "I am the conservative alternative." Then, young Forbes aides leaped to the stage to pose for triumphant photographs around the chart with the vote tally. It must have appeared to the Bush folks, for just a moment, as if the Visigoths had sacked Rome.

The immediate beneficiary of Bush's somewhat lackluster result is likely to be Forbes, who now has a credible measure of public support to go with his personal fortune. He may well be able to spend his way into a two-man race now. Finishing in second place at Ames, he far outpolled Bauer, the other semiplausible candidate of the religious right. If Forbes can consolidate conservatives, he'll make Bush's life miserable. After all, the conservative candidates in Ames—Forbes, Bauer, Buchanan, Alan Keyes, and Quayle—garnered a combined 47 percent of the vote, not far behind the 53 percent for the more moderate Bush, Elizabeth Dole, Alexander, and Hatch.

Cheering for Forbes to weaken Bush will be Dole and John McCain. Dole, the third-place finisher, will now be seen, along with McCain—who sat out the straw poll—as a viable, mainstream alternative to Bush. They both assume that the conservative Forbes, though he may hurt Bush, is incapable of getting the nomination. The poll also cleared the field of Alexander (who has dropped out of the race) and Dan Quayle, who is determined to continue as a sideshow along with Hatch and Keyes. For Buchanan, who had a fair showing in fifth place, it's now decision time. The Iowa Republicans clearly endorsed the big-money, free-trading internationalism of Bush and Forbes, giving Buchanan good reason to bolt the party, perhaps to run on a populist Reform Party ticket.

On straw poll day, I spent less time with the candidates than with the caterers. My theory was that the candidates who served the most lunch would receive the most votes. This was not a simple calculation to make, though, because the candidates served different portion sizes. Forbes, for example, used 3,000 pounds of pork to feed 7,000 people, according to his caterers, but Bush tried to stretch 4,000 pounds of meat to serve 13,000 people by supplementing it with 1,150 quarts of coleslaw. Alexander's caterer believed 400 pounds of pork and 1,500 pounds of ribs would feed 3,500 people, while Dole and Bauer, who shared a caterer, together used a mere 1,500 pounds of pork loin. Buchanan served more than 4,000 sandwiches and 3,700 ears of corn, but no one touched an entire roasted pig. Nevertheless, I assembled a meal tally (see Exhibit A), which turned out to be a more reliable predictor of the results than conventional means, such as opinion polls.

With this information, we can draw the following conclusions about what Buchanan called the "main political event of 1999": (1) Dole and Bauer skimped on the pork loin; (2) many of those who ate Buchanan's corn and Alexander's barbecue did not vote for them. (That includes this correspondent, who was attracted by the shorter line at Alexander's tent.) But there are other, nonculinary observations that can also be made now that the Ames results are in. Here's how the Republican race will be reshaped by the straw poll.

Bush: The Front-runner Is Mortal

Forbes: Bush's Conservative Rival

During the week before the Ames poll, it was impossible to avoid Steve Forbes. When I turned on the radio, there was the Forbes ad, before the farm report. When Hatch went to make a live appearance on the evening news in Cedar Rapids, there was the Forbes ad. There was even some trouble trying to schedule a candidate debate Friday evening because Forbes had bought a half-hour of the debate-hosting station's airtime for an infomercial. Driving down U.S. 169 in central Iowa, I overtook the two Forbes buses pulling out of a dirt road between two cornfields; on board were the candidate, his family, his campaign chairman, his pollster, his campaign manager, his communications director, a spokesman, the chairman of Sunglass Hut and the usual travel aides.

Forbes, poor fellow, hasn't improved his performance on the stump a jot. He continues to smile and bob his head while greeting supporters, as if he were on a business trip to Asia. During his speech, the head-bobbing stops and the energy goes to his forearms, which chop mechanically as he makes fists, except for two fingers on each hand, which point straight outward. Even his aides have begun to imitate him.

But all of this hardly matters: the real work was being done back at Forbes's Iowa headquarters, near the state capitol. The campaign, which is rumored to have spent $2 million on Ames (Bush spent $825,000), called more than 250,000 Iowans and reached another half-million by mail. Staffers sent postcards and placed radio and newspaper ads to bring people to bus tour events and to fuel calls to the campaign's 800 number, which overwhelmed the office's 17 phone lines. After participants signed up, they each received two letters and two calls. Another 300 were recruited on the Internet. All of the participants were entered into a database, and the Forbes staff, working 19-hour days for a month, developed a manifest and chose a captain for each of its buses. Once on the buses, participants watched a Forbes video and received a Forbes T-shirt and a hardcover copy of the candidate's new book.

The coordinated effort apparently worked. On straw poll day, thousands wearing orange Forbes T-shirts crowded the Forbes site. Inside the arena, Forbes's campaign launched an absurd display: *Stars and Stripes Forever* played while confetti and balloons dropped, sparklers and fireworks were ignited and horns blew. The balloon drop turned out to be a blunder, because other candidates' staffers popped the balloons while Forbes spoke. The place sounded like a bag of popcorn in the microwave. But the voting, fortunately for Forbes, was mostly over before his fiasco on the floor.

Dole and McCain: Mainstream Alternatives

Senator John McCain, who skipped the straw poll, picked up Dan Quayle's South Carolina advisers when they defected after Quayle's flop in Ames. McCain denounced the poll as a sham, concentrating instead on New Hampshire.

Dole's strong showing in Iowa is the work of what she calls her "invisible army" of young professionals, who are wealthy, well educated and, in most cases, female. A few days before the vote, I met some of them at a Dole reception for businesswomen held in West Des Moines. Dole, not terribly spontaneous on the stump, was actually lively there. She put in a sisterly quip about Bob Dole ("he's home making the bed") and won the biggest applause for a line demanding 100 percent deductibility of health insurance premiums for the self-employed. After her speech, the 60 women attending presented her with a doll wearing a T-shirt emblazoned with the slogan "Someday a Woman Will Be President." Dole's female supporters would deliver a more important gift at the straw poll: 45

women from local chapters of the National Association of Women Business Owners and Business and Professional Women USA would fill a bus to Ames for her. "I've never done this before," said Kathi Koenig, one of the organizers.

Dole continues to get no respect from the press. Part of this, no doubt, is plain old sexism. One reporter, returning from a one-on-one interview with Dole on her campaign bus, told his colleagues, "She looks great naked." But there's also a legitimate beef to make about her unwillingness to answer questions. When I started talking with her about the upcoming straw poll, she replied: "Well, we're having a great time. Isn't this a wonderful state? Great people." She pointed to the horizon. "Isn't this beautiful? The rain cleared. That's good. Well, they need the rain. But maybe after the parade. Isn't it beautiful?" You can just see Bob listening to this over breakfast while reading his newspaper, muttering, "Whatever."

Still, I must confess: I like Dole more each time I see her. She seems, over time, a fetching combination of the maternal, the ordinary, and the Thatcheresque. Yet her poor image among opinion-makers caused her to be underestimated in Ames. Her tent wasn't nearly as spirited as Buchanan's, with its whooping peasants. At one point, supporters complained that her music was too loud. A "Dole Rocks" banner on stage seemed to be hung in irony. Inside the arena, Dole didn't get much of a reception; the real cheers came when her husband joined her onstage. So, almost everyone in the place was astonished when she came in a strong third. Soon, the reason was revealed: two-thirds of her supporters were women. They came, voted, and left.

Buchanan and Bauer: Populist Irritants

Buchanan made few campaign stops in Iowa before the Ames poll, so it's telling that one of them was at a farmer-owned ethanol plant in Blairstown. After the obligatory photo-op with guys in hard hats, Buchanan launched into an attack on big agricultural concerns. With his shirt ripped and his dress shoes muddy, Buchanan lambasted the "Hollywood lawyer" (Mickey Kantor) and "some academic" (Charlene Barshefsky) who, he claimed, run Clinton's trade policy. Thus did he stake his populist claims: anti–big business, anti-Hollywood, anti-lawyer, anti-academic.

Buchanan aims to be the last friend of the working stiff in either party this year; the problem is, there aren't many Republican working stiffs. When I remarked to him that there were plenty of blue-collar Democrats who had no way of expressing support for him in a GOP primary, he replied: "There sure are." Buchanan did nothing to dismiss the third-party talk when we spoke; the night before, he'd said on television that he had "impure thoughts" about bolting from the GOP. Conventional wisdom says that Buchanan, if he joins the Reform Party, will hurt Bush in the general election by stealing the social conservatives, but I bet he would steal an equal number of blue-collar workers from Gore or Bradley.

As if to underscore that point, six tractor-trailers and about 400 Teamsters joined the Buchanan tent at the Ames straw poll. The union had bought tickets for its members, and though the Teamsters didn't officially endorse Buchanan, he was clearly their man. Buchanan, drawing cheers from the truckers, decried the "big banks" trying to "deindustrialize America" before turning to the topic of Mexicans. "You put Pat Buchanan in the White House, and we'll put that border back up, and those trucks will never enter the United States of America," he said. The Teamsters, many of them Democrats, then marched over to vote.

The race's other populist, Bauer, was able to place fourth in Ames by rallying church groups. His 21-year-old daughter has been lobbying youth groups across Iowa, and the campaign has advertised on Christian radio. Bauer, who headed the Family Research Council, a Christian interest group, also has benefited from the infrastructure of the group's state affiliate, the Iowa Family Policy Council.

A diminutive figure himself, Bauer makes his stump speech about—what else?—the little guy. "The littlest guy of all," he says, is the unborn child, and the "second littlest guy" is the family farmer. But somehow it is difficult to picture Bauer as a serious prospect. He simply doesn't have the resources to contend with Forbes to be the conservative challenger to Bush. Bauer, who wears an impish grin, does seem to possess a rare sense of self-awareness. When his volunteers-on-wheels sang melodies at the state fair parade, Bauer walked away, embarrassed. "I can't believe I'm actually doing this," he said. "I'm standing in the middle of the street and there are people singing songs with my name in them."

Keyes, Quayle, Alexander, and Hatch: The Irrelevancies

Hatch's candidacy promises to be the most exciting event in presidential politics since the Dick Lugar campaign of 1996. The man has it all. Media praise: "My dog has a better chance of getting the nomination," writes the *Washington Post*'s Tony Kornheiser. Conservative friends: "If presidential candidates are driven by an abundance of ego, Senator Hatch is overqualified," opines the *Manchester Union Leader*. And a proven ability to close the gender gap: Remember when he waved around a copy of *The Exorcist* at the Clarence Thomas hearings to discredit Anita Hill?

Hatch's declaration increases the ranks of Republican candidates to an astounding 12 (although rumor has it that Senator Bob Smith is ready to quit the Republican race for a third-party run). In its first days, though, the Hatch campaign still needs to work out a few kinks. Appearing on NBC's *Meet the Press*, Hatch managed to refer to himself both in the first person plural ("We plan on running for president. . . . We're going to give it everything we have") and in the third person ("Reducing taxes is a very, very important part of Orrin Hatch's agenda"). He used words like "frankly" and "to be honest" to preface statements that were, frankly, less than revealing.

But, frankly, we are being too hard on Hatch, and, to be honest, being hard on Hatch is not part of Dana Milbank's agenda. Despite having become a figure of fun for lefties during the Anita Hill craziness, the Judiciary Committee chairman is actually a pretty serious man, a respected lawmaker, and a straight-shooting, thoughtful figure in Congress. The once-fierce conservative is now showing admirable flexibility, becoming a leading architect (sometimes in tandem with Ted Kennedy) of health care policy.

What's more, Hatch's background contrasts nicely with George W. Bush's. Hatch grew up in poverty, not privilege (the senator once worked as a janitor), and he has had far more experience in government (23 years' worth) than the Republican favorite. Bush *fils* "has been a governor for four years in a state that has a constitutionally weak governor," Hatch told me in an interview." He's going to have a tremendous learning curve, and that's what people are going to center on. This is a very complex day and age. Do we want somebody like that leading us into the new millennium?"

This should be a potent argument—except that the 2000 campaign has taught us that voters don't care much for the experienced candidates. The most experienced guys in the race are Hatch, Al Gore, Bill Bradley, Lamar Alexander and, to be sure, Dan Quayle. Just look how they fare in matchups against Bush. Experience, it seems, is a liability. No wonder there's a clamor for a Jesse Ventura candidacy.

Hatch, oddly, had been counting on two constituencies to get him through the straw poll: Mormons and chiropractors. Both, he found out, are insufficient supporters. There are about 16,000 Mormons in Iowa, but not many of them came to the straw poll for Hatch. On the other hand, "there are 1,200 chiropractors in Iowa," all of them of voting age, said Hatch spokesman Jeff Flint. "Our first contacts in many of these places are chiropractors. At one event, the chiropractors started going wild." Hatch's staff says the back-crackers like him because his health insurance legislation has helped them qualify for reimbursement from insurance companies; I suspect it has more to do with his ramrod posture. The chiropractors were indeed a force at the straw poll. "I think we probably got two hundred," Flint said.

Unfortunately for Hatch, he failed to motivate others in similar proportions. He placed dead last among the participants. And yet, there he was on the coliseum floor after the tally, claiming victory. "New Candidate Hatch Has Solid Iowa Showing," read a statement from his campaign, clearly printed before the results came out. "He exceeded expectations considerably." Really? With 2 percent of the vote? I asked Flint what the expectations had been. "One percent," he said.

The goal of any candidate is to avoid winding up like talk-show host Alan Keyes, a political nonentity who seems to be running so he can rant in front of crowds. At Ames, he shouted past his time limit, continuing to holler and gesticulate madly even after his microphone was turned off.

In danger of joining the Keyes category is now Quayle, who, painfully, polled even lower than Keyes. It was obvious something was wrong early in the week, when just 15 farmers showed up to talk with Quayle at a farm event and the only camera waiting when he arrived was one from PBS. The event was five days before the poll, and Quayle already sensed trouble. "I can't imagine any campaign deciding to stay in or get out based on the straw poll," he said. "This is a straw poll, and I emphasize the word 'straw.'" The crowds grew slightly for Quayle during the rest of the day, but people seemed more curious than devoted. A columnist from the Cedar Rapids paper thumbed through the sign-in list at a Quayle reception in that city and said, "I guess if you've got an endangered species on your property, you want to show him off."

Alexander, who gambled everything on Ames and lost, has taken a more dignified route: he quit. The candidate was reportedly upset by my profile of him in *TNR*, which depicted him partially nude and was described by the *New York Times* as an "obituary." Actually, the piece was sympathetic to Lamar's quest, a noble but doomed endeavor to run a grassroots campaign at a time when money is everything. Bush spent just ten days campaigning in Iowa, but Alexander, who spent 39 days in the state, finished a distant sixth. Alexander knew this was happening, and his last day of campaigning before the poll, at the Iowa state fair, had the whiff of a valedictory. He took a turn as "honorary chef" at the Iowa Pork Producers tent and played *God Bless America* on the piano for fairgoers. At the Republican booth, I picked up an invitation to his straw poll festivities, written during happier times. "This campaign's really cooking!" it said.

The Ames results have made it clear that George W. will have a fight on his hands for the Republican nomination. At the same time, he is falling victim to the same malady that hurt Gore earlier on: his overwhelming front-runner status (fueled, in Bush's case, by an unprecedented war chest) has had the unintended effect of narrowing the field. The beneficiaries of Bush's success: McCain and Forbes.

The fact that Bush's great pile of money has made him more vulnerable, rather than less, should be particularly interesting to Senator Mitch McConnell of Kentucky, who has been keeping busy in Congress by killing measure after measure to clean up campaign finance. He relishes his role as friend of fat cats and tormenter of clean-government types, so much so that in order to do something really scary for Halloween I dressed up as McConnell, wearing horns, pitchfork, tail and cash-stuffed pockets. My wife dressed as McConnell's omnipresent partner, Soft Money, in a green foam-rubber ensemble.

McConnell figures free-flowing funds will help Republicans. But he ought to consider the latest victims of big-money campaign funding. The cash craze has driven Elizabeth Dole out of the race and has given Pat Buchanan an excuse to leave the Republican Party altogether. It caused presidential candidate Gary Bauer, lion of the Christian right, to side with finance reformer McCain, McConnell's nemesis. And now, ironically, it seems that McConnell's candidate, George W. Bush, has fund-raised so many challengers into oblivion that he's allowed McCain, the man left standing, to mount a serious challenge.

We begin this tale of woe with poor Pat Buchanan, a man not usually worthy of sympathy. But even xenophobes can be pitiable. First, big money contributed to his decision to bolt the GOP. Then, just as Buchanan was to announce his Reform Party candidacy, big money, in the form of Donald Trump, again trumped him. Trump declared that he, too, was quitting the Republican Party in anticipation of a Reform Party bid. Finally, today, Buchanan's low-budget Reform Party kickoff event has turned into a disaster.

Outside the Doubletree Hotel, protesters greet Buchanan with a sign announcing "To Adolf With Love." Inside, moments into Buchanan's announcement speech, the sound flickers and fails, eliciting from the Buchananites cries of "Sabotage!" and crude insults directed at the sound system: "Made in China!" and "Union microphone!" The sound, once repaired, breaks again midway through the speech, leaving Buchanan to fiddle with it for what seems like forever until his sister, Bay, finally fetches a technician. The disaster-prone Buchanan, it seems, will fit in just fine in the Reform Party.

Maybe Buchanan couldn't raise much money because he has wacky ideas and marginal support. But, cleverly, he sounds a populist theme in his Doubletree speech. "The day of the outsider is over in the Beltway parties; the money men have seen to that," he bellows. "Let me say to the money boys and the Beltway elites who think that, at long last, they have pulled up the drawbridge and locked us out forever: You don't know this peasant army." If Buchanan gets the Reform nomination, of course, this particular peasant army will have $13 million in public campaign funds to play with.

Five days before Buchanan bolts, Dole calls her own meeting in a hotel, this one the tony St. Regis, to announce that she is quitting the race. Instead of a peasant revolt, this is more of an upscale wake. "What did you do for Mrs. Dole?" a reporter asks a staffer, in hushed tones. "I did direct mail," replies the grieving employee. Yes, we know that Dole had been suffering terribly, and that she's probably better off where she is now, but does she have to go so soon? I had even marked November 7 in my calendar as the start date of her presidential kickoff tour—a plan that would have had Dole announcing her candidacy at exactly the moment that her failure seemed assured.

The funereal mood disappears instantly when the candidate appears with her husband, the cutup who voiced doubts about his wife and support for her rival McCain. Now, at his wife's pullout, Bob Dole steals the show again, winking at a friend and offering a wry remark off microphone. He grins at inappropriate times, a ham for the cameras.

But no amount of Bob's clowning can obscure the central reason for Liddy's failure. "The bottom line remains money," she says. Like Buchanan, if she'd had a better message (or, really, any message at all), she might have won more support and therefore more dollars. But in pulling out of the race, she argues that she would have done 108 fund-raisers this year, and even then Bush and Steve Forbes "would enjoy a 75- or 80-to-1 cash advantage," she says. "Perhaps I could handle 2-to-1 or 10-to-1, but not 80-to-1." Though beaten by the lack of spending limits on Bush and Forbes, Dole used her farewell speech to join McCain's call for an end to soft money.

The only Republican candidates not affected by Bush's decision to break the spending limits are the irrelevancies—Bauer, Hatch and Keyes. The losers get their moment in the spotlight tonight, before the cameras of New Hampshire's WNDS-TV and all 6,600 of its viewing households. The major candidates are skipping the debate, and their lack of response necessitates the use of substitutes, including a Reform Party official and 1996 vanity candidate Morry Taylor, who prepares by drinking a beer in the back of the studio.

The debate, full of miscues, looks more Wayne's World than presidential forum. Even Hatch cancels, leaving the diminutive Bauer to battle the demonstrative Keyes on such key questions as, "How would you persuade a Buddhist or a Muslim that they are part of your America?" Taylor, known as "the Grizz" and wearing a grizzly bear tie, goes on next. Mercifully, the debate ends after an hour—and is followed promptly by a Forbes ad.

"They're all fringe characters here," says the Grizz, who should know. But Taylor, whose long gray hair makes him look like Buffalo Bill, says he will not shake up the race by running again. "I spent my money, had my say," he says. Spend money, have say: the two are now one and the same. Even Bauer has joined the criticism of the money system. When McCain asked other candidates to support a ban of soft money, Bauer obliged with a letter on October 19. "Those unlimited special interest funds distort the legislative process and they have been egregiously abused," he wrote.

Bush's money chase has knocked out Dole, Buchanan, Dan Quayle, Lamar Alexander, John Kasich and Bob Smith—which has helped McCain climb in the New Hampshire polls to 27 percent (from 10 percent this summer) against Bush's 39 percent. But the Texas governor's vulnerability appears to be growing. A recent *Newsweek* poll found Bush up only nine points over Gore and five over Bradley. Of course, this is nothing a few million dollars' worth of Bush advertising won't fix. But because Bush's candidacy is based on inevitability, he'll be in trouble if these numbers persist.

Bush's opponents, meanwhile, are getting smarter. Forbes, running second to Bush in Iowa, is essentially in cahoots with McCain, who is strong in New Hampshire. Buchanan is shrewdly playing down abortion to curry favor with his new Reform constituency. Gore, for his part, is readying an arsenal of barbs for Bush on health care, the environment and problems in the Texas border region; he is even planning a big campaign finance reform push for next spring.

Until now, Bush has responded to the threat with a parade of endorsements—Gore's losing strategy against Bradley. His first ads will help. But Bush's play-it-safe style is wearing thin. He still uses his five-month-old stump routine, urging that the American dream "touch every willing heart" and then shaking every willing hand. He refuses to engage in political give and take, saying he won't participate in the smashmouth politics of our time. Only the rare flourish takes him from his script, and the ad libs usually aren't an improvement.

Bush delivers a special message in Newport and at his next stop, in Keene, "for those of you supporting one of my erstwhile opponents, and I emphasize *erstwhile*: Don't work too hard." Perhaps he should stop emphasizing *erstwhile* until he looks the word up. Moments later, he promises "an administration of decent and honorable people trying to do what's right for Texas—America." Finally, asked about vice presidential candidates, he declares, "It is incredibly presumptive for somebody who has not yet earned his party's nomination to start speculating about vice presidents." Now, Governor, you are the presumptive nominee, so it wouldn't be all that presumptuous.

But malapropisms are not the message. Money is the message. Asked in Newport whether campaign finance will become a big issue in the 2000 race, Bush lists a few token reforms he supports, and acknowledges, "I think it's an issue." But compared to his top priorities, he adds, "I don't think it's as big an issue." Apparently not. When McCain asked for a letter of support for his reform legislation from the other candidates, a Bush spokesman said that all the governor would be sending McCain was a "Bush for President" bumper sticker.

Bush continues to sail above the fray, even as it's clear McCain is making a serious run at him. He seems oddly unwilling to engage, as if he operates by different political laws. Though this has worked well enough with some of the more feeble challengers such as Kasich, Hatch and Dole, who refused to take on Bush in any serious way, it's not going to work as well with McCain, who isn't afraid to mix it up with Bush.

McCain is that rarity among truth-tellers: a plausible candidate with plausible ideas. He increasingly finds himself the chief rival to Bush. Dole's money problems, staff departures and reluctance to take stands have removed her from the race; Dan Quayle has also quit, and Pat Buchanan is leaving the party. That leaves McCain as the mainstream alternative to Bush (and Forbes, who has plenty of money, as the conservative alternative).

McCain, like Bradley, is a favorite of the national press, in part because reporters love challengers and in part because both men are heroes. But while Bradley appears aloof, McCain is an ordinary guy, without artifice—or perhaps he's just very good at artifice. This week, he asked an aide to move so I could sit with him and his wife on a flight from San Diego to Phoenix. He talked about politics, but also about the ordinary—a war buddy fallen on hard times, the MTV awards, his son's lacrosse team.

Still, the main reason the press loves McCain is his gruff honesty. At his California kickoff at the Ronald Reagan Library, McCain speaks freely about Russia ("very much like their leader, an alcoholic who has to hit bottom"), military bases ("we have too many"), low military pay ("responsibility lies as much with Congress as it does with the president") and, most of all, abuse of soft money ("this is an incumbent protection racket"). McCain told me that he's inspired by Morris Udall, the late liberal Democratic congressman from Arizona. When Udall lost a bid for House majority leader, McCain relates, he declared that the difference between a cactus and a caucus was that "in a cactus, the pricks are on the outside."

McCain's obsession with campaign finance reform—which he shares with the other truth-tellers, Bradley and Beatty—is arguably the main source of his popularity among reporters. "A lot of them cover Congress," McCain says. "They see the effects of money. They see the tax breaks and who gets priority." Reporters may disagree with McCain on social issues, but they share his belief that campaign finance abuse is so big a problem that it colors all else. And that's the core of McCain's appeal. Americans who quarrel with McCain's stances on abortion, gay rights, labor or the poor may still find reason to support him, because if he were to lessen the overwhelming influence of money in politics, chances are the government would adopt policies more in tune with the needs of people who don't have a lot of money. Even abortion policy, McCain says, should be seen through the campaign finance prism. "It's the special interests that make a business out of it and prevent the issue from being resolved," he says. Instead, they could be solving the problem by promoting more adoption. McCain himself has adopted three children, including a daughter who is from Bangladesh.

Mark Penn, Gore's deposed pollster, has advised Clinton and Gore that campaign finance reform doesn't interest voters. Bush seems to be getting similar advice. McCain disagrees. "Mark Penn is mistaken—he asks the question in terms of campaign finance reform," McCain says. "But if you frame it in terms of special interests and corruption in Washington, it is a big issue out there." Let's hope McCain is right. But, at his speech this week in San Diego, where three hundred Naval Academy alumni cheer him heartily, he gets no applause for his attack on the campaign finance system.

McCain is not one to be deterred, however. A few hours later, in Arizona, the truth-teller is doggedly hammering away again at "special interests" and "corruption." Campaign finance reform, he says, simply must happen. "Until I draw my last breath, I will fight for it," he vows. It's no wonder so many in the press wish McCain long life. And it's time Governor Bush recognized this challenge.

10

★ ☆ ★

"The Biggest Caper in History"

It's primary night in New Hampshire, and a photo of President George Herbert Walker Bush is keeping vigil over the Presidential Suite of the Nashua Crowne Plaza Hotel. Bush would not be pleased to be witnessing a scene such as this one, however. For just beneath the Bush portrait is a television tuned to CNN, which is reporting some unhappy returns for Bush's son, George W. At the moment, the Presidential Suite is occupied by John McCain and his family and top staff.

McCain, reveling with a couple dozen aides and family members, spies me in the back of the suite, a gin and tonic in my hand. He tells me he got my postcard, the one I sent from Iowa with a cartoon of various pigs saying "Welcome to Iowa" and my observation that "you're not missing much here."

"We may be proving that correct," the candidate tells me. That's for sure. McCain took the unorthodox step of sitting out the Iowa caucuses last week, and it doesn't seem to be hurting him here in New Hampshire. The first exit polls came in around 1:30 this afternoon, showing McCain with a 12–15 point lead. McCain's own aides, expecting a close race, were baffled. "It'll tighten," said Mark Salter. But it didn't. The next round of polls had McCain up 20 points. By 5 p.m., the word had pretty much filtered out, and boisterous McCain supporters were already crowding the ballroom downstairs. "They've hit a major 'berg and they're in trouble," Mike Murphy, a McCain strategist, is telling the reporters. McCain mouthpiece Todd Harris is smug. "I'm waiting for all those backdated letters to arrive at the office," Harris says, "and the calls from Senator So-And-So: 'What do you mean you didn't get my endorsement?'"

Upstairs, however, McCain looks serious, almost grave. It's only when somebody shouts "Timber!" and "The landslide has begun" that McCain indulges in a laugh. When NBC's David Bloom, in the incessant chatter that precedes the results, suggests that "many people don't believe the Texas governor is prepared to be commander in chief," the candidate's wife, Cindy, screams: "Oh, yes!" Cindy, unlike her husband, is outwardly ecstatic. She watches herself on television, remarking, "I can do a Nancy Reagan stare." McCain himself, however, talks to me about his nap that afternoon; he asks John Weaver if it's OK to step into the hallway outside his suite, where a few of his guests are milling around a bar. Weaver is amused that the man now a giant step closer to the presidency needs to request permission to walk between rooms. "He's always uncomfortable with success," Weaver says.

That should be difficult tonight. At 7 p.m., as the polls close, CNN flashes McCain's face on the screen with the projection "*Winner*." Cheers of "whooooooh" erupt in the suite as McCain and a few aides pump fists in the air. When CNN's Jeff Greenfield talks about voters hitting Bush "upside the head," another round of cheers erupts. When Greenfield adds, as a caution, "We'll have to wait for South Carolina," the cheers change to groans, and Rick Davis, the campaign chairman, scolds, "Oh, Greenfield." Aides round up McCain's children to congratulate their dad. Salter, nearly in tears, hugs Weaver, while Lanny Wiles, McCain's advance man, is openly tearful. Cindy McCain, overcome, keeps touching her hands to her face, as if making sure all this is real. Only the candidate himself seems to hold back; he closes his eyes, as if fighting off emotion, then gives in to a few smiles and nods as he watches the television.

Just after 8 p.m., Karl Rove calls to talk to McCain. Weaver, Rove's arch-enemy, tells an aide to inform Rove that "consultants don't concede to candidates." Rove backed down, and a few minutes later, Bush himself called; the talk lasted all of 90 seconds. On television, meanwhile, the exit polls showed McCain beating Bush by 41 points among independent voters and, more surprisingly, by 10 points among GOP voters. "The volcano has erupted," says Ken Khachigian, a former Reagan man advising McCain. Lindsey Graham, a South Carolina congressman, comes in and hugs McCain. "Firin' up, firin' up," McCain says in his phony-candidate, wheeler-dealer voice. Karen Hughes, Bush's powerfully built communications director, is on the tube, explaining the "bump in the road." The room erupts in cries of "Sasquatch," the McCainiacs name for Hughes.

McCain retreats to the bedroom, where his wife is putting on makeup. Now Bush is on TV, making his concession speech. He goes on and on with excuses, about how McCain spent more time here, about the bump in the road, and more. McCain watches, holding the back of a chair, growing increasingly irritated as Bush drones on. McCain, on his way out of the room, shakes his head and says to me, "Sometime in this election I'm going to lose a primary. I'm going to say, 'Thank you, congratulations, good night,' and exit stage right." With that, he heads to the elevator, down to a dangerously crowded ballroom, where the naval hymn is playing.

Amid the hubbub, John Weaver reclines on a sofa in McCain's hotel suite, drinking his trademark bottle of Budweiser. He flashes an impish grin. "This is like, Holy shit, Batman," he says. "We've just pulled off the biggest caper in history."

That may be a stretch. But this much is true: nobody believed McCain could inflict such a lopsided defeat on Bush, with his huge war chest (now $70 million) and his vast organization. Nobody, that is, except for Weaver.

Weaver, who orchestrated McCain's triumph here, was able to exploit a flaw in Bush's campaign. The front-runner, taking the high road, essentially ignored McCain, refusing to mix it up, avoiding debates where possible and spending little time wooing voters. Bush responded weakly to McCain's charges that his tax cut was too big, that he didn't leave enough money for Social Security and that he invited corruption by refusing campaign finance reform.

In New Hampshire, Bush learned a crucial lesson: the Mr. Nice Guy routine doesn't work. Now, Bush must engage McCain. He must fight to win.

You could tell immediately that this was no ordinary day in New Hampshire when you saw Carmen and Priscilla Gangi walking down Manchester's main drag at high noon—accompanied by their eight-month-old goat, Butch.

"They told us to get out the goat—I mean the vote," said Carmen Gangi, as Butch, a purebred La Mancha, gnawed at his leash and Priscilla Gangi's shopping bag. The animal had two Alan Keyes yard signs tied to its midsection. "We're patriots, and he's the closest thing we've found to the Founding Fathers," said Carmen Gangi, a local farmer. He was talking about Keyes, not the goat.

Primary Day 2000 in New Hampshire is like no other day here. Bill Donovan drove up from Boston so he could stand on a busy street corner here wearing a rubber Clinton mask and carry a sign that says, "I believe Paula Jones." "Today's the big day," said Donovan, in Bush T-shirt, Bush stickers and Bush buttons. Just a block away, a man handed out fliers describing how "you can legally stop paying income taxes." He's for Keyes, naturally.

The candidates themselves have no time for such frivolity on Primary Day. They must do serious things. They must visit *Imus in the Morning*.

Don Imus is broadcasting from New Hampshire this week, and John McCain rose before dawn, so he could bask in the I-man's endorsement in front of a crowd of a thousand packed into a Concord auditorium. Imus is to politics what Oprah is to book publishing, which explains why Jeff Greenfield, Tim Russert, Dan Rather, Tom Brokaw and McCain were all on the show this morning. Bill Bradley called in Monday.

The candidates, for the most part, were playing it safe in the final hours. Bush canceled an event in Exeter on Monday, leaving CBS's Rather high and dry. This morning, he dropped by a polling place in Bedford, causing a traffic backup in all directions. Bush stood in the parking lot of McKelvie Middle School, trying to talk to voters, who are few, and avoid reporters, who are many. "How ya doin', Buddy?" he greeted one man, before realizing Buddy was a reporter.

The candidates didn't want to make news, because news made at this stage was likely to be bad. Gary Bauer learned this when he fell off the stage during a pancake-flipping event. His campaign spent the rest of the day in damage control, arguing that, in fact, he had caught the pancake in his bare hand.

Vice President Gore, opting for a sterile environment before the election, invited reporters over to his Manchester headquarters Monday while he joined a phone bank. Even this backfired, because the people Gore called suspected a hoax. "No, it's not a joke. I really am Al Gore," the vice president told one person on the phone. "How can I prove it to you? . . . No, it's me, Al Gore. . . . Mary, it's Vice President Al Gore. . . . No, it's *not* Michael."

Even the demonstrative Keyes seemed tame. For his finale, he hired the Drifters to play at a Nashua hotel, raising the possibility that the fiery moralist is softening. Keyes blasted a rival for admiring the group Nine Inch Nails, and now he calls in the Drifters. (They weren't talking about tax policy "Under the Boardwalk.")

The campaign staffers, their work done here, are nursing their wounds, which in this case seem to be mostly from influenza. In the past month, Steve Forbes's senior New Hampshire adviser, Paul Young, lost eight days of work to the flu. Dan Robinson, Forbes's state press secretary, was out for a week, while Graham Shafer, his New Hampshire director, and Alan Raymond, his deputy national political director, also were felled by the virus. The candidate himself, who took the trouble to get a flu shot and carries a bottle of Germ-X hand cleaner, hasn't succumbed. "Not yet," Forbes said last weekend, knocking a Germ-X-treated hand on his bus's wood veneer wall.

Word from George W. Bush's campaign is that Press Secretary Mindy Tucker came down with a hard case a couple of weeks ago and felt as if she'd been hit by a truck. The bug also ravaged the Bush press plane.

John McCain's *Straight Talk Express* is a roiling, roiling petri dish of infection. After the candidate contracted something nasty a few weeks ago, he passed it on to his friend Congressman Graham, who promptly came down with pneumonia. Campaign Manager Rick Davis, meanwhile, has been terrorizing colleagues with his particularly unpleasant cough. Todd Harris, who fainted on the bus a couple of weeks ago, reported a new sore throat yesterday.

From Bill Bradley's team we hear that Press Secretary Eric Hauser was cut down for two days. On the vice president's JugGoreNaut, colleagues of New Hampshire Director Nick Baldick ordered him to stay home last week—and away from them—after he caught the bug. And Press Secretary Chris Lehane is fading fast. "Low-grade fever, sore throat," he confided, pulling from his pocket a capsule of his secret weapon. "Echinacea. I could be their poster boy."

At lunchtime on Primary Day, the action was at the Merrimack Restaurant in downtown Manchester. This is where reporters interview patrons to see how the election is going—an informal exit poll. Problem is, the cashier estimated it was 75 percent out-of-towners today. An NBC crew was in front of the restaurant, a radio crew in back. ABC's political director was sharing a booth with a man from NBC.

"It's gone from the sublime to the ridiculous," said L. A. Williams, one of the few locals eating lunch here. From her office at a nearby bank, she has seen "Captain Climate" in a red cape, banjo players at Steve Forbes's headquarters and someone dressed as a phallus following Bush. "A lot of people are going to be real happy to see it over," Williams said, wishing the waitress good luck on her way out. "I've only got two more hours," the waitress replied.

The other Primary Day institution in town is the Webster School polling place. McCain, Bauer and Bush all went this morning, the poll-watchers say, and Forbes had plans to come by, too. A soldier from the old Pat Buchanan Brigade collected signatures. Five girls from Manchester Central High, bracing against the cold, stood nearby. "Have a Bradley cookie," one of them offered, displaying a box full of treats with B's in icing. Who baked them? "His wife, Ernest," said one girl. "That's Ernestine," her friend corrected. A few paces away, Satoru Suzuki, Washington bureau chief of Japan's TV Asahi, used the Bradley girls as background noise for his broadcast.

The Bradley girls were part of an army of local volunteers driven by motives both civic and social. At the Carpenter Center, a polling place in downtown Manchester, the talk was about who's moving in and out of the neighborhood. "It's fun—we get to see all our neighbors," says Doris Genest, a Forbes backer. Out-of-towners join the act, too. Leo Giacometto spent the day waving Bush signs on a street corner. Unfortunately, he forgot his hat and gloves, and his mustache collected icicles. "Yesterday I was soaking wet going door to door," he said.

Not that he was complaining—because he would soon be celebrating at the Bush victory party. Actual victory is no prerequisite for the victory party. Everyone says they beat expectations. "We'll claim victory no matter what happens," confided State Director Baldick, noting that Gore has been outspent here.

Bradley seemed to have the same idea. Hours before the polls close, Bradley workers were unloading tables and setting up risers for Bradley's victory party in the gymnasium at New Hampshire College. But what if Bradley loses tonight? "It's still a party," said Tim Allyn, the event coordinator, eating a McDonald's breakfast sandwich and sending out for more duct tape. "I'm from Los Angeles. We party win, lose or draw."

But the fun of Primary Day in New Hampshire is immediately replaced by the bitter contest to come in South Carolina, the next primary state for Republicans. Bush immediately changes his tactics, taking on McCain directly and fiercely. McCain, he charges, is a phony reformer, while Bush is, somewhat implausibly, a "Reformer With Results." McCain, furthermore, will "say one thing and do another," a new mantra for Bush. The switch by Bush to the smashmouth politics he so recently deplored reflects his new reality: he has to fight to win. For anybody who still believes in the tooth fairy, Santa Claus and the inevitability of Bush's ascent to the presidency hasn't yet considered the case of J. W. Hendrix of Lexington County, South Carolina.

To the naked eye, Hendrix is a solid Bush man. The former county councilman and Republican activist has planted "George W. Bush for President" signs on his front lawn and at some of the six trailer parks he owns. But Hendrix's Bush sympathies are only skin-deep. The yard signs, it turns out, were given to him by his state senator, who asked Hendrix to put them up as a favor (and business owners don't want to offend the local senator).

Hendrix probably won't even vote for Bush in Saturday's South Carolina primary; he's leaning hard toward McCain. His friend Billy Oswald, another former councilman, has accompanied Hendrix to a county Republican meeting and says he knows several others who are displaying Bush signs but will vote for McCain. Oswald will, too. Why? "I think McCain will be a stronger candidate in the end," Oswald told me.

The meeting, unfolding on the top floor of the county administration building, should terrify the Bush campaign. It's evidence that the post–New Hampshire rap against Bush could be true: his support, impressive on the outside, might be hollow at the core. Last December, reporters on the campaign trail were already beginning to speculate that Bush might not have what it takes to win the presidency; in our speculation, however, it was assumed that the Democrats would upend him, not his fellow Republicans. Now the once-unthinkable seems plausible: Bush might not survive the primaries. Could it be that the Bush campaign is smoke and mirrors, largely the creation of businessmen who bet their money on a sure thing who isn't?

That thought could prove wildly premature or downright foolish; Bush is, of course, still the formidable front-runner for the GOP nomination. He's also still the best financed, although he's already spent more than $40 million of his record $70 million campaign chest. But the Republican establishment that anointed Bush last summer is now splitting and second-guessing. As Al D'Amato, the former New York senator and an early Bush backer, said Wednesday, "I have endorsed Governor Bush, [but] it doesn't keep me from marveling and enjoying and living vicariously through McCain."

South Carolina is a case in establishment angst. Statewide, McCain has only half as many state legislators backing him as Bush does, and McCain slyly talks about how the entire GOP establishment is against him. But McCain's supporters include two of the state's four Republican congressmen, the state House speaker pro tem and majority leader. On paper, Bush has the benefit of former Governor Carroll Campbell's political machine. But now there is talk that Carroll's organization may have as much trouble delivering votes here as Senator Judd Gregg's machine did in New Hampshire.

Loyal Republicans have given Bush their endorsements but not necessarily their hearts. To see this phenomenon, stop in at the meeting of the Lexington County Republican Party, the most loyal Republicans in the most Republican county in this largely Republican state. This was the first county in the state to go Republican in the 1960s; if there is a GOP "establishment" in South Carolina, it's here. And sure enough, the crowd of 150 is roughly 3 to 2 for Bush. But it quickly becomes clear that its loyalty to Bush isn't very strong.

Here's why:

To begin with, the Republican establishment doesn't hold much sway over the party faithful. Eileen Rodriguez Harding, for example, is a young party activist who intends to run for office herself. She cast her lot with Bush early. "I was bouncing around with the higher-ups in the state," she says. "I went with Bush because they all were." But then she did some reading. She went to a debate. She prayed. And two weeks ago, she showed up at McCain's headquarters here to volunteer. A turncoat! Even now, she says she feels guilty about leaving Bush, whom she likes. "He's taken several pictures with me," she says. "But all he's got is the name recognition. McCain's a maverick. I don't think Bush is as strong. He's got the money, but it's his daddy's coattails."

McCain has the support of a couple of county officials, the Lexington mayor and the county GOP chairman, Tommy Windsor—who is a McCain volunteer, no less. It's perilous, of course, to extrapolate a national shift from one small pocket of Republican strength. But the national establishment's new nervousness about its chosen candidate is also on display here.

At the meeting, Marilyn Bundrick, the county GOP treasurer and a Bush supporter, turns to Art Guerry, the county auditor. She assumes he also is for Bush. Instead, Guerry gives her a lecture on why McCain may be stronger against the Democrats than Bush. "I looked at people supporting Bush, and their support was really for his father, not for him," Guerry says. "The Bush people are thin—they're easy to push over. I've seen a lot of people stop working for him. The McCain people are much more committed. I've got a strong feeling a lot of Bush supporters are going to vote for McCain."

Disgusted, Bundrick turns away. "I'm going to pray for you tonight, Art," she says.

But the auditor has a point: McCain could be a tougher challenger for Al Gore, the likely Democratic nominee at this point. And Gore's aides, though cheering for McCain to weaken Bush, don't actually want McCain to defeat him. The governor's credentials play to Gore's strengths—experience, foreign policy expertise, relative moderation (particularly now that Bush is wooing the conservatives)—and few of his weaknesses. The Bush money machine can't easily make an issue out of the Clinton-Gore 1996 campaign finance abuses, and a Bush certainly can't accuse a Gore of being born with the proverbial silver spoon. Perhaps that's why the governor, who led the vice president by almost 20 percentage points nationwide in polls last year, is down to a single-digit lead in some surveys and now trails Gore in the crucial electoral states of New York and California.

Also, Bush's singular advantage, that he's a sure winner for the GOP, no longer exists. Several recent national polls show McCain matching or outperforming Bush in head-to-head contests with either Gore or Bill Bradley. With his aura of inevitability gone, Bush has lost the central foundation of his candidacy. And this isn't lost on the loyal Republicans of Lexington County. "The strongest thing Bush had going was that he could contribute to a landslide," says Ken Clark, who wore a GOP elephant tie to last week's meeting. "Now that's not so obvious."

Clark says he's still a Bush man, but more out of obligation than passion: "I'm hesitant to switch to McCain because I've been supporting Bush." Nearby, a state representative, Elsie Rast Stuart, says McCain's rise has helped her resist pressure from legislative peers to back Bush. "I was really leaning toward Bush because I thought he could do so much for the party," she says. "Now I don't know."

Even those still backing Bush here in Lexington should give the Bush campaign cause for alarm. Their reasons for supporting the governor are fuzzy, the sort of soft impressions that could easily be reversed in the electorate by a Democratic opponent. A sampling: "He's well-educated, he has class, he's sincere . . . he's had a good upbringing . . . his father was a great president and his mother was a great first lady . . . he's charismatic, well-organized, I like his record." There was virtually nothing about the vision thing, a cause around which voters can rally.

McCain supporters, by contrast, are far more vigorous. Even some of the Bushies acknowledge the difference. Dot Pappas likes Bush, but confesses that her fondness for him doesn't come close to the intensity that her husband, Jim, feels for McCain. "I think McCain would be better against Gore," Jim Pappas says. Bush, like Bob Dole in '96, "doesn't have that fire in his belly. I think McCain does."

Surprisingly, Dot agrees. Turning on her candidate, she says McCain "can excite people more, the way Reagan did." But then, catching herself, she pulls back. "I'm with Bush," she says, "for now."

The truly loyal Bush supporters in the Lexington County council chambers tend to be those who identify themselves as religious conservatives. They see Bush as the more conservative of the two candidates, and Bush has encouraged this thinking. But even this could ultimately means bad news for Bush. While he woos the far right, he's giving up the claim to the middle he staked out so persuasively last year. If he does become the GOP nominee, this could hurt him in November. And while Bush courts the Pat Robertson voters here, McCain is again luring independents and Democrats. Bush's conservative backers grouse that the Democrats, who don't have a primary on the same day, are busing in their own to tilt the South Carolina primary in McCain's favor. But this gives the Democrats too much credit: maybe Democrats are supporting McCain because they like him. And maybe they'll like him in November, too.

Bush seems to be stuck in a campaign of inevitability, mustering daily displays of institutional support. On the day after his New Hampshire defeat—which his campaign blamed on that state's quirkiness—Bush trumpeted his endorsement by Dan Quayle. The following day, the campaign hauled out a bunch of veterans to vouch for the governor and then issued a news release announcing the backing of Jim Gibbons of Nevada, "the

175th Republican member of the House of Representatives to endorse Governor Bush." Next came word that "Utah Leaders Give Sweeping Support to Governor Bush."

Problem is, a lot of Republicans in Lexington County don't much care what's doing in Nevada or Utah. They're waiting for Bush to give them a reason to be passionate. So far, he hasn't. Bush needs a more aggressive attack—and fast.

Part III

★ ☆ ★

The Rise of Smashmouth
Gore's Recovery

11

★ ☆ ★

Shakeup

> "A (expletive) good guy! Is he with us? . . . That (expletive) (expletive) is trying to take me out. He (expletived) himself . . . No one's gonna (expletive) with Matty. Who is this (expletive)? . . . I've had enough of that (expletive)."
>
> —Michael Whouley, in an overheard phone conversation

For Michael Whouley, it all began with a message in a Chinese fortune cookie. "Bill Clinton will be in your future," it said. That was 1991, and Whouley, a young Clinton operative, arranged for a cookie with that fortune to be given to each participant in a Florida Democratic straw poll; the participants also received a wake-up telephone message from Clinton in their hotel rooms. Those gimmicks, and some old-fashioned politicking, handed Clinton an upset victory in the straw poll and vaulted him into serious consideration as a presidential candidate.

From there, Whouley rose to become Clinton's national field director and, in '96, Al Gore's campaign manager. Now he's the man Gore calls his "brain," a top strategist who was brought in to rescue the struggling Gore operations in New Hampshire and Iowa. Within a week or so, the campaign is expected to announce that Whouley will become Gore's point man at the Democratic National Committee, the man responsible for coordinating the Democratic Party's national effort with that of its presidential nominee.

Whouley is notoriously publicity-shy; even Gore teases him about his invisible image, and his own mother-in-law complains that he won't even walk past a C-SPAN camera so she can see him on television. A product of Boston's ward-an-precinct political system, he considers himself "an old-style operative, and proud of it," says Patty Foley, a friend and former colleague. "He's the quintessential blue-collar Democrat," says John Marttila, who knew Whouley as a tactician for Senator John Kerry. But while Whouley has a back-to-basics style, he has also been known for his political stunts. In addition to his fortune cookie brainstorm, he devised Clinton's door-to-door delivery of videotapes in New Hampshire.

Whouley grew up the son of an engineer in the St. Peter's Parish neighborhood of heavily Irish Dorchester, Massachusetts. He became a campaign volunteer as a teenager and the ward boss in a mayoral race when he was 20. Today, he retains an almost clannish code of loyalty. After Clinton's victory in 1992, he briefly took a job as the White House personnel director, making sure all those who helped him in the field landed jobs in the administration. On the night Gore won the New Hampshire primary this year, when the candidate and his top staff flew out of town, Whouley stayed behind to go to a bar with his field staff. "He gets the most out of people because he demands loyalty," says Bobby White, Whouley's mentor in Boston politics. "That's where he gets his strength." His wife jokes that his pals from Dorchester could be murderers and he'd still defend them.

Whouley's intensity is legendary among colleagues, some of whom live in fear of what they call the "Whouley stare" when they haven't done a job right. His heavy Dorchester accent (Gore is "Gaw") is sprinkled liberally with street language. In a nod to the world outside of Dorchester, Whouley likes to wear fine suits, everything from Brooks Brothers to Brioni. Colleagues recently caught Whouley wearing a $2,200 suit—a fact they knew because he accidentally left the price tag on it. "You can take the kid out of Dorchester," Lehane says, "but you can't take Dorchester out of the kid."

★ ☆ ★

The news came over the Labor Day weekend. The unthinkable had just happened: Bradley had passed Gore in New Hampshire, according to a new poll in the *Boston Globe*. The loping challenger, once dismissed by Gore aides as Michael Dukakis with a jump shot, was now a real threat to take the Democratic nomination.

At Gore headquarters, alarm bells went off. Clearly, Gore's above-the-fray, Mr. Nice Guy routine had not worked. Bradley, ignored by Gore, had sneaked ahead by portraying Gore as a small-thinking vacillator with few ideas. Gore, now realizing himself to be in need of some bare-knuckle politics, called up Whouley. The man from Dorchester would take over the Gore operations in New Hampshire and Iowa, effective immediately.

Whouley, with license to be Gore's Mr. Fixit, has wasted no time. In New Hampshire, he has killed Gore's practice of lining up minor endorsements, instead urging the candidate to do door-to-door canvassing. He has created "town-hall meetings," borrowing a leaf from McCain's book, to show a more accessible Gore. He has told headquarters to leave the local Gore operations alone, free to pursue their own mailings and phone calls. He has quietly arranged the endorsement of Governor Jeanne Shaheen, who will soon announce her backing and tape telemarketing messages for Gore.

In Iowa, Whouley is overhauling the sluggish Gore operation. He has begun a rigorous vote-counting machine, assembling an aggressive phone-bank shop that targeted even solid Bradley backers. He called out 20 of his political-operative friends from Boston, and 20 others from around the country, and he presides over them in a smoke-filled back room in Gore's Des Moines headquarters, as if commanding a Viking ship.

The results are immediate and dramatic. Gore is engaging Bradley—finally. At the Jefferson-Jackson dinner for Democrats in Iowa, Bradley is cool and cerebral. But when it's Gore's turn to speak, he bluntly demands weekly debates. "What about it, Bill?" Gore challenges, walking out in front of the podium and looking down at Bradley. "If the answer is yes, stand up." Bradley doesn't budge. Gore aides have circulated posters reading "Stay and Fight" to his supporters, whom the vice president leads in a chant. "Some walked away," Gore shouts, referring to Bradley's departure from the Senate in 1996, "but I decided to stay and fight!" Even Bradley supporters cheer. The stay-and-fight idea, which will appear in TV ads, isn't a bad theme; it questions Bradley's past, addresses doubts about Gore's tenacity, and suggests continuity of Clinton policies without naming Clinton.

As Gore duels with Bradley upstairs, the Gore campaign's vast minions are engaging the smaller army of Bradley staffers in a skirmish downstairs. Gore spokesman Chris Lehane confronts Bradley's communications director, Anita Dunn, who is refuting Gore's claims to a *Boston Globe* reporter. "I won't debate you," Dunn tells Lehane as she retreats. "You're just like your candidate," Lehane calls after her. After the speech, the Gore operation again outguns Bradley. Moore works on one *Times* reporter while Whouley buttonholes another before moving on to ABC News. Lehane zeroes in on *U.S. News & World Report* and then the Associated Press. Dunn races, without much luck, to keep up. Not that it matters.

Gore would get good reviews, for once, and even one Bradley adviser, after the spin is spun, confides the improbable truth about Gore's night: "He was terrific."

When future historians assess the Gore campaign's turning point, they might point to Whouley's role in Iowa and New Hampshire. But they would also be wise to recall the moment when the cleaning crew got the upper hand in the Gore campaign men's room.

The reference, aficionados of toilet humor will recognize, is to Mark Penn, who has been dumped as Gore's top pollster. *Reason* magazine, in an article picked up in the *Washington Post*'s gossip column, accused Penn and his firm of keeping their office bathroom messy. The firm denied it, and my own inspection of the premises revealed an unflushed toilet and water spilled on the counter but an otherwise tidy operation. Still, the charge had a familiar ring. The rumpled Penn, nicknamed "Pigpen" by his Clinton '96 colleagues, is known to be a bit bizarre. Penn's colleagues say he misplaced an untold number of cell phones during the '96 campaign (he admits to "four or five"). Longtime Gore adviser Bob Squier tells of finding Penn's suit jacket and greeting him the next day while wearing it.

"How do I look?" Squier asked.

"OK," Penn responded, gruffly.

"Like this jacket?" Squier nudged.

"It's OK."

"Look familiar?"

"No."

"It's yours."

"No, it's not."

"You lost it yesterday."

"No, I didn't."

"Try it on," Squier offered.

Penn did. "Hey, my pen's in the pocket!" (Penn still denies it's his jacket.)

But Penn's idiosyncrasies didn't hurt the vice president. His advice did, Gore loyalists say. Last year, Clinton aides blamed Penn's rosy reports for the president's failure to beat impeachment. Penn encouraged Clinton and Gore not to push campaign finance reform—though Bradley has, with much success. He persuaded Gore to enumerate a profusion of policies rather than a few big ones, something Bradley has countered well. And, they say, he downplayed the Bush and Bradley threats. On top of that, his long client list—which includes Bill and Hillary Clinton, Gore, and Bill Gates—makes him look like a mercenary.

Now comes an October 9 *New York Times* story in which Penn washes his hands of Gore's failures. The story said that, back in April, Penn presented Gore and his aides with a memo recommending that Gore take on Bradley. Gore decided not to—an obvious mistake, in hindsight. But the Bradley recommendation was just one of several, including a call to take on Bush ("start the general now") and to roll out policies. According to others at the meeting, engaging Bradley was not Penn's top priority. Now, Gore and his advisers see the article as Penn's revenge for his firing. "If there were ethical standards in the polling industry, he'd be disbarred," says a Gore aide. Penn may be just another of Campaign Chairman Tony Coelho's scapegoats. But even if that's true, Penn's willingness to exonerate himself in the *Times* at Gore's expense suggests his top priority isn't Gore's election.

The replacement of Penn, along with a plan to do less polling, is evidence that Gore is finally acting decisively. It's not clear whether the changes have come too late. But at the moment, Gore seems to be back in business. Consider New Hampshire, where Bradley leads Gore. Shaheen will soon back Gore, possibly shifting the momentum in his favor. Meanwhile, the Gore campaign, aware that its lists of petty endorsements are useless, has canceled an event with one hundred state representatives in New Hampshire. Instead, on October 21, Gore will hold an unscripted meeting with undecided voters.

The evidence of change is all around. "Lease—Excellent Rates," reads a sign at 2131 K Street in Washington. In front, movers load the contents of Coelho's office onto a U-Haul truck. The move to Nashville will allow Gore 2000 to cut headquarters staff. The campaign is also toning down lavish events and sending fewer aides on Air Force Two. As Gore sheds advisers who don't move, he's picking up some new ones—including one of Clinton's early scandal managers, Mark Fabiani, as communications director. Even Michael Whouley got into the spirit of the move by wearing cowboy boots to Iowa.

Gore's shift to the heartland sometimes borders on the absurd. When reporters joined Gore's caravan in Iowa last weekend, they were given packages containing home-baked cookies, a hand-bound scrapbook with snapshots of Gore, a piece of Iowa's official state rock ("which like Al Gore is seemingly plain on the outside, but quite interesting inside") and an ear of corn with a note from a farmer.

But whether or not it's genuine, Gore is simulating with increasing skill the mannerisms of a normal human being. In a Des Moines neighborhood, he surprised his own advance team by leaving a press conference and marching door to door for a couple of blocks. "We've got sort of a renegade candidate here," said Press Secretary Kiki Moore, who worried that Gore would be bitten by a dog.

It would be premature to celebrate a new Al Gore simply because Whouley is in and Penn is out. Even Naomi Wolf couldn't add much spice to the vice president in his October 27 debate with Bradley. The two candidates haggled over price tags and magnified small distinctions. Typical of the night were the five "Reality Checks" the Gore campaign distributed to reporters during the debate. "Reality: Bradley failed to support a bill to reduce logging in the Tongas forest," said one. So the Democrats' bid to differentiate themselves had come to this: nitpicking in New Hampshire over an obscure bill about an Alaskan forest.

Fortunately for Gore, Bradley wasn't flawless, either. When asked for his models of leadership, he offered Jimmy Carter, Woodrow Wilson and Mikhail Gorbachev: a moralizing loner, a failed egghead and a Communist who presided over his empire's collapse. Bradley, it seems, simply can't play the kind of tough politics he must to get traction against a newly aggressive Gore.

While Gore begins to steal loyal Democrats away from Bradley, John McCain seems to be stealing the independents who might vote for Bradley over to the Republican side. Some 37 percent of the New Hampshire electorate are registered independents, and both men are focusing on that group. Asked whether he's competing with Bradley for independent voters, McCain replied: "I think so. . . . I think there may be a kind of a second contest going." McCain even needled Bradley about his reversal on ethanol subsidies. "He may have found himself on the road to Damascus—or the road to Des Moines," McCain said.

Of course, Gore is only cheering for McCain to a point. If the Arizona senator were actually to defeat Bush—still a remote possibility—he might prove a more formidable opponent in the general election. McCain has more experience, both in foreign policy and overall, than Bush does. And McCain can co-opt Democratic issues—notably campaign finance reform— and highlight Gore's vulnerability on the Clinton administration's fundraising abuses. "McCain does a better job of appealing to independents, so Bush is probably the candidate we'd rather face," reasons Jim Demers, a Gore activist in New Hampshire. McCain's reform talk, he admits, "does hit a nerve."

Bradley's advisers, though they acknowledge competing with McCain, say that few independents are genuinely free of party leanings.

"It's way overblown," says Mark Longabaugh, Bradley's New Hampshire man. Bradley, when I asked about vying for independents, replied: "I'm not segmenting the market."

In the space of a few weeks, the Democratic campaign has undergone a reversal. Now Bradley is the aloof one who doesn't want to mix it up, and Gore is more of a street fighter bearing down on his foe. Bradley advisers recently approached their candidate with a new line of attack against Gore, responding to Gore's more aggressive charges against Bradley. They want Bradley to ask Gore, in a debate, "How can people trust you to tell the truth as president if you don't tell the truth as a candidate?" It could be a withering line, but we may never find out. Soft-touch Bradley, so far, refuses to use it.

12

★ ☆ ★

Strange Bedfellows

Michael Feldman, a senior adviser to Al Gore, was riding on Marine Two, the vice president's helicopter, when he reached into his briefcase and, much to his surprise, found a zucchini.

"What's that?" Gore asked, as Feldman pulled the vegetable from his bag.

Feldman knew instantly what had happened. "It's Lehane's zucchini, sir," the aide reported. Chris Lehane, who has just been named press secretary for Gore 2000, had surreptitiously placed the vegetable in Feldman's briefcase.

This is not as uncommon an event as one might expect. In fact, just about everybody who works for Gore has a complaint about Lehane. For example, Paul Cusack, Gore's personal aide, arrived at his Chicago hotel one night to discover that all the furniture had been removed from his room. Lehane, posing as Cusack, had called the hotel, demanding that his room be completely cleared out before he arrived.

Maurice Daniel has a beef, too. The vice president's political director found that he'd been hauling the Los Angeles Yellow Pages around in his luggage for two days after Lehane had stashed it there. Spokesman Alejandro Cabrera is not amused, either. When Lehane was recently interviewed by Swedish television, he added a personal note about how much he loved Sweden, urging any and all Swedes to call him. Lehane said his name was Alejandro Cabrera and provided Cabrera's phone number.

Lehane, who was Gore's official mouthpiece and is now his campaign flack, has established himself as the court jester in an operation sorely in need of comic relief. Though his title is press secretary, his unofficial duty is far broader: he's helping Gore relax and lighten up—letting Gore be Gore, as he often puts it—which, in turn, brightens the dour mood in Gore 2000.

As the primaries approach, the staff silliness is a serious matter. Gore's main problem is his inability to be himself, or to act normally. By lightening up the atmosphere, aides like Lehane and Feldman, with help from some higher-ups like Tipper Gore, have been trying to inject a bit of fun into the Gore operation.

Insurgent or fiercely ideological campaigns don't require this kind of injection of spirit. Steve Forbes and Gary Bauer inspire bands of young conservatives, while Bill Bradley attracts alienated liberals and John McCain brings out reformers. George W. Bush, like Bill Clinton in 1992, attracts partisans who want to save the party. But Gore draws none of these. Although often charming behind closed doors, in front of crowds he is alternately described as reserved or phony. So Lehane's job is to take the loose, private Gore public. "I want Americans to see Gore the way I see Gore," he likes to say.

The Gore campaign staffers are constantly battling two negative images: that they don't have any fun and that they are a bunch of mercenaries with questionable loyalty. Lehane, a 32-year-old smart aleck with slicked-back hair who cut his teeth in the White House scandal management operation, provides an antidote to both. "There's no passion inside the campaign," says one Gore loyalist, voicing a common complaint. "There aren't a lot of people willing to lay their body down on the tracks for him." But while a number of Gore's advisers and consultants have divided loyalties and interests, Lehane is all Gore. "You want him in the foxhole next to you," says Mark Fabiani, who worked with Lehane in the White House Counsel's Office.

At the moment, Lehane is turning his Gore 2000 foxhole into a haven for merry pranksters. He persuaded Roger Simon of *U.S. News & World Report* to leave a gag phone message for the famously press-shy Feldman saying that he was working on a major Feldman profile; Feldman, on a bus tour with Gore when he got the message, went into a panic. Lehane's objects-in-luggage gags have now become routine: a burrito, numerous bananas, and a Jabba the Hutt paperweight in Feldman's briefcase, a dog biscuit and salad tongs in Deputy Chief of Staff Monica Dixon's bag. The vice president, noticing Dixon's dog biscuit, felt compelled to inquire. But any hard feelings were eased by the leftover bottle of wine Lehane appropriated from a wedding reception in Providence, Rhode Island, and placed in Dixon's bag; an inscription said: "A toast to you from far and near, from Brenda and Todd." Lehane also annoys his colleagues with unflattering nicknames: a slight fellow becomes "Pipes" and the display on Gore aide Tom Rosshirt's cell phone morphs from ROSSHIRT to HAIRSHIRT.

Nor are the shenanigans strictly for internal consumption. For some time, Lehane has been engaged in a daily game of bingo with the press, trying to convince publications to print certain strange words—say, trying to get *aardvark* into the *Chicago Tribune*. For years, he's been hoping to get *officious intermeddler* into print. (He finally landed it in an October 23 *New York Times* story on Bradley.) But he has yet to achieve the Holy Grail of spokesman's bingo: getting a quote published with the word *rimbamboo* (supposed meaning: a fool) in it, which he claims is in the writings of *L. A. Confidential* author James Elroy.

Along the way, Lehane's one-liners have made him a regular in various quote-of-the-day compilations. When asked, after a Gore speech on guns, whether Gore meant to criticize Bush, Lehane replied, "If the holster fits, wear it." Last week, after Bush flunked a reporter's foreign policy quiz, Lehane commented on Bush's recently leaked college grades: "I guess we know that C at Yale was a gentleman's C." Earlier, after a Bush foreign policy speech, he quipped: "The governor's foreign policy expertise begins with Slovenia and ends with Slovakia."

If there's a problem with Lehane, who has degrees from Amherst College and Harvard Law School, it's that he's too clever by half. His barbs sometimes sail over his targets' heads. When Republicans tried to kill Gore's Earth-filming satellite, Lehane called them "troglodytes." James Sensenbrenner, chairman of the House Science Committee, responded that he didn't like being called a dinosaur. Lehane pointed out that troglodytes were early humans, not dinosaurs, telling reporters, "This is further proof of why they should be for the Clinton-Gore education plan."

Lehane's tomfoolery not only loosens up Gore; it also soothes a hostile press corps. For instance, after reporters hounded Lehane with questions about Gore's Palm Pilot, Lehane, Feldman and Gore loaded it with phony information and inside jokes; then Lehane persuaded Ceci Connolly, a *Washington Post* reporter, to ask Gore about the Palm Pilot in public. Gore happily revealed his programmed to-do list: lunch with *Brill's Content* concerning Connolly, ask the FBI to investigate Connolly's pilfering of Gore campaign literature and "remind Lehane of who he works for." Back in private, Lehane, Gore and Feldman exchanged high fives and later retold the story for a Gore staffer like giddy schoolboys.

Perhaps the most remarkable thing about Lehane is that he still has a job at all. Gore's press shop is haunted by the ghosts of spokespersons past: Larry Haas, Pat Ewing, Marla Romash, Kiki Moore, Roger Salazar. The press operation is but a microcosm of the overall campaign, in which a number of Gore's top advisers—Bob Squier, Mark Penn, Ron Klain, and

Craig Smith—have been replaced. Though the campaign still has its share of highly paid consultants who also work with other clients, a small band of fierce loyalists has risen to prominence. Michael Whouley, the chief strategist, and Donna Brazile, the campaign manager, are, like Lehane, Gore fanatics, as are Dixon and Feldman on Gore's official staff. Kathleen Begala, Paul Begala's sister, just hired as Gore's campaign communications director, is from the same mold: a lower-profile adviser with no professional interest other than Gore's. "Anyone with Begala chromosomes is going to be a . . . solid soldier for the cause," says Bush's ad man, Mark McKinnon, who knew Kathleen Begala at the University of Texas.

Lehane's loyalty to Gore isn't the wide-eyed hero worship or cult-of-personality kind that other candidates inspire. "You can't imagine a more cynical guy," says a friend of Lehane's, and yet "he's unflaggingly loyal." The loyalty comes from Gore's highbrow appeal: he's serious, demanding, contemplative and futuristic. But these same characteristics make him a lousy candidate, and as a result, only those closest to Gore feel intense loyalty. "We see a part of him that not everyone gets to see," says Dixon. Watching Gore cope with 20-hour days and relentless adversity, she says, "bonds you to him. You'd kill for him."

In his intensity, Lehane is very much like Gore. He talks to reporters hundreds of times a day on his cell phone, and when his battery dies, he switches it with the charged battery of an unsuspecting colleague or simply takes the colleague's phone. His fierce devotion to work has caused his girlfriend to implement what she calls the "weekend rule," which prohibits the returning of pages while out to dinner on weekends. On a trip to the Caribbean last Christmas, Lehane received a page and, because his cell phone didn't work, knocked on a villager's door and begged to use a phone. Even while jogging, he returns pages from pay phones.

A native of blue-collar Lawrence, Massachusetts, with Irish and Italian roots, Lehane moved to Maine as a child and, despite his five-foot-eight stature, became captain of Kennebunk High's basketball team. In law school, he spent much of his time working on campaigns; a classmate recalls that Lehane once tore the plastic wrapper off his textbook for the first time as he began an exam. He wound up in Washington, doing tax policy in the bowels of the Treasury until Fabiani put him to work as a scandal manager. There, he drafted a report about the "communication stream of conspiracy commerce," or how Internet rumors reach the mainstream media. The report, ridiculed as sophomoric at the time, seems more relevant since the rise of Matt Drudge and the fall of Monica Lewinsky. After a stop at Andrew Cuomo's HUD, Lehane joined a Gore operation still submerged in the no-controlling-legal-authority era.

Today, Lehane is almost universally liked by reporters, particularly for his Mike McCurry–like sense of how to massage journalists. He knows which tidbit will fit in the *Wall Street Journal*'s "Washington Wire" or the *Washington Post*'s "In the Loop." "He's the ultimate matchmaker," says Laura Quinn, the vice president's White House communications director. Once Lehane makes a match, he tracks down the reporter; he found Mike Glover, the Associated Press's man in Iowa, working out at a gym on a Saturday. Invariably, Lehane identifies himself to reporters by his code name: Frank Serpico, from the Al Pacino movie.

Though it hasn't yet produced much measurable benefit, Lehane has built up considerable goodwill by entertaining the press and dealing openly with reporters who are hard on Gore. When a particularly tough story about Gore appears, Lehane tends to brush it off with a Bill the Cat "Ack!" sound. "He takes the long view," says a colleague. "You can lose a battle but win the war." When I wrote a critical story about the vice president, Serpico appeared on my voice mail: "Good God, man. Accusations are being leveled. Fingers are being pointed. Who lost Milbank?" The light touch works. In Texas with Gore, Lehane met a group of Spanish-language reporters who wanted sound bites. Lehane speaks not a word of Spanish, so he called a member of his staff to ask for a phrase and then left his cell phone on so the staffer could hear the reporters howl with laughter as Lehane repeated the same phrase, with a terrible accent, in answer to every question.

Even if Lehane's antics don't yield favorable coverage, they have lifted morale. One Gore aide, in retaliation for a Lehane gag, set Lehane's hotel alarm for 3 a.m. on a recent trip and then ordered additional wake-up calls at 4 a.m., 5 a.m., and 6 a.m. Lehane's wardrobe—he bought a closetful of Armanis and Zegnas after he joined Gore's press staff—has also become a subject of mirth. When one Iowa farmer saw his threads, he remarked, "You're not from here, are you, son?" Lehane responded, "No, I'm from Ottumwa," a nearby town. The incident wound up in the *Des Moines Register,* and Feldman, using Lehane's computer, sent an e-mail message in Lehane's name to Gore staffers with the story and a note saying, "I am as well known as I am well dressed."

★ ☆ ★

Lehane has a crucial ally in his bid to make the vice president lighten up: the veep's own wife.

Something about Tipper Gore makes a political trip feel more like an outing with Mom in the family wagon. So what if the family, in this case, consists of a half-dozen White House aides, and the wagon is a jet on loan from NASA? As the plane idles on the tarmac in Nashville, Mom (that's Tipper) chats on a cell phone while the kids (her aides) chortle and bounce noisily in their reclining seats. Earlier, Tipper passed around her Walkman with the Beatles' *Rubber Soul* CD. She talked college basketball. Strolling the cabin now, she sneaks up behind a bald-headed aide and pretends to polish his pate. She gives a shoulder rub to her press secretary and socks her security chief playfully on the jaw. "Disregard all of this," she shouts over to me. "Soon this will all be a distant memory."

Not likely. A moment later, she sits down next to me just as the plane is taking off, and when the jet begins to climb, she stands and leans into the takeoff, hovering almost parallel to the floor. For her next act, the vice president's wife distributes barbecue sandwiches and salad to all the family—and then returns to pick up our trash. It's hard to imagine Dad doing the same on Air Force Two.

Welcome to the free-spirited world of Tipper Gore. This Mrs. Gore, you might observe, is somewhat different from the one we first met in the 1980s: the "prudish housewife" (as the *New York Times* put it) and "cultural terrorist" (as Frank Zappa put it) determined to protect our virgin ears from all those nasty rock music lyrics. The Ramones even wrote a song about her: "Censorshit." She earned herself the description of a "high-collared prude trying to Lysol the world," and in her 1996 photo collection, *Picture This*, she acknowledged that her crusade hurt her husband's '88 presidential hopes. "Please rein her in," she recalls one of the senator's advisers telling him. "This is killing your campaign."

A decade later, Al Gore is again hitting the presidential campaign trail, and Mrs. Gore is no longer a liability. She's now the one who livens up her too-earnest husband. If only she could do more.

Tipper—or "Tipster," as they call her on Air Force Two because she allegedly demanded they stock Bailey's Irish Cream—gives the sense she is always conspiring to violate protocol. Each of the other "principals," as the Clintons and Gores are known, has a Secret Service abbreviation: POTUS (President of the United States), VPOTUS (Vice President of the United States) and FLOTUS (First Lady of the United States). Mrs. Gore is, simply, MEG (Mary Elizabeth Gore). On a recent trip, MEG arrived at Washington's National Airport wearing blue jeans and a denim jacket, and greeted her staff with a tomboyish "How ya doin'?" She skipped an official trip to Switzerland with the vice president for an economic conference so she could go to a friend's mental health event in Nashville. "She balances protocol with who she is," says Jane Siena, a friend.

Her first stop on a recent trip is Clarksville, Tennessee, where she inspects recent tornado damage. She's wearing hiking boots (GoreTex, of course) and carrying a Nikon, which she uses to photograph the building and workers. "I wasn't prepared for that," says John White, Jr., an emergency worker, after Mrs. Gore insisted on taking his picture. "I was going to take *her* picture." She makes a brief speech, but words, as always, are not her strength. She is saying something boosterish and unmemorable about "the need for, um, readiness and, um, awareness," and declares that FEMA, the Federal Emergency Management Agency, is "an absolutely fantastic agency." Mrs. Gore often stumbles over words in her speeches and, when straying from her prepared text, tends to get tangled in syntax.

But she compensates with a personal touch. In Clarksville, she puts away her speech and begins to take photos of the townsfolk, the mayor and a cop in front of a school, residents in front of their destroyed homes. The mayor is so smitten he can't seem to keep his hand off Tipper's back.

Behind the scenes with staff, she's part wise guy, part chatterbox. She teases them about yet another barbecue lunch, wonders if they've exceeded an elevator's weight limit, muses about traffic. After a quick shower at the Loews Hotel in Nashville (Loews' owners, the Tisches, are friends of the Gores), she rushes from her room, buttoning her cuff, to make her way to the next event, a roundtable on mental health. After a few minutes there, she hurries out for a series of interviews, then grabs a friend for a brief talk. "See how much fun we have?" she asks, with some irony, as she hops in an elevator for yet another interview. "Lots of variety."

Her travels favor the soft-focus photo-ops. Her trip to New York is typical. At an event to promote children's fitness, she gets together in front of a basketball-court backdrop with ESPN's Robin Roberts. "Can I call you Tipper?" the broadcaster asks. "It's such a sports name. I can see it on ESPN: Tipper up for two!"

★ ☆ ★

As the campaign wears on and the combatants grow weary, the antics of Serpico, Feldman and the Tipster have infected much of the staff. As Gore gets panned in his reviews for his stiff demeanor, his campaign staff has come to resemble something out of a fraternity house.

One night, Feldman, assigned as usual to share a hotel room with Lehane, was trying to get some sleep. But Lehane was snoring loudly and incessantly. Finally, Feldman could stand it no more. He stood over the spokesman and shouted, "Lehane, you're snoring!"

Lehane stirred long enough to shout back three words: "Feldman, you're flatulent!" With that, the press secretary to the vice president of the United States resumed his snoring.

The Gore campaign, it seems, is full of strange bedfellows. Last fall, when the campaign was hemorrhaging cash, Campaign Manager Donna Brazile set out to cut costs. Gore lost some use of his helicopter, and consultant Bob Shrum was reduced to flying Southwest Airlines. But the most disruptive requirement was the one forcing traveling staffers to share hotel rooms.

The belt-tightening worked: Gore finished the primaries with more money than George W. Bush's campaign (which doesn't require senior staff to share rooms). But the room-sharing policy also changed the lives of Gore's aides in unpredictable ways. Sleeping together for most of the past ten months, the Gore staffers have learned more than they ever wanted to know about one another. "My life is an open book more than I ever imagined," says Gore speechwriter Eli Attie. "An open book and an open bed."

Nathan Naylor knows all about that. The Gore advance man has a reputation for such ferocious snoring that when David Morehouse, Gore's trip director, found that he would be bunking with Naylor, he plunked down his personal credit card to get his own room. Even the formidable snorer Lehane paid for a room to avoid Naylor. "Windows crack, plaster falls," Lehane says of one "sleepless night" in Naylor's presence. ("My wife still loves me," Naylor replies.)

Making things messier, staffers have access to one another's rooms. (The Secret Service secures the entire floor, so room doors are often open.) Consider the case of Matthew Bennett, at one time Gore's trip director. His colleagues sneaked into his room and called the hotel operator claiming to be him. "I need a wake-up call every hour during the night," the Bennett impersonator said. "I'll yell and scream, but pay no attention. I have a sleeping disorder, and that's the only way I can get up in the morning." They also set his alarm for the middle of the night and removed all the light bulbs in the room. (Bennett, coincidentally, has since found other work.)

Some Gore staffers wonder if the room-sharing savings justify the sleep deprivation. One night, Attie and Austin Brown, who works for a Gore consultant, were sharing a room, one in a bed and one on a pullout couch. Over the two hours after they turned out the lights, three more Gore-affiliated strangers came in, one taking a spare bed, one toting a mattress and the other one curling up on the floor. As the five men drifted off to sleep, one of the unknown staffers "started snoring like a maniac," Brown reports. Attie finally threw a pillow at the offender, to no effect.

The proximity makes the Gore aides unusually familiar. They know that Gore's opposition researcher, David Ginsberg, keeps spoiled food in his hotel rooms. They know that Brazile likes to sleep with the television on. They have witnessed Lehane doing affirmations in the mirror, repeating the mantra "top 1½ percent" (of what, he doesn't say). Gore himself sometimes prowls the staff hallway at night waking aides who answer the door in boxer shorts. Along the way, the antics have boosted camaraderie and eased tension. "There's a lot of inner bonding that happens," says Sarah Bianchi, a Gore policy adviser.

Then there's the delicate matter of bathroom time. Brazile complains of a woman who spends way too much time in the bathroom getting ready. She won't name names, but three Brazile roommates—Bianchi, former communications director Laura Quinn and policy chief Elaine Kamarck—deny being the one. ("I'm one of the fastest dressers you'll ever find among the female type," says Kamarck.) That leaves Gore scheduler Lisa Berg, who declines to discuss her nocturnal habits.

The campaign keeps hotel rooms single sex, to maintain propriety. But it's not unusual for a top Gore aide to be assigned to share a room with a total stranger. One night, Attie arrived at a room occupied by another Gore worker who had been there for two nights. "It looked like a college dorm room: this horrible stench of unwashed laundry, stuff on the floor and toothpaste all over the sink," Attie says. "This guy needed shock therapy, if not better breeding."

Even among friends, the rooming situation can raise tensions. Morehouse, for example, won't share a room with Lehane because of a particularly bad night. "I refuse to spend another night with that miserable little man," Morehouse says with a laugh. "He sleeps annoyed. He grimaces. He yells at you in his sleep. He shouts vulgarities if you open the window." Lehane, however, offers another version: "I thought I was spending the night with a carnival worker. He stands over my bed at 3 a.m. like the Karate Kid. He says he's stretching his hamstring." (Morehouse says he had a cramp.)

Lehane has found a somewhat more compatible partner in Feldman, who suffers his abuse more calmly. Feldman doesn't mind the booby traps his roommate sets for him, such as turning the shower head so it sprays Feldman in the face when he turns the water on. Each night, Feldman kicks open the bathroom door to see if a wet towel falls on him. He pulls the sheets off his bed to inspect for objects. He checks to see if there is any silverware in his pillowcase. "One night in the dark I encountered a banana," he says. Feldman once retaliated by inviting a Japanese TV crew to film Lehane sleeping early in the morning. But Lehane invited the same crew back into the room as Feldman emerged from the shower.

The two roommates spend most nights listening to each other's cell phones ring and pagers buzz. Once, in Los Angeles, tensions boiled over and Morehouse was forced to mediate a screaming match between the two outside the door to their room. "I've always assumed the campaign was performing an experiment on me about the ability to withstand prolonged exposure to Lehane," Feldman says. Even after one night, their room is in chaos; other Gore aides must step over socks and underwear to enter the room.

Brazile, responding to Feldman's pleas, has finally agreed to loosen the roommate requirement. She has agreed to give them separate rooms after next month's Democratic National Convention. But Feldman would be premature to believe his roommate troubles are over. Says Lehane, "He'll only be a doorway away."

13

★ ☆ ★

Fisticuffs

Jen O'Malley wasn't looking for trouble. She had come to the Democratic presidential debate in New Hampshire to cheer for her man, Al Gore, and to wave a "Gore 2000" sign in front of the TV cameras. But suddenly, things turned ugly.

A pack of Bill Bradley supporters, intent on waving their signs for the cameras, knocked O'Malley to the ground, injuring her knee. Fearing a trampling, she curled up in the fetal position, enduring a kick in the back before being rescued by police. "I came to the debate to show my support—I had no idea I'd end up at the bottom of the mosh pit," says O'Malley, Gore's volunteer coordinator in Manchester. "Those Bradley kids are tough."

When it comes to hooliganism, the Gore partisans are no slouches, either. The same night, Bradley's New Hampshire spokesman Mo Elleithee attests, a Gore partisan pushed a Bradley staffer in front of a moving minivan.

The police, who once again intervened, are as baffled as anybody by the fisticuffs. "I expected more of a Grey Poupon crowd," says Sgt. Tim Goulden, a station supervisor for the Nashua police. "These are two of the mellowest candidates in the world."

Not anymore. What began with an escalation in Gore's verbal attacks on Bradley has escalated into actual violence of a sort. In recent weeks, the Democrats' campaigns have picketed and disrupted each other's events. Gore folks have assigned a six-foot ear of corn to "stalk" Bradley when the New Jerseyan comes to Iowa; earlier, the Gore campaign sent a human chicken to a Bradley fund-raiser in New York (demonstrating Bradley's alleged fear of debates) and dispatched senior citizens—"our Gray Panthers," says a Gore spokesman—to do jumping jacks at a Bradley event in

131

Iowa (mocking his idea that exercise would cut Medicare costs). Bradley isn't innocent, either: a Bradley disruption outside Gore headquarters in Nashua prompted a call to the authorities.

Presidential politics has always been a nasty business, of course. But while the trend on the Republican side has been toward cordiality—Steve Forbes, the tiger of '96, is more of a pussycat this time—Democratic rudeness seems to have escalated. Ray Buckley, the deputy Democratic leader of the New Hampshire House, told the *Manchester Union Leader* that protests by Bradley supporters at a Gore event with Governor Jeanne Shaheen descended to a level not seen even in the McGovern-Muskie or Carter-Kennedy battles. "What were they so angry about?" Buckley wanted to know.

What, indeed? Let's put the question to John Rauh, one of Bradley's top activists in New Hampshire. "It's the childishness, the lack of respect," he says. The vice president of the United States is "immature, rude and not telling it like it is." Still, Rauh's disgust has its bounds. After much prodding, the Bradley man confesses he'll back Gore, rudeness and all, if he wins the nomination.

Therein lies the strangest element of the Democratic fight. With few exceptions, there is little history of bad blood between the Gore and Bradley operatives. They've spent years working on the same side of campaigns, and many of them are pals. Anita Dunn, Bradley's communications director, is a business partner of Bill Knapp, a Gore strategist. Knapp, in turn, counts among his best buddies Mark Longabaugh, Bradley's New Hampshire director.

David Ginsberg, Gore's research director, is thick as thieves with Bradley's researchers. Michael Whouley has fought side by side with Longabaugh, and Gina Glantz, Bradley's campaign manager, goes all the way back to the Mondale campaign with her friend Donna Brazile, Gore's manager. Matt Henshon, Bradley's special assistant, believes his law school pal Chris Lehane went to work as Gore's campaign spokesman because "he's trying to make up for all those times I beat him in intramural basketball."

Even while the insults and accusations fly, the two sides can't help but fraternize. In December, the New Hampshire staffs for the two campaigns got together for their second basketball competition. (The Bradley forces won, of course.) "We'll all be friends again in April," Ginsberg says.

And why shouldn't they get along? Their bosses are fairly similar: both mushy moderates at heart, and both by necessity playing to the party's liberal base. They're not split over life-and-death issues such as abortion. Instead, Gore and Bradley are hurling invectives over the intricacies of health care policy.

Some of the combatants realize that the intensity of their spat is farcical. "It's really not about the issues," says Russ Nadler, a 22-year-old volunteer troublemaker for Gore. "We've got two centrist, free-trading Democrats." But that doesn't stop Nadler from driving to a Bradley appearance at a shopping mall in Nashua, his pickup truck carrying Gore placards and a sound system—tools of disruption. When Bradley arrives, Nadler's gang waves Gore signs and chants "Gore! Gore! Gore!" until a security guard informs them, "This is a shopping mall. Please behave yourselves."

Back in his pickup, Nadler says the heckling is retaliatory: Bradley, Nadler insists, is the one who made this campaign nasty. "They show up at all our events," he complains.

True enough, admits Longabaugh, Bradley's man in New Hampshire. The very morning of the mall attack on Bradley, Bradley partisans showed up at Gore's hotel to abuse the candidate when he went for a jog. But Longabaugh insists it's Gore who started the nastiness. "I don't see how you could have any other interpretation," he says. "They panicked, and Al Gore started attacking us."

It was not always like this. For most of 1999, Gore's strategy was to ignore Bradley, and Bradley spent his days talking about "big ideas," making only implicit reference to Gore. But that changed in the fall, when Bradley passed Gore in the New Hampshire polls and Gore began to tell America that Bradley's health care plan would bust the budget, wound the elderly and infirm, and bring about disaster generally. The Bradley campaign largely ignored the assault—until early December, when Bradley partisans released their pent-up anger.

Longabaugh, who had unsuccessfully been urging Bradley headquarters in New Jersey to take a tougher position against Gore, sent out a letter calling the vice president "disingenuous" and "cynical" and said the Gore campaign was guilty of "utter fabrication of the facts, and the vice president knows it." A couple of days later, Bradley loyalists were handing out fliers at New Hampshire pharmacies accusing Gore of "uncontrollable lying." The Bradley campaign apologized.

Since then, the campaigns have deteriorated into a so's-your-old-man volley of accusations. Bradley gives a speech declaring that during his presidential announcement, "Al Gore spoke 2,836 words, but never were the three words 'campaign finance reform' mentioned." Gore forces retaliate with their own number: "Bradley waited 6,219 days after joining the Senate to author a campaign finance reform bill."

Pettiness is no obstacle. Gore puts out a press release to say "New Jersey's Frank Lautenberg Endorses Gore." Bradley responds with a statement titled "Senator Frank Lautenberg Already Endorsed Gore." Bradley puts out a partial transcript of an NBC report about Gore's "distortions." Gore responds by releasing a fuller transcript of the report, which includes the line "Bradley has gotten it wrong too." At the New Hampshire debate, Gore forces fire off four "Reality Checks" of Bradley statements, and Bradley forces counter with three of their own reality checks, including a reality check of a Gore reality check.

A few days later, Bradley has moved on to attack Gore about agriculture policy. While Iowa farmers suffer, he says, "after seven years, the vice president has offered nothing more than negative attacks and distortions."

Precisely three hours and 11 minutes later, Gore forces in Iowa announce that they are about to unveil "Corn Man," a six-foot-tall human ear of corn. Corn Man will be "stalking" Bradley at his Iowa appearances to give the candidate an "earful" about Bradley's unwillingness to debate. "There's a farm crisis going on, and it's shameful that Bradley won't even let Iowans know where he stands," Corn Man says in a prepared statement.

It was perhaps inevitable: In this nasty campaign, even the vegetables have become rude.

To trace all of the nastiness and bad blood between the Gore and Bradley camps, here's a hint: check out the candidates themselves. There is, of course, the vice president, whose heightened and near-hysterical rhetoric about Bradley has allowed Gore to take the upper hand in the Democratic race. But there's also Bradley, whose self-pitying complaints about Gore's attacks have become a negative attack of their own.

We begin in Raphael's drinking club, tucked in a back alley of Manchester, New Hampshire. Raphael's is a haven for the city's last few Irish and German industrial workers. It's just a few blocks from downtown on the other side of the Merrimack River, where the hulks of abandoned textile mills are being converted to dot-com offices. The dot-com crowd doesn't even know about Raphael's; it's a place for guys to get a Budweiser and throw some darts after shift change.

On this frigid January night, however, the mood at Raphael's is beginning to turn ugly. The beer has been flowing steadily, and the bartender is busy coaxing a drunk out into the snow. The rest of the crowd, a gaggle of men in union shirts and caps, is spoiling for a fight. They gather around their leader, a portly, graying fellow who is waving his fist in the air and shouting madly. "Let's go kick his ass!" he shouts to his beery followers, who respond with a roar and go to pick up two-by-fours for the coming showdown.

At any other bar, I'd be asking for my check about now. But tonight, I am staying; I've come to march with these hooligans. The leader of the mob is one Bill Shaheen, the husband of the governor of New Hampshire. The posterior he wishes to kick belongs to Bill Bradley, the former senator from New Jersey. And the person in whose name he will do the kicking is Al Gore, the vice president of the United States. The union workers, many of them local firefighters, aim to give their man a little support by waving signs and standing down Bradley supporters at tonight's debate. "The vice president has been fighting for you," one of the union chiefs shouts to the crowd. "It's up to us to fight for him."

The mob, accompanied by a couple of bagpipers and drummers, marches across the river and over to the studios of WMUR-TV, scene of tonight's debate. "Pipes up! Make way!" come the orders, as Gore's icicle-covered bus pulls up. The workers chant Gore's anti-Bradley slogan: "Stay and fight!" Gore hops out and greets his comrades. "Oh, man, I love it," he shouts, and then rallies his troops with a wave toward the studio, directing them to battle. "OK, let's go, guys!"

From my vantage point in a snowbank, the whole scene—the rowdies from the bar, the stay and fight chants, the defiant, pugnacious Gore preparing for verbal battle with his opponent—strikes me as just the right mood for a campaign on the eve of the primary. Passions are hot on this freezing night, and we are preparing to watch a titanic clash of ideas. But from the moment I enter the WMUR complex, it becomes quite apparent that I've got it all wrong. Bradley, the debate moderators and hundreds of reporters seem to be unanimous in their view that Gore is doing something very, very bad.

"Attack, attack, attack, every day, the people are fed up with it," Bradley tells Gore, accusing him of "unfair and misleading" tactics. The dirty rat. "You're the elephant of negative advertising." The rotten scoundrel. "You know better, but you continue to do what you know is untrue." Horrors! "Why should we believe you'll tell the truth as president if you won't tell the truth as a candidate. . . . If you're running a campaign that's divisive, your presidency will be divisive." And the debate moderators pile on: the first two questions to Gore are about his negative distortions.

In the WMUR press room, my colleagues laugh derisively at Gore's offensives and prepare to write stories defending his poor victim from such assaults. But I keep coming back to the same thought: What is Bradley whining about?

The "attacks" in question are hardly defamatory. Gore, as he himself points out in the debate, has never used Bradley's name or likeness in an ad. And his "negative" campaign is all in the fair-game category. Bradley's claims of attacks involve arcane matters of nursing home standards and whether benefits replacing Medicaid would be a capped voucher or a subsidy with a weighted average. Many neutral observers side with Bradley on the facts. But so what? This is hardly a case of attack politics.

"It's strange," Carter Eskew, Gore's message maven and author of the supposed attacks, tells me after the debate, as he works the press room. "It hasn't been a negative campaign. There haven't been, to my knowledge, any negative ads, negative mail, negative phoning. The voters don't have any perception at all that it's been negative. People at home are saying, 'What negative campaign is that?'" It may be self-serving for Eskew to say this, but it also happens to be true.

It occurs to me that I've stumbled across a dirty little secret about the negative 2000 campaign: it isn't negative. The volleys between candidates are no more vicious than usual, and probably less so. There's certainly been no Willie Horton equivalent (though Bradley tried to blame Gore for bringing it up in '88) and none of Lyndon Johnson's mushroom clouds. The only thing that seems to have changed is that candidates are more likely to accuse their opponents of "going negative" and the press is more likely to echo the complaint, reporting claims of "negative campaigning" or "personal attack" whenever such charges are made. "Keep your fingers crossed that this Mr. Nice Guy stuff lasts," writes David Nyhan of the *Boston Globe*, land of the Puritans.

But why? Why is everyone so obsessed with being nice? What's wrong with questioning a rival's record, or poking holes in his proposals? Isn't that what politics is all about?

Not for the moment, apparently. This time, everybody's making at least a show of purity. Gore, Bradley, John McCain, George W. Bush and Orrin Hatch all signed a "civility pledge" in December vowing "respect" for opponents and promising to avoid attacks that "demonize." In Michigan, earlier this month, McCain and Bush shook hands promising not to run negative ads.

Bradley says the "radical" idea of his campaign "is that you don't have to go out and . . . smash the other guy so that people will vote against him, but that you go out and give people a positive vision of where you want to take the country."

How nice. For example?

Let's see the "positive vision" of Senator Bob Kerrey of Nebraska, campaigning recently for Bradley. "Please don't tell me that I ought to give you a round of applause for sticking around and fighting Newt Gingrich," he said about Gore. "You brought us Newt Gingrich. That would be like asking me to thank the arsonist after he sets the house on fire because he sticks around and helps us put out the blaze."

Now that's a different kind of campaign.

The Gore folks, predictably, have used Bradley's lapse into the negative to steal the victim label from him. "He has raised another phony issue: condemning negative attacks while launching negative attacks," Gore told a gathering of high-tech workers here yesterday. "I don't see how he can, in one breath, condemn so-called negative attacks and, in the other, launch real negative attacks."

Bradley's campaign chairman, Doug Berman, notes with amusement how Gore is turning the tables on his man, inventing a "Potemkin negative campaign" with which to accuse Bradley. "Asserting that something is an attack, he hopes, will make it true, merely by saying you're the victim."

Sound familiar?

Gore's invigorated style and sharp attacks on his foe have had the desired effect. Gore has finally galvanized his own supporters and given them some reason to feel passionate—a quality that had been utterly elusive for months.

I knew things were looking up for Gore when Warren Reynolds rolled into Manchester in his 1990 Honda Civic a couple of days after New Year's. The 76-year-old retired State Department historian worried that Bradley was closing in on Gore. The polls were looking bad. Gore needed volunteers. So Reynolds left his home in Washington and drove north, stopping in a motel off the Garden State Parkway on the way. He showed up unannounced at Gore headquarters.

Reynolds grew up in such a Republican household that his full name is Warren Harding Reynolds, assigned him when he was born a day after President Harding's death in 1923. He remembers putting up signs for Alf Landon when he ran against Roosevelt in 1936. "Dad, do you really think Landon can win?" he asked. "My father said, 'of course he can win.' He took two states, two fucking states," Reynolds recalled. Reynolds soon became a Democrat, but this is his first campaign working as a volunteer since 1936, a 64-year break.

Reynolds, working from Gore's Manchester office, is a man possessed. He has Gore stickers on his frayed sweater and spends 12-hour days folding campaign literature and driving students around to distribute it. He makes phone calls and goes to retirement homes to drum up enthusiasm. He shouts in the cold outside the debates. Called "Dr. Reynolds" by the young volunteers in the office, he sings, over and over again, a one-line tune he wrote. "Go-o-ore, for president!" "It's from one of these goddamn musicals," Reynolds explains in his loud, raspy voice, which he punctuates by pounding on tables.

Reynolds has such uncommonly blind loyalty to Gore that he utterly lacks perspective. Gore's debating? "Transformational." Gore's style? "He's a country boy, you know, a country yokel." Gore's temperment? "He's in control. He's cool. He's courtly." And beware all those who cross Gore. "Why is the *Post* so goddamn tough on him," he demands of me as we lunch at a greasy-spoon diner. And what of Gore's foes? Bradley: "His heart is not that well." Bush: "He's a bully."

Reynolds admits it's a bit strange that Gore, of all people, inspires such passion in him. "I wondered why," he says. "Is it because I'm an old man? Am I an old fool? Then I thought No, you're thinking of your country, your children, your wife. I think he could carry us further along than Clinton has been able to because Clinton got hamstrung by his own appetites." Gore himself hasn't been able to make such a clear case for his candidacy yet.

One day, while Reynolds is stuffing envelopes in Gore headquarters, Sam Watterson, the star of the TV show *Law and Order*, stops in to volunteer in front of the cameras. Reynolds begins to sing. "Go-o-ore for president!" Watterson remarks: "He's a one-man campaign." Another volunteer tries to apologize for Reynolds, noting that he's a "piece of work," but Reynolds demands of Watterson, "Come on, Sam, sit down here." When he does, Reynolds gets a good look and blurts out, "I know you. Oh, that's wonderful, unbelievable!". After learning Watterson missed a debate, Reynolds scolds him: "I hope they have a tape of it back at your studio. It's very affirming."

The passion of Warren Harding Reynolds is something Gore will need to find in much greater quantity if this campaign is to be a success. But slowly, the signs of truly committed loyalists are beginning to grow.

The passionate Gore-backers began as a lonely band last October. The vice president had joined 75 firefighters to do some neighborhood canvassing. Gore and Mark Oulette, president of the Professional Fire Fighters of New Hampshire, were invited into one home to talk. Unbeknownst to Gore, the family dog sidled up to the vice president as he spoke, Oulette recalls, and treated the candidate as if he were a hydrant.

Muffy's indiscretion Gore took in stride. "I've been in politics for a long time," he said. "I've had to walk through a lot worse than this for a vote."

The firefighters promptly took the vice president, soiled pant leg and all, over to the Lake Street fire station, where they bestowed on him their union's endorsement. It was the sort of rescue they've performed often for their candidate.

When hecklers disrupted Gore's presidential announcement in Manchester last June, a group of firefighters in the audience tore down the protest banner and moved to rough up the hecklers before the Secret Service intervened. When Bill Bradley was pulling ahead in the New Hampshire polls, the Manchester firefighters soothed him by cooking a spaghetti dinner for more than three hundred in his honor. And when Gore seemed outclassed by a nimbler George W. Bush, the firefighters handed him a p.r. coup: after Bush canceled a school visit in Rhode Island to attend a fundraiser, the firefighters quickly scheduled an event for Gore at the school.

Now, a resurgent Gore, clobbering Bradley in New Hampshire, again leads in the New Hampshire polls, and the firefighters are leading his parade. Before Wednesday night's debate in Manchester, a band of a hundred firefighters, some wearing kilts and playing bagpipes and drums, stood for an hour in freezing temperatures waiting to walk Gore into the studio.

It is fitting that, for a campaign that spent much of last year putting out proverbial fires, its most ardent supporters have been real-life firefighters. Their zeal beats the rap that still haunts the vice president: that he's a nice but blah fellow who doesn't inspire passion in his followers. The firefighters, at least, are fired up.

When one thinks of political powerhouses, teachers, teamsters and auto workers come to mind before the International Association of Fire Fighters. In New Hampshire, the union has only 1,200 members and 700 retirees. But when an Atlanta firefighter dangled from a helicopter to rescue a man from a crane last year, the hero, interviewed on the *Today* show, plugged Gore. When several firefighters were killed in Worcester, Massachusetts, union leaders insisted the vice president attend the memorial. The IAFF was the first union to endorse Gore last spring, at a time when labor's support looked shaky.

Here in New Hampshire, the 35 IAFF locals help with most Gore events. "The firefighters are the most active organization in the city of Manchester," says Bill Cashen, a longtime alderman. It's the same throughout the state. A couple hundred firefighters do regular volunteer work for Gore: stuffing mailings, placing phone calls, putting up yard signs, using their trucks to hang lights and signs. Some attend Gore townhall meetings and ask softball questions.

All this for Al Bore?

Harold Schaitberger, a national IAFF official who flew to Manchester for the debate this week, says the relationship dates to the mid-'90s, when there was a fire in the Gore home in Arlington, Virginia. "Our guys did a helluva job," Schaitberger says.

Since then, Gore has done a helluva job for the firefighters. He championed the Occupational Safety and Health Administration's "two in, two out rule" on the number of firefighters required inside and outside a building fire to improve safety. He backed a federal investigation into all on-duty deaths by firefighters. At the union's request, he met with child burn victims at the White House. He supported national collective bargaining for firefighters and better pay for firefighters on military bases.

At Engine Company 2 in southwest Manchester, four of the "Twos" on duty one afternoon this week proclaimed their fealty to Gore. (The fifth, a Republican, likes John McCain.) "If you stick with us, we stick with you," said Mike Bouchard. "He's been there for us—we're used to politicians who only want to meet when it's crunch time," says Bill Clayton. The men are awed by their proximity to Gore. "If you haven't met Gore twice, you just haven't been out of your house," Clayton says.

But the firefighters' passion seems to go beyond constituent service. "I was thinking about this last night at the firehouse," David Lang begins. "We're the nation's first response. We see the ravages of a poor economy, of poor health care, of lower-income areas. We really get to see America at 2 a.m., and most people don't."

What Lang sees now is a booming economy, lower crime, fewer needy kids at charity drives. And the problems he still sees—children without health coverage, old folks in cold homes—happen to be part of Gore's campaign agenda.

14

★ ☆ ★

Dollar Bill Devaluation

Though it is far too early in this chapter to be discussing frozen bull semen, let us just say, for now, that Al Gore has made some very impressive efforts to befriend the Iowa farmer.

There was the day Gore showed up at the McKinney farm in blue jeans, denim shirt and cowboy boots. He spent nearly an hour working on the tractor, then joined a potluck supper and slept overnight in the farmhouse. And many an Iowan has heard the vice president brag about his farm in Tennessee or lament the low price of a bushel of corn.

Sure, Bill Bradley can accuse Gore of living in a "Washington bunker." But last week, Iowans heard Gore offer to help a farmer who complained about getting butted by a 300-pound ram whenever the farmer was working with the ewes. Last year, Gore visited the Iowa state fair and won the support of the woman who sculpted a life-size cow from butter. "I wonder what people will think of Iowa when they read in the *Washington Post* that the lady who carved the butter cow is a Gore precinct captain," worries Steve Hildebrand, a South Dakotan who is directing Gore's campaign in Iowa.

Let them wonder. Gore is doing exactly what he must do to triumph in the parochial Iowa caucuses. He is shamelessly pandering to the farmer. And he's using a new brand of tough-nosed politics to paint Bill Bradley as a foe of the farmer. Probably the most pivotal moment in the Democratic primaries came in a debate in Iowa recently, when Gore called on a flood-ravaged farmer to ask Bradley why he opposed flood relief. Bradley responded, weakly, "This is not about the past." Bradley's numbers plunged overnight. The senator still hasn't recovered.

"The past does matter," says a Gore strategist in the candidate's headquarters here. "Even though Al Gore grew up in the Fairfax Hotel, he represented a rural district." For that reason, Gore's agricultural pandering comes a bit easier than it does for Bradley, the former senator from New Jersey, when he has his photo taken in front of a cartoon of a "genuine Iowa pig." Or when Bradley visits a three-story bull in Audubon named Albert. Or when the former NBA star talks daily about his small-town roots or flips pork chops with the Iowa Pork Producers. Surely, they are impressed by his road-to-Des Moines conversion on the virtues of ethanol and his ability to speak the language of "terminator seeds" and "GMOs" (that's genetically modified organisms, for you city slickers).

In Iowa these days, it feels as if the suburbanization of America never happened. Both gentlemen vying for the Democratic nomination—Gore of St. Albans and Harvard, Bradley of Princeton and Oxford—are farm owners. Neither seems to have a clue what happens on these farms. But never mind: they are outdoing each other in farmer friendliness as Monday's caucuses approach.

So resumes the time-honored ritual of pandering to the Iowa farmer, a mainstay of presidential politics since the first-in-the-nation caucuses began in 1972. Every election year, some Americans complain that the Iowa caucuses, with their heavy emphasis on agricultural issues, don't represent urban, industrialized America. And now, the Iowa caucuses are not even representative of Iowa.

Agriculture's share of income in the state has declined from 15 percent in 1965 to about 3 percent today. Fewer Iowans work in agriculture than in manufacturing. And though the farm economy is now in crisis—prices are at historic lows—the Iowa economy has hardly noticed. Unemployment is 2.1 percent, half the national average, and personal income is growing at a 7 percent clip.

"Any candidate tries to create an issue," says Harvey Siegelman, the state economist. But while small, family farmers feel the pinch, he says, the truth is this: "There really isn't very much misery."

And yet the candidates continue to build a bridge to the nineteenth century. Earlier this month, Gore flew a New Jersey grain farmer, Roy Etsch, here to tell his farmer brethren in Iowa that he doubts Bill Bradley "understands the difference between corn and soybeans." Gore also got Iowa Senator Tom Harkin to scold Bradley, while not directly naming him, in television and radio ads for voting against flood relief, farm credit, crop insurance and ethanol subsidies. Last week, Gore and Bradley traded barbs from rival barns.

Why the farm obsession? In part, it's nostalgia. "It's a symbol of Iowa, it's hearth and home," says Dan Lucas, Bradley's Iowa manager, who usually lives in Arlington. "What are we tied to, if not the land?" Bradley looks at rural life and "gets in a very Jeffersonian state of mind," Lucas says.

There's another, simpler reason for the agrarian anachronism. A *Des Moines Register* poll found that 41 percent of likely Democratic caucus-goers come from farms or towns of under 5,000. Using more conservative estimates, Gore's Hildebrand figures that 14 percent of Democratic caucus-goers are directly affected by agriculture. That's equal to the number of caucus-goers in Polk County, the largest in the state. And among farmers, Hildebrand figures, Gore is ahead by more than 2 to 1.

This is one reason why Gore, by most reports, is far ahead of Bradley in Iowa. For all Bradley's talk about running a different kind of campaign, the caucus is still about the nuts and bolts of old-time politics: lock up labor, lock up the farmers and get 'em to the caucuses. When it comes to organizing farmers, Gore has more machinery in Iowa than John Deere.

Bradley, for sure, has done everything to stop Gore but don overalls and hold a pitchfork. He has had at least 25 meetings with farmers, including six farm visits. He persuaded agriculture officials from the Kennedy, Johnson and Carter administrations to send a letter to newspapers comparing Bradley to Jack Kennedy, another "urban state" Democrat who did right by farmers. Bradley has even hinted he'd select Iowa Governor Tom Vilsack as agriculture secretary.

Mostly, though, Bradley has been trying to convince farmers that Gore and his boss have been doing a lousy job. "Are Iowa farmers better off today than seven years ago?" is the question Bradley asks everywhere, in person and in mailings. The campaign offers statistics on the crisis: a 24 percent inflation-adjusted drop in farm income, a 36 percent drop in hog prices, 6,000 farms gone, all since 1992. He blasts Clinton and Gore for the Freedom to Farm Act, which caused much of the problem by reducing government payments to farmers. This line of attack is blunted only by the fact that Bradley voted for it, too.

It was nearly a year ago that Gore, in a flight of pastoral embellishment, remarked on his youth spent on the farm in Tennessee plowing fields, shoveling manure and the like. Suddenly, the senator's son who grew up in a Washington hotel was portraying himself as Farmer Al—to near-universal ridicule. Gore's farm story, along with his claims of Internet paternity, became a symbol of his floundering campaign.

Yet a year later, Gore is a certified friend of the farmer, and he has eyewitnesses to prove it. Gore's campaign has come up with a couple of Iowa farmers who attest to boyhood work as a farmhand. Berl Priebe, 81, remembers seeing young Al at a cattle show. "He was cleaning up behind the cows," Priebe attests. "At least he knew what end of the fork to use."

And that's where the frozen semen comes in.

It was November 1965 when Max Mugge and his father, of Cherokee, Iowa, entered into an agreement with the senior Al Gore. "We ended up with a bull together," says Mugge, who still has the papers. The Gores kept the bull on their farm in Carthage, Tennessee, and sent the dividends to the Mugges in Iowa, frozen and packed in liquid nitrogen. "We got the semen," Max Mugge says. And Gore will get his vote.

These days, Mugge is happy to vouch for Gore's farming credentials. "He has a little bit of farming background—not a lot, but some," Mugge says. "I'm sure he was out on the Gore farm enough that he knows a little about what's going on." To demonstrate his support for Gore, Mugge used a 20-acre field to carve the letters G-O-R-E with a cornstalk cutter. The letters are "35 rods up and down," Mugge reports. That's 577.5 feet high, city dwellers.

Of course, Gore would have known that.

Gore's take-no-prisoners strategy against Bradley in Iowa came with the expected result: a lopsided victory. Even a narrower Bradley loss in New Hampshire the following week could do nothing to reverse the man's slide. While everybody follows McCain's New Hampshire triumph and the possibility that he could upset Bush, the once-menacing Bradley is all but forgotten.

When Al Gore called Bill Bradley "desperate" in Monday night's debate, he didn't know the half of it. So starved for attention is Bradley's presidential bid that the candidate has come to contemplate a life of crime.

"I need an event," Bradley said late last week, as his motorcade traveled down I-95 in Connecticut. "I should hold up a bank."

Of course, Bradley, a banker's son, isn't really considering grand larceny. But continued inattention, fueled so far by the McCain phenomenon, could be fatal to his campaign after consecutive losses in Iowa and New Hampshire. "I've told as many people as would listen—and there haven't been that many—that if anybody had been paying attention, the last two weeks in the Democratic race would've been fascinating," says Eric Hauser, Bradley's press secretary.

Finally, Bradley got some attention in Monday's debate, but the Democratic race was immediately eclipsed again yesterday by Republican primaries in Michigan and Arizona. With those primaries done, Bradley's people are hoping the buzz will return to the Democrat.

"At some point, people have to come back," says a hopeful Doug Berman, Bradley's campaign manager. If not, Bradley may resort to increasingly desperate measures. On Saturday, Bradley finally found a way to get on the evening news: His plane, reporting possible landing-gear trouble, made an emergency landing in St. Louis.

Other than that, the Bradley campaign has little to show for its recent efforts. Bradley denounced Gore with such vehemence that one report described him as "red-faced and almost speechless with anger." A few days earlier, Bradley rolled out ads featuring the endorsement of basketball god Michael Jordan. Next, Bradley flew off to South Carolina in a naked attempt to steal some of the TV cameras that were in the state to cover the Republican primary. And still, for the most part, the front pages and the nightly news eluded him.

Bradley aides have tried just about everything for publicity, including press releases announcing "Bradley Campaign Opens Three (3) Additional Offices in New York State," and "Arnold Pinkney Named Bradley Ohio Campaign Director." But the packet of newspaper clippings distributed at Bradley events contains only one story written after the New Hampshire primary, and that's a column from the *Wall Street Journal* noting that Gore, though dastardly, is "trouncing his Democratic challenger."

The lack of coverage has frustrated Bradley's party of traveling press, some of whom, in their ample free time, have fashioned halved basketballs to wear as hats. A man from one of the networks called his wife from the press bus to complain about his bosses. "I'm in a vacuum—it's a waste of time," he said. "They don't have any interest at all. We're gonna have to come back with some naked pictures or something to get on TV."

One Bradley reporter even tried subterfuge, telling her editors that people at a Bradley event were demanding to know why the networks were not putting him on the air. The editors didn't bite. "They laughed," she said. But you can't really blame them; editors are watching the polls. Bradley doesn't lead in any of the 15 states holding contests on March 7, and in all important California, he's at 13 percent in the polls, less than a quarter of Gore's 54 percent. The result is a vicious cycle of coverage: Poor polls beget light coverage, which begets more poor polls.

Not surprisingly, Berman thinks this phenomenon, aggravated by the Democrats' lack of a contest before March 7, is unfair in light of Bradley's performance in New Hampshire. "Bill came closer than any challenger in the history of the Democratic primaries against a sitting vice president with the governor at his side and the governor's husband running the campaign," he says.

Hauser is equally miffed. "We almost won New Hampshire," he says. "We needed attention and, given the normal rules of politics, earned it with the New Hampshire performance."

Bradley's invisibility comes just as the candidate has assumed the trappings of a major contender. Bradley accepted Secret Service protection after his narrow New Hampshire loss. The result: Bradley arrives at each event in a blaze of flashing lights and sirens, only for a lackluster reception.

This was the case on a recent morning in Boston, when Bradley was to address supporters at a community health center. The meeting was scheduled to start at 8:45, but at 8:41 there were only two cameramen, one TV truck outside, and three reporters, one of them reading a story in that day's Boston Globe proclaiming, "Bradley Bemoans Campaign's Lag in Capturing Voters' Attention."

The Boston visit gave little reason for encouragement. Children, journalists and Secret Service agents outnumbered Massachusetts voters. Even the few genuine Bradley supporters there didn't seem optimistic. "I wish he could win, but I just don't think he can," said Gerard Hurly, whose wife works at the center.

Bradley's next stop, in Providence, Rhode Island, appeared at first glance to be a large, enthusiastic crowd packed into a high school gymnasium. But most of those present were students whose attendance was required, and most of the others were from nearby Brown University—undergraduates from across the country and therefore unlikely to be registered to vote in the state's March 7 primary. One of the few local voters in the crowd, Dan D'Alessio, came with John McPhee's book about Bradley, a book by Bradley, two Bradley trading cards, and copies of a poem D'Alessio wrote about Bradley. But even he was not hopeful, putting the odds for Bradley at "2 to 1 against him."

Bradley's next stop was a diner in Old Saybrook, Connecticut, which was stocked with youngsters from Old Saybrook High School, just a few blocks away. "I'm a big Bradley supporter," said Evan Brown, a senior at another area school, Old Lyme High. There was only one problem: "I'm too young to vote," Evan said.

The story was much the same at Bradley's next stop, a nightclub near the Yale University campus in New Haven. One of Bradley's warm-up speakers made the mistake of asking how many in the crowd were registered to vote in Connecticut. Only a few hands went up.

But the candidate pressed on to an event at Manhattanville College in New York. There, stacks of folding chairs were hidden behind a divider, forcing several in the crowd to stand and giving the false appearance of a packed house. Bradley droned on for a couple of hours, even as his listeners made for the exits. In the back of the room, reporters fought off sleep or talked on cell phones. It had been another 15-hour day, covering four states and a couple hundred miles—and once again, neither candidate nor press corps had much to show for it.

★ ☆ ★

It was, Gore aides thought, a sign of the times: a few days ago, a reporter told a senior Gore adviser that the candidate's hair appeared to be growing back.

Alas, it was not so. Gore's bald spot has become a patch covering much of the vice presidential cranium. But his aides say it wouldn't surprise them if it were true. "When things are going well, everything falls into place," said press secretary Chris Lehane.

Today, on Super—no, Titanic—Tuesday, everything fell into place for Gore. The only question, as the voting began, was whether the once-formidable Bill Bradley could pull off a face-saving victory in one state. Connecticut, maybe? Vermont? Somewhere? Anywhere?

Apparently not. As the results flowed in, first from the South, then the Northeast and finally the West, it was all Gore. His quest for the Democratic presidential nomination had ended up much as it had first appeared: a sure thing. Just after 8 p.m. local time, Gore descended from his suite to the ballroom of the Loews Vanderbilt Plaza Hotel, where he announced he'd received a concession call from Bradley. "Friends," he told the crowd, "they don't call it Super Tuesday for nothing."

Gore's triumph in the primaries is so much the sweeter because of all the misery he experienced in the past year. He isn't exactly gloating, but he's savoring his victory over the doom-sayers. "Maybe they'll write again that the move to Nashville was a gimmick," he joked to me today as he pored over early exit poll results with Tony Coelho and Donna Brazile, his campaign chiefs, at his headquarters here. At that, Brazile reached out and gave the candidate a high-five.

It was as if the past 14 months had never happened. Gore was transported back to a time before the infighting that led to the switching of his staff chief, campaign manager, ad man and pollster. Before he closed his struggling operation's K Street office and moved it to Nashville. Before Bradley edged ahead in funds as Gore hemorrhaged cash. Before Bradley rode his "big ideas" to a lead in the New Hampshire polls. Before Gore claimed paternity of the Internet and bragged about his youth as a farmer. Before Naomi Wolf and her earth tones tried to turn Gore into an alpha male. Before Pat Moynihan endorsed Bradley, saying Gore couldn't win. Before Clinton publicly doubted Gore's campaign strategy.

But enough about the past. Gore today has executed the political equivalent of a flawless full gainer. Or, more appropriately, a full Gloria Gaynor: He will survive. To commemorate this moment, let us pause to review some of the reasons he was never supposed to reach this day in the first place.

Remember the dreaded Y2K bug? "Unable to process the next millennium, computers threaten to bring the international economy crashing down with them," wrote the *American Spectator* in August 1998. "And government is still not responding adequately. Among the casualties could be Al Gore's presidential aspirations." Or maybe not.

If the Y2K bug didn't kill Gore, campaign staff squabbles were sure to do him in. "The civil war is likely to rage on," Dick Morris wrote in the *New York Post* last May. "Nobody will have time to fight Bradley, much less Bush. The casualty will be Al Gore." Other observers (including this reporter), citing Coelho's heavy hand, said much the same thing. "Oops," the campaign chairman taunted playfully when reminded of those forecasts today at Gore headquarters.

How about the Russian money-laundering scandal with the Bank of New York, a supposedly crushing blow? "Gore, who's the administration's point man in Russia, gets the brunt of the blame," said a Washington pundit on the *Beltway Boys* show. George W. Bush piled on, and Steve Forbes blamed Clinton-Gore for the scandal. Now the scandal is gone, and so is Forbes.

Gore's Republican rivals have been particularly flawed prophets when it comes to predictions of his demise. Dan Quayle and Elizabeth Dole both blamed him for the spy scandal at the Los Alamos nuclear lab and for general botching of China policy. And both rode the issue to an early dropout from the race. Republicans also figured Kosovo, the "Clinton-Gore War," would bring ruin. A wire service reported last year that Pat Buchanan's spokesman, Bob Adams, "predicted that Kosovo would be key to the 2000 election and that Gore's outspokenness could doom his chances." Well, Kosovo isn't an issue, Adams is gone from the Buchanan campaign and Buchanan is gone from the Republican race.

Hillary Rodham Clinton's run for the Senate was supposed to doom Gore, too. Likewise, U.S. membership in the World Trade Organization was supposed to sour the trade unions on Gore, and the Kyoto environmental accord was to become a Gore albatross. We're still waiting for that—and for the bumper sticker recommended in an article in the *National Review* related to the vice president's environmental and urban-sprawl efforts: "Stuck in traffic? Blame Al Gore."

Even some of the truly damaging developments haven't packed the wallop one might have expected—at least not yet. There's campaign finance, of course. "Gore's opponents are salivating over the possibility that he'll enter the presidential campaign season under investigation," *USA Today* wrote. They sure were. But it didn't happen. There are now dire warnings about "Clinton fatigue" bringing Gore down just as the president's popularity has been climbing.

Some of the doomsday scenarios now seem a bit far-fetched. Did Republicans really believe in the curse of the "Gore Glitch," a plan to blame him for the lack of high-speed Internet access? And what of the backlash against the "Gore Tax," the vice president's "e-rate" surcharge on phone bills for the wiring of schools to the Internet?

Now on the verge of victory, Gore's staff delights in all the bullets it dodged. Lehane enjoys listing the various demonstrators who have shown up at Gore events blaming the vice president for a variety of humanity's ills. There were protesters at Gore's announcement seeking AIDS drugs in South Africa, Utah wilderness advocates in New Hampshire, people dressed as vegetables in New York protesting genetically engineered crops, animal rights demonstrators dressed as rabbits, U'Wa Indians protesting oil drilling, and more. "It's a sign you're relevant," Lehane says. "Everybody has to exact their pound of flesh."

Even before the Super Tuesday balloting began, Gore and his aides were sending signals that their troubles—at least their primary troubles—were behind them. Some Gore advisers, confident of a quick finish to the primary contest, were already booking vacations for late March and April. On Monday night, the campaign released a schedule for today indicating that the press would be invited to Gore's suite at 6:10 p.m. to watch the election returns with him—a sure sign of anticipated victory.

Gore made a token effort throughout the day to keep up his mantra that he's "taking no vote for granted." But as he examined the early exit polls at his headquarters here, I asked for his impression. He repeated his mantra, but then smiled and added, "It's a comfortable margin."

Later, sitting on the couch in his hotel suite, his left arm around his wife, Gore watched CNN as the network projected victory for him in eight states. Again, he teased reporters about taking no vote for granted, but his confidence was beginning to seep out. "My principal concern now is to build suspense for the speech I'm going to make in the ballroom," he said. "I'm not taking anyone's applause for granted."

Finally, in the Loews ballroom, Gore, in a dark suit—no earth tones!—ceased his tease. "My heart is full tonight," he bellowed to the boisterous crowd as a screen flashed CNN's latest projections of his victories. "Hear me well: You ain't seen nothing yet."

Gore advisers—most of them, anyway—had little doubt this day would come. "There's a huge sword-in-the-stone element in the primary battle," Ron Klain, the candidate's former staff chief, said on the eve of the New Hampshire primary. "You can be a scrawny little runt, but once you become king of England, everybody bows down."

For now, Gore is king of England. That will change, of course, when the Gore Glitch gets him.

Part IV

★ ☆ ★

The Rise of Smashmouth
Bush's Recovery

15

★ ☆ ★

Dreaming My Life Away

Candidate debates are one of political journalism's great hoaxes. Hundreds of reporters have convinced our editors (and will soon convince our readers and viewers) that we must go to "watch" each GOP presidential debate. But in fact we do nothing more than hang out, eat sandwiches and brownies, and watch television. The candidates are in another room, and we see them on screen, just as we would have done at home, only not as comfortably. Worse, I usually forget to reserve a seat in the mosh pit—er, press room—so I am relegated to the back, a couple of rows behind Japan's Asahi Shimbun.

It may be utterly pointless to watch presidential debates, but here I am on a five-hour flight to Phoenix for the next one. Tonight, though, I have a plan: I leave the press room, wangle a ticket to the debate from one of the campaigns, put away my press badge and walk right into the debate as a private citizen, a guest of the Arizona Republican Party. Suddenly, my whole perspective changes. I can see the gilded theater, the shades of gray in the candidates' suits. I can see Judy Woodruff's legs behind the podium (note to Al Hunt: not that I'm looking). Most important, I can see the candidates' body language when they're off camera and hear the murmurs and titters in the crowd. And, from this vantage point, things do not look good for George W.

Even before tonight, Bush's paint-by-numbers campaign has at times verged on the farcical. For the last several months, Bush has begun almost every speech with a story about a discussion he's supposedly just had with his wife, Laura, before leaving Austin. As he tells it, his wife advised him, "When you get up to Washington, New York, New Hampshire, [fill in the blank,] don't go showing off and pretending you're witty and debonair." Since he flunked the world-leader pop quiz, Bush has been telling crowds

153

that Laura further counseled, "And don't go naming all the world leaders, either." It is hard to imagine Laura Bush, a sensible woman, making
the exact same joke to her husband before every single trip.

Tonight, the stump-speech excerpts the governor uses to answer questions don't seem to work. He starts by declaring, "If the poorest of the
poor remain in trapped schools"—an inadvertent reversal of the script,
which calls for the phrase "remain trapped in schools." As candidates take
potshots at Bush—for using public school money for vouchers (John
McCain), for "looking for somebody else to put words in your mouth"
(Alan Keyes)—Bush shifts his weight, taps his foot, slouches left, looks
bored, moves his hands, tilts his head, drinks from a water bottle, tilts his
head again, grins weakly, shifts his feet again and jiggles his leg. He's
clearly not enjoying himself. Asked to expand on his reading of a biography of Dean Acheson, which he'd mentioned at the previous debate, Bush
doesn't even pretend to try, launching instead into a stump-speech snip-
pet about how "we must promote the peace." McCain then slyly relates a
story about Acheson telling President Harry Truman that North Korea
had invaded South Korea.

When Gary Bauer presses Bush on China, the front-runner, briefly
thrown off his script, stammers and makes mention of the need to export
"Arizona farm products." (Cactus?) Forbes surprises Bush by asking him
about the oil supply—a trick question, since it's one a Texas governor should
be able to answer but not one that he would have been prepped for. Bush
says twice in his answer that natural gas is "immune from OPEC." McCain
then shrewdly mentions how the Chechnya situation affects the oil supply.

Other candidates use the "debate" to ask questions of their rivals,
advance their own causes or put others on the defensive, but Bush stumbles. He asks Orrin Hatch to praise his "compassionate conservatism." But
Hatch turns on Bush. "Frankly, I really believe that you need more experience before you become president of the United States," he says. "You'll
make a heck of a president after eight years"—as vice president to President
Hatch. Amazingly, the GOP audience loves it, many actually laughing at
their front-runner. It only gets worse in Bush's closing speech. He wheels
out his favorite lines: "no child is left behind" and "match our conservative minds with our compassionate hearts." Titters and laughter begin in
the back of the room and ripple forward as the clich,s are recognized.

Bush's squirming is amusing but, in truth, fairly predictable and not
headline-making. The candidates' debate performances have by now
become standard: Bush scripted, Hatch boastful of obscure legislative
accomplishments, Bauer zealous and Keyes mad. And Forbes? Five more
"also too"s tonight. No wonder nobody but McCain has been able to give
Bush a challenge.

★ ☆ ★

In the smashmouth world of politics, if you don't differentiate your-self and say what's wrong with the other guy, you aren't going to win. Nor should you. The plausible, mainstream Republican candidates in the race other than McCain—Liddy Dole, Lamar Alexander and Orrin Hatch—are so gentle on Bush as to seem as if they are auditioning to be vice president or a cabinet secretary. In drawing such a gentle group of challengers, Bush has been blessed by his enemies.

Nobody but McCain and the dark horses of the far right has been will-ing to take Bush on. It shouldn't surprise anybody, then, that the candi-dacies of guys like Hatch and Alexander were disasters. If you don't dif-ferentiate yourself with tough, harsh politics, you can't win. Here's how Hatch and Alexander, two qualified and respectable but overly polite men, learned that the hard way.

We begin in Osceola, Iowa. It is just before the Iowa straw poll in the summer of 1999, and Lamar Alexander stands in the back of a borrowed Winnebago with his shirt off and his pants unbuttoned, in full view of the press corps (which, in this case, consists of me). As he dresses hurriedly, the Lamarmobile careens down a highway in southern Iowa at 70 miles per hour, trying to get the presidential candidate to a TV interview.

Only moments ago, Alexander was to have done a conference call with ten New Hampshire reporters, but his cell phone conked out, sending the bug-spattered Winnebago on a harrowing backroads hunt for a telephone. Finally, the RV pulled into the driveway of the Clarke County Farm Bureau, and the presidential aspirant, emerging from a cloud of dust, begged to use a phone. "For those who say the race is over, I'm saying it's just starting," Alexander argued into the receiver as he sat in the borrowed Farm Bureau office. "It has to be earned, and I'm out here earning it."

That's for sure.

It's been a rough ride for Alexander on the campaign trail. The man who became a contender here in '96 and who many once thought would have a serious shot at the presidency in 2000 has recently been deluged with phone calls from supporters urging him to drop out. Practically broke, Alexander has had to lay off staff and move virtually all his workers to Iowa. I had planned to meet with his Web expert, but the poor fellow was sacked before I had the chance. And as I travel with the candidate, Alexander's vaunted field team in Iowa has been struggling to draw more than a dozen spectators at many events.

When I catch up with Alexander's "Iowa Homecoming Tour," which will take the Winnebago (borrowed from a supporter) to 60 Iowa counties before the Ames poll, he is in Council Bluffs, in the western part of the state. "So, how you been?" the bartender at Dirty Harry's restaurant asks the candidate as Alexander arrives for yet another event in the tavern. Lamar's 20-year-old son, William, who has been stuffing envelopes late into the night, is struggling to tape an Alexander sign to the front door. Finally, he makes his way upstairs to the event, which is a politician's nightmare: there's practically nobody there and a CNN camera is rolling.

I turn to one woman and ask her if she's for Lamar. The woman, Mary Jones, laughs; she's a local organizer for Dole. "I don't look at him as a threat at all," says Jones, enjoying the free lunch. "When he has an event at twelve noon and there's six people here, it works for me." About two minutes into Alexander's speech, the CNN crew breaks down its equipment and shuffles out noisily. He turns and watches like a lounge singer seeing the last patron walk out on his act. Moments later, the local radio reporter has had enough, and she steps in front of Lamar to remove her microphone. When I check the sign-in book, there are only three names, including one person from Florida and one from Nebraska. Dennis Warm, a Republican eating lunch downstairs with his wife, doesn't bother to listen to Alexander. "What we want now is a winner," says Warm, likely a Bush man. "There's nothing he can say to me that would change my mind."

At this moment, the Lamarmobile, retreating from the embarrassment in front of the CNN camera in Council Bluffs, is heading south to Sidney, a town of 1,200, which, according to the locals, hasn't had a visit from a presidential candidate in at least 30 years. But Alexander is looking everywhere he can. He stands before a crowd of 18 in AJ's Steakhouse and Saloon, where the bar stools are swiveling saddles and peanut shells cover the floor. The audience is a typical Iowa crowd: several older folks, many of them heavy-set, and lots of men in baseball caps. Alexander's speech is sensible, complex, intelligent—and uninspiring. I take a walk to Casey's General Store across the town square. "You going to see Lamar?" I ask the woman behind the counter.

"Who?" she asks.

"Lamar Alexander."

"Never heard of him."

"He's running for president," I tell her.

Another woman working at the store shrugs. "I never heard of him, either." A stop at the drugstore produces the same response.

After his speech, Lamar tucks into a chocolate pie and works hard on a corn farmer for ten minutes, talking about trade, corn prices and ethanol. "He's got my interest," the farmer says later. So will he go to Ames? The man hesitates. "I got a lot of farming to do," he says. The local organizer approaches Alexander's son, William, looking apologetic. "The pledge cards aren't getting filled out," she says. "You want me to follow up with phone calls?"

Back on the Winnebago, Alexander looks on the bright side. He drew 18 people in a town of 1,200, he says, doing a calculation in his head: "In New York, it would be as big as a Garth Brooks concert in Central Park." As the Lamarmobile pulls away, a local man shouts at the driver for going the wrong way on a one-way street. The candidate, from the back, offers a wry suggestion: "Why don't we tell him we just blew in from Texas? Is this Dez Moinez?" Away from the public events, Alexander reveals some of the bitterness he feels toward Bush, who he thinks has bought the election. What infuriates Alexander is not losing but being denied a chance to compete, the chance underdogs Jimmy Carter and Ronald Reagan got in '76, George Bush Sr. got in '80, and Pat Robertson got in '88. "For the last thirty years, the Iowa caucus has been a way for a guy who's not rich and not famous to run for president," he vents. "Take that away, and what's the pool? People who have an inherited advantage, like Forbes or Bush. Or people who are very well liked by the Washington media, like Bradley or McCain. It's the rich and famous. In 2004 the Iowa caucus will evaporate, and it'll be Ted Turner versus Donald Trump."

As his campaign founders, Alexander has resolutely tried to keep his spirits up. "Who else can see America this way?" he says aboard the Winnebago. "Interrupting people at breakfast, sleeping in their houses." He delights in trivia of the road ("You know, Lewis and Clark went right by Council Bluffs," he tells his son) and in sharing the troubles of middle America (he actually seems to enjoy the endless discussions about gasoline additives and corn prices). He has become the Charles Kuralt of politics.

Our next stop is Clarinda, Glenn Miller's birthplace, where Alexander peers through the window at the venue for his next rally, Vaughn's Cafe. "Ugh, more food," he says, slowly taking his jacket from the closet. There are 14 spectators here and a local reporter, and Lamar, now that the cameras have stopped rolling, gives a fabulous performance. When a questioner wants to know how he can compete with the Bush dynasty and Forbes's "modern marketing," Alexander replies, "I'm going to shake a lot of hands." After his talk, a friend who had written a column for the *Des Moines Register* makes the pitch for Ames. Amazingly, eleven of the 14 people in attendance pledge to go to the straw poll with Lamar.

At dinnertime, the Winnebago pulls into Shenandoah, a small, depressing town that long ago produced the Everly Brothers. Lamar brings his keyboard to play some tunes, and 50 or so locals crowd the restaurant, where Alexander signs are taped to beer kegs. Here the candidate is at his best, telling folksy stories about the Everly Brothers, Teddy Roosevelt and eastern Tennessee. After a painless stump speech, he rolls up his sleeves and begins the concert, singing first "Tennessee Waltz," then "Bye Bye Love." The Iowans love it, singing from their song sheets, some of them swaying arm in arm, others holding hands. Alexander closes with the Everly Brothers favorite "All I Have to Do Is Dream." It seems fitting for Lamar, a dreamer himself in this quixotic campaign: "The only trouble is, gee whiz, I'm dreaming my life away."

A few minutes later, the dream is over, and we're back in the Winnebago, heading for a $38-a-night motel a couple of hours down the road. Alexander whistles a tune, sings a few lines to himself and drifts off to sleep. And the Winnebago rumbles between cornfields into the dark Iowa night.

Lamar's sad demise repeats itself for Orrin Hatch, when I meet him in Iowa just before the caucuses. A blizzard has blown into northern Iowa with 40-knot winds and sub-zero temperatures. Trucks are jackknifing on the highways, and cars lie abandoned in ditches. But one Chevy Blazer barrels along at breakneck speed, a former race car driver at the wheel. In the passenger seat, in suit and tie, sits a presidential candidate, zipping between meetings with the *Marshalltown Times-Republican* and the *Mason City Globe-Gazette*. Neither snow nor wind nor gloom of polls can stay the presidential quest of Orrin Hatch.

How could they? For, in his breast pocket, the senator from Utah carries a letter from Pierre Salinger that he quotes to audiences. At the moment he is reading it into his cell phone for a reporter from the *Kansas City Star*. "I feel very strongly that you are the best Republican candidate for president," wrote President Kennedy's press secretary. "You have done incredible work in the Senate for years, something that makes me feel that you would be an important president."

It's hard to picture George W. Bush or John McCain bragging about a letter from a Democrat famous for spinning plane crash conspiracy theories on the Internet. But Hatch will take support wherever he can get it. "I thought it was pretty neat," says Hatch, who called Salinger to thank him for his $144 contribution.

Hatch's candidacy, never a likely proposition, isn't quite living up to expectations. Instead of a million "skinny cats" sending Hatch checks for $36, only 15,000 did. "That's about 985,000 less than I need," he allows. Instead of climbing to second or third in the polls, as Hatch hoped, he's dead last in sixth, with a whopping 1 percent, even behind radio commentator Alan Keyes and Christian activist Gary Bauer. Hatch figured voters would come to view Bush as unready and McCain as phony, and some have, but they still haven't warmed to Hatch, who suggests he'll quit if he can't place fourth or better in the Iowa caucuses Monday.

And now this: the senator's campaign consultants, led by Sal Russo, have dumped him. Hatch hired Russo's firm to run a soup-to-nuts campaign: directing strategy, organizing events, launching ads and handling the press. The Russo gang quit earlier this month when Hatch turned down nearly a million dollars in public matching funds, for which the campaign proudly announced its qualification in November.

"Why would I turn to the taxpayers to finance my election?" Hatch asks. Russo's firm told him that he'd look like a fool running around Iowa with no ads but the cheaply done infomercials he already ran. "It may be stupid, but that's how I am," says Hatch, riding through the blizzard with his volunteer driver. The campaign, which moved its "national headquarters" to West Des Moines with all of five paid staffers, will go broke in days. Hatch acknowledges it wasn't worth Russo's time without TV ads. "I don't blame them," he says.

As a result, the mighty senator, lion of the Judiciary and Finance Committees, is forced to live as an also-ran in Iowa, accepting even the lowliest appearances. He gets up early to be on a shock-jock radio show in which the host, immediately before Hatch's segment, is talking about "big mud flaps on a chick." His first question to Hatch is about Bob Dole and his "penile dysfunction," then a query about Hillary Clinton allegedly having sex with Vince Foster, then one about President Clinton allegedly raping Juanita Broaddrick, then something about "orgies going on in the White House." Hatch calmly responds with "It makes me sick" and "You're absolutely right," all the while struggling to weave in bits about his vast experience. ("I'm the author of the balanced-budget amendment!")

Hatch himself appreciates the irony of his position: one of the most serious men in Washington is getting no respect on the campaign trail. "I'm starting to get the word out. My wife said just this morning, 'I hear you're running for president,'" Hatch quips at a speech to Principal Financial Group employees in Des Moines on Wednesday.

Instead of first-class tickets and lunches at La Colline, Hatch often finds himself flying in coach, middle row. Other candidates stay in luxury hotels; Hatch gets $59-a-night specials. When he hops into his Blazer on Wednesday, a Burger King fish sandwich is waiting for him. "It's still warm!" he delights. "I've had my first two Wendy's hamburgers in 15 years, and Taco Bell and Burger King," he said. "Junk food really does appeal to me." This is a guy, after all, who survived poverty in Pittsburgh. Even now, when a button fell off his coat before a New Hampshire event, Hatch, to the amazement of onlookers, pulled a sewing kit from his pocket and stitched it back on.

On Wednesday, Hatch is driving more than 100 miles through a snow-storm just for an interview with the 35,000-circulation *Times-Republican* at Mr. G's Restaurant in Marshalltown, then on to another interview with the Mason City paper. There are no greeting parties, no supporters, no organization. The reporters, in person or on the phone, invariably inquire about the hopeless nature of his quest. Hatch is getting used to it. Wednesday night, it's Brian Williams on MSNBC. "He probably wants to know why I'm doing this since I can't win," Hatch says. "It's fascinating to people that I keep going."

What went wrong? Some reasons he lists are obvious: started late, didn't raise much money, from a small state, not exactly a live wire. And he complains of anti-Mormon discrimination from fundamentalist Christians.

But there's also an unusual amount of complacency in the electorate. Often, at this stage in the campaign, there's a sense of buyer's remorse, a feeling that all the candidates are losers. But this time, according to a USA Today/CNN/Gallup poll, fully 75 percent of Americans think one of the current candidates would make a good president, up from 40 percent in '92 and 57 percent in '96. Hatch figures that people, feeling fat and happy, aren't focusing on the election. "Let's call it a Ritalin experience," he says, eating an apple after the fish sandwich in the Blazer.

Hatch blames the press for his status as an also-ran, even though he knows reporters are just tracking the candidates' bank accounts and poll numbers. "Almost every interview I've had, they say, 'You're a giant in the Senate, why are you doing this? You don't have a chance.'" Hatch mentions this to most every crowd. "The media's all but written me off—they say it's a two-man race," he likes to say. "If I were a resident of Iowa and I wanted to send a message to the Eastern-liberal-establishment press, I'd vote for Orrin Hatch. This would startle the whole country."

That's for sure.

Hatch, many in Washington agree, is a decent, smart and powerful man. But as a candidate on the stump, the four-term senator doesn't exactly deliver a barn-burner. He tells Iowa crowds about "HCFA" and "penumbras and emanations" and the "strict-scrutiny view of any claim for quotas" and about how "it was not germane, so I had to get a super-majority"—as if he were addressing lobbyists. Mixed in is the aw-shucks language: "Gimme a break," "I've gotta tell you," "Doggone it." To the annoyance of his staff, Hatch continues to speak about himself in the third person: "Orrin Hatch has one litmus test . . . Orrin Hatch gets it done! . . . I gotta tell you, Orrin Hatch woulda voted with them . . . Orrin Hatch does have more experience and a better record of accomplishment . . . Orrin Hatch has stood up for the Second Amendment for 23 years."

Leaving Washington, where it feels like everyone knows his record, to stump in Iowa, where nobody much cares, is a struggle for Hatch. The result is a candidate who blows his own horn. He utters the word "experience" hundreds of times a day, and often recites his legislative resume. "I had 41 bills in the last Congress," he tells the workers at Principal Financial. Then he proceeds to name his greatest hits: the nursing facility legislation, the Hatch-Waxman bill, "which actually created the generic drug industry," the Hatch-Harkin bill on dietary supplements, the "three AIDS bills along with Ted Kennedy."

"Let me just mention one more," he pleads, then names several: child health insurance legislation, the Satellite Home Viewer Act, the "cyber-squatting" bill. By the time he gets to the Digital Millennium Act, the hostess is signaling an end to the talk. As the crowd files out, one reporter grumbles, "I wanted to hear the rest of the 41 bills."

Hatch, during the recitation, is aware that he's gone too far in his self-promotion. "If you tell the truth, you're not lacking in humility," he tells the crowd. (Hatch, an accomplished songwriter, penned a campaign ditty titled "I May Be Vain, but I'm Not a Liar.") Later, in the Blazer, Hatch reproaches himself. "I started talking 1,500 miles an hour," he says. "I said to myself, 'Slow down,' but I couldn't. I worried I sounded arrogant, because I'm not."

In an ideal world, this boastfulness wouldn't be necessary. There was a time, not long ago, when a powerful senator entering the presidential race would have been taken seriously. But legislative experience no longer defines the "serious" candidate. And it is difficult for Hatch, for the first time in 23 years, not to be taken seriously. "It absolutely kills me to have to do it," he says of the legislative boasts. "I hear people say, 'I know your name but I don't know who you are.' I think, my gosh, I've been there 23 years, I've done so many things for you that you don't even know about."

On the trail, Hatch seems incredulous that his achievements aren't known or don't count for much. "I've been there, I've done it, I'm not just making promises." It burned Hatch up when conservative activist Phyllis Schlafly praised Steve Forbes as the leading anti-abortion candidate, while also acknowledging Bauer. "She doesn't even mention me—the first to bring a constitutional amendment to the floor!" Hatch fumes. He was enraged to hear that media outlets were seeking a Bush-McCain debate. And it galls Hatch particularly that Keyes, Bauer and Forbes are put in the same category with him—or higher. "They have a right to run, but I believe you should be elected to something first," he often says.

Ever since Hatch announced his surprise run last summer, his candidacy has inspired something of a parlor game in Washington: Why does he do it? Even his closest allies were doubtful. "I said, 'Well, I feel anxious for you,'" recalls Kevin McGuiness, Hatch's former chief of staff, who took a leave from his law practice to volunteer as campaign manager.

Some speculate that he's running for a Supreme Court nomination or appointment as attorney general. Some think he's doing it for a bit more TV time. Some say it's because he hates McCain (who "in particular does stick in my craw," he admits). Still others think it's a secret plan to help Bush by fragmenting the opposition. And, of course, there's the stated reason: the senator simply sees himself as more qualified than the other guys.

But there's another explanation that may outweigh the rest. Hatch is 65 years old, and this is perhaps the last time he could run for president. One gets the sense that he wants to tell his 19 grandchildren that he reached as high in life as he could, that he even had a go at the highest office in the land.

"If the people don't want me as president, I can live with that—in fact, I can easily live with that," Hatch says. Too easily, perhaps. "I will never regret doing this," the candidate declares, looking at a map of Iowa and ticking off all the towns he's visited. Would he regret it forever if he didn't try to be president? "I would feel like I hadn't at least given it what I should."

McGuiness puts it this way: "It is better to try and fail than not to try at all. The only thing that holds you back is your pride, and once you get rid of the fear, eliminate the pride, you're liberated."

As he presses on through the snowstorm to another meeting with another skeptical small-town newspaper reporter, wondering if he can find a Wendy's baked potato for dinner, Hatch seems to have suppressed his pride fairly well. "Look, the Lord has never made my life easy. I didn't have enough to eat when I was young. I worked hard my whole life."

But then again, Hatch also makes things hard on himself: Surely he doesn't have to be out here in a snowstorm, campaigning for president and sleeping at the Mason City Holiday Inn. He could be tucking into a nice steak at the Palm. Hatch disagrees. "I feel I do have to be out here," he says. In a few days, mercifully, his obligation to posterity will be fulfilled, and he can go back to being a giant again.

16

★ ☆ ★

Capitalist Retool

It's a bitter winter night outside the studios of WMUR-TV in New Hampshire, scene of the Republican candidates' debate. Several hundred rough looking youths have come to the debate just so they can stand outside the TV studio, in their orange T-shirts, waving Steve Forbes signs and harassing the other candidates and their supporters. They are mostly 16-year-olds: too young to vote for Forbes in the February 1 primary but not too young to shout for him. I ask one of them why he's backing Forbes. "I want to keep more of my tax dollars," the boy replies.

You pay taxes? (Pause.) "I used to. I got fired."

Forbes's young warriors, a fixture at the debates, are everything their candidate isn't: fierce, energetic and cool. They have spiked hair and pierced bodies. They march in formation. They beat drums. They wield wooden sticks with Forbes signs. They taunt would-be presidents. They are scary. "We've thought about calling them F-Troop and Orange Crush," says Graham Shafer, Forbes's New Hampshire director. But after watching a group of them march into the press room and disrupt candidate interviews at a recent debate, a bystander gave them another name: *die Jungen*. Indeed, there is something very Germany 1938 about them.

That's how Dave Lenhart feels. A mild-mannered county commissioner from Maryland here to cheer for George W. Bush, Lenhart finds himself surrounded by pro-Forbes youths on the sidewalk outside the debate. "You have to move," an orange-clad tough orders. When Lenhart responds with something legalistic about a "public easement," the thug returns with more toughs and megaphones. "We own this sidewalk!" they chant at Lenhart, who takes a good look at them and retreats from his public easement.

Alas for Forbes, the tough line his toughs take in the street is nothing like the pussycat demeanor Forbes assumes inside—and throughout much of this campaign. Bush, as I've noted, has been blessed by his choice of inept opponents. But this isn't limited to mainstream candidates such as Hatch, Alexander and Dole, who declined to paint a stark and tough contrast between Bush and themselves. Even Steve Forbes, the terror of '96, has turned into a tame animal this time.

On the eve of the 1996 New Hampshire primary, the local ABC affiliate, WMUR, opened its new headquarters in New Hampshire, an 80,000-square-foot, $3.6 million palace of broadcasting. The station's marketing literature calls the place, with its lavish studios and advanced digital capabilities, "the best and most innovative broadcast facility in the country." But the nation's political operatives have another name for it: The House That Forbes Built.

"We've heard those rumors," says Karen Brown, WMUR's news director. "It's not true. All we dedicated to him was one pillar out front."

Forbes went wild in the '96 race, spending millions to batter and bruise the Republican front-runner, Bob Dole. But it wasn't just the sheer dollar value of the attack; it was the effective nastiness of the campaign. Forbes mercilessly attacked Dole as too soft on the matter of taxes, essentially a fat-cat Republican who didn't believe in limited government. That helped Forbes, and it also helped other conservatives, such as Pat Buchanan.

Forbes spent a ton of money in New Hampshire again this time, but it wasn't nearly as effective. In part, this is because Bush shunned the public financing system that limits a candidate's budget in New Hampshire; Bush could go dollar for dollar with Forbes. But the volume of Forbes's ads weren't the problem. It was a matter of tone. Instead of tough ads about Bush, Forbes indulged in homey, black-and-white ads that painted Forbes as a warm-and-fuzzy man. The idea was to make himself look presidential, no longer an attack dog. In retrospect, the commercials were a flop.

Forbes has turned into an old softy. And it's no coincidence that he hasn't been able to draw blood as he did in '96. Bush has deftly encouraged Forbes to stay "positive" by warning about nastiness to come while effectively running him out of the race with a deftly negative campaign. Bush, like Bradley on the Democratic side, is constantly complaining of nonexistent unfair attacks by Forbes. Voters are so disgusted by past nastiness, he figures, that all a candidate need do is cry foul and, voila, the opponent is the bad guy.

"The Bush campaign uses the accusation of negative attack to be its own negative ad," says Bill Dal Col, campaign manager for Forbes, who launched a devastating series of ads against Bob Dole in '96. The press, meanwhile, has changed the nomenclature, he says. "They used to call it a comparative ad or a debate ad. Now they call it an attack ad."

Bush has been displaying his victim status eagerly. The Republican Leadership Council, a Bush-friendly group, has been running ads assaulting Forbes for "a history of unfairly attacking fellow Republicans—and now he's doing it again." Senator Charles Grassley, a Bush backer, took to the airwaves in his home state of Iowa to knock Forbes: "Some presidential candidates are trying to win Iowa votes by slinging mud and distorting records." The Bush people even accuse Forbes of doctoring a Bush photo in a brochure to make the governor's ears look bigger. "It kind of looks like Ross Perot," Eric Woolson, a Bush spokesman, said.

The essence of the Forbes "attack" is that Bush proposed raising certain taxes and fees in Texas. The legislature rejected the idea, which, Forbes fails to point out, was part of an overall tax cut. "If being negative is telling the truth, I will continue to tell the truth," Forbes said when challenged at a debate. "We deserve an open and vigorous debate."

Bush's piety is hard to square with some of his own actions or inactions. Bush-friendly Grover Norquist and his Americans for Tax Reform have been running ads claiming McCain helps "labor unions, trial lawyers and pro-abortion groups," even morphing McCain's likeness into Clinton's. Bush isn't running these ads, but neither is he doing anything to stop them.

Even as he warns this week about "ugly politics" to come from Forbes, the governor is getting a taste of his own politics—from McCain, who is stealing the victim label from Bush. McCain trucked out a former Bush volunteer who claimed she left the Bush campaign after she was asked to criticize McCain's tax plan in an ad. Now, McCain is blasting Bush for a new ad saying McCain would tax $40 billion in employee benefits.

Bush says it wasn't negative at all: "We've got a policy disagreement. . . . An honest debate about how to cut taxes is important for the Republican Party." In response to earlier McCain complaints about negativity, a Bush spokesman argued: "He's going to discuss with the American people the issue differences between the two candidates. . . . That is issue-oriented." The spokesman is absolutely right. But it's the same technique Bush used to drive Forbes into irrelevancy.

Bush didn't drive Forbes from the race alone. Forbes had much to do with his own demise. And one of his biggest miscalculations was that new technologies, particularly the Internet, would make the 2000 presidential race like none before. Forbes bet on a high-tech campaign. And he was wrong.

Let's return to early 1999. In a dark basement somewhere beneath downtown Cincinnati, Rick Segal presents the attack plan. "The fact of the matter is it's war," he is telling a group of followers, who scribble notes. "It's a black-and-white world of wins and losses." He flashes war movie clips on the screen and discusses the techniques of today's smartest warriors: Hamas, the Mexican Zapatistas, Asian triads and other amorphous, stealthy networks. "Bastions, redoubts and empires are subject to implosive attacks and ambush," Comrade Segal tells his men. Quoting from a Pentagon report, he adds: "In an information-age 'battlespace,' massed forces will simply form juicy targets for small, smart attackers."

The scene might prompt an eavesdropper to call the FBI if the basement weren't a conference room in the posh Queen City Club, if the attendees weren't a bunch of corporate suits and if Segal weren't sporting a polka-dot bow tie beneath his chin. In fact, Segal, the head of a local marketing firm, is talking about network warfare, or "netwar," which, done his way, involves no bloodshed. As the world advances beyond the industrial age of mass production, he believes, small and nimble enterprises can use technology to leave their larger, slower competitors in the dust. The concept isn't unusual in business circles; what's strange is Segal's latest client, the man who introduced Segal's war games speech: Forbes. Segal, using the same high-tech methods he employs to sell refrigerators, flooring and telecom services, believes he can help Steve Forbes launch a guerrilla attack on the massed forces of George W. Bush.

The Forbes netwar, an effort to wrest the Republican presidential nomination from the favorite in 2000, is an opening salvo in what will be the first presidential campaign of the information age. Forbes is calculating that technology will redefine political campaigns in 2000 much as television did in the late 1950s and early 1960s—and he isn't alone in this forecast. The Gore campaign and both national political parties are making similar assumptions in their 2000 strategies. Why? For one, 76 million Americans are online already, according to the Nielsen ratings, and 70 percent of voting-age Americans will have Internet access by Election Day, according to a survey by Dataquest. At this time in the '96 campaign, only 11 percent of Iowa Republican caucus-goers and only 14 percent of New Hampshire Republican primary voters were online, according to Forbes's internal polls; now some 57 percent of Republican caucus voters in Iowa and 68 percent of primary voters in New Hampshire have computers, and most use the Internet regularly.

But the Web is just the beginning. At the same time, vastly expanded consumer databases and enhanced computing power have put an unprecedented amount of information at the candidates' fingertips. If you're a registered voter, chances are the candidates know not just your name, address and voting history but also your age and the age of your children, whether you smoke cigars, where you shop, where you attend church, what kind of car you drive, how old it is, whether you're on a diet and what type of pet you have, to cite just a few examples. Using artificial intelligence and an array of new software programs, campaigns can target and contact their likeliest supporters with unprecedented precision. The trend is further aided by the replacement of the giant national TV networks with cable channels, independent stations and local news, which allows political spots to be targeted right down to a few hundred voters. In California, for example, there are some 180 cable systems from which a candidate can choose.

Many of the new-fangled techniques are still too expensive for most campaigns. But for Forbes, a wealthy publisher willing to spend some $50 million on the primaries, these new technologies are crucial. Forbes launched his campaign over the Internet and uses the Web to advertise and promote sponsorships. He created an organizing tool called the "e-Precinct," which encourages participants to enroll friends, forming "e-Blocks," "e-Neighborhoods" and even an "e-National Committee." On June 16, he held a virtual fund-raiser in which participants had a private online group chat with Forbes—after making a $10 credit card contribution. Later in the campaign, Forbes will speak live, his image broadcast over the Internet, to a town-hall meeting in New Hampshire while he has a half-hour of downtime in Iowa. Just as Clinton pioneered the rapid response in the '92 campaign, the Internet allows Forbes 24-hour interaction unfiltered by the news media.

Though the Forbes camp won't say what it spends on its online campaign (aides insist it's less than the $500,000 that industry experts have estimated), it's enough to fund five staffers full-time for the website alone. The website, which began at 670 pages and has expanded to include "photoscopes" with digital images, is easily the largest of all the candidates' sites. Technology is also shifting Forbes away from conventional polls to "database surveys." Rather than pose 50 questions to 300 randomly selected people, pollsters pose a few questions to thousands of people found on consumer-marketing databases. Forbes pollsters then do a computer analysis of dozens of personal characteristics—including age, family structure, consumer habits, home ownership and magazine subscriptions—to figure out whether you will vote, how susceptible you are to persuasion and what pitch will appeal to you most. Already the Forbes campaign is running targeted 2000 ads, using such vehicles as the History Channel, tailored to cable systems in early primary states. "We've gone from mass media to demassified media," says John McLaughlin, Forbes's pollster and media strategist. "People are overloaded with information. If you don't talk to them directly, they're going to lose interest." Campaign manager Dal Col says this changes the whole nature of campaigns. "You don't have to shotgun anymore," he says. "You can now bullet."

What all these techniques have in common is an effort to establish a personal, one-on-one relationship between the campaign and each supporter based on the supporter's preferences. Call it the Customized Campaign. Instead of mass media and mass marketing, it's about individual interaction and personalized politics fostered by technology. Instead of the old demographics, campaigns are now getting inside voters' heads to track "psychographics."

Forbes aides argue that the e-campaign makes Americans feel more involved. Technology, though it can alienate, might also revive a Tocquevillian America, in which civic groups thrive online. "We're reconstructing the old-fashioned ward and precinct system," Segal says. "I may not be the first person to invent a political machine, but I may be the first to create a political machine that's really a machine."

One mailing the campaign already sent enclosed a survey on various issues—missile defense, the United Nations, term limits, morality and others. If somebody scribbles a line about tax reform, the campaign will later personalize a form letter with a postscript from Forbes, saying, "Thanks for writing me about that tax issue last month. I put it in one of my speeches." That's a simple way to create a personal touch.

Others worry that e-campaigns will invade individual privacy, a danger when there's so much personal information for sale. Campaigns are taking some measures to reassure the public. Forbes's campaign, for example, says it won't use "cookies" or other devices to collect information about visitors to the site without their permission. Other campaigns say they won't send "spam," or unsolicited e-mail.

Segal says the Forbes campaign will send unsolicited e-mails to potential voters who meet the Forbes profile, but to avoid complaints, the campaign will try not to send more than one unsolicited e-mail to each prospect. A more obvious way to avoid the privacy problem is to use information people supply themselves. Segal eventually will send up to eight e-mails a day with messages written according to the recipient's preferences. The website is gathering such preferences at every turn, requesting information about job, income, education, fraternity and civic groups. "What's important to you?" the website asks at various points, offering 49 choices that cover everything from school prayer to Kosovo, crime to Y2K.

Often, those who are individually targeted won't even know it; they'll just see their junk mail as more relevant. In 1997, while working for the Republican gubernatorial candidate in Virginia, McLaughlin singled out upper-income professionals in northern Virginia for a pitch on lowering the state's car tax. The campaign similarly delivered a pitch to mothers of school-age children about hiring 4,000 new teachers, while in rural southern Virginia it sent a tailored tobacco message to every tobacco farmer.

The privacy and democracy problems will become more pressing as the technology becomes more pervasive. For now, the debate will be about the merits of the technologies themselves. Though few doubt that they work, some doubt whether they work well enough to justify the cost. Some political commentators have proclaimed e-campaigns overblown, arguing that candidates won't be able to reach enough of the voters they need via the Internet and that people don't go to the Internet for politics.

However, those who dismiss the Internet's role often assume e-campaigns are just about websites, which, in truth, are little more than electronic yard signs. The Internet is only a means of gathering and organizing information, and e-mail is just one way to deliver highly targeted messages. The point of e-campaigning is to use the information gathered through the Internet in order to better target people, not only through e-mail but through more traditional means, such as regular mail, phone calls, television and door-to-door visits. And the Forbes campaign's techniques are already showing some promise in that regard: a recent review of the campaign's phone calls to potential supporters in an early primary state showed that, because of targeting, the calls had had an unusually high success rate of 20 percent.

The Forbes campaign is also working on new ways to attract those who wouldn't ordinarily surf the Web or seek out political sites. Forbes's Internet banner ads, which are already in use, will eventually be custom-delivered using Internet service providers' customer profiles so that the ads only appear on the screens of those people the campaign wants to reach—say, registered Republicans who live in Iowa.

More significant, though, is the use of Steve Forbes "pavilions" on popular websites. Segal pictures a "constellation of websites" linking voters to Forbes. Doctors for Forbes, Teachers for Forbes, North Dakotans for Forbes and the like will use virtual bumper stickers that link viewers to the Forbes site. Such sponsorships face fewer legal restrictions than TV ads. Among the results of all these efforts: in its first six weeks, Forbes2000.com enrolled 12,720 volunteers and 1,620 e-precinct leaders while racking up 20.3 million hits in 377,000 separate visits to the site.

Forbes advisers are the first to admit that all this won't be enough to win the nomination by itself. If the race isn't close, e-politics won't do much good. But if Forbes's $50 million can somehow get him close to Bush, his futuristic campaign might make a difference. "Since 1952, most Republican presidential candidates have approached campaigns like

Eisenhower: mass the troops," says Segal. Bush's advisers "are going to be tempted into the security of the last playbook, what happened last time." In the information age, Forbes figures, the old playbook may be no match for a couple of guerrillas with laptops.

The Bush campaign, though weighing using an artificial-intelligence method to predict voter turnout in one early primary state, otherwise appears to be ceding the high-tech campaign to Forbes. Bush has spent only $15,000 on his website. Of course, Bush is currently leading the polls with the support of 54 percent of Republican primary voters, while Forbes can boast of the support of 6 percent. "A lot of that is, frankly, overrated," Bush adviser Karl Rove says of Forbes's computer techniques. "It's just a matter of sifting through the voter files." David Beckwith, who is over-seeing Bush's website, figures Forbes's high-tech advantage won't be decisive. "I can't disagree that with extraordinary resources an electronic campaign can get an extra few points," he says, "but he's not going to be in the zone."

As it turns out, Beckwith was right. Steve Forbes is not in the zone. Not anywhere near it. His campaign buses have been racing through their final rounds across New Hampshire before the primary, but they have been unable to outrun a disturbing impression following Forbes wherever he goes: that the candidate's good showing in Iowa didn't matter.

When Forbes placed a strong second to George W. Bush in the Iowa caucuses with 30 percent of the vote, the candidate, who had spent huge resources in that state, declared it a three-man race between him, Bush and Arizona Senator John McCain. Forbes manager Dal Col had predicted, boldly, that Bush would finish third in New Hampshire. With the traditional "bounce" from favorable publicity after Iowa, and with relentless plugging from the *Manchester Union Leader* (which has endorsed Forbes and attacks Bush daily), Forbes figured he'd immediately vault into contention here.

It hasn't happened, and time is running out. Instead of squaring off with Bush and McCain in last week's GOP debate, Forbes took on CNN's Bernard Shaw for not giving him enough time. Public polls have put Forbes's support in the range of 11 percent to 17 percent, while Bush and McCain both score above 30 percent.

The Forbes campaign, however, is defiantly optimistic. "I know what the polls say—we all do," said Robert Lawsom, a weekly newspaper owner, as he introduced Forbes to a rally here Saturday. "The national news media has been declaring this a two-man race for months. But look what hap-pened in Iowa. They were wrong then, and they're wrong now—because we've got momentum." Forbes, taking the stage, seconded the theme. "Tuesday night you're going to show the world that the pundits, polls and media . . . are the new lagging indicators," he said.

Still, these rallying cries couldn't overcome the skepticism in the crowd of 150. "What you say makes so much sense," said the first questioner after Forbes's stump speech. "How come it's so difficult to get your message out?"

One problem is the press has pretty much written him off. Only four reporters climbed onto the Forbes bus in Nashua for Saturday's trip; McCain had left from Nashua earlier that day with more than 50. Forbes hasn't been drawing large crowds in New Hampshire, as he did in Iowa, and his old friend Jack Kemp just endorsed Bush, suggesting Forbes become treasury secretary. Forbes finally seems to have dispensed with conservative rival Gary Bauer, only for Alan Keyes to surge.

Meanwhile, a Bush-friendly group and Robert J. Dole are attacking Forbes for his supposedly negative tactics. There are signs that Forbes, after winning over the social conservatives in Iowa, has had trouble closing the deal with his natural constituency, the economic conservatives. There have also been reports that he isn't spending much on advertising before the primary (though Dal Col said Forbes's ad purchase, about $600,000 in the past week, is bigger than Bush's).

But Forbes continues to predict a surprise in New Hampshire. "We have fun redefining the conventional wisdom," he said in an interview on his campaign bus. "We're getting a good response. I got firm credibility out of Iowa. Now we have a three-way race, and we're gaining strength." Dal Col argued that between 20 percent and 30 percent of GOP primary voters will be undecided Monday morning, and "the undecideds have been breaking our way."

"We could finish second," he predicted, arguing that Forbes's New Hampshire polling and phone calls have been giving him the same signals he got before his impressive showing in Iowa. The Iowa bounce exists, Dal Col said. "You'll see it Tuesday."

Forbes has taken the unorthodox strategy of playing up his anti-abortion message in New Hampshire, which tends to favor economic conservatism. He continues, of course, to give his anti-tax pitch. Speaking Sunday in Nashua, he railed against Bush's "wishy-washiness," citing the governor's remarks that he would pass his tax cut, "hopefully, in the first term."

At the same time, Forbes has been trying to neutralize attacks by Bush loyalists that his negative politics have hurt the party. Before a Forbes speech to a GOP group in Nashua Friday night, he was introduced as a friend of the party in 1996: "During the general election he campaigned loyally for the Republican ticket."

Dal Col also argued that the Forbes organization will, as in Iowa, get its supporters to the polls in higher percentages than others. "It's not as intense as a caucus, but you've still got to get them up out of their chair and in to vote," he said. Forbes volunteers have been covering the state in yard signs and arranging a get-out-the-vote push that will beat expectations Tuesday. "I don't believe the polls," said Charles Setaro, a Forbes supporter in Nashua.

But Forbes, for all his organizational prowess, still hasn't inspired the electorate. His speeches sounded as if he were reading, angrily, from a history book. He continued to chop his forearms mechanically while keeping the rest of his body eerily still, and tripping over words. Speaking about foreign policy, he declared: "This is not a military issue, this is not a moral issue. I mean money. This is not a military or money issue. This is a moral issue." An hour later, he tried again in another speech: "This is not a military issue. It's not a moral issue. [Pause.] It's fundamentally a moral issue, not an issue of military or money." Finally, speaking in Nashua Sunday, he got the line right.

Finally, visiting the Lake Region of central New Hampshire, on the eve of the primary, Forbes escalated his attack. "George W. Bush says he's pro-life but straddles, refusing to make such clear, pro-life pledges," a Forbes statement said. Bill Dal Col, Forbes's campaign manager, said the renewed emphasis on abortion is intended to "drive passion among our base" in New Hampshire.

Forbes's latest assault on Bush's abortion record dovetails with radio ads the publisher has been running for the past few days in New Hampshire. One accuses Bush of "acting like a pro-life pacifist afraid to offend." Another radio ad picks up the straddling theme, accusing Bush of having it both ways on spending and taxes in Texas.

But it seems to be too little, too late to even the most committed Forbes supporters. Joe Guthrie, a Hampstead selectman and a devoted Forbes man, wasn't surprised when there were almost no Forbes supporters at a GOP event the candidate spoke to in Manchester. "It just happens that way, I guess," he said. Forbes would be a serious threat in New Hampshire, he said, without Keyes and Bauer. "You almost have to add Keyes and Bauer's support to his," Guthrie said. Unfortunately, that isn't allowed—and Guthrie doesn't expect a miracle on the order of the one Dal Col predicted. "We can't expect any better than third," he said.

That's just not enough to keep Forbes going. It's impossible to know, of course, but I can't help but believe Forbes would be more of a contender in New Hampshire if he had the bravery to run the tough sort of campaign he ran here in '96.

17

★ ☆ ★

The Right Cracks Up

Lucky, lucky George W. First he gets a pass from his mainstream Republican opponents, as Libby Dole, Lamar!, Orrin Hatch and John Kasich make nice in hopes of staying in Bush's good graces. Then Forbes wastes his money on a mushy, positive campaign. There's a third stroke of luck for Bush, too: the hopeless splintering of the religious right. Forbes, Dan Quayle, Gary Bauer and Alan Keyes, instead of aiming their attacks at the front-runner, are busy carving themselves up.

The carving of the religious right begins almost two years before primary season, in the spring of 1998, at the annual gathering of the Harris County, Texas, Republican Party. This is no place for moderates. It begins with a 7 a.m. prayer remembering the millions of innocents slaughtered in the womb, followed by a concert of religious hymns sung by a home-school choir. Throughout the day, presidential aspirants— Quayle, Missouri Senator John Ashcroft, Bauer—cross the stage to rehearse moral themes while attendees line up in the back to buy bumper stickers saying "Lorena Bobbitt for White House Intern." Bush sent his regrets. Local party leaders speculate, with some pride, that he doesn't wish to be linked to the religious conservatives who dominate Republican politics here.

But another would-be candidate has no such qualms about associating with the true believers. This fiery moralist takes to the podium late in the day and rouses the crowd to three standing ovations. They shout with joy as he quotes from Moses to the Israelites and praises the Promise Keepers. They hoot and cheer when he condemns the president's morality and calls for spiritual renewal. Finally, his demand to ban the "infanticide" known as partial-birth abortion brings the house down. "This ban will be the first step toward putting abortion on the road to ultimate extinction in the United States of America," he thunders from a stage in the University of Houston's basketball arena. "The law protects not only the strong, the healthy, and the rich but also the weakest among us—the old, the infirm, and the unborn."

And just who is this Texas evangelist, this protector of the unborn and friend of the common man? Why, it's New Jersey's own Malcolm Stevenson Forbes, Jr.—the same Malcolm Stevenson Forbes, Jr., who once called Christian Coalition founder Pat Robertson a "toothy flake" and who was quoted during the '96 campaign as saying, after his anti-abortion credentials were challenged, that the Christian Coalition doesn't speak for most Christians. And it's the very same Malcolm Stevenson Forbes, Jr., who, during that same campaign, antagonized conservative activists by, they said, supporting gay rights and displaying a Robert Mapplethorpe photo on his 151-foot yacht.

The very public spiritual awakening of Steve Forbes is a peculiar tale. Here is a candidate who talked about nothing but the flat tax in '96 suddenly positioning himself as the right's new moral voice. Here is a businessman worth a reported $440 million who flew around in a plane called *The Capitalist Tool* recasting himself as a populist hero. And here, remarkably enough, are Christian conservatives embracing him as one of their own. To complete the irony, they say they're drawn to the famously robotic Forbes by his folksy personality.

"He's a real person, like you and me," says Billy Wayne Moore, who wears an anti-abortion infant-footprint logo on his lapel at the Harris County convention. Moore, coordinator of the Christian Coalition's Houston chapter, didn't like Forbes last time. "He's changed his tune quite a bit since '96," says Moore, a heavy-set retiree. "I like what he's saying. He sounds genuine, and he doesn't neglect the social issues." In fact, Moore adds, "there's only one thing about Mr. Forbes that bothers me greatly: It's his flat-tax proposal."

Forbes's Bible Belt appeal is confounding some leaders of the religious right. They would like to unite the movement behind an older friend like Ashcroft, Quayle or Bauer, but voters of the religious right are clearly willing to forgive Forbes's past disdain for their views. "There's a reason why in the Gospels Christ refers to his followers as sheep," says one religious political leader, marveling at Forbes's success. Yet even some of the religious right's political operatives say they're flattered by Forbes's pandering, which implicitly acknowledges that any Republican candidate needs their members' votes to win the nomination.

In truth, Forbes's success thus far may have less to do with God than with mammon. Forbes and his issues advocacy group are spending significant sums of money on Christian causes, candidates and leaders to win their support. He's offering consulting contracts to Ralph Reed and other well-known religious conservatives who opposed him last time. Could it be that the religious right is for sale? "A little sweet-talking and a lot of money can go a long way," says one social conservative who hopes to be a presidential candidate in 2000. "He's just looking at the electoral map and seeing what he has to do." An adviser to another likely Republican contender grouses, "He's become a sugar daddy for conservative causes, buying tables at all the right events."

But rivals can complain all they want. Forbes's conversion is convincing where it counts: with the movement's foot soldiers. "Regardless of whether you look at it cynically or uncynically, he's doing it with a degree of success I would not have thought possible," says David Keene, a GOP consultant and chairman of the American Conservative Union. Indeed, in a late February straw poll of delegates to the Southern GOP Leadership Conference, Forbes placed second only to Bush, ahead of Quayle, Fred Thompson, Ashcroft, Alexander and Newt Gingrich. In a late March Fox News poll, Forbes beat Quayle in a matchup against Al Gore. In a leaked poll of Christian Coalition state chapter leaders, Forbes placed behind only Ashcroft among serious candidates, ahead of Quayle and the other usual suspects.

One can find all sorts of wisdom in Steve Forbes's regular column, "Fact and Comment," in *Forbes* magazine. He recommends the "potato tart fused with spiced ham and lobster" at Bouley Bakery and insists Zarela has "the best flan ever tasted." He tells us he found the novel *The Magician's Wife* "intriguing" and that Walter Mosley's mystery *Gone Fishin'* has "plenty of adventure." Forbes also writes that the World Series "underscores how quintessentially American baseball is."

But one thing not to be found in these columns is evidence of longstanding social conservatism. He first condemns partial-birth abortion in December 1995, with a graphic description of the procedure—followed by a list of "All Star Eateries," in case anyone still has an appetite left. In 1984, he talked of "our unnecessary brouhaha about abortion" at a population conference; in 1979, he seemed to mock a tour guide in China for praising the public humiliation a woman had to suffer before getting an abortion.

In 1996, Forbes seemed to do everything possible to distance himself from moral conservatives, and they reciprocated. Forbes was hurt badly in Iowa when the state's Right to Life Committee said he was "not pro-life," and he did little to dispel the belief that he opposed a constitutional amendment banning abortion. The Christian Coalition distributed flyers noting Forbes's support for President Clinton's "don't ask, don't tell" policy on gays in the military. Forbes was asked on *60 Minutes* about his father's alleged homosexuality, and a group opposing gay rights spread the word about the Mapplethorpe on his yacht. (It's a picture of a beach.)

When I sat down to talk religion with him before a recent speech, he seemed ill at ease. "I've always believed. I do attend church, and when I don't, I pray," he said, as if answering questions at a deposition. Which prayers does he favor? "There are many prayers for particular occasions," he replied. Any specifics? "You share it with the Lord," he said. So, he thinks up his own prayers? "The Lord recognizes when you're doing it mechanistically and when you're truly seeking his guidance." And so on.

Jude Wanniski, a supply-side guru and one-time Forbes friend, says that Forbes once believed economics would drive social policy. "If we push the economy in the right direction, the economy would drive all else and in the end we'd get to where pro-life people want to get," he says. "That was essentially his position." Wanniski, who had a falling out with Forbes over the management of the '96 campaign, says Forbes's more recent pronouncements are "paying his respects to the Christian conservatives to patch things up." If Forbes had his choice, Wanniski believes, "economics is all he'd want to talk about, and the International Monetary Fund, and world economics, and the gold standard."

In my interview with Forbes, I posed the hypothetical case of a President Forbes able to enact only one of two policies: overhauling the tax code or banning abortion. Which would he choose? "Life is basic," he replied. "If you don't have a foundation of life, a moral foundation, all else is ephemeral. Taxes can be raised and taxes can be cut, but if you value life, you won't be subject to individual whims." Taxes can be raised and taxes can be cut? Those are fighting words to economic conservatives. "That shocks me," Wanniski says of Forbes's reply. He's equally surprised that Forbes backed a failed proposal that would have denied Republican Party money to any candidate who didn't favor a partial-birth abortion ban.

Forbes is spreading the gospel at a rapid clip: He's delivered 260 speeches since November 1996, almost always mentioning partial-birth abortion. He's met frequently with the likes of Don Hodel and Randy Tate of the Christian Coalition, Dobson and Bauer, Phyllis Schlafly, and Heritage Foundation leaders. But he's also doing what a Forbes does naturally: spending money. For example, his issue advocacy group, Americans for Hope, Growth, and Opportunity, which began with $100,000 in Forbes-supplied seed money and now has $4.1 million, bought a table at a fund-raising dinner honoring Ralph Reed held by Regent University's Robertson School of Government. Forbes also spoke at events for candidates who are clients of Reed's political consulting firm in Kentucky, South Carolina and Pennsylvania. Forbes has offered Reed a contract to consult for Americans for Hope, Growth, and Opportunity, and he's actively recruiting Jerry Keene, state chairman of the Christian Coalition in Georgia, a key electoral state. Reed, clearly in Dole's camp in '96, has warmed a bit to Forbes.

Similarly, Forbes's group gave the Catholic Alliance, a Christian Coalition offshoot, $10,000 in April 1997 for a partial-birth abortion campaign. "We would welcome more, and we're working with him," says Keith Fournier, president of the Catholic Alliance. Perhaps not surprisingly, Fournier has come to like Forbes. He was quoted as praising a Forbes speech at Heritage later last year. "He's striking a chord with the real people, the dock workers, the people who don't shave sometimes and don't look perfect," Fournier says. "It's an amazing phenomenon." Forbes also threw some cash at Heritage, buying two tables for its 25th anniversary dinner after the conservative think tank's journal published his article; his issues group has given between $10,000 and $15,000 to Heritage in all. (Both deny a quid pro quo.) The Heritage folks are impressed. "Here you have the walking embodiment of capitalism saying capitalism is not enough to maintain a free society," says Heritage's Joseph Loconte. "Among religious conservatives, he's going to have a very good showing. It's the right cultural moment for Steve Forbes."

Toward the end of our interview, I asked Forbes if there are any biblical passages he finds inspiring in political life. The question put him on the spot, but he eventually found a suitable response. "There's a quote, not from Scriptures, but Bill Bennett told me it years ago," he said. "Every saint has a past, every sinner has a future." I asked him to elaborate. "It means you can always do better, and you shouldn't cease to try to do better," he said. "Always look to the future, do not be burdened by the past." That idea should serve him well in his next presidential campaign. Steve Forbes has atoned for his sins against the religious right, he has bought himself an indulgence, and he has been forgiven.

Now, in the heat of the campaign, Forbes's purchase of the religious right has the *real* religious-right candidates wringing their hands.

"So, when are you going to write something nice about us?" Gary Bauer's senior adviser, Jeff Bell, chided me during one of his candidate's campaign stops in New Hampshire. Bell's needling is much deserved. Looking back through my stories, I found nothing but gratuitous mockery of the barely five-foot-six-inch former director of a middlebrow Christian think tank who now fancies himself presidential timber.

When Bauer marched in an Independence Day parade in New Hampshire, I observed that he and his aides couldn't even "persuade some spectators to shake the candidate's hand and take his leaflets." When he placed fourth in the Iowa straw poll this summer, I dismissed him as "diminutive," noting: "It is difficult to picture Bauer as a serious prospect." This fall, I mentioned that Bauer was planning a trip to California, "not that anybody cares." Next, I sought to analyze his 1 percent showing in the polls.

In short (so to speak), my coverage of Bauer has been nasty and brutish, and I hereby apologize. To set the record straight, Bauer is a solid, well-intentioned man, a sensible speaker, a fierce debater and a wily candidate. Instead of criticism, he deserves high praise, in particular for the great service he is performing for his country: he is overseeing the demise of the religious right as a political force in the 2000 presidential race. Now, Bell may not consider this a nice thing to say; Bauer, after all, is supposed to be the religious right's hero, not its Czar Nicholas II. But I mean it as the highest compliment. Bauer's candidacy has fragmented social conservatives. And for that, Americans should be grateful.

For conservatives, these are not the best of times. The only serious Republican presidential contenders are George W. Bush and John McCain, both of whom are running as moderates. The Democrats are favored to regain the House, while the fallen Newt Gingrich, his mistress exposed, joins the ranks of GOP hypocrites. The president of Hillsdale College, a conservative beacon, stands accused of an affair with his daughter-in-law, who subsequently killed herself. Senator Bob Smith, applauded by the far right when he quit the godless GOP, dismounted from his high horse and crawled back to the party when offered a committee chairmanship. As the conservative writer David Brooks put it in a *New York Times* op-ed piece, American conservatism is "flamboyantly cracking up."

So, who killed the far right? Pat Buchanan, of course, has done his share by quitting the Republican Party. But at the moment, the greatest damage is being wrought by the Bush-Forbes-Bauer love triangle. George W. has stiffed the conservatives on most issues, throwing them only a few bones. Forbes, his critics believe, is an impostor, stealing votes from more legitimate conservatives. And finally there's Bauer, whose candidacy prevents the right from unifying behind Forbes.

Forbes, if you measure by polls and bank accounts, is the conservatives' best chance against Bush, and he's trying to prove it. Last week, he assembled a group of top conservative activists including Lyn Nofziger, Brent Bozell, Richard Viguerie and Paul Weyrich; calling themselves "Conservatives for Forbes," they plan a road show in Iowa and New Hampshire. Advisers to Forbes dismiss Bauer, a bit too hopefully, as "a nonfactor" and "a wasted vote." Bauer and his followers, of course, insist he's in the race to win. But others attribute another motive to Bauer: he wants to emerge from the race as king of the religious right. The post is up for grabs, with Jerry Falwell and Pat Robertson aging and Ralph Reed quitting the business. "Bauer's not running for president; he's running to be the next Pat Robertson," says Greg Mueller, Forbes's communications director and a former Buchanan operative.

Forbes wants badly to ignore Bauer and gun for Bush. He routinely scolds George W. for his "New Democrat" education policy, his "typical Washington" Social Security plan, his "spending growth twice the rate of Clinton-Gore," his "nothing on the table" health care policy and his China coddling. "There's more to life than fund-raisers," Forbes told the absent Bush at an Arizona debate on November 21, ridiculing the Texas governor for his "teleprompters" and "tutors." When a Bush-friendly group ran anti-Forbes ads, Forbes, in a curious inversion of '96, bemoaned Bush's "negative smear tactics."

But Bush has a surprising ally in his fight against Forbes: Bauer. Bauer hammers Forbes for his free-trade views, calling him the "son of a tycoon" who is "trying to pull a fast one." He charges that under Forbes's flat tax "a lot of Fortune 500 companies would pay zero tax while waitresses, truck drivers and others pay who-knows-what." By pillorying Forbes, Bauer keeps both mainstream candidates, Bush and McCain, from having to contend with a united attack from the right.

To be sure, splits in the religious right are nothing new; even Ronald Reagan wasn't its unanimous choice. But Bauer has enough support in churches to maintain his candidacy until the Republican convention, and Forbes has the money to do the same. That leaves little hope of conservative unity any time soon. "It's not going to happen," Bell says.

Much of the conservatives' disarray can be traced to the craftiness of the Bush campaign, which has cleverly signed on strategists such as Ralph Reed and lured top conservative activists to Austin for the royal treatment. Robertson and other Christian conservative leaders have made a calculation much like the one liberals made in 1992 when they backed Bill Clinton: though Bush isn't one of them, they'll settle for half a loaf in the hope that Bush's administration would be marginally friendlier than Gore's or Bradley's. But to keep these conservatives on board, Bush must tiptoe around delicate issues—hence the increasingly comical scripting of his public appearances.

"No questions," a Bush press aide reminded the assembled media as I caught up with the candidate's entourage here in Stratham, New Hampshire, last week for a tour of the Timberland Company's headquarters. Bush then proceeded through the tour as if he were acting in a short play. In Scene One, he met with a group of young people, telling one of them, "You're an articulate dude." In Scene Two ("OK, let's move on to the next part," the press-handler said), Bush wore safety goggles, inspected a shoe prototype and kissed a supporter. In Scene Three, Bush delivered his stump speech to a captive group of workers. For an encore, he was led to a nearby farmhouse, where he met with locals. Spying reporters in the house, Bush conferred privately with an aide, who asked the journalists to step back and, a few minutes later, declared: "Can we ask all members of the media to exit the house now?" A photographer bristled at the command. *"Sieg heil!"* he muttered as he filed out.

Still, Bush, perhaps stung by the recent doubts about his intellect, felt a need to go beyond his usual script in Stratham. When a Timberland worker asked him about military pay, he wandered off into a display of his vast knowledge of policy: a discussion of the earned income tax credit, marginal rates, and entitlements. "And then, fourthly," he continued, "I want to make sure the education system functions in America." After this dizzying transition, he apologized for his ostentatious display of wonkery. "I took advantage of your question to head off into the wild blue yonder," Bush said. Show-off.

When Bush does reveal himself, his thoughts form a pattern—and it's not a conservative one. The purpose of his visit to Timberland was to praise its sponsorship of City Year, a community service organization that happens to be part of Clinton's AmeriCorps program, which anti-government conservatives loathe. When I asked Bush about this afterward, he replied: "I support a broad range of volunteer programs. This is one approach, not *the* approach." It's this kind of packaging—progressive tendencies wrapped in conservative rhetoric—that has allowed the moderate Bush to subdue the religious right so effectively.

Bush, however, gets only part of the credit for the conservative quiescence. Some of it must rest with Forbes. The departures of Quayle and Buchanan have given Forbes an opening. But his millions haven't won him double digits in the polls anywhere but Iowa, and there he's battling for second place with McCain, who isn't even an official competitor. One explanation for Forbes's slump is that voters are rejecting damaged goods. The Republicans who have been national candidates before—Buchanan, Quayle, Lamar Alexander—have all flopped. But Forbes also faces lingering distrust among the social conservatives he offended in '96, when he dissed the Christian Coalition in Iowa.

Alan Keyes and Orrin Hatch are doing their best to siphon off parts of the conservative vote, too, but with little success. Keyes is too broke and bizarre to be much of a threat, and Hatch is just plain hopeless. But Bauer has enough church-based support and money to make Forbes miserable. Last week, Bauer's campaign spent $130,000 for TV ads in Iowa. Bauer hopes to pick off Forbes for second place there; more likely, all he'll do is harass a fellow conservative.

Yet Bauer soldiers on. Wretched poll ratings? Dim prospects? So what? "Where I grew up, I was taught that if you were in a fight and you were the last guy standing, that meant that you won," Bauer likes to say. But the Republican nomination is not, in the end, a street brawl. It will take a team effort for conservatives to pose a serious threat to Bush, and Bauer so far prefers to play singles.

To nobody's surprise, Bauer flops dismally in Iowa and New Hampshire, with few votes outside his extended family. The only attention he gets is when an online reporter with the flu licks the doorknobs in his campaign office.

And it only gets worse in defeat for Bauer, who decides to back out of the race and support, of all people, John McCain.

Just before Super Tuesday, Bauer was due in Los Angeles to campaign alongside McCain. But at the last minute, the former presidential candidate decided to stay home in Virginia, as one McCain adviser put it, "catching holy hell."

From his own friends, no less. In the conservative religious world Bauer had called home, his endorsement of the Arizona senator was considered an act of betrayal—and that was before McCain gave a speech, with Bauer in the front row, calling Pat Robertson and Jerry Falwell "agents of intolerance." (McCain followed that up the next day by calling the two Christian leaders "evil.")

Suddenly, one of the movement's angels had become a heretic. The organization Bauer had led, the Family Research Council, turned against him. And his mentor, James Dobson, a man he once talked to almost daily, sent out a critical letter without telling him. The research council "has received over 800 calls since Gary Bauer chose to endorse John McCain, and all of them have disagreed with Gary's position," Dobson wrote.

Next came fax attacks from Falwell and others, complaints from old friends that he sounded like a Democrat, and about 150 e-mails from supporters saying some version of "How dare you!"

But the barrage had one obvious upside. Bauer's swift excommunication from the conservative religious movement has achieved the one thing that eluded him during his presidential campaign: attention.

Bauer flopped as a candidate, his support stuck in the single digits. His most enduring moment was an accidental plunge from a stage while flipping pancakes in New Hampshire, where, he jokes, he received so few votes that he knew all his supporters' names. Then, instead of quitting the race quietly, he backed McCain, who tanked.

The last month was just a final step in his departure from the conservative religious orthodoxy. At its most idealistic, it was his effort to salvage a movement and a political party he has come to see as misguided and tainted by money.

"It wasn't just a matter of Gary breaking out of the box he was in. It was getting the religious conservatives to break out of the box they were in," says Bill Kristol, the conservative publisher who is a friend of both Bauer and McCain. Kristol points to Robertson's broadcast business in China as an example. "Seeing Pat Robertson defend unfettered trade with China without mentioning his own interest there, to see Pat totally sell out to the corporate interests of the Republican Party, horrified Bauer and led him to reform instincts."

But a brief campaign scandal made Bauer a laughingstock. Some religious conservatives criticized him for spending too much time behind closed doors with a female staffer. So he held a press conference, with his wife and children, to refute the accusation, giving real attention to a matter nobody had even heard about.

Still, no Bauer miscue could compare to his backing of McCain, a man loathed by the religious right. A partial list of grievances: McCain's campaign finance bill would suffocate groups such as National Right to Life; he said he would respect his daughter's decision on a hypothetical abortion; he agreed to meet the gay Log Cabin Republicans; he admitted he cheated on his first wife.

Then came what Bauer calls "this very unfortunate thing." Bauer had seen a draft of McCain's speech on the plane—he swears he thought he was on his way to a veterans event—but because it had already been distributed to reporters, he couldn't delete anything. He did add some lines, to soften the blow, praising Dobson and Charles Colson. He later defended the speech as making a distinction between certain leaders and grassroots Christians.

The nuance got lost in the uproar. Willing or not, Bauer sealed his fate as a heretic. And in retrospect, he does not regret it. "When I made the decision, my number-one question was what's best for the country," he says. "And in the long term, I'll be proven right."

Now, though, Bauer is no longer welcome at the Family Research Council. Instead, he plans to write speeches, opinion pieces, maybe a book; he even thinks about another run at the presidency. He'll continue to operate his political action committee and maybe collaborate with Kristol, who foresees ominous things for his Republican Party.

"Conventional wisdom is he made a terrible decision," Kristol says of Bauer. "But sooner or later, he will be vindicated. Maybe after November, many religious conservatives will realize getting in bed with George Bush and surrendering to the corporate interests in the party was a mistake."

Meanwhile, Bauer is relearning Harry Truman's lesson, which McCain often cited: If you want a friend in Washington, get a dog. "I don't in any way feel sorry for myself about my fate," he says. "I live in a great city in a wonderful country. My family loves me—and I've got two reasonably good dogs."

18

★ ☆ ★

Keeping Up With the Bob Joneses

Finally, the background noise has disappeared. Forbes, Dole, Bauer, Hatch, Alexander, Kasich and even Keyes (though he won't admit it yet) are all history. After McCain's crushing victory in New Hampshire, the GOP primary battle is a two-man race.

McCain's side is positively giddy. His staff is passing out "Road to Victory" T-shirts with a drawing of the *Straight Talk Express* heading from New Hampshire to South Carolina, scene of the decisive February 19 primary. The McCainiacs, as they call themselves, feel as if the campaign has become a long-running fraternity prank.

On a Tuesday night in February before the primary, top McCain advisers sit down with journalists for a late-night dinner at Magnolias, an upscale restaurant in Charleston, South Carolina. The trouble starts when McCain spokesman Todd Harris hurls a sugar packet at unsuspecting advance man Lanny Wiles. Believing Harris's fib that political director John Weaver threw the sugar, Wiles tosses an ice cube toward Weaver but hits the *Houston Chronicle*'s Cragg Hines. Suddenly, there is a barrage of wine corks, bread rolls and other missiles. Alan Murray, the *Wall Street Journal*'s Washington bureau chief, throws a hunk of bread into Weaver's chest. I see *Newsweek*'s Michael Isikoff launching missiles, and I manage to land a packet of Equal in the wine glass of *Newsweek*'s John Dickerson.

McCain, asked to explain the incident, replies, "That's what happens when you get your staff from prison work-release programs."

At other times, I have seen Lanny Wiles carrying exotic drinks in test tubes and giving attractive young women tours of the bus. Mike Murphy, McCain's flashy sidekick, once invited a female McCain admirer to accompany him and Weaver to dinner in Charleston, but while they were walking down a street, Weaver ducked into an ally and fled, leaving Murphy to contend with the annoying woman himself. Even Cindy McCain, the candidate's wife, conspired with Weaver to dupe her husband: she called McCain on his cell phone to declare that she was having her photo taken sprawling on the hood of a race car painted with the Confederate flag.

Then there's the Spring Hill Lizard, of course. If McCain wins the South Carolina primary, more than a few staffers will attribute victory to the reptile.

The lizard, believed to have mysterious powers, is the property of Wiles, who used it to help Texas A&M beat Nebraska and to force a golfing opponent to miss a $100 putt. He employs the lizard (which isn't a lizard at all but a certain spell cast by wiggling the right pinkie) only on rare occasions. "We use it only if we're at Def Con One," says Weaver.

This isn't the first campaign to honor strange superstitions. During Bill Clinton's '92 run, campaign manager James Carville was known to wear the same underwear for days at a time when things were going well. But this time, there's a new twist: the candidate himself is the leading shaman. He keeps on his person a lucky compass, a lucky feather, a lucky penny and, at times, a lucky rock. He assigns Weaver to carry his lucky pen, a Zebra Jimnie Gel Rollerball (medium, blue), at all times. For added luck, he wears his magical L. L. Bean rubber-soled dress shoes.

"I'm wearing my lucky shoes from today till Sunday," McCain says from his bus on a Wednesday. At the moment, his pockets contain the compass, feather (from a tribal leader) and penny (flattened, in his wallet). When McCain once misplaced his feather, there was momentary panic in the campaign until his wife found it in one of his suits. When the compass went missing once, McCain assigned his political director to hunt it down. Weaver found it, and it remains safe, knock wood.

Primary Day requires additional rituals. Steve Dart, McCain's lucky friend, will fly to South Carolina from California. He has been present with McCain for every Election Day since McCain first won a seat in Congress. McCain must sleep on a certain side of the bed, particularly before an election (and he never puts a hat on a bed: bad luck). Rain is good for Election Day, as are motion pictures. McCain requires himself to view a movie before the vote is counted. He fell asleep in his hotel room in New Hampshire before he watched a movie on Primary Day, but his staff didn't panic. "We have superstition fire walls," says Todd Harris, a spokesman.

That's for sure. Even some foods carry special powers. McCain insists that he and his staff eat barbecue—"our lucky food," says Cindy McCain—

before each debate, sending Wiles out to find ribs or pulled pork even in New Hampshire or Michigan. "It's in the ancient tradition of slaughtering the hog before you slaughter the opponent," explains Murphy.

McCain's staff and family have embraced their candidate's hocus-pocus. Cindy McCain may well don her lucky purple suit, and Rick Davis, the campaign chairman, will likely sport his lucky tie, with the state of New Hampshire on it. Murphy should bring out his magic Hawaiian shirt and "the lucky khaki socks with the palm trees." And Weaver may even send for his lucky football ("I save it for the big enchilada," he maintains). But one thing is for sure: Mark Salter, McCain's chief of staff, will not shave his beard, grown during McCain's New Hampshire surge, until the nomination battle is over.

McCain's superstitions have origins in the military. His grandfather, during World War II, kept a lucky crushed cap, and the whole crew on his ship believed in its powers. "When it would blow off, people would dive for it," says Salter.

McCain himself, when flying in Vietnam, insisted that his visor be cleaned by his parachute rigger immediately before each flight. "A lot of guys are superstitious who are aviators," the candidate says. "It's either a pilot thing or a stupid thing."

Don't tell Jim Merrill it's a stupid thing. Merrill, McCain's South Carolina director, blends secular rituals with the sacred. "I try to hit confession prior to the election—I don't want anything to be blamed on me," he says. Yes, and then what? "I hit one bucket of golf balls in the morning." Merrill didn't observe this superstition during his last race, a gubernatorial campaign, and his candidate lost, needless to say.

Even those who never entertained superstition in their lives succumb to the voodoo. "I've started wood knocking," says John Raidt, McCain's policy guy. "You see everybody else doing it." McCain staff meetings must sound like a game of knock rummy.

McCain and his aides, so absorbed in their supernatural arts, haven't stopped to consider that their practices might seem a bit bizarre to the uninitiated observer. Weaver is surprised such a question would even be asked. "We've never read chicken entrails or anything like that," he says. Pausing thoughtfully, he adds: "Maybe when we get to Michigan . . ."

When I first met John McCain on the campaign trail, in early 1999, it was strictly a low-budget affair. There was only one other reporter—the *New Yorker*'s Joe Klein—and we sat in the back of a minivan with the candidate as his New England director drove us down a bumpy road to a small radio station. Along the way, John Weaver shook his head while his boss fired off one impolitic remark after another.

McCain's rise has been arguably the most exciting story of the campaign so far. And yet I kind of miss those early days when the Arizona senator was still a dark horse. In mid-December, Klein and I again found ourselves in the McCain entourage here in Cambridge, Massachusetts, but this time we were joined by a battery of twelve cameras, a gaggle of reporters and political advisers, and a hall so packed with McCain admirers that overflow signs had to be posted outside to direct latecomers to a standing-room-only section. After the event, we piled onto McCain's coach, which was fully equipped with satellite television, fax machine, leather armchairs, kitchen, couch, and bathroom with shower and telephone. Two Norwegians, a team from National Public Radio, a man from ABC and various other journalists crowded into the back of the bus to talk to McCain, forcing me, Klein and a fellow from the *New York Times* to wait in front for our turns. When the appointed time came, a spokesman emerged to say, with mock gravity, "The senator will see you now."

McCain, who confesses he is fatigued by his endless chat sessions with an ever-growing corps of reporters, also feels a certain fondness for his early, less popular days. "I remember it with great nostalgia," he says. That's no surprise. These days his aides' ears are constantly stuck to their cell phones, and the candidate and his advisers are surrounded at all hours by an insatiable press mob. Well-wishers climb aboard to shake the candidate's chapped hand. "It's a combination of *The X-Files* and *The Boys on the Bus*, says Weaver, surveying the scene on the bus. Chief of staff Mark Salter feels he's losing control of the press beast: "You can't move, you can't go to the head, you can't signal McCain to shut up."

Not that these guys are complaining. The McCain campaign has gone from obscurity to front-runner status in just a couple of months. Early on, McCain's candidacy was fueled by a clever notion: provide abundant access to reporters, and you'll get a bonanza of free publicity. But with the rising poll numbers, crowds and financial contributions come an unwieldy press corps and a cumbersome, full-fledged campaign complete with baggage calls, filing times and press passes. Now McCain is suddenly confronting a new problem: how to behave like a scrappy insurgent when you're the favorite.

McCain is surrounded at all times by cameras, microphones, reporters, and supporters demanding autographs. The minivan has been replaced by two coach buses. McCain's bus, dubbed the *Straight Talk Express* and painted with the campaign's logo, is now often trailed by a press bus, nicknamed *Bullshit One* by staff wags. Reporters are given laminated "credentials" to wear around their necks to identify them as part of McCain's traveling entourage. At an event in New Hampshire not long ago, McCain aide Todd Harris proudly showed me the lengthy manifest for the next day's bus tour, including such luminaries as the anchor of the *CBS Evening News*. "Dan Rather!" Harris gushed. "On the bus manifest!"

McCain Inc. has become so huge a conglomerate that the candidate risks losing the authenticity label that has propelled him so far. He is another big-time pol now. He doesn't hold events; he performs "stunts." "How can you, with a straight face, say this is not a political stunt?" was the first question out of Ted Koppel's mouth as he moderated the McCain-Bradley campaign finance event in Claremont, New Hampshire. It was a stunt, to be sure, although the blame was as much Koppel's and ABC's as McCain's. The evergreen woods in the on-screen background turned out to be potted shrubs. When there was a technical glitch, Koppel told the candidates to repeat their answers, saying, "We can pretend that none of this happened." Who's performing stunts now, Ted?

But Koppel doesn't need to come off as an ordinary guy. By contrast, a politics-as-usual appearance could blunt McCain's challenge as he enters the political big time. His appeal depends in large part on his ability to talk directly and frankly with reporters, who then give him favorable coverage. And he is struggling mightily to keep this up. When I hitched a ride on the *Straight Talk Express*, McCain was obviously tired; when the bus took a wrong turn, the candidate lost any hope of getting some down time without reporters before his next event. "I'm keenly aware that the fundamental mistakes of campaigns are done under fatigue," he said. Still, he added, "I can't change. The one thing is, don't change." And so, since he doesn't have time to service all the eager journalists these days, he rotates them through his bus, and some must settle for conversations with his staff. He has so far refused security, another potential barrier between him and the press. "I won't take security. I don't need it . . . I don't want it," he told me.

The senator's laid-back personal style is about to collide with presidential-contender reality. But McCain keeps trying. As reporters crowded around him on the bus, he went through his usual shtick, as he had a hundred times before. He talked on the phone with his wife and children. He clowned with his aides. And he didn't refuse a single question—even when a Norwegian reporter asked, "Are women interested in you?" He talked about sports ("I'd watch the Thumb Suckers play the Bed Wetters") and about his dislike for the French ("Queen Victoria said the poor will always be with us. Well, the French will always be with us"). When a reporter asked him how he keeps up his energy, he deadpanned, "I throw a temper tantrum." I asked if it helped to hurl chairs. "Throw a few chairs, bust a window, beat up on my wife," he said. The reporters dutifully scribbled it down. McCain's spokesman, overhearing his boss, put his hand to his face and shook his head in disbelief. For a moment, it felt like old times: we were back in the minivan, McCain was still in single digits and everybody was having fun.

I'm sitting on a park bench with John Weaver outside a McCain event in Spartanburg, South Carolina. We've heard the speech too many times before, and it's too boring to face it again. But late in the event, Mark Salter comes running from the auditorium, his face a mixture of outrage and delight. "A woman in the crowd got an earful last night on the phone about how McCain is a hypocrite and a liar!" Salter shouts to Weaver. Weaver dashes inside. "Find that woman!" he calls.

This, both men believe, could be a turning point. Bush, as McCain has already learned, is taking a much tougher line against McCain now that it's a two-man race, attacking the senator daily and shoring up his conservative base with such ill-considered events as a visit to Bob Jones University, known for its racist, anti-Catholic views. And now this: Bush (or at least his campaign) caught red-handed telling an impressionable Boy Scout that McCain is a liar.

The fuss begins when Donna Duren tells McCain and an auditorium of people that her teenage son, whom she says regarded McCain as a hero, had received a telephone call that described the senator as "a cheat and a liar and a fraud." "He was push-polled," Duren tells the audience, using the terminology for negative calls made by political campaigns. "He was so upset." After describing the contents of the call, she adds, "I was so livid last night I couldn't sleep."

McCain seems genuinely upset by Duren's story and promises to call her son later today. As he leaves the auditorium, he holds a news conference to denounce Bush.

"I'm calling on my good friend George Bush to stop this now. Stop this now," McCain says. "He comes from a better family. He knows better than this. He should stop it. I'll pull down every negative ad that I have. . . . We're not in the business of harming young people."

The Bush campaign says it's been making calls to voters, but not using the language of hypocrites and liars. To back up its claims, the campaign releases a script of the message, which says that the South Carolina race "has turned ugly" and blames McCain for "negative campaign tactics" and ads "comparing Governor Bush to Bill Clinton." The script also quotes South Carolina Senator Strom Thurmond, a Bush supporter, condemning McCain.

Weaver isn't satisfied. "Any staff that would be low enough to make calls like that is low enough to have a phony script and lie about it," Weaver said. Bush rejects McCain's demand to halt the attacks, claiming the Arizona senator is guilty of the worst excesses.

This, ladies and gentlemen, is what we've been waiting for. Bush, backed into a corner, has gone on the attack, and it's working. He's dumped the Mr. Nice Guy routine, and he's attacking McCain directly. He's also simultaneously accusing McCain of being the nasty guy, the same strategy he used so well against Forbes.

Since the candidates left New Hampshire ten days ago, the campaign has fundamentally changed character and now threatens to leave both candidates sullied before one emerges with the GOP nomination. This is good for Bush, because, as McCain's Murphy puts it to me, "when there are two pigs in the mud, it's hard to tell them apart."

The mudslinging particularly hurts McCain, because he has an above-the-fray reputation. The McCainiacs figure Bush's negative campaigning will suppress McCain's support by making voters disenchanted while rallying the conservatives to Bush. And they're almost certainly correct.

Both candidates have been running attack ads, with Bush airing spots criticizing McCain's ties to lobbyists and accusing McCain of misrepresenting Bush's tax cut plan. McCain has been running ads implying that Bush would be as untrustworthy as President Clinton.

Bush has been laying the groundwork for a tough, negative campaign in South Carolina for some time—even before he lost in New Hampshire. It begins in January, in Sumter, South Carolina. And it's being carried out by men such as Jim Gunn.

From the moment Gunn swings his blue Ford wagon into the parking lot of Big Jim's coffee shop in Sumter, there is no mistaking this man's priorities. One clue is the decal on his car from the Citadel, the military academy his granddaddy and 15 other relatives attended. Another is the sticker from the Camden Military Academy, his son's alma mater, just up the road. There's also the U.S. Marines sticker, the POW-MIA sticker, the American Legion ("paid-up-for-life member") decal, and the special-issue veterans license plate with the American flag.

Gunn's person is similarly adorned. He wears a Marines pin on his lapel, and scars from Korea on his scalp. "My head looks like the road map of Chicago," says Gunn, who directs a retired veterans organization here, a group started by a pilot who served as a prisoner of war in Vietnam with John McCain. Gunn—that's Sergeant Gunn to you—is a walking cliché, and proud of it. "I'm the guy who eats tacks for breakfast," he tells me at Big Jim's. "Had 'em in my cereal this morning."

It would seem natural, then, for Gunn to back McCain, the war hero—turned-senator-turned-presidential candidate. But then you would have to ignore two other items that appear on Gunn's bumper: twin "George W. Bush for President" stickers. It's true: Gunn is backing a National Guardsman.

"John McCain did a lot of heroic things. I'm not knocking him," says Gunn, as he and a friend, sipping coffee in Big Jim's, prepare to do just that. "But he's presenting himself like he's the only one who suffered in the military. McCain is saying, 'Because all these things happened to me, you've got to vote for me.'"

Strange though Gunn's disloyalty to his fellow warrior may seem, it's not half as odd as the explanation: Sergeant Gunn is convinced Captain McCain, a protégé, of Barry Goldwater, is some sort of liberal.

"He's just like Clinton and Gore," says Gunn. "He's not part of the solution. He's the problem." On abortion, for example, McCain is "a jerk," Gunn ventures, despite his anti-abortion voting record. "It's murder, it's destroying our country, and McCain isn't strong on this at all." Of the senator's vociferous support for campaign finance reform, Gunn says, McCain "is taking away my rights as a free-thinking American—and this is what I laid my life down for." McCain is even a dud on veterans and military affairs, according to Gunn.

Call it the McCain Mutiny. Veterans like Gunn are causing problems for McCain with his most crucial constituency. As the state's February 19 primary approaches, Bush's soldiers are doing their best to convince veterans that McCain isn't conservative enough for them. The charge is questionable. But, ominously for McCain, it appears to be sticking.

Warren Tompkins, Bush's man in South Carolina, boasts that the campaign's polling shows Bush is getting a larger share of veterans here than McCain. And McCain aides don't dispute there's a problem. "We probably don't have as much of the veteran vote as we should," says Phil Butler, a retired colonel who has just been named McCain's veteran coordinator in the state. "People don't know who he is, and secondly, there's some misinformation out there." There sure is. People here have somehow swallowed the implausible notion that McCain is Ted Kennedy in a flight suit.

The town of Sumter, in central South Carolina, is dominated by Shaw Air Force Base, just down the road. At McCain's town-hall meeting today, eight posters of the former Navy flier in uniform adorn the walls inside the hall, and McCain himself enters to a Sousa march. The introduction is a standard one: how McCain was shot down over Hanoi, how he spent years in solitary confinement. McCain starts off by praising a local man who served in Operation Desert Storm, and introduces a man in the crowd "with whom I had the privilege to serve in the Hanoi Hilton." He jokes about how he "intercepted a surface-to-air missile with my own plane."

McCain talks at length about World War II veterans. "The good news is we're beginning to appreciate them," he says, trumpeting Tom Brokaw's best-seller *The Greatest Generation* and the box office hit *Saving Private Ryan*. "The bad news is we're not taking care of them. We're not giving them the health care we promised them." This generates the first applause for McCain, and he follows up with a similar line: "How are we going to get another generation of Americans to serve if we don't take care of those who already have?" The applause gets louder. He promises to restructure the veterans health care system. "It's the highest priority," he says to more applause.

Speaking at another event, in Camden, McCain stands in front of a larger-than-life poster of himself in his flight suit. Red, white and blue balloons form arches over his listeners, many of whom are wearing their veterans caps. "It is a national disgrace," he says of the veterans health care system. Then it's a call for higher military pay. "There will be no food stamp army when John McCain is president of the United States," he shouts. Next, he blasts Clinton's national security team, "not one of whom has ever spent one minute wearing the uniform of this country." He closes by telling the veterans in the crowd, "I am honored to be in your company."

The crowd loves it. "I've got to vote for a military man," says Jennifer Neitzel, wearing a McCain sticker on her Air Force sweat shirt. She served in a medical unit during Vietnam and has two sons in the military. Bob Wolf, an Army veteran of Korea and Vietnam, walked into the McCain office in Columbia recently to offer his services. Asked why, Wolf talks at length about McCain's capture by the Vietnamese and all the gory details of his ordeal: the broken limbs, the stab wounds. "He's proven he can stand up to anything, being a prisoner of war for five and a half years," Wolf says. "He's proven he's a man."

To make sure all South Carolina veterans get those details, McCain has named veterans coordinators in each of the state's 46 counties, all reporting to Butler, an artillery battery commander in Vietnam. The campaign has sent out mailings to veterans ("I ask you to join me for one last mission"), has distributed a nine-minute video to veterans' households, and will call at least 50,000 veterans. On January 26, a group of McCain's fellow prisoners from the Hanoi Hilton will begin a three-day bus tour of the state. Lindsey Graham, a popular South Carolina congressman who backs McCain, has been touting the senator as "the conservative who will stop Bill Clinton's betrayal of our military." Graham thinks the message will get out. "He's literally their commander," he says. "I've seen people come up to him and salute him."

Harder to explain are the many veterans who leave meetings with McCain unsatisfied. In Sumter, several of those filing out of the McCain meeting voice their displeasure.

George Thom, a prisoner of war in Germany during World War II, isn't impressed with McCain's military appeals. "I put in 187 days in solitary confinement, one piece of bread and one glass of water a day, so I have a good idea of what he's been through," says Thom. "But I'm going to vote on the issues. I want to know what he's going to do, not what he did." Thom came to McCain's speech with a business card listing his concerns: base closures, survivor benefits and military health care. But McCain's answers don't satisfy. "I think I'll go to Bush," he concludes.

His difficulties with veterans don't surprise the candidate himself. "You've got to proceed on the premise that in '92 and '96, Bill Clinton took the majority of veterans' votes," he says. "The Bush people were astonished back in '92—I was with him—saying, 'How come these veterans aren't rallying to our side?'"

There are about 400,000 of them in South Carolina, potentially enough to dominate the Republican primary, in which only about 300,000 people are expected to vote. But only about 100,000 of the 400,000 are registered Republicans, and they don't vote solely on veterans affairs any more than, say, Jews vote solely on policy toward Israel. Even in a best-case scenario, Richard Quinn, McCain's South Carolina consultant, hopes to pick up two-thirds of the 100,000 Republican veterans and register up to 40,000 more in time for the primary.

But so far, McCain doesn't have the numbers he needs. And a lot of that has to do with George W. Bush, whose campaign has been waging a successful propaganda war here. Searching for a fire wall to contain McCain's conflagration in New Hampshire, where the senator leads in the polls, the governor has settled on South Carolina. This is one of the most conservative states in the Union, and its veterans are among its most conservative constituencies. Bush, therefore, has been doing everything he can to appear more conservative than McCain—on taxes, gay rights, abortion and campaign finance.

Never mind that the idea of Bush as arch-conservative and McCain as bleeding heart is preposterous. The "liberal" McCain has received ratings of 76 percent to 93 percent from the Christian Coalition in recent years for his Senate record; he has opposed gay employment rights, the Clinton budget and gun control while backing missile defense, a balanced budget amendment and Clinton's impeachment. The "conservative" Bush, meanwhile, is blamed by some Democrats for ripping off their education, technology and defense policies.

Still, the McCain-as-liberal image spreads. "McCain is a Democrat-Lite," says Wayne Cockfield, a disabled Vietnam veteran who sits on the board of South Carolina Citizens for Life. Cockfield's group spreads vitriol about McCain because of "flip-flops" on abortion and campaign finance reform, which the group calls a "free speech restriction act." "I'm a pro-lifer," Cockfield says, "and most pro-lifers in this state are supporting Bush." (McCain's Senate votes received rankings ranging from 80 percent to 93 percent from the National Right to Life Committee, but he has antagonized some anti-abortion activists by saying they are mainly interested in perpetuating conflict over the issue.)

The McCainites are well aware they're being outflanked on the right. Congressman Graham, his conservative credentials secured by his impeachment heroics, has been braving pneumonia to vouch for McCain in appearances in the state. "You get conservative interest groups attacking him, and when y'all guys"—that's the media—"treat him with respect, it makes people think he's a Democrat."

Another problem is that many veterans hold McCain, because he is a veteran, to a higher standard than other candidates. If anything has gone wrong for veterans in Washington in recent years—and plenty has—why not blame McCain? Bush, after all, wasn't anywhere near Washington. McCain, therefore, feels veterans' wrath for cutbacks in the medical services available to retirees at military bases and for substandard Veterans Affairs hospitals. Some object to McCain's efforts to improve relations with Vietnam. Some POW-MIA activists have even convinced themselves that McCain is covering up the truth about the missing—perhaps because he was brainwashed by his captors. "They're just mad," says Weaver.

At Big Jim's, Blane Lawson, a retired Air Force man, confesses he doesn't know much about the issues, but he says Gunn has convinced him that "Bush would be more conservative than McCain."

Even Big Jim Karvelas, the coffee shop's proprietor, gets an earful. Karvelas is only vaguely aware that the candidate is coming to town. "What's his name, McNair?" he asks. The conversation turns to McCain's wartime heroism, and Karvelas seems to be coming around. "I might vote for the McNabb," he says. "If he's a war hero." Gunn, however, will have none of it, and Karvelas backs down quickly. "Oh," he tells Gunn, apologetically, "I thought you were for him."

★ ☆ ★

Now, after McCain's New Hampshire triumph, Bush's hard-nosed attempt to paint McCain as a liberal toughens every day. And McCain is hitting back just as hard.

Bush hits McCain for past votes in favor of public financing of elections. (Bam!) He says McCain "says one thing, does another." (Splat!) McCain accuses Bush of "savagery." (Bop!) "They've got 200 staffers trying to comb John McCain's voting record," the Arizona senator says. (Pow!)

Behind the sparring, something important has happened. Bush has regained the offensive, and McCain is in the awkward position of answering attacks. McCain is peppered by reporters on his bus with questions the Bush campaign has raised about his Senate record. McCain said some of his moderate votes in favor were necessary compromises. "That's the essence of legislation," he said, arguing that Bush is doing the same thing to him that Steve Forbes did to Robert J. Dole in 1996. (And it worked.)

Bush, at a news conference, takes issue with McCain's complaint. "How can he call it savagery if the man made five votes, legitimate votes, on the floor of the Senate?" the Texas governor asked. "It's not savagery, it's what we call full exposure, full disclosure."

But Bush keeps up the attack. Saying Republicans want to "get rid of the Clinton era, not reinforce it," he calls McCain's views on some issues closer to Clinton's and Gore's than to his own. "There is no clear philosophical difference on tax cutting between Vice President Gore and John McCain," Bush charges.

Bush and McCain are comparing each other to President Clinton, someone akin to Lucifer here in South Carolina. "The Washington establishment is in a panic mode, and loading all their guns, and shooting all they can," McCain says at one event. The senator says that Bush is an "agent of the status quo" because he "refuses to address campaign finance reform."

Bush says Republicans should not doubt his toughness, pointing to his 1994 victory in Texas over incumbent Democratic Governor Ann Richards. "Am I tough enough to win?" Bush asked rhetorically. "I guess my answer is, just ask Ann Richards." McCain, meanwhile, is the one now trying to make peace. "We're not having anything to do with negative campaigning," he says at one event. "I hope the people of South Carolina will reject that." Even his aides say that's a huge risk.

McCain promises to pursue a campaign "all of our supporters and friends can be proud of." But he knows that's probably not a winning campaign, and he doesn't rule out the possibility that he would run ads featuring victims of the "push poll" calls he says Bush partisans have been making, encouraging South Carolinians to vote for Bush by giving negative information about McCain. "We'll do ads [in which] we talk about the value of positive campaigning," he says.

Bush, to his credit, shows no sign of easing up. Greeting supporters after a town-hall meeting, Bush agreed when State Senator Mike Fair told him that he needs to go after McCain's "soft spots," but he added, "I'm not going to do it on TV."

When the McCain camp learned about what Bush thought was an off-camera remark, McCain's Weaver tells me on the bus, "It's clear that he is talking about some effort to discredit or defame John McCain, and if he is not going to do it on television, what other way does he have but the telephone?"

Privately, McCain aides say they're hearing about phone calls from Bush supporters that go over the line: things about Cindy McCain's drug use, allegations that she has mob ties, charges about an abortion in the McCain family and accusations that McCain has illegitimate children. This, by any measure, is an attack gone too far, but there's no evidence Bush is behind it.

McCain voices hope that the alleged Bush tactics will backfire. "It's amazing, the number of people" who have told him they're switching to him because of the attacks, he tells me. At each stop on a cold and gloomy Saturday, another victim of Bush push-poll calls steps forward, first at a home that McCain visits while going door to door in a neighborhood here, and then at a NASCAR race in Darlington. There, a man named Ed Cheek tells his story. "I didn't like it," he says of the call. "I called and complained to Bush headquarters."

But McCain is beginning to realize that whining about being attacked isn't enough to blunt the attack. He admits he can't compete with Bush's TV campaign, which he said "may be the largest buy in the history of South Carolina." McCain claims he's being outspent "seven, eight, ten to one."

He suggests that if Bush were to gain an ugly victory that turns off the electorate and keeps independent voters away from the primary, he would hurt GOP hopes in November. Reaching out to Reagan Democrats, according to McCain, "is the way you govern, and that's the way you win general elections."

Perhaps, but this is still a primary. And Bush has found the right formula: tough, harsh attacks that expose weakness in policy and character. McCainiacs continue to hope that South Carolinians will miraculously reject the Bush method, but they know from experience this probably won't work.

On Primary Day, I check in with Dan Schnur, McCain's communications director, just after noon, to get the results of the first wave of exit polls, the ones that can't be broadcast until the official polls close. "The early results are notoriously unreliable, and that's a good thing," Schnur says. McCain is down by about 10 percent. And it won't get better.

McCain, thus dethroned in South Carolina, will revive briefly in Michigan a couple of days later, but the damage is done, and his aides know that Super Tuesday will be his last day in the race before heading to the red rocks of Sedona, Arizona, to pack it in.

Part V

★ ☆ ★

Spring 2000
Bush Wins the Silly Season

19

★ ☆ ★

Veep of the Week

The polls had just closed in California on the night of March 7, Super
Tuesday, and the predicted Gore sweep had happened. I filed my story,
went off for a couple of whiskies with Tennessee Congressman Harold
Ford, Jr., and then made my way back to the bar at the Loew's Hotel in
Nashville. There sat a senior Gore aide advising a group of reporters (off
the record, of course) on which person Gore might select as vice president.

It seemed absurdly premature, and the names mentioned—Frank
Raines, Dennis Archer, Bob Rubin, Zell Miller—seemed outlandish. But to
my amazement, those very names began appearing in press reports in the
coming days. The veepstakes was on. And so, I decided to play.

The game is pretty easy: get somebody to mention a name, and add
the name to the speculation. There's no way to knock down speculation—
Gore and Bush won't comment or make their choices for another four
months—and there's little penalty for being wrong, because everybody will
forget that you had said back in April that Wayne Gretsky would be the
next v.p. (Somebody actually picked him, though his Canadian birth would
require a constitutional amendment to get him through.)

I decided to start my own cottage industry in v.p. picking. It would be
called Veep of the Week, "your headquarters for groundless vice presidential speculation," and each week a new candidate would be mentioned.

April 5. Welcome to Veep of the Week, in which we respond to mindless
and irresponsible speculation about possible presidential running mates
with . . . more mindless and irresponsible speculation. This week's pick:
New Jersey Governor Christine Todd Whitman. Her name has been
floated by an "administration source" (the White House chef?) to *Time*

magazine as a running mate for Al Gore. But of course: a woman and a popular governor, Whitman would be a brilliant choice for the Democrats.

There are a few wrinkles. Whitman, astute readers will recall, is a Republican. She has endorsed George W. Bush. But these are not insurmountable obstacles. Perhaps Whitman is playing hard to get—a clever effort to land herself on the Democratic ticket. Let's ask her spokeswoman, Steffanie Bell:

"I'd have to, you know, uh, I'm just sort of stunned, that's my gut reaction."

See? Not a denial! It's Gore–Whitman in 2000.

APRIL 13. Surgeon-cum-Senator Bill Frist may be nationally invisible, unlike fellow Tennessee Senator Fred Thompson. He's perhaps best known for saving the life of the Capitol gunman. But give him this: in the delicate art of running for vice president, Frist is first.

It all began when reporter Clint Brewer of the *Lebanon* (Tenn.) *Democrat* reported "talk" of Frist as George W. Bush's v.p. Never mind that such talk was generated by people suspiciously close to Frist, among them his former chief of staff. The senator himself slyly confided to Brewer that he'd "heard the talk, too" (What big ears you have, senator!), and the Frist boomlet was born.

When Bush, at a campaign event with Frist in Tennessee, was asked about the possibility, "Frist laughed and feigned a double-take," according to the *Knoxville News-Sentinel*.

Feigned is right. For this triumph of self-promotion, Frist is our Veep of the Week.

APRIL 22. It is unjust that it has taken so long in the vice presidential mentioning game for one of the most promising Democratic contenders to get his moment. But it has finally happened: Parris Glendening has made the list.

In recent days, news reports have said the Maryland governor "is angling for a position in a possible Gore administration" and is "confiding to intimates that he hopes to be Gore's running mate." What a fine idea! This could be Maryland's best contribution to vice presidential politics since Spiro Agnew (unless Barbara Mikulski throws in her hat).

Glendening, a charisma-challenged former professor, isn't an obvious pick. He's a semi-popular, low-profile governor from a state Gore should win anyway. Maryland's Democratic Senate president once likened him to a baboon. But give Glendening this: if Gore wants somebody who absolutely, positively will never outshine him, he has found his man.

APRIL 28. Colin Powell exhibits no interest in being George W. Bush's vice president, yet he is among the candidates most mentioned. Why?

Look carefully at the general's demurrals—(it helps to do this after a drink or two) and you'll see he is not, to any degree of epistemological certainty, ruling out a run.

"He stands by his 1995 decision not to run for president and is not seeking an elective office," says his spokeswoman, Peggy Cifrino.

Yes, but he could be tapped for vice president without seeking the office.

"I doubt he would."

So he's not ruling it out?

"He's very happy and engaged in his youth crusade."

Unpersuaded by this non sequitur, we looked up Powell's recent denial. "I have no desire for political office," he said. Hounded further, he responded, "Since I last heard, the vice presidency is an elected office, so it falls into that same category."

Hmmm. The vice presidency falls into the category of something he doesn't desire—but something he might do if pressed? We returned to Cifrino. "I don't want to speak for him," said the spokeswoman.

But we do. Powell has left himself a loophole big enough to drive a vice presidential motorcade through.

MAY 6. The talking heads have been chewing up vice presidential frontrunners at an alarming rate. The Elian fracas led Chris Matthews to strike Senator Bob Graham from Al Gore's list. Senator Evan Bayh was riding high until Patricia Ireland decreed him "a bad idea." When Governor Tom Ridge suggested that the GOP change its abortion platform, Fred Barnes labeled his comment "dumb."

But fear not. The veep pool perpetually replenishes itself. George W. Bush just named Dick Cheney, his dad's defense secretary, to lead the search for a vice president—and, notably, didn't rule out the searcher. This brings to mind Warren Christopher, who led Clinton's Cabinet search and made off with the State Department.

W. called Cheney "as solid a citizen as America has ever produced" and declared, "I trust Dick Cheney's judgment." So Bush should have no argument when Cheney, after exhaustive searching and intensive screening, determines that none of the prospective candidates holds a candle to . . . himself.

MAY 10. John McCain, asked this week if there's anything that could convince him to become the Republican nominee for vice president, replied, "Nothing that I can imagine."

George W. Bush mistakenly took this as a lack of interest on McCain's part. But perhaps it's just a lack of imagination. If Dubya were to throw in some sweeteners, we feel certain McCain could imagine himself on the ticket. Bush could:

—Move the vice president's office to the White House press briefing room.

—Reserve a parking space on the South Lawn for the *Straight Talk Express.*

—Adopt campaign finance reform and tell McCain, during the inaugural address, "You the man."

—Hire McCain's favorite band, Nine Inch Nails, to perform at state dinners.

—Name Pat Robertson to the new post of ambassador to Antarctica.

McCain's office, asked about these potential sweeteners, declined to comment. What? A "no comment" from McCain? He must be reconsidering.

MAY 20. Fifty-seven percent of Americans characterize the Bush vs. Gore campaign as "dull," according to a CBS News–*New York Times* poll.

We need somebody with pizazz to liven up the ticket. We need a little excitement. We need . . . George Pataki.

Consider the balance and intrigue George E. could bring George W. Whereas Bush was Yale '68, the New York governor comes from a different era: Yale '67. Before politics, Pataki did fascinating work as—now get this—a lawyer! On Wall Street!

He has experience: a big-state governor and one of Peekskill's best mayors. And how about that Pataki humor? He's another Jay Leno. "I wouldn't go that far," says his spokesman, Mike McKeon. "He's a serious man who takes his job seriously."

The explosive Bush–Pataki combination would be unstoppable—unless Gore picks Evan Bayh. Picture it: The first all–St. Albans ticket against two Georges from Yale.

MAY 27. When it comes to veeps, Al Gore has a woman problem. He needs one to keep the gender gap intact. But who? Dianne Feinstein? Risky. Kathleen Kennedy Townsend? Inexperienced. Barbara Mikulski? Short.

One woman, however, has it all. She's a 40-year-old Harvard graduate, a noted feminist, a diva of the environmental movement, a nursing mother and a Native American. Her name? Winona LaDuke.

Gore must overcome the fact that LaDuke is already Ralph Nader's running mate on the Green Party ticket. But if Mr. Earth in the Balance could prevail, he might win back voters out West who plan to vote Green.

Gore spokesman Chris Lehane issued the following statement after hearing LaDuke's name: "I don't know her." Told more, Lehane added, obligingly, "From what you describe, she would bring many strengths to any ticket."

Would LaDuke be receptive? "It's worth asking," she says. But, she adds, "I won't stay by the phone. I've got a few errands to run this afternoon."

June 3. In the battle for No. 2, William Cohen has just launched a major escalation. The defense secretary, already a routine mention on v.p. lists, blasted George W. Bush's military plan on *Meet the Press* and offered to brief the governor. When Bush declined, the Gore campaign crowed: "It's frightening that Bush . . . refused a briefing from the U.S. secretary of defense."

What's really frightening is how craftily Cohen, a Republican, has made himself an ideal Democratic veep candidate. Cohen made Bush look wimpy on war while giving Al Gore a bipartisan cloak. And he's a one-man melting pot: Jewish father, Irish Protestant mother, African American wife. Maine isn't an electoral mother lode, but surely this Bangor boy could beat a Kennebunkport kid at home. And how about the benefit of having a published bard on the ticket? "It would add to the already poetic tenor of the campaign," says Gore spokesman Doug Hattaway.

Still, should the Democrats try to beat the Republicans by running one? Bush spokesman Ari Fleischer sighs: "It'll only be a matter of time before Al Gore reinvents himself again—as a Republican."

June 16. Poor Tom Ridge. Once he was the most mentioned of GOP vice presidential candidates. Now, conservatives such as James Dobson and the *National Review*'s editors are trashing the Pennsylvania governor, and the whisperers who traffic in v.p. speculation are striking him from the list.

This is a travesty of a mockery of a sham. Ridge is an ideal veep: a moderate from a swing state, a six-foot-two, broad-shouldered, Bronze Star–winning, all-American guy. Even *National Review* Editor Rich Lowry raised his Ridge opinion after beholding his "sheer physical mass" in person. "There's a magnetic sort of thing going on," Lowry confides.

Here's Ridge's problem: he's just a guy who can't say no. Were he to rule out being veep, as ex-Senator John Danforth did and Senator John McCain did—again—this week, the ensuing media frenzy would demand his nomination. Apparently, nobody told Ridge the drill: Be coy. Appear not to want it.

Instead, Ridge is begging to be No. 2, even lending his name to a Bush press release yesterday attacking Gore's economic record.

It's not too late, governor. Just say the magic words: "No, thanks."

June 24. As the Captain Ahabs of the press continue their quest for the Great Veep, the *Philadelphia Inquirer* has landed an alarming scoop. A Bush adviser, the paper says, hinted that the actual nominee "might not be among those publicly mentioned" so far.

This is troubling, considering that media outlets have named most every conceivable Republican choice, from the usual suspects (Representative John Kasich) to the up-and-comers (Representative Chris Cox) to the dark horses (Wayne Gretzky). Is it possible the real veep hasn't been "publicly mentioned"?

Yes, actually—until now. The *Post*'s Tom Edsall, speaking this week with Tom Daschle spokeswoman Ranit Schmelzer, learned that the Senate Democratic leader has been traveling in Texas. Asked whether those travels might take him to Austin, Schmelzer replied, "Don't you know? He's on the list." So that's what the Bush adviser was hinting about. It's Bush-Daschle in '00.

JULY 1. Why is Nebraska Senator Chuck Hagel so high on George W. Bush's veep list? Some point to his Vietnam heroism. Others cite his ties to John McCain, with whom he shares a maverick's knack for antagonizing Trent Lott.

But there's a better reason to pick Hagel: lineage. Hagel, it turns out, has nominal ties to Georg Wilhelm Friedrich Hegel, the nineteenth-century German philosopher. Hagel's great-great-grandfather was a German named—get this—Friedrich Wilhelm Hagel.

Admittedly, that's the extent of the relationship. Still, Bush's selection of such a famous name would answer complaints that he doesn't value intellectual heft. Bush could then adopt as his platform the Hegelian dialectic, which influenced Karl Marx. (Bush doesn't have to brag about that part.) Gore, to keep pace, would be forced to launch a desperate search for kin of Immanuel Kant.

A modest Hagel claims his ancestors were "poor peasants." But he does quote a philosophy passed down by generations of Hagels: "Don't worry about the mule. Just load the wagon."

Is that a metaphor for the Republican ticket?

JULY 8. The veepstakes is getting religion. George W. Bush, the veep-whisperers say, likes a fellow named Frank Keating, who is allegedly the governor of the so-called state of Oklahoma. His main qualification: he's a Catholic who sticks closely to the Vatican line on abortion.

While Bush flirts with Catholics, Gore woos Jews. On his list, speculators speculate, are Senators Joe Lieberman of Connecticut and Dianne Feinstein of California, and former treasury secretary Robert Rubin. Defense Secretary Bill Cohen is also in the hunt, but he doesn't count: he gave up Judaism when his rabbi requested a ritual circumcision before his bar mitzvah.

It's nice that the candidates care so much about minority religions. But they would be bolder to skip mainstream religion entirely and name a Scientologist. Gore, specifically, should choose John Travolta. The man already played a presidential candidate in *Primary Colors*. And just this week, Gore bemoaned his own lack of dancing skills.

For that, Travolta is just the ticket.

July 15. George W. Bush continued his vice presidential head fakes this week, posing with Tom Ridge in Pennsylvania, George Pataki in New York and Christine Todd Whitman in New Jersey. (No, she didn't frisk him.) But don't believe any of it. The man Bush really wants is Strom Thurond.

That's the signal Dubya has been giving this week. First, the Bush campaign put out a statement in Thurmond's name saying that Al Gore is "no Harry Truman." Then, the *Post*'s Michael Powell gave Bush spokesman Ari Fleischer every opportunity to distance Bush from Thurmond's white separatist past, even a teensy bit, but Fleischer wouldn't do it.

This all makes sense. The 97-year-old Thurmond has everything Bush craves. Maturity? He's twice the age of Representative John "Pick Me Please" Kasich. A military record? He was a paratrooper on D-Day. Foreign policy experience? Refer to his over-the-top support of the Bay of Pigs invasion. Extemporaneous speaking? His 20-hour filibuster set a Senate record.

Most of all, Bush wants a No. 2 who won't upstage him. Again, Strom is perfect. He'd spend most of his term napping.

July 22. The veep speculation industry is in chaos on the eve of the GOP convention. NBC likes Dick Cheney. *USA Today* has a hunch about Lamar Alexander. The *Dallas Morning News* is talking up Richard "The Animal" Lugar. Virtually everyone continues to be mentioned—even John Danforth. In other words, after four months now, the speculators are right back where they started.

John McCain, earlier named Veep of the Week for his crafty nondenials, is once again tweaking his old nemesis, George W., by letting word slip that he would take the job, after all. McCain is gambling that Bush would rather lose the presidency than pick an insubordinate No. 2 who would turn the entire West Wing into a briefing room and doughnut dispensary.

No, Bush needs a more loyal v.p. than McCain would be. He needs a man with Washington and foreign policy experience. He also needs a win-at-any-cost man who has a proven ability to outshine Gore and to steal Gore's credit for the economic boom. Bush especially needs a deputy whose words can discredit Gore in the press. Yes, you've guessed it: Bush needs Bill Clinton as his veep.

Now, as we reach the moment of truth, the veepstakes speculation has reached a crescendo, and even the candidates themselves are toying with the press. Asked recently what his biggest challenge is in the selection process, Bush replied, "Making sure information doesn't leak out."

"There's just a lot of wild speculation in Washington, D.C.," Bush said, professing his sympathy for reporters under pressure to produce news about the selection. "I feel for you. I really do."

Now, finally, it has happened. Bush has picked Cheney and Gore has picked Lieberman. Not to crow too loudly, but Veep of the Week picked 'em both. Cheney was the man back on May 6, and Lieberman was mentioned on July 8 (although he lost Veep of the Week honors to Travolta). But this achievement is not entirely one to be celebrated. The purpose of the Veep of the Week was to parody the selection process with fanciful choices. Now fantasy is reality; the selection process is a parody of itself.

20

★ ☆ ★

Air Trump and UFOs

This is the dead time of the campaign. The Democratic and Republican nominees are clear, but it's months before their coronation. What's a political journalist to do? He can speculate on vice presidents, of course, but I've already done that. Or he can go off in search of third-party candidates, the blessed souls who believe their talents too great for our two-party system.

I've known there would be such a dry spell in the campaign, so I've been nurturing my sources in the loony-tune community for some time. We begin at the Reform Party's national convention in Dearborn, Michigan, in the summer of 1999, where things are getting desperate. Why, Reformers wonder, doesn't anybody want the party's presidential nomination? Jesse Ventura, who missed his speaking slot at the convention because bad weather grounded his flight, calls to tell delegates they shouldn't even think about nominating him. Colin Powell won't do it, and Donald Trump and Pat Buchanan don't seem serious about it, either. Ross Perot now seems too goofy to be credible, and Lowell Weicker, who is seriously considering it, is hardly a franchise name.

But those who fear for the Reform Party's future haven't met Erik Thompson. A quiet, bearded man in blue jeans, Thompson approaches me at a reception and offers me his business card. "Candidate for President, Reform Party," it reads, along with his name and slogan: "No War Now!!" Candidate Thompson tells me that the combination of his message (abolishing the standing army) and experience (three months in a federal penitentiary for trespassing at a nuclear installation) should give him a 30 percent chance of winning the Reform nomination. "I'm going to do what Jesse did in Minnesota," he vows. Ventura's victory has made Thompson giddy. "What if I win?" he wonders excitedly.

Thompson won't win, however, unless he's able to conquer the indomitable Jerry Beck. "I am the front-runner," says Beck, who ran as an independent in 1996 but with "not very good" results. (He claims to have made the ballot only in his hometown of Windsor, Missouri, which is not legally possible.) This time Beck plans to go all out. "We have a full political seminar set up, and we take five musicians with us," he boasts. Beck's chief rival is Charles Collins, who has no musicians but does have a big idea. "You could eradicate $6 trillion in a single day," he tells me, simply by buying the stock of the Federal Reserve so "you wouldn't have to pay the debt." Collins, holding forth poolside at the Hyatt Regency, says his scheme would cost $462 million, and he has a 1966 letter from Senator Russell Long to prove it. Collins would also "triple GDP in one year" with a simple plan: eliminate all taxes.

Still not sold? Consider pulling the lever for Harvey Carroll, Jr., who totes around a campaign sign painted by his brother and hands out business cards on photocopy paper. He ran for the state legislature as a Democrat but became a Republican during the Bush years because, he believes, he was secretly directing Bush's foreign policy by faxing advice to the CIA and the State Department. "I actually put words in both Bush's and Gorbachev's mouths," he says, then hesitates. "This is sort of classified. If you can water it down, that's cool."

This, unfortunately, is becoming the story of the Reform Party. Ventura's gubernatorial victory has convinced party members that just about any wild scenario (such as a Trump candidacy) is now possible. The party's ballot access, along with $12.6 million in federal campaign funds for 2000, has attracted the usual assortment of characters: note perennial left-wing fringe candidate Lenora Fulani's interest. At the convention, a fellow mutters to himself as he circulates a petition for low-power radio stations. After one press conference, a party member shouts about "goddamn Communists" and about how the CIA killed JFK. Odd characters always show up at conventions, of course, but here they seem to *be* the convention. I expect to find water fluoridation protesters at any moment; one reporter whispers during a session, "Where's the UFO meeting?"

One of Ventura's strategists explains that the loons who have been drummed out of the other parties have flocked to the Reform Party, and it has yet to weed them out. "I have been banned from all Democratic bulletin boards because I dared to discuss issues," reads an e-mail on one of the Reform Party listservs, which are full of rants. "I have been stopped from posting to any Republican bulletin board for the same reason." Thus another Reform Party activist is born.

Reformers seem incredulous that their star, Ventura, won't run for president. "Sorry folks, it's not going to happen," his website proclaims.

And yet they yearn. Max Shaffer, dressed up as Uncle Sam in a beard, top hat and matching bow tie, wears his "Draft Jesse" button, like so many others who have gathered in Dearborn. "He's been an actor for how many years?" Shaffer asks. Maybe he's just faking his lack of interest now. Or maybe not. Trump, likewise, has ignored calls and faxes to his office from Tim Whitcomb, a Reformer who seeks to draft the millionaire. But this hasn't stopped Whitcomb, who's declared himself a "co-chairman of Trump 2000" and has been distributing fliers in Trump's name. The rump Trump committee even rents a "hospitality suite" for Friday night, and a rumor spreads that The Donald is coming. But all that's in the suite are several plastic bowls of peanuts and pretzels, a few gallon jugs of Inglenook wine and some disappointed delegates.

Trump isn't the only celebrity with unauthorized supporters here. One woman from New Jersey collects signatures to draft Ralph Nader (she has ten when I meet her), and another woman is drafting Buchanan (she has four). Ted Turner has some fans here, as does former Oklahoma Senator David Boren. Boren's booster, Oklahoma Reform Party Chairman Greg Brown, grabs me in a headlock and puts his hands around my neck, urging me to "see the light." He allows me to leave after I accept an autographed copy of a Boren endorsement he wrote for the *Norman Transcript*. Nearby is a booth to draft Colin Powell. "We're going to get a million signatures," says Drake Beadle, the man at the table. How many so far? "Just these," he says, showing me 16 names. The next day, the Powell contingent hosts a press conference. "Many of you have asked me why we would do this, since he has said he would not run," the self-appointed chairwoman begins, and it goes downhill from there. Any pipe dream, it seems, is possible. "Why not have a ticket of Jesse Jackson and Pat Buchanan?" asks Robert Bowman, who, like a dozen or so convention participants, is running for president himself. (In his candidacy statement, he identifies himself as "Most Rev. Dr. Robert M. Bowman, Lt. Col. USAF, Ret.")

Actually, Buchanan, however zany his views may be, is probably the Reformers' best fit. He appeals to the Reagan Democrats alienated by their party's free trading and to the religious conservatives alienated by Republican front-runner, George W. Bush. The party needs a big name to keep its public money for 2004, when Ventura might run. "If we don't have a 5 percent vote in 2000, the money's gone and the party's over," says Whitcomb, the unrequited Trump admirer.

There is, to be sure, something noble about the Reform Party gathering, with its clear message of power to the people. If only each one of the people wasn't demanding quite so much power. Everybody in the Dearborn Hyatt, it seems, is running for something; every person is a would-

be governor, senator or president. Their campaigns are all the more perplexing because none of them actually wins. One fellow hands me a card
with a smiley face announcing "Wierzba Wierzba '99," a husband-and-
wife team running for mayor and a borough council seat in their New Jersey town. A man from Florida running for the Senate distributes photos of
himself with former President Reagan. Walking out of one session, I am
approached first by a Minnesota Senate candidate, then by a man who just
ran for governor of Ohio. He stands with a beer-bellied friend, and I ask
if the friend is running, too. "No," he replies. "I'm a kingmaker."

The amateur quality gives the convention the feel of a student government meeting, right down to the cash-and-carry lunch. As the convention begins Friday night, two men walk into the display hall with what
looks like an enormous dead bird but turns out to be the party mascot, an
eagle. Its wings, packed in a separate cardboard box, have yet to be assembled, and the stand has yet to arrive, so the bird carcass is left belly-up
on the exhibition room floor while TV cameras film it. It seems an
apt metaphor for the party's bush-league feel. Pat Benjamin, running
for party chairman, distributes pamphlets stating that she's "got the
resources" for the job, because she had a second phone line installed in her
home and "she also bought two more computers." On Saturday morning,
the convention erupts into a bitter floor fight between two groups both
claiming to be the New Jersey Reform Party.

The convention's finest moment comes neither from such antics nor
from Perot's address but from the speech of an 89-year-old campaign
finance reformer known as Granny D. At the podium Friday night, she
stokes the true populist themes that unite the otherwise divided party.
"Democracy is something we do not have because we cannot speak," she
preaches. "We are shouted down by the bullhorns of big money." Granny
D. compares Michael Eisner to Khrushchev and Tito as the crowd erupts.
The devotion to campaign finance reform is the party's noblest trait, and
yet the party only exists because of Perot's millions; the only reason it
remains relevant is the $12.6 million it has for 2000. Though the speak-
ers, one after the other, attack the establishment attitudes of the other two
parties, the Reform Party itself looks similar. An upstart member, Jack
Gargan, backed by an upstart patron, Ventura, is running for party
chairman against the establishment favorite, Benjamin, backed by the
party's founder, Perot. It's little different from the struggles of Bradley
vs. Gore or Everybody vs. Bush. Gargan, in a press conference, accuses
the party establishment of shutting him out by refusing to give him a full
list of delegates.

The contest for party chairman is crucial. If Gargan wins, Ventura is
free to recruit a big-name candidate; if Benjamin wins, Perot will likely

choose the candidate—namely, himself. On Saturday night, Perot delivers a typical stump speech, saying he's willing "to participate in any constructive way." I doubt that means licking envelopes.

In the end, though, there's a refreshing difference between the Reformers and the Democrats and Republicans: the Reform Party, true to its roots, elects outsider Gargan over insider Benjamin. Alas, the new party chairman is not exactly free of the crazy-aunt problem. A retired financial planner and unsuccessful congressional candidate, he lives, as the *Washington Post* reports, on Florida's Cedar Key because it will be safer during the depression and anarchy he's expecting. "You've got to come 24 miles down that road to get here," Gargan has said. "You could defend the No. 4 bridge and only let in friends and relatives, or no one at all."

But Gargan himself isn't important. What matters is that Perot's stranglehold on the party has been broken, and that bodes well for its chances of finding a serious candidate in 2000. Still, Gargan will carry on at least part of the Perot legacy. The new chairman, I notice at Gargan's press conference, has enormous ears.

My quest for the third-party candidate, the Perot of 2000, next takes me to California, in the fall of 1999. This is a hardship assignment. I am posted in a $340-a-night room at the Beverly Hilton Hotel, wearing a terry-cloth robe and slippers. I just had a soak in the hot tub beneath the palm trees and lounged poolside in a cabana. Yesterday, I strolled on the Santa Monica and Venice beaches. In a couple of hours, Angel, the hotel's driver, will take me on a complimentary stretch-limousine ride down the street to a reception, where I will sip Chardonnay with Dustin Hoffman and, more important, Warren Beatty: the next president of the United States.

My plan to travel to the Beatty event in the hotel limousine proves a bit awkward. As Angel and I approach the hall, I see dozens of cameras at the entrance. As I try to sneak away from the limo, I get a call on my cell phone from my mother, who has just seen me on *Rivera Live*. Presently, there is a barrage of flashbulbs, and I hurry to catch a glimpse of Beatty. But it turns out to be Larry Flynt, who has just emerged from his Bentley (license plate: HUSTLR). Shortly before seven o'clock, the time for maximum exposure, Beatty, trailed by Garry Shandling, arrives with Annette Bening. He wades through the scrum and greets George Stephanopoulos, who is posing as a journalist, notebook and all. In the strobe light of flashes, I can see the inevitable merging of political and celebrity journalists into one indistinguishable mob.

Then, disaster. The Beatty event is being hosted by Americans for Democratic Action (ADA), an increasingly marginal group of liberals and one not accustomed to attention. The tickets arrive late, and there aren't enough tables, causing many guests to have to wander around hungry. "If they run a campaign like this, we're lost," says George Winard, an older ADA member who has been searching for seats for himself and his wife for more than an hour. I spy Marc Cooper of the *Nation,* and we agree that this is what the world would be like if liberals were in charge. At just that moment, Dustin Hoffman approaches us, drink in hand, to deliver a Beatty sound bite: "If he were in Nixon's position, he would've burned the tapes. If he were in Bush's position, he would've had a better line than 'I was out of the loop.' If he were in Clinton's position and he got a blow job from his intern . . ." Well, you get the idea.

The proceedings feature a video of Roseanne describing the would-be candidate as "a nice piece of ass." Norman Lear declares, "I'm here to endorse what could be a powerful populist voice." But the powerful populist is noncommittal and self-indulgent. He calls himself an "unrepentant, unreconstructed, tax-and-spend, bleeding-heart, die-hard liberal Democrat." That ends his candidacy, and he knows it. "I have no problem professing this," he says, "because I love my day job—making movies. I want to keep on making them." He proceeds to deliver a sermon about the rich-poor gap and the "slow motion coup d'etat of big money's interests." Legitimate issues. But if the situation is so dire, then surely Beatty will run. Nope. "Keep the spirit," he tells us. Thanks, Warren.

It is now winter, and I still have not found a third-party presidential candidate of any stature. But there are rumors that Donald Trump will be making a campaign swing through California. I sign up for the trip.

Ridiculing Donald Trump—billionaire, presidential candidate, lounge lizard—has become so easy that it is no longer sporting. *Doonesbury* recently featured Trump squeezing a busty blonde and reciting his stump speech: "Biggest! Best! Me! It's unbelievable! Biggest! Mine! Tallest! Biggest! Me!" The *New York Times*'s Maureen Dowd described him as a "high-rolling plutocrat," and the *Weekly Standard* called him a "Chump on the Stump."

I have come west determined to be contrary: I will take the developer and his nascent presidential candidacy seriously. It isn't easy.

First, there's the problem of Pee-Wee. A Yorkshire terrier of slight proportions, Pee-Wee is the pet of Roger Stone, Trump's political consultant, and Stone's wife, Nydia. The couple has placed Pee-Wee in a piece of luggage and taken him aboard Trump's 727 for the California tour. But Pee-Wee proves to be a logistical nightmare for Trump's Australian advance woman, Diane, who is overwhelmed by a 35-person press contingent. While Diane herds the journalists, the Yorkie escapes from his bag and runs wild on the press bus.

Then there are Pee-Wee's owners. Back in 1996, tabloids linked the Stones to ads, in various swinger publications, seeking group sex. There were photos of her in a black negligee and him bare-chested, and there was an enumeration of her personal measurements. Stone said he had been set up, but he was forced to step down as an adviser to the Dole campaign.

And finally there is the vehicle for Roger Stone's rehabilitation: Donald Trump himself. An incorrigible show-off, Trump delights in taking us aboard his plane (the one with the winged "T" on the tail and a mirrored headboard over the bed) for an utterly unnecessary, 15-mile flight from Los Angeles to Long Beach. Those who drive to Long Beach arrive a full hour before we did.

Yet, despite these obstacles, I am still determined to take Trump at his word. The guy says he's willing to spend $100 million on his Reform Party bid, and that would knock out Pat Buchanan. He has scheduled a press conference with Jesse Ventura, the Reform kingpin. He has hired signature firms to gain ballot access. He has done polls.

And he is shaking hands. A germ freak, Trump has said he doesn't want to touch the diseased masses. His campaign passes out half-ounce bottles of hand soap, with Trump's website address taped to the necks. On board his plane, though, Trump walks up to me and extends his hand. It is a good, firm grip.

As part of his California trip, Trump tours the Simon Wiesenthal Center, where he is led from one disturbing display to another: hate speech, Bosnia, Rwanda, the civil rights struggle, the Holocaust. But Trump seems detached, focusing his attention on the presentation rather than the content. Shown a video of a racial confrontation, he remarks, "Good actors." He spends an hour or so wandering around the exhibits, muttering "fabulous" and "unbelievable" and "brilliant execution" and "extraordinary" and "outstanding." The mood is occasionally broken by Roger Stone's telephone, which plays the *Grande Valse* whenever there is a call.

After a guide asks the TV cameras to leave, Trump quickens his pace, galloping through the Warsaw Ghetto and the Holocaust in about three minutes. Rejoined by the cameras, he slows down and is handed a guest book to sign. He pauses thoughtfully, as if searching for the perfect sentiment, then scribbles two words in the book: "Great Work!" He underlines "Great" three times and dots his exclamation point with a loop. He then contrasts his own tolerance with the "racist" views of his potential Reform opponent, Buchanan, whom he links to Hitler. But even here Trump sounds like a developer. He marvels that Hitler came to power "so brilliantly." Fabulous! Great work, Adolf!

Later, in Anaheim, Trump delivers a speech at a motivational conference for 20,000 entrepreneurs. Before his talk, for which he earns $100,000, Trump paces backstage. I can make out the first sentence of the handwritten text: "All my life I've been successful." It goes downhill from there. Trump notes that he flies the Concorde, owns the Empire State and General Motors buildings, and likes the United Nations because "it's right next to my 90-story building."

In private, Trump isn't as bad. He talks plainly and plausibly. Asked about the debates, he says he was appalled by Bush's showing. "And they say I'm not prepared?" he marvels. Furthermore, when you look at the policy positions Trump has taken so far, he's amassed a fairly sensible agenda: more regulation of tobacco and alcohol, no more soft money, no Social Security funds in the stock market, a missile defense system and universal health care.

But if Trump is serious about his run, he'll have to make his candidacy less about himself. In other words, he'll need to undergo a personality transplant. Recently, he met with Reform Party activists and, inexplicably, insulted them. Asked about the Reform Party platform, Trump ridiculed his adopted party. "Nobody knows what the Reform Party platform is," he said, eliciting boos and prompting one activist to offer him a copy of the document. Trump sounded every bit the plutocrat running on a populist ticket. If he wants to be taken seriously, he'll have to lose the limousine with the 1ALPHA license plate, the mirrored headboard on the 727 and the phone that plays the *Grande Valse*. If he's really serious, he might even think about finding a kennel for Pee-Wee.

In the middle of 2000, the election year, the Reform Party is no better off, little closer to having a candidate than it was in 1999. Ventura has quit the party in disgust. Leaders have been overthrown, then their overthrowers overthrown. Buchanan, after he dropped out of the Republican Party and went Reform, seemed to have things locked up. But at the Reform Party convention in Long Beach, which was to be a Buchanan coronation, a rump faction (or is Buchanan's the rump faction? Too many rumps in this party) bolted and set up its own convention across the street, with its own delegates and its own nominee. Now the Reform Party has two presidential candidates, a fierce battle over the $12.6 million in federal funds, and no known voters.

As a large-eared former presidential candidate might say, the crazy aunt is out of the attic.

This week, at the Alexandria Hilton just off I-395 outside Washington, D.C., the party of Ross Perot is becoming the party of His Holiness Maharishi Mahesh Yogi. Perot is not in attendance himself and neither is the Maharishi, a Hindu guru from India who created Transcendental Meditation and the accompanying skill of "yogic flying." But the remnants of Perot's Reform Party who have opposed Pat Buchanan's hostile takeover have formed a "coalition" with the Natural Law Party, founded eight years ago by followers of the Maharishi.

It's not an obvious match: the party of inner peace and tranquillity has united with the party of red-faced shouting and fierce litigation. Jim Mangia, leader of the anti-Buchanan Reform faction, says the sound of the two parties merging will go something like this: "Ommmmmmmm—point of order!"

The Natural Law Party, being based on meditative calm, calls in its platform for "conflict-free politics. . . . the Natural Law Party advocates an end to negative campaigning and partisan politics."

By contrast, the anti-Buchanan Perotistas split with the Buchanan wing of their party at their own convention in Long Beach a few weeks ago in a melee reminiscent of a fistfight in the Taiwanese legislature. They're now fighting Buchanan in the courts, at the Federal Election Commission and in most every state to determine which faction is the real Reform Party.

Despite last month's party split, the Reform people here are in a marrying mood and think the two parties—the non-Buchanan Reform Party and the Natural Law Party—will soon be one. Some state Natural Law parties have already changed their names to Reform, Mangia says. "At next year's convention you may see a full-fledged merger."

But they'll have to iron out a few differences in philosophy. Like the role of yogic flying, which involves "hopping," "hovering" and finally taking to the sky. The process is said to lift the practitioner's body off the ground by an inch and possibly move it forward a couple of feet. It may also bestow powers of invisibility and immortality.

"I don't know anything about yogic flying, but I had a sled, an American Flyer, when I was a kid," says Russ Verney, once Perot's right-hand man and now in attendance at the Natural Law convention as part of the Reform delegation. "I have nothing against people thinking peaceful thoughts," Verney says.

Lenora Fulani, the far-left activist who joined with Buchanan, then turned against him, says she has not learned to levitate. "I don't even know what meditating is," she says, "but I support everybody's right to do that."

And who knows? Fulani is open to learning the ways of the Maharishi. "I'm looking," she says. "Politics is stressful."

You've come to the right place, Ms. Fulani. The Natural Law Party platform states the following useful information about Transcendental Meditation, or TM: "Research has found that EEG brain wave coherence increases dramatically during TM-Sidhi Yogic Flying. . . . Forty-two scientific studies have shown that such coherence-creating groups (constituting as little as the square root of 1 percent of the population) promote highly significant decreases in violent crime and other negative tendencies and increases in positive social and economic trends."

The platform offers meditation as an answer to virtually every policy question, including education, crime, health care and drug abuse. Foreign policy? "The Natural Law Party would support the establishment of groups practicing the Transcendental Meditation . . . in key areas of the world. These programs have been uniquely effective in dissolving social stress and preventing the outbreak of armed hostility and war."

Revitalizing inner cities? "The establishment of coherence-creating groups practicing the Transcendental Meditation" would lead to "significant reduction in negative tendencies, such as crime, violence, sickness and accidents, and a strengthening of positive social and economic trends." The party also calls for the United States to create a group of 7,000 meditation experts "engaged in creating coherence throughout society."

Doug Friedline, Jesse Ventura's campaign manager and an old Perot guy, just signed on to manage the Natural Law presidential campaign without reading the platform. As such, he was surprised when he heard somebody ask the candidate, John Hagelin, if he could fly. "He said no," Friedline says, reassured.

The Natural Law folks are trying to move their agenda beyond the mystical. As such, their convention was so conventional as to be dull, with long speeches on preventive medicine, alternative fuels and school innovation. There was an oompah band playing patriotic marches, a stage with stars and plants, and delegates arranged by state.

"We're just finally trying to have a political party that's got a lot of issues," says Robert Roth, the party's spokesman.

Roth insists the Natural Law Party isn't linked to the Maharishi's Natural Law parties in various foreign countries, though party members have participated in international conferences and the U.S. party shares some platform planks with the Maharishi's International Council of Natural Law Parties, formed in 1992.

Still, Roth says the party isn't concealing its roots. During a Q&A with delegates, Hagelin explained that he started meditating at age 17, when he was in a motorcycle crash and an orthopedist recommended it.

He later found that meditating cleared his head to study physics. A physicist, he has taught at the Maharishi University of Management in Iowa.

And the original Natural Lawyers say the party can't shed its philosophy. "This party can't deliver what it promises without that," says Valerie Janlois, a TM instructor from northern California. She ran for Congress as a Natural Law candidate in 1992, gaining 33 votes. She admits to being "angry about not being able to convince people about this very simple mental technique." But she doesn't look angry. She looks perfectly serene. Jane Meade, another party original and a fan of meditation, says, "I don't think it can ever get lost. It's the main thing."

Hagelin, in his acceptance speech, didn't mention meditation directly, but he did note that "the unified field percolates infant universes at the rate of 10 to the 143rd per cubic centimeter per second." Cosmic.

Perhaps this is just what the pugilistic Reformers need. In speeches to the Natural Law convention, Mangia compared Buchanan's candidacy to Hitler's rise in Germany (take a deep breath and exhale slowly, Jim) and Fulani declared that "Pat Buchanan is a criminal element" (think happy thoughts and repeat your mantra, Lenora).

Will these political warriors find inner peace and harmony in Natural Law? As the Hagelin 2000 slogan says, "Anything's Possible."

21

★ ☆ ★

Gonadal Politics

All across Washington—nay, all across political America—a plaintive cry is being raised: What do we do now? We have been sentenced, cursed, to suffer eight months of Bush-Gore, or simply Bore. No McCain, no Beatty, no Ventura, no Trump: just two cautious, uninspiring establishment figures facing off in the longest presidential campaign in history. "I'm bored by it and I'm disgusted by it," says Bernie Palicki, a retired engineer who works in the hardware section of the Home Depot in Huntsville, Alabama. "Is this the best we can do?"

Afraid so, Bernie. It's a two-man race now. All the papers say so.

But Palicki knows this is not true. And he can prove it empirically: Palicki himself is running for president. He formed the Spirit of '76 Committee to Elect Bernard Palicki (Bernard Palicki, treasurer) and registered with the Federal Election Commission as a candidate. "I'm still in this race," the candidate says. In fact, the only thing standing between Palicki and the White House is a little respectability. "All you have to do is quote me," he says. "Write me up in the *Washington Post* and I could be on a roll."

Consider it done, Bernie. Palicki believes that certain corrective actions need to be taken in the federal government, and he has therefore created the Corrective Actions Party (actually, an Internet site dubbed it that, but Palicki uses the name because he hasn't come up with anything better). His main issue is the New World Order (he's opposed). Friends, Palicki tells me, say, "Bernie, knock off the New World Order stuff," but he won't hear of it.

Instead, Palicki blames the media for his lack of success. "It's their fault—they're not looking at these other guys," he says. Meantime, "these bozos"—that's Bush and Gore—"are getting free publicity."

The man has a point. Those who declare this a two-man race are clearly not doing their homework. The FEC has a list of 211 Americans who have announced their candidacy for president. Although some of the more marginal candidates among the 211, such as Elizabeth Dole and Bill Bradley, have quit the race, many others are still going strong. Well, maybe not strong, but going. Among those who have filed with the FEC are Clay Hill of the Populist-Democratic Viking Party, one Samuel B. Hoff (slogan: "Get Aroused"), Caesar Saint Augustine of the Get Even with the State-Federal & Local Level Committee, and the nominee of the Charles E. Garinger We Give a Darn About Our Fellowman Committee.

Just before Al Gore on the FEC's alphabetical list is Benjamin Gleitman, c/o Benjy's Presidential Dreams and Hopes committee. If that sounds too modest, you might prefer Freddy Irwin Sitnick, whose committee is called Messiah for President. Hard to vote against that. Still, Mensa members might pull the lever for the guy on the Genius at Work ticket, while golfers will be pleased to know there's a candidate under the National Tee Party banner. Taking the long view? Consider the Julian Starr for President in 2016 committee. There are Greens, Libertarians, Socialists, Reformers and Natural Law regulars, to be sure, but also campaigning this year are candidates for the Buffalo Party, the Internet Party, the Veterans Industrial Party and, simply, Mike's Party.

I confess to a certain weakness for Jeff Costa, whom I met at one of the primary debates in New Hampshire. He was wearing a red cape and red lobster-claw mittens. Turns out Costa is campaigning for president as Lobsterman on the Crustacean Liberation Party ticket. Lobsterman has a banner that reads "Lobsterman for President 2000," but he apparently forgot to run his spell-checker—the banner states that he is a "Crustacian."

Inexplicably, Costa was not allowed to participate in the presidential debate, so he had established himself in a parking lot across the street, where he projected a Lobsterman campaign video onto a brick warehouse wall. "These people think they have denied me the opportunity to speak to you!" Lobsterman bellowed. "Why? Because these people are called the mainstream. The Lobsterman does not come from the mainstream. The Lobsterman comes from the ocean, the home of the crustaceans. . . . Puritans—remember them? Were they mainstream? Uh-uh. I don't think so." Costa, who is a professional wrestler when he's not campaigning, went on to discuss his platform. "We don't have a problem with gun control," he declared. "We have a problem with maniac control." Apparently so.

While it is debatable whether these fringe candidates deserve publicity, it is undeniable that the lack of it is what's keeping them on the fringe.

"The media is taking it on themselves to say there's only two parties," claims Edison McDaniels, 76, whose answering machine says, "This is Edison McDaniels, candidate for president of the United States." "Nobody else gets the publicity, and when they print something, they print it in a kooky fashion so it makes the challenger look like a fool."

This has got to stop. The inattention has all but destroyed McDaniels's presidential aspirations. He hatched a plan to take a train from his home in San Bernardino, California, on a cross-country trip to "speak to every hamlet and village" about his candidacy. He put this on the Internet and pleaded for money for his big ride: "For the sake of America, and the future of your children, GIVE!" But nobody gave. Now there's no train.

"The presidential election game is a fraud," grouses McDaniels, one of seven candidates vying for the Libertarian nod in July. One opponent, David Hollist, plans to abolish taxation in favor of "contract insurance." His website offers reflections on a variety of subjects, including, "One sunny day, I stepped into an outhouse" and "I am a thinking animal." Another Libertarian, L. Neil Smith, has a warning on his website: "Not everybody likes L. Neil Smith. Some folks find that he sends them into shivering conniption fits." Talk about high negatives.

If the mainstream candidates seem a bit timid, don't despair. Among those who have stated their intentions to the FEC, most every position can be found. Al Hamburg of Wyoming, whose campaign photo shows him in a military helmet, proposes giving "all dopers and illegal aliens" ten days to move south of the border, or else they "would be sterilized and forced into Mexico." David McReynolds, a Socialist, takes a different tack. He would impose a "maximum wage" of four times the minimum wage.

Some candidates are quite obviously acting on a lark. Jim Taylor (slogan: "Because everything is crappy") is making a film about his presidential quest: *Run Some Idiot.* His platform includes a 30-hour workweek. Another contender, David E. Wyatt, scheduled a campaign swing through the Eastern states. "If you are planning a party or just want to party with your future president, please e-mail me and I will try to be in your neighborhood around that time," he wrote on his website. "I love to party!"

Others seem more serious. "I've been stumping primarily in the Midwest," said Joe Bellis, who formed America's Party and wants to kill income taxes and most government programs. "My California organization is trying to arrange some speaking engagements." The California operation consists of a college poli-sci student making some calls. Bellis has spent $60,000 of his own money, he says, but hasn't raised any. This has forced him to postpone the bumper sticker rollout. "I've got a design for one," he says. "I'm waiting for some money to come in so I can print them."

Least viable of all are those candidates who declare their candidacy on the Internet but don't bother to mention anything to the FEC. Two gentlemen, Bruce and Mike Muckian, have superimposed their photos over the White House with the catchy phrase "The Mucks stop here." More earnest is Stephen Gaskins, who hopes to challenge Ralph Nader for the Green Party nomination. "I want it to be understood that we ARE a bunch of tree huggers and mystics and peaceniks," his statement says. He adds: "My main occupations are Hippy Priest, Spiritual Revolutionary, Cannabis Advocate, shade tree mechanic, cultural engineer, tractor driver and community starter. I also love science fiction."

For the long-shot candidate, no amount of discouragement can kill a presidential dream. Consider bookstore owner Heather Harder, a Democrat who boasts she's so tough she has "leather ovaries." Harder plans to stay in the race all the way to the convention in August. "Right now, it looks good for Al Gore," she allows. But, she adds, "there's still a lot of excitement out there, and anything could happen before the Democratic convention." She claims she fought her way onto the ballot in Arizona and Minnesota and is now working on New Jersey. Still, she toils in obscurity. "The whole process is biased," she complains. "Wake up! How many people have heard me?"

Maybe more than she realizes. Harder, in a campaign statement, declared that her belief in UFOs was so strong that "no amount of government denial" would sway her. "Daily hundreds, and perhaps thousands, of contacts are being made which prepare us to meet our cosmic neighbors," she wrote. "We must begin now to prepare for open and direct contact with many extra terrestrial beings."

If only Harder could register them to vote, Gore would be in serious trouble.

It is a sad commentary on this election year that the only plausible third-party candidate with a reasonably stable party is that too-familiar face, the Green Party's Ralph Nader, whose '96 campaign went nowhere and whose 2000 campaign promises to go only slightly further. I catch up with Nader at Occidental College, a small liberal-arts school here in Los Angeles, which should be fertile ground for Ralph Nader's presidential campaign. The campus is so politically correct that it boasts having the first non-sweatshop clothing zone in its campus bookstore. When Nader comes to speak, the college president introduces him by comparing him to Martin Luther King, Jr.

And yet, when the 66-year-old consumer advocate finishes his favorite lines about "government of the Exxons, by the General Motors, for the

DuPonts," a student rises to ask why Nader's issues reflect "white, middle-class interests," not gay, nonwhite or youth concerns. Nader retorts, "There's plenty of injustice for everyone, isn't there?" The applause goes to the questioner, not to Nader.

"He doesn't talk about poor people very much—he talks about cars," complains Susannah Straw-Gast, an Occidental senior. "He is speaking to the white middle class." Straw-Gast, who wears a bandanna and a tattoo and participated in the protests at the Democratic National Convention, should be a natural Nader supporter. But if the election is close, she says, "I'll vote for Gore."

A swing with Nader through California finds similar doubts at almost every stop. In San Diego, a caller to a public radio show hosting Nader complains that he represents "white progressives" who don't care about race. In Santa Barbara, Neil Coffman-Grey carries a sign protesting a Nader remark denouncing gay concerns as "gonadal politics" and another sign declaring "Vote Nader, Elect Bush." Coffman-Grey says that on gay issues "Gore is more progressive."

Al Gore more progressive than Nader? Nader an anti-gay candidate indifferent to the poor and minorities? It seems absurd on its face, and yet it haunts Nader.

Herein lies a cruel irony: Nader is failing to rally the far left for the same reason Gore failed. Many in the badly fragmented left wing are suspicious that Nader is soft on some of their favorite causes: civil rights, animal rights, gay rights. And many on the left, rejecting Nader's argument that he's the only untainted candidate in the race, don't want him to sink Gore and elect Bush. Gore, after all, has proved happy to pander to special interests of the left.

Not Nader. His only enemy is the corporation. "The left has become heavily concentrated on identity politics—gender, race and homophobia," Nader says. "It's devolved itself into grievances. Slights are magnified, and they tend to implode on themselves. It's a real dilemma."

Particularly for him.

High in the hills over Santa Barbara stands a gated manor with a commanding view of the Pacific. You can sit by the pool, listen to the fountains and gaze into the valley. Or you can park your car near the Mercedes, Jaguar and Volvo in the driveway, where a golf cart is available to take you to a fund-raising party inside. Here, a corporate chieftain is hosting guests who paid between $100 and $1,000 to attend.

The occasion for such luxury? Why, it's a fête for Nader, scourge of corporate America, patron saint of consumer protection. Last night, Nader, celebrated for his monastic frugality, slept here. He stands behind leather furniture to give his speech—then hands off to an aide, who asks for more money.

"I'm not a revolutionary; I'm a business guy," says the host, Russell Palmer, a recording equipment executive who calls himself a Republican. "I don't want to tear things down, and I don't believe he does, either. He's a legitimate guy." Back in the 1970s, "we saw him making strong and surly comments on TV," Palmer says. "I thought he might be that older surly guy—but he's not. What a gentleman!"

Huh? First the lefties are calling Nader anti-gay and anti-poor, and now a wealthy Republican is calling him a gentleman? This can't be right.

Ah, but it is. As he runs for president this year on the Green Party ticket, Nader is doing many things that seem a bit out of his ascetic character. It's not that Nader is changing his behavior but that his presidential campaign is showing the world that Nader was never the cultural hermit that myth made him out to be. He eats fatty foods at midnight, he breaks the speed limit, he watches television and indulges in air conditioning.

At a fund-raising stop at a San Diego home ($250 per person for a buffet of rolled tofu tacos, soy cheese quesadillas and vegan cookies with carob chips), he grants his hostess's request for a photo of him in a '64 Corvair—the car he vanquished in *Unsafe at Any Speed*. "You see what I do for a campaign?" he asks, as the cameras click. "I want to put it in my scrapbook as an example of how far I'll go."

If some vehicles are unsafe at any speed, all vehicles are unsafe at certain speeds—including the Nader campaign van at 90 mph. Nader has only one hour and ten minutes to travel the 144 miles from San Luis Obispo to Salinas. When his van driver cranks the speedometer over 90, Nader protests gently: "You can't go over the speed limit."

When an aide in the van urges the driver to step on it, Nader puts his hand to his face in mock horror. "Let it be recorded that I object," he says. The driver slows. The aide tells him to put the pedal to the metal. "You're contradicting my lifelong devotion to lower speed limits," Nader says, but then drops his argument. The speed limit is 65; the van is going 93.

The scene underscores the tension Nader faces between his personal mythology, developed over 35 years, and a less neat reality. Some picture him as a modern-day Gandhi, his bed a mattress on the floor of a cheap rented room. In truth, he has few possessions. No car. No wife. No children. He devotes most of his energy to work, donating most of his income to his organizations.

He does play to the myth on occasion, refusing to eat at McDonald's and snubbing tap water to protest lax purity standards. Bill Hillsman, who designed a Nader TV ad spoofing MasterCard commercials, told reporters that "we did have to explain that to Ralph—he doesn't watch much TV."

But the truth is more complicated. In fact, Nader had seen the MasterCard ads, and he has even seen an episode of *The West Wing*. He wears leather shoes, eats meat and junk food, drinks wine and reads novels. He's an avid Yankees fan and goes to Orioles games monthly. He listens to Bonnie Raitt, and he laughs at George Carlin jokes. He hikes in New England and likes movies and flamenco music. Though he lives modestly, he invests in Cisco Systems, and his net worth is at least a $3.8 million. He talks on a Motorola cell phone. He even jokes with his staff: "The last time I heard a yawn like that, the emitter had four legs," he tells an aide.

Waiting in a TV station green room before an appearance, Nader is approached by an admirer who assumes he eats no animal products. "You're vegan, aren't you?" she asks. Nader points to the turkey and roast beef sandwiches he's eating. "Not when there's stuff like this," he says.

To Nader's Raiders, the idealists who passed through one of Nader's public interest law groups out of elite colleges or law school, none of these revelations about Nader's comfort in the consumer culture is surprising. He was always that way, never a saint or a martyr. "Exaggerations and embellishments," Theresa Amato, a Naderite turned Nader campaign manager, says of the myths. Tarek Milleron, Nader's nephew and campaign adviser, laughs about the "old raincoat and rumpled suit" that reporters assign Nader in their stories (unless they catch him acting normally, in which case he's a "hypocrite").

In truth, he's neither holy man nor hypocrite. "He's devoted to a cause," says Carl Mayer, another old Raider. "He hasn't taken a Gandhian vow of poverty." Nader himself doesn't see any martyrdom in his lifestyle. "It's not an ordeal," he says, as his van travels up the California coast. "What is the pursuit of happiness? You can't pursue happiness if you're oppressed. Justice is the bulldozer that clears the highway of happiness. Day after day, it becomes happiness itself."

But to Nader's would-be allies in the Green Party and among the far left, the realization that Nader is tainted by compromise and corporate culture comes as a disappointment. The merger between the Greens and the Naderites has never been easy. The Naderites are good-government lawyers who believe in advocacy and congressional hearings. The Greens are radical activists in sandals who would rather replace the system. A gathering of Greens attracts a vast array of oddball causes, from Malthusians to a group called Beaver Power! that wants to install hydroelectric generators in beaver dams.

And like the angry radicals at some Nader events, some Green leaders believe that Nader's cause is different from their own. "There are different agendas," says Tom Linzey, a Nader adviser in '96 and a current Green Party candidate for Pennsylvania attorney general. "He never moved beyond the regulatory. People wish he would move." Nader, he adds, is just "putting out spot fires."

While some Greens and other left-wingers see Nader as insufficiently pure, the Naderites worry about moving the radicals into the political process, which is "not as sexy as shutting something down," as Nader adviser Ross Mirkarimi puts it. "It's inside the system. You're reorienting them. It's going to take a hell of a lot of sweat equity just to get them to the polls."

A third-party candidate for president must be willing to suffer certain indignities and miscues. For example, when Nader holds a news conference in Los Angeles to announce the endorsement of AFSCME Local 1108, the union reps don't show up as promised. When the candidate's van attempts to get to a rally north of Los Angeles, the Russian immigrant driver insists on going south from downtown and continues several exits before Nader staffers finally persuade him to desist.

Why would Nader subject himself to the unseemly game of fringe politics? After all, he has a reputation and fame that most politicians could only dream of.

Three decades ago, he was one of the most admired men in the world and was touted as presidential timber. He virtually created the field of public interest law and forced the passage of consumer protections that have saved thousands of lives. A phone call from Nader could get an article in the papers or a hearing on the Hill.

But now, Nader can't even get into the presidential debates. "It's so much harder now," he says.

That explains his presidential run: a way to gain some publicity for his moribund issues. For Nader, there's little downside in this quixotic campaign. He'll either build a viable third party (unlikely), force Gore to adopt some of his positions (more likely) or get a lot of press.

Nader, after a half-hearted presidential bid in '96, has put together all the elements to keep his campaign in the news. He has raised $2 million and hopes for $5 million, visited all 50 states and expects to be on the ballot in at least 45, and is drawing crowds in the hundreds and the thousands (including 10,000 in Portland, Oregon). He claims high-profile supporters such as Don Imus, Susan Sarandon, Woody Harrelson and the Indigo Girls. He has a paid staff of 55.

And he loves the microphone. His hour-plus stump speeches put him in league with Castro. At a utility deregulation event in San Diego, Nader rambles from the "Chimpanzee Channel" to TV weather broadcasts to Alan Greenspan to Justice Brandeis to Bill Gates, back to Brandeis, then to Thomas Jefferson and finally to Cicero. When aides point out to him that he's late for a flight, he walks off the stage dragging the Nader presidential banner from a string around his ankle.

So obsessed with news coverage is Nader that while driving through the central California town of San Luis Obispo, he spies a man with a video camera on the street. "Hey, there's a TV camera!" Nader exclaims. "Ninety percent of people get their news from television. Get out and get that guy." The van pulls over, until aides gently convince Nader that the cameraman is probably doing a project for film class.

The Nader campaign is based on a simple premise: there is no difference between the two major parties. This is true if you stand far enough away from the two parties—in the same way New York and Tokyo would look similar if you were standing on the moon.

But look closer and you'll see the two sides disagree over taxes, Social Security, education, health care, abortion, conservation and gun control. And just as the Greens and the far left don't necessarily embrace Nader as their own, they don't necessarily buy his argument that there's no difference between Bush and Gore.

As a result, Nader can't escape the question of whether his campaign is simply stealing votes from Gore. Nader offers a dozen reasons why this isn't so or doesn't matter. He cites the Clinton record ("How could the Republicans have done worse?") and points out that a Democratic Senate allowed Clarence Thomas to join the Supreme Court. "When you vote for the least worst, you get the worst," Nader likes to say.

Yet the spoiler questions persist. "I thought that would've stopped," Nader says. "It gets tiring listening to this." The questions linger, in part because union leaders have toyed with endorsing Nader as a way to wring concessions out of Gore, and Republicans are thrilled to exploit a Nader candidacy.

But the questions persist also because Nader himself seems to suggest that he wants Bush to win. A "provocateur" like Bush, he says, would rally the left more than a smiling "anesthetist" like Gore. "Is it better to have a James Watt, who galvanizes the environmental movement, than Clinton-Gore, who anesthetize the environmentalists?" Nader asks.

Whatever the cause, Nader can't dodge the spoiler rap in his recent trip through California. On Bill Maher's *Politically Incorrect*, a conservative guest tells Nader that there are "Republicans out there actively campaigning" for him to hurt Gore. At his next event, a $150-a-head fundraiser at the House of Blues in Los Angeles, a questioner wants to know if "a vote for you is a vote for Bush." The next morning, Nader calls in to San Diego radio talk shows, and Mel from Hillwood declares that "Nader is the best friend George Bush could have."

The question surfaces even at seemingly friendly venues. One night, Nader's name is in lights outside Ventura College, where an impressive 1,300 people pack the gymnasium to hear him. Police escort him onto the campus.

Nader is buoyant. "The guys back in Washington are worried," the guy from Dupont Circle bellows.

But the crowd, though big, is more curious than enthusiastic. Local organizers had invited all the liberal groups in the area to bring their members and set up tables outside.

Susan Vinson, a local activist, came to promote the county hospital, not to support Nader. "I don't see any point in splintering off the vote and ending up with Bush," she says. "Gore needs all the help he can get."

Charlotte Jensen, a student at the U.N. Club table, explains that many students have come because they "get extra credit" for attending. She's for Bush.

Of course, Nader always can count on a small band of passionate followers who don't much care if Nader hurts Gore. "I'd like to punch Al Gore in the guts—I'd like to see his guts fall out," says Liz Hush, an activist at a Nader fund-raiser.

At a rally in Santa Barbara, an admirer hands over a $25 contribution with a note: "Diogenes would be as proud of you as we are." The ancient Greek philosopher, a Cynic, had contempt for possessions and believed that only virtue brought happiness. He begged for food, lived in a tub and walked barefoot through Athens with a lamp, looking for an honest man.

Yes, Diogenes probably would have liked Nader. Problem is, he died 2,300 years ago, and he is not registered to vote.

22

★ ☆ ★

The All-Starch Diet

Political reporters find strange occupations to keep themselves busy during the dead time. Some venture north to cover the Hillary-Lazio (née Hillary-Rudy) race in New York. My editor at the *Post* has corralled me into a couple of those stories, one about Hillary's date on the *Letterman* show and one about Hillary's luck in Giuliani's demise. But I will not be distracted from the presidential race, no matter how torpid.

Most political reporters spend dead time engaged in the game of Follow the Bouncing Polls, in which reporters give great meaning to meaningless changes in polls. Bush up in Ohio! Gore pulls even in Florida if he picks Graham! Bush surges in Pennsylvania if he runs with Ridge!

Problem is, none of this means a thing. Each week, the Vanishing Voter Project at Harvard sends us e-mail reminders that nobody in America is paying attention to the presidential race. Maybe it's 15 percent, or 18 percent in a good month. But I'm not sure. I'm not paying attention, either; I started the spring by taking a week's vacation in the Caribbean.

On my return, I've decided to look for signs that would tell me which candidate is really ahead. My criteria: First, which candidate serves the best food to reporters—an indication of favorable coverage, which will help a candidate surge. Second, which candidate do the bookmakers favor. And third, which candidate is doing the best job of patching things up with his primary foe.

For reporters covering the presidential campaign, every day is Thanksgiving.

Check in with the Bush campaign's traveling press corps on a recent day. In the last five hours, we have consumed mashed potatoes, baked ziti, grilled chicken, beef brisket, chicken soup, cauliflower, broccoli, crab-stuffed mushrooms, shrimp and steak kebabs, pizza, chicken Caesar salad, cookies and pastries, cheese and crackers, rolls, ice cream and candy bars. At the moment, we are swarming around a table with egg rolls and vegetables left over from a fundraising event. "Come on, animals," says a Bush staffer who herds us to the press bus.

Waiting in our seats on the bus is a menu detailing our next meal, at our hotel: striped lobster ravioli with red salmon caviar, beef Wellington and cheesecake. The journalists on the bus, elated at our good fortune, chant the name of the Bush aide who assembled the feast: "Silvia! Silvia! Silvia!"

Who said journalists are cynical and negative? All it takes is a little care and feeding. Okay, a lot of feeding. Like six meals a day. But it's a small price to pay. "We're so easy," NBC producer Alexandra Pelosi says amid the celebration on the bus. CNN correspondent Chris Black concurs: "You hate to be shallow and say food matters, but food matters."

Political campaigns know the obvious: Hungry reporters are cranky and aggressive. Bloated reporters are docile and content. "A well-fed press corps, both in quantity and quality, is a happy press corps," says David Morehouse, Vice President Gore's trip director. "It's not going to win or lose the campaign, but it helps."

It's a case of sustenance over substance. "They give us food instead of news," says Patricia Wilson, a Reuters Bush correspondent. Reporters following Gore believe the quantity of campaign food is inversely proportionate to the number of press conferences. In their quest for journalistic gluttony, the campaigns come equipped with both major food groups: sweets and starch (which cause blood sugar to rise, then crash, and which trigger the release of insulin). This, says Monika Woolsey, a Phoenix area dietitian, raises the level of the brain chemical serotonin, making us calm— "the Prozac effect," Woolsey says. Turkey sandwiches fill us with tryptophan, making us sleepy.

Then there's the sheer quantity. "It tends to put a lot of your metabolic activity toward your bowel and away from your brain," she says.

Further evidence of a conspiracy is the fact that campaign aides get less food and therefore are more energetic. Are campaigns making the press fat and happy and the staff lean and mean? "I think you're reading too much into it," says Greg Jenkins, who handles the press arrangements for the Bush campaign. But consider that Jenkins and at least two other members of the Bush staff are on high-protein, low-carbohydrate diets.

Which campaign serves the best—and the most—food? The question is important. If good feeding keeps reporters happy, the best-catered campaigns should get the best news coverage.

Bush himself, chatting with reporters on his plane, notes that "the food has improved dramatically." His campaign has dined the press with a cappuccino bar in Atlanta, a Mexican fiesta in San Diego and lobster in New England. Gore's campaign has done its best to keep up. Gore himself played waiter and served salmon and wine on his plane.

The *Washington Post*, which, like other news organizations, pays dearly for the meals the campaigns provide, sent this correspondent to spend an overnight on each campaign and review the food. Meals were rated on a scale of one to four drumsticks, based on the food's potential to produce favorable coverage of the candidate. Following are the results of this investigation:

Wednesday, 12:15 p.m. Reporters on the Gore campaign have two culinary options today: Fly on a press charter plane or on Air Force Two, both en route to Philadelphia from Washington. I am on the charter flight, where I sample Pepperidge Farm cookies (four months past their expiration date) and a well-balanced meal of a Blazin' Blue Fruit Roll-Up, Ghirardelli chocolate and orange juice. My colleague on Air Force Two, Dan Balz, receives a tired chicken-salad sandwich, which he mistakes for tuna and leaves untouched because of the warm mayonnaise. A hungry Balz is a bad omen for coverage.
Drumsticks: 1.0

Wednesday, 1:35 p.m. The lunch buffet at the Philadelphia Convention Center features, among many other things, Phillie cheese steaks. Dick Polman of the *Philadelphia Inquirer* passes up the steak and makes himself a sandwich of bread and pasta. "It's good—just reinforced starch," he says. That should make him too sluggish to write anything hostile about Gore this afternoon.
Drumsticks: 2.0

Wednesday, 6 p.m. Our next meal is also lunch, our third lunch of the day. It awaits us on the planes, now en route to Cincinnati. The press charter serves more cheese steaks. I fly on Air Force Two, which serves chicken fettuccine Alfredo, cheesecake and more. (I also discover that Air Force Two lavatories are stocked with Rolaids and Alka-Seltzer, just in case.) David Kennerly, the veteran *Newsweek* photographer, is pleased with his consumption. "A well-fed press is a happy press," he says. If Kennerly is happy, Gore should be happy with *Newsweek* this week.
Drumsticks: 2.0

Wednesday, 8:15 p.m. Dinner at Gore's event in Cincinnati is a culinary improvement: roast chicken, with delicious steamed asparagus and breaded eggplant. Complementing the meal is a Drouhin's Saint-Veran '98, a well-made white Burgundy. Then, at 10:40 p.m., aboard Air Force Two again, we dine some more on fruit and candy. A steward, asked which wines are available, pronounces Merlot with a hard "t" and produces some Gallo. I order a beer. After my two drinks and two helpings of apple pie, Gore could visit a Buddhist temple fund-raiser tonight and I wouldn't notice.

Drumsticks: 3.5

Thursday, 8:35 a.m. The morning brings a major oversight: No food in the hotel in Chicago. At the first campaign event, we find two small trays of supermarket doughnuts and pastry. The coffee is undrinkable. Bush would have served two hot meals by now, reporters grumble. "Not that that would affect my coverage of the stingy bastards," the *Financial Times*'s Richard Wolffe says of the Gore campaign.

Drumsticks: 0.5

Thursday, 11:10 a.m. Lunch at a Chicago convention hall is a significant improvement: a three-pasta orgy. I select the cheese tortellini and the striped mushroom ravioli instead of the fettuccine. Both are high quality, as is the cheesecake. Next, at 5:05 p.m., Air Force Two serves roast chicken breast and potatoes. The slaw is pleasantly crunchy. The corn bread suffers from microwave overheating, but this is forgotten when the Dove Bars come out. The reporters, sated, may forget their morning hunger, and anger.

Drumsticks: 3.0

The following Thursday, 12:45 p.m. The trip with George W. Bush begins on Bush's airplane with spinach-and-tomato omelets. I join Bush at his first stop, a Radisson Hotel in suburban Pittsburgh. Here we enjoy grilled chicken and beef, accompanied by mashed potatoes and (overcooked) ziti. One complaint is the inexplicable absence of dessert. Still, NBC correspondent David Gregory pronounces the meal "a bit starchy." Starch makes us lazy. Thus, Bush should get soft coverage.

Drumsticks: 2.0

Thursday, 3:40 p.m. Another lunch on the Bush plane. The crab-stuffed mushrooms and the shrimp kebabs seem to be in a state of decay. I opt for the pizza, which is too cheesy but not bad. After lunch, attendants circulate ice cream bars, cookies and health bars. My choice, a Protein Revolution, has 22 grams of protein. Serving protein is bound to make reporters pay more attention, a bad move.

Drumsticks: 1.0

Thursday, 5:10 p.m. We leave the plane in New Jersey and get on a campaign bus, where Tropicana orange juice awaits to raise our blood sugar and then lower it just in time for the next event, at 5:40 p.m. at the East Brunswick Hilton. The huge buffet is not technically for the press, but this does not stop us. The pasta is nicely al dente, the egg rolls crunchy and greasy. This should keep our minds off Bush.

Drumsticks: 1.5

Thursday, 7:40 p.m. Back at the hotel, we sit down to the fourth meal since noon. The food, at our Newark Airport hotel, doesn't live up to its billing. The ravioli is cold and the filling doesn't resemble lobster. The rolls are stale. "I'm hungry—that's all you need to know," says NBC's Pelosi. "I had a five-course meal, and I'm starving." A malnourished Pelosi is bad news for Bush; still, she appreciates the effort.

Drumsticks: 2.5

Friday, 7:45 a.m. The Bush campaign redeems itself in the morning with a superb breakfast, including a selection of breads (I recommend the pecan pastry) and a crepe station offering a choice of fillings (avoid the crab meat). The scrambled eggs, crispy bacon and the rest are near perfect. "Yummy" is the verdict of *Time*'s Margaret Carlson. "One thousand points of cholesterol." Carlson asks that her return trip to the buffet be considered off the record. This suggests we can expect a favorable column in *Time*.

Drumsticks: 3.5

Friday, 8:30 a.m. Reporters voice surprise that there is no spread at Bush's morning event, and most file stories based on a hostile questioner's exchange with Bush. But our mood improves at 11:40 a.m., when we get to the Sheraton New York, where we tuck into chicken breast, beef stroganoff, cold cuts, antipasto and more. The *Boston Globe*'s Jill Zuckman notes that the raspberry dressing is too sweet and the chicken tastes like ham. But we still gorge ourselves, which is good for Bush.

Drumsticks: 2.5

Friday, 2:05 p.m. The press departs for another lunch aboard Bush's plane. I return home and go to the gym.

So who wins? If campaign food is indeed a predictor of campaign coverage and Election Day success, Bush is favored: he gets 13.0 drumsticks overall to Gore's 12.0. The journalists' consensus is that the Bush campaign's dining experience, after a poor start in the primaries, has now surpassed Gore's. It is perhaps no coincidence that while Gore enjoyed more favorable coverage than Bush in February, when Gore's food was better, Bush now serves better food and receives generally friendlier coverage.

Still, the overall food quality is fairly close. Where Bush pulls ahead is in quantity (the missing breakfast in Chicago cost Gore) and in service (Air Force Two desperately needs a sommelier). The feeding picture, in short, is the same story as the campaign generally: Gore lags, but he is close enough to make a race of it.

Now, what are the professional investors saying? First, I checked with them as the primaries were all but done. Almost everyone believes politicians can be bought and sold. There's actually a market to facilitate the transaction. Investors, trading in a presidential futures market over the Internet, play the spreads between bid and ask prices, hold short positions, hedge their investments, engage in risk arbitrage, and win or lose money on the candidates. "They are a commodity," says Stuart Sweet, an adviser to investment funds. "It's just like wheat and gold and silver."

Or pork bellies.

Sweet is a well-diversified investor. He has shares in Human Genome Sciences, Lockheed Martin, a Brazilian mutual fund—and 250 contracts of George W. Bush. Sweet bought the governor when his shares were trading at 69. "On March 14, Bush will be in the high nineties," Sweet predicts. Some 4,350 traders have invested a total of $113,000 in the Iowa Electronic Market, a political futures market run by the University of Iowa business school. Joyce Berg, an accounting professor, expects that amount to more than double by convention time—and it would be much higher if there weren't an individual investment limit of $500. The small size of the market keeps away commodities regulators. But the market, which began in 1988, expanded this year, its first time available to anybody on the Web (www.biz.uiowa.edu/iem/markets), making it a more reliable barometer of the political zeitgeist.

That's not to say there isn't real money in presidential futures. Bill Bradley, for example, was trading at under 4 cents in the Democratic race in late February. Because the winning contract will be worth $1 in August, a $500 bet on Bradley would yield $13,500 if he were to win the nomination. Or do you think McCain is more likely to get the Reform Party nomination than Buchanan, Trump, Ventura or Perot? Put $500 on that hunch and you could wind up with $4,500. Or, you could lose it all.

More cautious investors might go with Al Gore, trading at 94 cents on the dollar yesterday, or Bush, who, at 75 cents, leads McCain, at 25 cents. The market also has Hillary and Rudy futures: he's worth 60 cents, she 34 cents. Buchanan, at 72 cents, leads all others in the Reform Party. Investors favor a Democratic House and a Republican Senate, and, in recent days, have bid the Democrats above the Republicans for the first time in the presidential race.

The market has attracted such Wall Street luminaries as Lazard Freres' Steven Rattner, a top Gore fund-raiser. He takes time out from billion-dollar deals to monitor his presidential futures account balance, which has climbed from $500 to $613. "I just checked," he says from his New York office. "If this weren't limited to $500, God knows what I would do." His secret? "I'm very long on the vice president," he said. He bought Gore early, at 65 cents.

But Rattner is prudent. "I own some Bushes and some McCains," says the Democrat. "It's partially hedged." He invests in everything but the Reform Party. "I'm prepared to predict rational events, not irrational events," he explains.

As in the hog and soybean markets, every investor has a plan. There are market-makers, such as Arch Crawford of Arizona, who writes an investment newsletter. "When the spreads are very large, I fill in with a buy below the last and a sell above the last," he says. "The same thing happens on Nasdaq." Crawford says he bought some McCain for 12 cents the night before the Michigan primary, when McCain shares nearly tripled. But Crawford also bought Forbes on the way down, not realizing Forbes would keep falling. "Some people play canasta," he says. "I do this."

Then there's the value investor. Mitchell Wiegner, who works in derivatives in Chicago, hunts for bargains. For this reason, he stays away from Bush, who "is not worth it." Instead, he amassed 1,400 contracts of McCain at one point, grabbing 8 percent of the market. Wiegner also invests in the more liquid Gore. "I'm actually buying Al Gore as a money-market instrument," Wiegner says, figuring Gore will climb from the low nineties now to $1 in August, a 15 percent increase with low risk.

Of course, somebody might argue that Gore, at 94 cents, is a bit over-priced. But Gore's spokesman, Chris Lehane, is talking up Gore futures. "Some candidates are blue-chip candidates—they grow over the long term," he says. "Others are like junk bonds."

Still others employ technical analysis in their presidential futures. David Caldwell, a computer programmer from Cleveland, figures he has spent 150 hours so far in this campaign, trading and writing programs to determine congressional election probabilities. His conclusion: "The best buys in the market were the sweeps" in which one party wins both the House and Senate. All this labor (which luckily complements his day job) has earned him just $75.

The political futures market has its problems. Because volume is relatively low, a few players can manipulate the prices. There's also no way to force losers to pay up. But it's believed to be the only market in presidential futures with real money involved. There are bookmakers, but they don't allow the selling of candidates after bets are placed.

So far, presidential futures have closely tracked campaign events. McCain stood at a lowly 10 cents per contract after Bush won in Iowa, but soared to 38 cents after his New Hampshire win. The day of his South Carolina loss, McCain plunged to 15 cents, until his Michigan victory took him back up to 32 cents. Bradley, likewise, was at 40 cents in mid-October, when Gore was at 63 cents. But in mid-January, when it appeared that Gore would win Iowa, Bradley plunged to 17. Bradley contracts fell to 10 cents immediately after Iowa and, other than a slight uptick after his narrow loss in New Hampshire, have been fading ever since.

The market in politicians has begun to gather a following beyond the traders involved. Various media outlets cite the prices as signs of a candidate's strength or weakness. And political junkies check the market regularly. One such soul is Tom Skinner, a Bethesda venture capitalist who doesn't trade, and doesn't even vote (he's a British subject). Yet he checks it obsessively. "I'm just a junkie," he says. "It's more exciting than anything I've ever known."

Anything?

"Anything I've ever known in politics," he corrects. Like the food quality method, the political futures market is proving a considerably more reliable barometer than the opinion polls. In the month of June, while Bush leads Gore in the polls by double digits, the wise futures traders have the race at a steady 48 percent to 47 percent, in Gore's favor. All year long, the two have been in a tight band, in contrast to the polls and the news coverage, which would make it seem as if the election's over. Come Labor Day, when the polls matter more, the futures traders will prove to be right on the mark.

And how about Bush's and Gore's ability to make nice with their vanquished foes? This, too, must indicate something about their ability to solidify their "bases" of partisan supporters.

Now that the presidential nominations are all but sealed, it's time for the ancient charade of "party unity," in which the losers are expected to swallow pride, close ranks and embrace their conquerors. This is never easy, but for John McCain and Bill Bradley it means a particularly large and unsavory feast. The vanquished challengers, each of whom has vowed to support his party's nominee, must now eat all those nasty words they said about their opponents.

The time has come, for example, for Bradley to answer his own question to Gore: "Why should we believe you will tell the truth as president if you don't tell the truth as a candidate?" So, too, must McCain answer the question he posed about Bush: "Do we really want another politician in the White House America can't trust?"

As a public service, then, here are some suggested talking points for McCain and Bradley, drafted in consultation with political speechwriter Mark Katz of the Sound Bite Institute. This should help them explain why those pesky, hard-to-rationalize quotes were not their final answers.

Offending McCain quote: "You don't understand the role of the president of the United States."

Recommended explanation: That comment was made in defense of the kaiser roll after Bush said he preferred a pumpernickel bun.

Offending McCain quote: "Governor Bush is a Pat Robertson Republican who will lose to Al Gore."

Recommended explanation: That was a misquote—traffic noise on the *Straight Talk Express*. He meant to say Governor Bush is a Paul Robeson Republican who will be loosed on Al Gore.

Offending McCain quote: "You are defending an illegal system. You are defending a system that has caused the debasement of every institution of government and it's got to be stopped."

Recommended explanation: Bush and McCain disagree strongly on NCAA office pools.

Offending McCain quote: "As this campaign moves forward, a clear choice will be offered, a choice between my optimistic and welcoming conservatism and the negative message of fear."

Recommended explanation: A negative message of fear, used appropriately, can be very compelling. As the Texas governor says, bring on the bricks and mortars.

Offending Bradley quote: "The point is, Al, and I don't know if you get this, but a political campaign is not just a performance for people, which is what this is."

Recommended explanation: He's a Performer With Results. Give him four stars and call it "the must-see hit of the season."

Offending Bradley quote: "You're the elephant of negative campaigning."

Recommended explanation: Hey—elephants never run attack ads. The vice president is a rare animal, pure as ivory, with a thick skin and a big heart.

Offending Bradley quote: "The watchword of this kind of politics is attack, deny, distort. It's the old politics that says the ends justify the means to win an election."

Recommended explanation: This was, in retrospect, a desperate ploy to attack, deny and distort Gore's record to win the election.

Offending Bradley quote: "You're in a Washington bunker."

Recommended explanation: So what's wrong with that? Bradley just spent $30 million trying to get himself inside a Washington bunker.

Apparently, such loaded rhetoric isn't easy to swallow. For while Bradley immediately offers his support to Gore, McCain waits a good two and a half months to lick his wounds. Throughout that time, McCain has continued appearances and press releases as if the primary race is still wide open. And now, after much fanfare, he is coming to Pittsburgh in late May to meet with Bush in an event scripted more like a summit meeting. It's time for somebody to tell McCain that his campaign is over.

Four McCain aides landed here today accompanied by a dozen journalists. The senator's advance man whisked them off to waiting rides to a hotel where they were to brief the Arizona Republican. After that, it was off to an evening news conference and a book signing.

The McCain itinerary was so much fun that it seems rude to point out the GOP presidential nomination already belongs to the other guy. Still, there were subtle signs McCain might have noticed. Gone was the 727, replaced with a delayed flight from Phoenix. At one of McCain's book signings during the campaign nearly 1,500 people came, some waiting for hours. Today there were 85 when he walked in the door.

Yet the permanent McCain campaign continues to show signs of life, like dismembered spider legs that continue to wiggle.

Even by normal standards for presidential races—in which substance invariably yields to fluff—the great "summit" here between McCain and George W. Bush is something special. The Tuesday meeting should be, if all goes well, the epitome of political theater: a substance-challenged photo op that ranks among the more celebrated non-news events of the campaign.

Consider the great fuss over the meeting's details: the brinkmanship over whether to have the meeting, the negotiations over the agenda, the careful choice of a city and date. The two sides were even careful not to use the same hotel. And for what? Is it conceivable anything important will occur here?

"It is conceivable—barely," says John Weaver, McCain's political director.

What, then, will happen? "Assume nothing," says Rick Davis, the former McCain campaign manager now serving as a liaison to Bush. "If George Bush had anything he wanted to talk to John McCain about, he'd pick up the phone and say it."

The oddly persistent nature of the defeated McCain campaign is symbolic of this entire stage of the 2000 race. It is a tightly scripted mass of symbolic appearances signifying nothing. The Bush and Gore events seem to have lost meaning, and yet the candidates go through the motions.

Forty years ago Nelson Rockefeller and Richard Nixon, beset by intraparty differences, sat down to reach the "Compact of Fifth Avenue," in which they hammered out crucial policy issues such as defense and civil rights. Barry Goldwater called it the "Munich of the Republican Party," and it undoubtedly altered the party in fundamental ways.

But the Parley in Pittsburgh?

Bush and McCain will chat for no more than 90 minutes—"probably less," Weaver says—and then get to the real business, a news conference. With luck, the spectacle will be up there with the Dayton Accords, the Bretton Woods agreement and the Treaty of Paris. Unlike Dayton, Bretton Woods and Paris, however, this one is set up to be "a big nothing-burger," as one Republican consultant puts it.

No matter. The story will wind up high in the evening news and on front pages. The reason: All three sides are complicit. Bush very much desires a McCain photo-op to woo independent voters. McCain wants badly to stay in the public eye (and to convince Republicans he plays well with others). And the press, in this lull in the presidential campaign, is desperate for a story.

Let us examine the potential that something of substance might happen Tuesday. There won't be anything useful about a joint ticket: McCain has made clear his contempt for the vice presidential job.

How about an endorsement? Well, he's always said he'll endorse Bush, so who cares?

Will Bush suddenly cave on McCain's demand to abolish "soft money" contributions? You're more likely to see the parting of the Monongahela River here.

Maybe a breakthrough on tax cuts? Maybe not. "Senator McCain has already said he's not going to Pittsburgh to negotiate or ask anything of Governor Bush," says Bush spokesman Ari Fleischer.

What remains, then, is the last act in a good bit of theater. First came the reports, nearly a month ago, that such a meeting would be held. Then came the McCain aides to describe the meeting as "tenuous." Then came the negotiations between McCain and Bush aides, held in the neutral confines of Bob Dole's office, to discuss what their bosses could discuss. After that came the inevitable declaration that the meeting, never canceled, was still on. There were even negotiations about who could be in the room with the leaders (resolution: nobody). It's a wonder we haven't heard about debates over the shape of the coffee table.

The thing resembles nothing so much as a striptease. "In the last month the two candidates have been taking off their primary clothing and putting on general-election clothing," says Davis. "This meeting with John McCain is the last symbolic act of taking off the clothing of the primary."

Symbolism is nothing new in campaigns. "I don't think there's anything new and different," pronounces Bob Strauss, the wise old man of the Democratic Party. Sal Russo, a veteran Republican strategist, concurs: "Everybody's always done it since the beginning of time." Political conventions have been largely symbolic gatherings since the Reagan-Ford showdown in 1976.

If it's possible to imagine, though, events are probably even more scripted in 2000 than in previous elections because of the constant news cycle created by cable television, which requires candidates to be on message all the time. Hence more prepared speeches and photo-ops.

The guy with the biggest interest in this Pittsburgh striptease is McCain. He formed a political action committee called Straight Talk America and moved many of his campaign staff onto its payroll. He's been traveling the land to give speeches and hold book signings. He went to South Carolina to atone for his Confederate-flag sins. NBC took him to Vietnam, where he visited the place where he was a prisoner of war. Some McCain enthusiasts even venture, privately, that the senator's reform movement (read: McCain 2004) would be better off if the Texas governor lost.

Bush, for his part, wants to walk away from Pittsburgh with footage of a firm handshake. "It's a wonderful show of Republican strength," Fleischer says. "It's newsworthy when two people who are arguably America's most popular politicians come together."

McCain aides are quick to point out that it was Bush who requested the session. "They didn't want an agenda, they didn't care about a meeting; they wanted a photo-op and an endorsement," Davis says.

If that's not depressing enough, consider this: The most likely outcome of today's meeting is an agreement by Bush and McCain to . . . schedule more meetings!

And the press can move on to more pressing matters. For instance, while Bradley has said he will "enthusiastically campaign" for Gore, he hasn't yet used the *e* word. Is something wrong? Let's go ask him . . .

23

★ ☆ ★

How Dubya Got His
Compassion Back

Of all the boneheaded moves in the presidential campaign so far, I think Michigan Governor John Engler's tantrum on the night of his state's GOP primary takes the prize. Engler, explaining why he hadn't been able to deliver Michigan for George W. Bush, whined about a hostile takeover of the Republican Party. "We've never seen a candidate like John McCain, who tried to go out and rent Democrats for a day," the governor complained. "John McCain isn't party building, he's party borrowing."

The implication, a shortsighted one, was this: The Republican Party is for Republicans only; independents and Democrats—the majority of American voters—should take their business elsewhere. Bush, momentarily echoing Engler's message, warned about Democratic spoilers trying to "hijack the election." Since then, phrases like "civil war" and "factional warfare" have spilled from Republican lips, as McCain angrily took on the religious right while Bush defended it. There's even talk among the bruised GOP faithful in South Carolina and Michigan about changing the rules to prohibit the "open primaries" that allowed independents and Democrats to vote in GOP contests this year—essentially evicting the reform-minded voters who gave McCain his victories.

This would be absurd, if not suicidal, for the Republicans. Bush and his advisers, after that incautious bit about the hijacking, have come to this conclusion themselves. (Nothing like a few primary wins to restore a candidate's sense of balance.)

If Engler's concern about the open primary is to be believed, Bush should have been in trouble in Georgia. The state's Democrats (an estimated 31 percent of the voters) and its independents (about 38 percent) could easily swamp the 31 percent who identify themselves as Republicans in polls. So what happened? Bush clobbered McCain.

The question now is whether Bush can keep those non-Republicans in the fold as he becomes the party's standard-bearer. If he doesn't make the necessary effort to appeal to reform-minded independents and Democrats, he'll become a doomed prisoner of his party's extremists. The fight with McCain depleted the funds Bush was going to use to pummel Gore this spring. And the nasty politics that have come to characterize the Republican race will make it hard for Bush to argue this fall that he's a different kind of politician.

The McCainiacs argue that Bush's right turn has already doomed him. "It's either President McCain or President Gore," Mike Murphy, a McCain strategist, tells me. "President Bush is no longer on the menu."

But that overstates things quite a bit. The McCain Democrats and independents are more of an opportunity than a problem for Bush. After all, the Republicans have attracted 4 million voters to their primaries so far, the Democrats (who have held fewer primaries) only 600,000. In exit polls from last Tuesday's Virginia primary, some 41 percent of McCain voters say they would vote for Gore in a Gore vs. Bush matchup, but only 6 percent would support Gore in a Gore vs. McCain contest. That means there has been relatively little of the mischief-making Engler claimed.

Bush's mission should be to win over these reform-minded voters, not shun them. This might not be so difficult. Though 41 percent of McCain's voters said they would go with Gore, the other 59 percent indicated they'd take Bush in November. Both Bush and McCain enjoy high favorability ratings among GOP voters. Karl Rove, Bush's strategist, tells me that by the time the nomination is settled, roughly half of the 4 million to 5 million vote McCain gets should be available to Bush. "Bush has time to win them back," Rove says.

To the pundits' surprise, Bush succeeded in convincing voters in both South Carolina and Virginia that he was the "real reformer," by a five-point margin in both states' exit polls. McCain finds this absurd. "If he's a reformer, I'm an astronaut," the senator likes to say. But this comparison proves the trouble with McCain's position. McCain isn't an astronaut, but he was a fighter pilot, the next closest thing. Bush isn't an obvious reformer, but he's a modestly innovative governor who, in a pinch, could pass as a reformer.

Already Bush seems to have improved his standing among independents. He went from a 16 percent share of the independent vote in New Hampshire to 31 percent in South Carolina and 33 percent in Michigan and Virginia. He also has done much better than McCain among women, 60 percent to 38 percent in Virginia, according to the exit polls.

But that may not be enough against Gore in November. Bush needs to move now to make an appeal to women, the elderly, the middle class and the poor. And he would be wise, eventually, to follow McCain in separating himself from Robertson and his troops. McCain may have been needlessly caustic, but his argument makes sense. "If your job is to go on kamikaze missions, then fine," he said. "But if you want to change that and start regaining the majority that we had in the '80s, then you've got to change the party."

Bush can follow that advice and do for his party what Bill Clinton did for his in 1992. Or he can ignore that wisdom and do for Republicans what Michael Dukakis did for the Democrats in 1988. You would think the choice would be obvious.

Now begins the process of restoring the compassion to Bush's conservatism. Bush, fleeing the memory of Bob Jones University, is seeking asylum on the grounds of Our Lady of Fatima Catholic Church here in Cleveland. Once more the compassionate conservative, Bush gushes to Catholic Charities heavies about "hope in people's hearts," a "universal call to love one's neighbor" and "miracles of renewal." "I'm a uniter, not a divider," Bush says for possibly the millionth time. "It may surprise you to hear a Republican say this."

But his listeners do not look surprised. Nor do they look impressed with Bush's attempt at his own miracle of renewal in the wake of Pat Robertson's carjacking of his campaign. There is no applause when Bush enters the room, and plenty of empty seats. The diocese has refused to allow Bush supporters to pack the house and won't hang the Catholic Charities banner behind Bush.

"We know we got the call on Sunday night only because of Bob Jones," says Patrick Grace, a diocesan official, at the Tuesday morning event. When the meeting ends, Bush, flanked by a Catholic priest, holds a news conference—but the journalists ignore the event's theme in favor of questions about the latest campaign bickering.

Therein lies the principle challenge for Bush as he embarks on his general election campaign for the presidency. His "compassionate conservatism" theme, a vague but pleasant message that got him through the early primary process, was replaced by a veneer of hard-right nastiness. "Somehow," says a top Bush adviser, "we lost our mojo."

Now Bush's team is asking a crucial question: How does George get his compassion back?

The governor himself doesn't think he'll have much trouble restoring his compassionate image. "I'm not worried about Bob Jones," he says in an interview. "I feel like I'm in good shape. It's me and my record. People will make up their own minds."

Bush believes that it should—and eventually will—be self-evident that he is compassionate to the core. "It's one thing to label yourself," he says of himself. "It's another thing to believe it."

So confident is Bush that he has made clear he has no regrets about his primary campaign and won't be rushing to emulate John McCain, who proved hugely popular with non-Republicans.

The candidate argues that his problem is largely with a press corps grown tired of his message, which, intentionally, hasn't changed much since he launched his candidacy. "I'm trying to fight through a filter that's very process-oriented," Bush says. "They'd rather write about the slugfest." While the local media tend to report Bush's themes, the national press wants to advance the daily back-and-forth between candidates. Bush believes he can prevail over the punditry by stubbornly sticking to his theme. "I need to put myself in front of crowds, to reinforce my message," he says.

But is this enough? Some Bush advisers don't think so. They argue that Bush can only recover the compassion mantle with a barrage of new proposals that convert slogans into a convincing governing agenda. After all, the fight against McCain is nothing compared with the battle Bush will likely face against Vice President Gore, who can't wait to clobber Bush for his alleged lack of compassion on Social Security, health care, abortion, gun control and more.

"It's not going to work simply to say, 'I'm dealing more with inner-city churches,' and have more photo-ops," says John DiIulio, who serves as a policy consultant to Bush. "I hope and expect that's not what they're going to do." Bush's policy experts, led by Steve Goldsmith, the former Indianapolis mayor, already have piles of proposals on Social Security, health care and other issues ready to launch. "We need to say new things and we need to say them comprehensively," insists Goldsmith.

Consider the images that have shaped modern presidential politics. Michael Dukakis in the oversize Army helmet symbolized a man too small for the job. Bill Clinton's Man From Hope was an Everyman who might help us feel better. Ronald Reagan chopping wood embodied vitality and power. Such symbols are everything. Few voters can be troubled to digest position papers and platforms. They make their judgments based on a stew of symbolic appearance, behavior and rhetoric.

From the start, Bush sought to make compassionate conservatism his defining symbol. The question, after he struggled in the early primaries, is whether this will still work. Does it feel true? Or is it a poor fit that can't stand up to the symbols of the far right with which Gore plans to tag Bush?

Bush's staffers vouch for his good heart. "Saying Bush is intolerant is like saying McCain isn't a veteran," argues Mark McKinnon, Bush's media adviser. "It defines his being."

Bush resents suggestions that he is not compassionate to the core, demanding that others not "judge my heart." Take my word for it, he is saying. Bush said he was stunned when his motives were questioned after his visit to Bob Jones University, with its racist and anti-Catholic associations. "I never dreamed my opponent would be making calls in states saying I'm an anti-Catholic bigot," Bush said.

But by framing the question as one of tolerance, Bush is knocking down a straw man. Few people would argue that he's a bigot. But if they are forbidden from judging his heart, voters still must judge whether Bush's stated compassionate conservatism truly reflects a concern for the poor and the weak. This requires moving beyond the visceral to assess the governor's words, the company he keeps and, particularly, his actions.

First, the words:

Bush has been bounding across the country with a stump speech full of the soft and fuzzy. He is knocking down the toll booth to the middle class. He is closing the gap of hope. He is leaving nobody behind. He is making sure the American Dream touches every willing heart. And, yes, he is rallying the armies of compassion. He is doing this over and over, without variation, at stop after stop. Undoubtedly, Bush is talking the talk.

From its beginning, the Bush campaign used compassionate conservatism as an implicit rebuke of traditional conservatives for not caring about the poor and the weak. Early in his campaign, Bush made the implicit explicit. He derided the "destructive mind-set" of conservatives who take "an approach with no higher goal, no nobler purpose, than 'Leave us alone.'" He adopted the language of the left, declaring, "Economic growth is not the solution to every problem. A rising tide lifts many boats—but not all." Bush also distanced himself from congressional Republicans who were trying to "balance the budget on the backs of the poor." And he trashed fellow Republicans for describing an "America slouching toward Gomorrah" and for confusing "the need for limited government with a disdain for government itself."

What about his fellow travelers? Are they as overtly committed to the compassion image as the candidate? Here, the evidence is mixed. Hard-edged ideologues are rare on the Bush staff. Goldsmith, Bush's domestic policy guru, for example, was an innovative mayor who helped to launch programs that strengthen a feeling of community; he is one of the original compassionate conservatives. Bush's economic adviser, Larry Lindsey, is a traditional tax cutter, but he, too, talks about the need to remove some of the tax code's regressivity.

On the other hand, Bush has also been keeping company with some controversial characters. In South Carolina, he stood with an oddball veteran as the man defamed McCain, and then was slow to distance himself from the attack. Similarly, Bush has embraced Robertson, allowing the religious broadcaster to deliver recorded phone messages supporting Bush. This is the same Robertson who in 1998 warned that the city of Orlando's display of rainbow-colored flags to commemorate a Gay Pride event would bring "earthquakes, tornadoes and possibly a meteor."

Even one of Bush's compassion advisers suffered a lapse in compassion. Bush counselor Marvin Olasky wrote a piece for a Texas newspaper about godless journalists who have "holes in their souls" and indulge in "Zeus worship." He listed three—all Jews. Olasky says he didn't know their religion. But this doesn't look good for Bush, who once got into trouble for doubting whether non-Christians could go to Heaven.

And what about Bush's actions? The governor has redoubled his earlier strategy of appearing among the poor and the nonwhite. In Los Angeles recently, he surrounded himself with mariachi music, Spanish-language signs and ex-gang members. "You're going to see a lot of events" along these lines, promises Karl Rove, Bush's top strategist. Adds McKinnon: "I think we'll say the same things. . . . We'll just be in a different auditorium with a bigger audience."

Bush can also point to his deeds in Texas. As governor, he demanded increases in education funding and opposed anti-immigration measures. He championed faith-based rehabilitation programs for prisoners. In his tax cuts, he favored reducing such regressive items as sales taxes on diapers and medication.

But Bush has recently done plenty to contradict his compassion image. After losing badly in the New Hampshire primary, he turned the campaign from education and charity to an ugly brew of Confederate flags, nasty phone calls and tough anti-abortion and anti-gay stances. He earned more criticism for allowing the execution of a great-grandmother convicted of murder who claimed domestic abuse. The most enduring symbol is Bob Jones U. By failing to condemn the school's denunciations of Catholicism and ban on interracial dating, Bush allowed McCain to create the impression that his compassionate words were at odds with his actions.

This complicated what was already a difficult sell for Bush. By talking to minorities and the poor, he is aiming for two solidly Democratic constituencies. His appeal is much like Clinton's efforts to woo business in

1992 by eschewing his party's soak-the-rich rhetoric. For Bush to win over this skeptical crowd, he'll need something tangible: either more government protections for the poor and the disenfranchised, or a convincing effort to get the private and nonprofit sectors to do the work.

Here, Bush faces two constraints. The first, one Bush created for himself, is his $1.3 trillion tax cut proposal (larger than even House Republicans could contemplate), which leaves virtually no money for new government spending. As a result, his proposals are by necessity thrifty. His tax credit proposal for charitable giving, for example, comes to $8 billion in the first year, an amount that disappointed Olasky, who wanted a credit twice as large. "We're trying to operate inside a realistic budget," explains Goldsmith.

There's also little evidence to suggest that churches and business, even if unshackled by regulation, would be able to do the entire job themselves. "You have to spend money," says Arianna Huffington, the conservative thinker who helped to popularize the "compassion" idea. "As I've learned the hard way, trying to just say the private sector's going to do it is not a happening thing. . . . As president, you can't just be head of the Red Cross."

Bush's recent ordeal on the campaign trail should prove to him that people won't automatically view him as caring simply because his heart feels it and his mouth says it.

At a high school near Columbus, Ohio, Bush is expressing compassion for the working poor, a standard part of his stump speech. "Our Republican Party better nominate somebody who hears their voices," he tells the students. "I'm the only one in the race who's talking about this. The hardest job in America is a working single mother." Bush's compassion slips only slightly when, asked about guns in schools, he neglects to mention a school shooting that occurred just hours earlier, instead talking about how "law-abiding citizens should be able to protect themselves."

There is trouble waiting for Bush at his next stop, in Cincinnati. Protesters stand outside with banners that say "Killer Bush" and "You're a Racist." The demonstrators chant: "Governor Bush, you racist-sexist. Governor Bush, go back to Texas."

Bush gets a friendlier welcome from the 700 GOP faithful inside the hall. With them, he's back on message. "The conservatives in the Republican Party insist that no child gets left behind," Bush tells them. "Ours is a plan that listens to all voices in society." Bush has never received a rousing response to such lines from Republican crowds. To his credit, he continues to use them anyway.

The next morning, Bush is at an event outside Atlanta. The speech, again, is laden with compassion. "It's unfair not to be listening to voices on the outskirts of poverty," he lectures. "We better nominate some-one . . . who can talk about the unfairness of the tax code in terms of the single woman." Instead of listening to such lines, though, some of the cam-eramen in the crowd are filming a few kids who have defaced their Bush poster so that it now says "Rednecks for Bush."

Bush next takes his entourage to a Catholic college in St. Louis. A priest opens the event with a prayer and then takes a seat behind the can-didate. Bush is all compassion, talking about education. "Our test scores are up [in Texas], particularly among our African American and Latino youngsters," he tells the mostly white crowd. "This country needs some-body who worries about the children in America." This time, in response to a question, Bush does talk about the previous day's school shooting, but awkwardly. "I know, it was sad," he says. "A young boy needlessly shot a young girl."

Still, Bush sounds far more compassionate than the union workers out-side, who are handing out fliers that say, "Bob Jones equals bigotry."

What exactly can Bush do to regain his compassion? Advisers in Austin, planning the candidate's general election campaign, will seek to reclaim his image on three fronts: public education, poverty and "inclu-sion"—namely, social justice for immigrants, whom Bush calls the "New Americans."

Step 1 is to outdo Gore on issues long dominated by Democratic con-stituencies. Already, contends McKinnon (a former adviser to Democrats), the combination of Bush's education plans to help the worst-off schools, his faith-based charity incentives and a tax cut that targets the working poor "offers more to typically Democratic constituencies than the tired, typical ideas offered by Al Gore." Still, a convincing anti-poverty program would probably require more extensive policies. One possibility that has been percolating in Bush's shop is to take on "corporate welfare," those tax breaks for business that have been a favorite target of McCain.

Step 2 is to offer a plausible alternative to Gore's plan to provide health care coverage to all American children. Bush can't outbid Gore, but he can attempt to offer a more efficient health care delivery system. Bush's plan is likely, for example, to concentrate on coverage of entire families liv-ing near the poverty level, not just children.

The third step is to introduce a new range of policies designed to pro-mote "inclusion" on matters of race, immigration and social justice—also typically Democratic issues. "We need to find a way to make tangible the kind of inclusiveness that Bush has done here in Texas," says a Bush adviser.

As he aims for inclusion, Bush will need to drift away from the con-servatives who rescued his campaign. Though he hopes to avoid it, he could also, in a pinch, attempt a "Sister Souljah moment," a phrase born when Clinton took on a rap singer's lyrics in the 1992 campaign. If he were to, say, name as his running mate Governor Christine Todd Whitman of New Jersey, a pro-choice moderate loathed by the Robertson-Falwell set, he could buff his compassion image in a hurry. Among Bush's conservative allies, that would cause earthquakes, tornadoes and possibly a meteor.

And that's just the point. If Bush is willing to defy his religious and corporate conservatives while making some serious proposals to win over the poor and minorities, he just might be able to solder his compassion and his conservatism back together.

To me, the clearest sign Bush is regaining the middle ground comes not from the candidate himself but from Karen Hughes, his communications director. Hughes, a tall and steely woman, is known for her unsmiling, unwavering defense of her boss and general hostility to reporters. So a conversation we have while waiting for a Bush appearance in Philadelphia takes me by surprise and indicates to me the Bush campaign *is* really changing for the better. It involves her footwear.

After I compliment her on a fine pair of purple shoes, Hughes confesses the following: she usually has to travel from Austin to Dallas to find quality ladies shoes that fit her exceptionally large feet. But recently, she found a shop in Austin that sells a wide range of large-size ladies' shoes, and she purchased several pairs. Eventually, she asked the proprietor why he stocked so many styles and colors; usually she could only find black and white in her size.

"Well," the proprietor replied, "we have a lot of men come in here who want to dress up as women."

It was a great moment: Hughes letting down her guard, showing some self-deprecating humor. It was a brief moment, but it changed my whole impression of her. Because I was part of the press "pool" at the event, I dutifully reported the conversation back to the reporters who weren't there—with strong advice not to print it.

On a larger scale, Bush also has been doing surprisingly well at shaking an unfavorable image. Come, amigos, let us hear how he is doing this. In short, he has returned to bilingual mode. "El gobernador George W. Bush" recently ate a taco at Fiesta Imperiale in California, where he also celebrated Cinco de Mayo and spoke Spanish (his is better than Gore's) with the crowd. Some of his campaign events have featured mariachi music, he taped a town meeting for Spanish-language television and he put out an ad declaring that he's "un hombre de familia" with "valores conservadores." (Gringos: read that "family man with conservative values.")

He named a Hispanic man to a top fund-raising job and visited a Latino community center in Ohio called El Barrio.

Perhaps you are wondering what this is all about. Perhaps you want to ask: ¿Que pasa, Jorge?

This is the year of the Latino voter, some members of the press corps tell us, and the Gore and Bush campaigns have been wooing the Latino vote aggressively. Though typical for a Democrat, this is unusual for a Republican.

As an electoral strategy, it doesn't make much sense. In the states where Latino voters have become powerful, the presidential race isn't much of a contest. And in the states where there's a contest, there aren't many Latino voters. The effort to recruit them this year, in fact, has more to do with the overall image of tolerance and sensitivity that candidates want to convey than it does with making direct appeals to Latino voters.

This is not to diminish the growing importance of Hispanics in politics. In some future presidential election—perhaps even the next one—they will be a decisive factor. Four years ago, Latinos comprised only 5 percent of the electorate; this year, the figure is expected to be 8 percent.

They are also, to some extent, up for grabs. Democrats have won roughly two-thirds of the Latino vote in recent years and have a 3-to-1 advantage in party identity. But many Latinos, particularly the most assimilated, tend to have conservative social positions that favor Republican policies. Bush, who won an impressive 49 percent of the Hispanic vote in the 1998 Texas gubernatorial race, has been holding his own nationally among this group in some recent polls.

Bush has taken pains to show that he disapproves of the anti-immigrant policies of former California Governor Pete Wilson, a fellow Republican. "El gobernador Bush es una nueva clase de republicano," says a press release from his campaign.

In recent weeks, Bush assembled Latino leaders in Pennsylvania's Lehigh Valley and attended a U.S.-Mexico Foundation breakfast in San Diego. During a stop in Santa Ana, California, he called himself Jorge and attended a Catholic mass, although he's a Methodist. In his first foreign trip as a candidate, he ventured a few hundred yards into Mexico to meet with that country's president. Bush also worked the crowd at the National Hispanic Women's Conference, and he visited Latino schools in Sacramento. Bush has made a practice of answering at least one question in Spanish at his news conferences.

Here's the electoral logic: If Bush can push his share of the Latino vote from the 30 percent that Bob Dole got to 50 percent, he gains some 1.6 percentage points nationally, which is a significant gain in a close race. But Bush isn't likely to duplicate his Texas success—that was a landslide in which he dominated virtually all demographics. In a poll conducted by the online political site Voter.com, Bush trailed Gore among Latinos by 12 percentage points this month; two months earlier, Bush led Gore by 6 points, which indicates "some core Hispanic constituencies are going home" to the Democratic Party, observed Ed Goeas, a Republican pollster.

The real obstacle to Latino clout this particular year is the Electoral College. Hispanic voters are a significant force in four critical states—New York (7 percent of the electorate there), California (11 percent), Texas (17 percent) and Florida (12 percent)—but none of these states is truly in play. Barring a national landslide, which neither side expects, California and New York should go to Gore, and Texas and Florida—home of the conservatively inclined Cuban community—should go to Bush.

Both sides know the election comes down to a surprisingly small collection of states—particularly Missouri, Michigan, Wisconsin, Pennsylvania, New Jersey, Illinois and Ohio—that have tiny Hispanic populations.

The real reason for Bush's Latino push, I believe, is his effort to improve his appeal to suburban swing voters by projecting an image of inclusion. "Whites, liberals, the gay vote, upper income, the Jewish vote—all of those people are heavily influenced by a candidate's broad sense of tolerance," GOP pollster Bill McInturff says. So the next time you see Bush or Gore speaking Spanish to janitors in East L.A., remember this: He's really talking to white soccer moms in Farmington Hills, Michigan.

Latinos are only one part of the Bush compassion restoration. There's also Bush's "bipartisanship week," a way to show how he reaches out to the other side. One morning, I fly with Bush to Greensboro, North Carolina, where he has invited supporter Sandy Kress, a lawyer and a former Democratic county chairman, to join him in front of the cameras. Bush, speaking to nearly 1,000 people at a North Carolina Department of Public Instruction conference, also goes out of his way to praise North Carolina Governor James B. Hunt, Jr., a Democrat and a possible Gore running mate. "He's an education governor," Bush says of Hunt, adding, "We need to check partisanship at the door when it comes to the education of our children."

He tells the educators that he and Hunt and their states are "part of a new movement in education." A Bush press release notes that "Texas and North Carolina have been praised by Clinton Education Secretary Richard Riley." Bush aides also note that Bush is being introduced by Phil Kirk, a Republican appointed by Hunt to chair the state's board of education, though Kirk's introduction is perfunctory and faint, leading Bush to quip, "I always like a short introduction."

To be sure, even in this week of Bush's bipartisanship tour, Bush has shown that comity has its limits. He asked guests at a luncheon fundraiser whether they wanted "a man who trusts the people or a man who trusts government," and "a man who grew up in West Texas or a man who grew up in Washington." Later, at a news conference, he cited a decade-old remark by Gore that he would "rip the lungs out" of his opponent. "I'll respond," Bush vowed, to what he perceives as Gore's attacks. Asked what he would do if Gore accused him of hypocrisy, Bush said he would laugh.

When a reporter notes that the Republicans attending Wednesday night's fundraiser in Washington gave him energetic applause for his partisan attacks but a lukewarm response to his peace overtures, Bush shrugs it off. "I made the right statements, applause or no applause," he says.

Soon after Bush's bipartisanship week, I join the governor on another trip though battleground states, in which he details plans to take the partisan poison out of Washington. (Okay, so he would do this in large part by transferring power from Congress to the president, who presumably would be himself.)

"If the discord in Washington never seems to end, it's because the budget process never seems to end," Bush tells about 600 people in brilliant sunshine outside the Knoxville Civic Auditorium. He decries an environment of "too much polling and not enough decision-making." "Americans look upon the spectacle of Washington and they do not like what they see," Bush declares. "I agree with them. It's time for a change."

His proposals are complex and geared more toward Washington insiders than swing voters. He wants to revamp the federal budget process to shift budget-making from an annual to a biennial exercise and to require the president and Congress to agree on spending targets early in the process, to prevent government shutdowns.

Again, as in the last bipartisanship tour, Bush and his supporters mix in a couple of partisan shots. "All we have heard from my opponent are the familiar exaggerations and scare tactics," Bush tells the crowd in Vice President Gore's home state. "Proposals he disapproves of are never just arguments; they're 'risky schemes.' This kind of unnecessary rhetoric is characteristic of the tone in Washington, D.C. It's the 'war room' mentality."

But the biggest offender is Republican Governor Don Sundquist, who introduces Bush by saying of his proposals, "You're right on every one and Gore is wrong." He must not have read the bipartisanship memo.

Or perhaps that's the strategy: Bush talks much about bipartisanship, but as a way to paint Gore as a partisan hack. This is a high-road form of negative campaigning.

A crucial piece of Bush's swing toward the middle and toward bipartisan bliss is his example in Texas, where he has, by all accounts, gotten along famously with Democrats, albeit conservatives, in the state legislature. In fact, his popularity among Texans, and Texas Democratic voters, is so high that the party seems well on its way to oblivion. There are hardly any Democrats left in his state.

Molly Beth Malcolm must feel like a Philip Morris salesman at an American Lung Association conference. Or perhaps a Serbian tourism agent in Bosnia. The difference is Malcolm's job is more perilous: she is Al Gore's chief cheerleader in Texas.

Being chairwoman of the Texas Democratic Party would be bad enough. Within months of taking the helm two years ago, she watched the Democrats lose the last of 29 statewide elected positions. Democrats have surrendered the Texas Senate and are just hanging on in the House. More than 100 elected Democrats have defected to the GOP since George W. Bush became governor. "It hasn't been an easy job," Malcolm allows. "This party has been through some tough times."

The worst may be yet to come. As the state party opened its annual convention yesterday in Fort Worth, Malcolm must contend with the governor's 47-point lead over Gore in the polls here. (Gore's lead in his home state of Tennessee, by contrast, is in the single digits.) Even some Democrats in the state legislature are backing Bush—and most of the rest don't dare criticize him. Making matters worse for Malcolm, Gore has adopted a campaign strategy of painting Texas as a polluted, illiterate, gun-toting, unhealthy backwater.

Just about everybody likes Bush here in the Lone Star State. "Space Alien Backs Bush for President," reads the headline in a recent issue of *Weekly World News*, displayed alongside *Newsweek* and the *National Journal* outside Malcolm's office. This same alien, a smaller head-line reveals, "Helped Clinton Win Top Job in 1992." Must be a swing voter. "That is a bad sign," Malcolm says, but quickly adds: "It doesn't disturb me."

No indeed. Malcolm is not the type to let a few bad polls and a meddling extraterrestrial get in her way. She is determined to make Gore's case in Texas—even if nobody else will.

"She's the best," says party spokesman Mike Hailey. "And the only."

Just listen to her partisan barrage:

On Bush's intellect: "He admits he doesn't like to read books!"

On his appointees: "Some very frightening ideas!"

On his equivocations: "I call him Governor Beat Around the Bush."

On his gun policy: "He is a political opportunist!"

On his pollution regulation: "Fox in the henhouse!"

And Malcolm is just warming up. "Let me get some talking points," she says, leaving her office. She returns with papers and continues the assault, now standing. "How handled is he? . . . He's got a canned talk! . . . That ought to raise concern. . . . What does he know?" Next, she's gesturing out her window, toward the governor's mansion across the street. "Out of touch with reality!" she protests.

Malcolm is not everybody's idea of a party chairman. "Molly Beth who?" is how *Texas Monthly* greeted her election. She is a former Republican who switched parties in 1992 after her husband lost a race for county GOP chairman to a candidate backed by social conservatives. A former teacher and school counselor, she became active in a Democratic women's group. Eight years later, at age 45, she sits in the party chair's office with a photo of Al Gore on the wall, a stuffed donkey on her desk and another one hugging her computer. "I left the Republican Party when everyone was going the other way," she says. "My parents didn't teach me to do what's popular. They taught me to do what's right."

Lifelong party members can't match her zeal. Two Democrats, State Representative Rob Junell and State Senator Ken Armbrister, recently traveled to Dayton, Ohio, to campaign for Bush, along with a couple of former Democratic legislators. The Democratic mayor of El Paso has signed on, too. For Armbrister, it's a safe bet. "If he wins, we'll have a direct voice to the president," he says. "If he doesn't win, you've still got to work with him as governor." (Bush's term runs through 2002.)

Local Democrats have also been offended by Gore's attempt to tarnish Bush's Texas. "If somebody takes on my state, I'll stand up to him," says Armbrister. Adds Junell: "It's hard to be for a guy who tells you you're part of a Third World country."

Malcolm wishes other Texas Gore-backers would speak up. But most politicians don't want to do it. "They say things quietly but won't say stuff on the record." It's almost an underground movement. "People say, 'I'll vote for him but I don't want to talk about it,'" she says, making a whispering gesture. "They fear retribution."

Not Malcolm. She wears a Gore pin and has a Gore bumper sticker on her car. She distributes pins of Bush with a Pinocchio nose. She appears before any camera that will record her lonely Bush critique. "There are people who say, 'Aren't you afraid of what he'll do to you?'" she tells me. "I can't live my life worrying about what George Bush would say."

Even Bob Bullock, the late Democratic lieutenant governor, backed Bush in '98 over Democrat Gary Mauro—though Bullock was the godfather of Mauro's children. This year, the party couldn't get a candidate of stature to run against Senator Kay Bailey Hutchison. President Clinton is coming here in two weeks for a fund-raiser for Democratic Senate candidates. But the Texas nominee, Gene Kelly, won't get any money because, as one event organizer put it in the *Austin American-Statesman*, "he has no chance to win."

"The Democrats are imploding," says a gleeful Kent Martin, who is coordinating the Texas GOP's campaigns in 2000. "Every year they become more and more irrelevant."

Rubbish, says Malcolm. "This party's demise is greatly exaggerated." For one thing, she vows, "Al Gore will do better in Texas than people give him credit for."

With Malcolm's hard work—and some divine intervention—Gore could win here. Even if he doesn't, Malcolm's reputation is assured. Texans, after all, love heroic failure. Remember the Alamo?

24

★ ☆ ★

Pandarus Albertus

Since the dawn of civilization, man has pandered. In the *Iliad* Homer introduces us to Pandarus, an unlucky Trojan warrior. Pandarus returns in Chaucer, and in Shakespeare's *Troilus and Cressida* Pandarus is a pimp, a "pitiful goer-between" of lovers. Happily, pandering has evolved into new species over the centuries. In the 2000 presidential race, we have two experienced panderers vying to honor the tradition.

We begin with Vice President Gore addressing a teachers' union convention in Philadelphia. He promises to "recruit one million new teachers," "raise teacher salaries," "give you all the training and support you need," and, of course, "never support private school vouchers." The beaming union president gives Gore a big hug. As pandering goes, however, the performance is fairly basic, employing primitive pandering known as the empty pander and the full-frontal pander (see Pandarus vacuus and Pandarus nudus, below).

While Bush pulls off a remarkable recovery of the middle ground this spring, Gore has gone the other way, returning to an unfortunate instinct to pander and to ponder, traits that got him in trouble early in the primary season. Gore and the Democrats left the primaries more united than the Republicans, but the candidate has pretty much squandered his advantage by avoiding tough and contentious politics—even as Bush deftly paints Gore as a partisan hack.

Gore's unfortunate intimacy with the pander dates back to the bad old days of the early primary campaign. In one week last year, Gore declared that he wanted to abandon the Clinton administration's "don't ask, don't tell" policy for gays in the military. Before anybody could figure out that one, Gore confounded his supporters again with a follow-up pander. Gore then broke with the Clinton administration to recommend "flexibility" in the use of marijuana as a pain reliever. A hit with the drug legalization crowd, Gore's new position went even further than that of his more liberal Democratic challenger, Bill Bradley.

You could hear the groans coming out of the Capitol Hill offices of the Democratic Leadership Council, the brain trust for the moderate "New Democrat" movement that carried Clinton to the White House. Gore seemed to be morphing into Walter Mondale and Michael Dukakis before their very eyes.

Donna Brazile, Gore's campaign manager and a former acolyte of Jesse Jackson, spelled it out last winter in her now-famous remarks to *Washington Post* political reporter Ceci Connolly: "The four pillars of the Democratic Party are African Americans, labor, women, and what I call other ethnic minorities." She then listed other "emerging constituencies": environmentalists, gays and the disabled.

Yet Gore's panderama continued. He objected to the Clinton deal with congressional Republicans that cleared the way for the United States to pay its withheld U.N. dues, worried that he would lose women's support because of the agreement's ban on U.S. money to international groups that advocate abortion rights.

He delivered full-throated defenses of affirmative action, aggravating Democratic moderates seeking new solutions. Rarely a day went by when Gore didn't attack Bradley's health care plan (a proposal that the DLC gave favorable reviews) as an assault on the poor, the disabled and minorities.

Now, in the quiet days of the general election, Gore has returned needlessly to pander mode. As Bush tries to raid Democratic constituencies, Gore, rather than raiding Republican constituencies, is trying to outdo Bush in overtures to the left. It's not so much that Gore is pandering and Bush isn't; it's that Bush is pandering smarter than Gore is.

George W. Bush, facing a skeptical NAACP convention in Baltimore, executes an expert pander. "While some in my party have avoided the NAACP," he says, "I'm proud to be here." He continues: "The party of Lincoln has not always carried the mantle of Lincoln. . . . What we need is a new attitude." Thus does Bush perform the Pandarus obliquus, an indirect appeal to white suburban soccer moms who will later see TV ads featuring the speech.

A popular view is that Bush doesn't pander, while Gore pimps for narrow interests. In truth, Bush is just a more evolved panderer.

It is time to praise the art of the political pander. That would be the practice of promising groups of people what they want, but not necessarily what they need. Consider what pandering has given us over the years: the Constitution (why else would Rhode Island have as many senators as

New York?), the Emancipation Proclamation, the eight-hour workday, Medicare, highways, parks and ethanol subsidies. There is pandering in most everything—every policy has its constituency—and even the most naked of panders can have an element of conviction.

"Pandering shows that politicians respond to the people," says Rick Stengel, a former Bill Bradley adviser and author of the book *You're Too Kind: A Brief History of Flattery.* Stalin, after all, didn't do much pandering.

Both parties appreciate an artful pander. "I always tell my clients: A man never stands so tall as when he stoops to kiss [a rear end]," says Paul Begala, a former Clinton adviser. John McLaughlin, a GOP pollster, concurs: "Pandering with a purpose really creates the debate democracy runs by."

A good pander should be unexpected, credible, sincere and have some broader justification. Columbia University's Robert Shapiro, co-author of the book *Politicians Don't Pander,* divides panders into bad and good, like cholesterol. Bad pandering satisfies the whim of one group. Good pandering, says Shapiro, "uses information about public opinion to make policies that do the public good."

In celebration of the pander, then, let us study the genus to see how we can separate the primeval panders (bad) from the evolved panders (good).

Bad Panders

- *Pandarus nudus:* The full-frontal pander. Leading this category is the Israel pander, a ritual for decades, in which the non-incumbent presidential candidate pledges to move the U.S. embassy from Tel Aviv to Jerusalem. Usually, the candidate changes this position once elected (see Pandarus dubius). Bush has made the obligatory pander. But Senator Orrin Hatch went one better: he slipped and called for "a united and indivisible Jerusalem as the capital of Utah."

   A subspecies of the naked pander is Pandarus nudus desperatus: the panic pander. Exhibit A is Gore's sympathetic line toward Elian Gonzalez's Miami relatives. This didn't do him much good with Florida's heavily Republican Cubans, and made him look foolish to everybody else.

- *Pandarus vacuus:* Substance-free Pander Lite. Consider Gore's remark to a Latino audience on May 5. "My grandson was born on the Fourth of July," he said. "If I have another grandchild, I hope he's born on Cinco de Mayo." The empty pander also has a tendency to backfire, as when Gore addressed a Jewish audience and mispronounced the Hebrew word for kindness, chesed. He replaced the guttural "ch" (as in *chutzpah*) with the soulid used to pronounce *cheese*.

* *Pandarus dubius:* This is the contradictory pander. Bush, for example, boasted that under his tax plan "the highest percentage cuts will go to those taxpayers with the lowest incomes." But Bush later cast doubt on his motives, saying he wanted to cut taxes more for the rich, but "I wasn't able to justify it." Gore's best example is his claim that his sister's death from lung cancer made him a crusader against tobacco; it turns out that after his sister's death, Gore continued to accept tobacco campaign contributions.

Pandarus dubius has been known to produce a mutant subspecies, the pander climbdown (Pandarus regressus). Most prominent here is Bush's Bob Jones pander, followed by a (pandering) letter to New York's Catholic cardinal explaining his visit to the anti-Catholic school. The gay issue often causes Pandarus regressus. Gore backpedaled almost immediately after suggesting that the Joint Chiefs must support gays in the military.

* *Pandarus mea culpa:* The grovel pander. This pander, rarely successful, requires the politician to admit wrongdoing. "Generally this one is performed at bayonet point in October," says Mike Murphy, a GOP strategist. Gore did this on campaign finance; he says he's learned from his "mistakes" and will make reform the first act of his administration.

* *Pandarus historicus:* Politicians use the historical pander to evade charges of flip-flopping. Hillary Rodham Clinton, for example, says she was always a moderate and a Yankees fan—but she apparently kept both good secrets. Bush prefers a subspecies, Pandarus antebellum: the states' rights pander. Grilled about the Confederate flag flying over the South Carolina capitol, Bush responded, "I trust the people of South Carolina." Asked if he had a personal reaction to the Confederate flag, he replied, "Not in South Carolina."

Good Panders

* *Pandarus obliquus:* The indirect pander is an evolved form of the fullfrontal pander, in which the politician makes a clear pander—but not to the group he is addressing. Gore, for example, addressing a Hispanic group, made a pander to National Endowment for the Arts enthusiasts, calling the arts as indispensable as air and water.

A more complex form of the indirect pander is the reverse pander, Pandarus contrarium, in which the panderer panders to one group by insulting a group on the other side. Clinton's Sister Souljah gesture in 1992, when he defied Jesse Jackson to oppose an inflammatory black rapper, was a pander to centrist Democrats. This time, Bush has done the same with his "compassionate conservative" label—implying that conservatives aren't usually compassionate—and when he criticized conservatives who complain that America is "slouching toward Gomorrah." Both were panders to moderate, swing voters.

* *Pandarus vulgaris:* The populist pander flatters the wisdom of large swaths of the electorate. Reagan often said he "never failed when I trusted in the wisdom of the American people." Sure, Lincoln may have talked about fooling all of the people some of the time, but these days voters want to be flattered. Clinton's empathy toward millions of Americans hurt by recession in 1992 ("I feel your pain") is in "the pander hall of fame," says McLaughlin, the GOP pollster.

* *Pandarus furtivus:* The crossover pander. Bush has demonstrated that full-frontal pandering can work—if you do it to the other guy's constituents. He's come up with a bunch of government giveaways usually associated with Democrats, such as money for new housing programs and disability research. Speaking to a Hispanic group, he made a strong defense of bilingual education and pledged reforms to make the Immigration and Naturalization Service friendlier.

Gore, too, has tried this form of pandering. During the primaries, he pandered to conservatives by suggesting that creationism could be taught in schools.

Pandarus furtivus is not to be confused with a less-evolved species, Pandarus subterraneus: the stealth pander. This is a full-frontal pander made secretly. Bush accomplished this with his hush-hush address last year to the Council for National Policy, which includes such members as Oliver North, Pat Robertson and Jesse Helms. When word got out that the meeting was recorded, Bush made sure the tape wasn't released.

* *Pandarus sincerus:* The candor pander was practiced by Paul Tsongas in 1992 and most recently by Bradley and McCain. The panderer promises to tell voters what they don't want to hear, often about balanced budgets and actuarial deficits. "You're pandering to the species Editorialus pontificatus," says Begala. "That gets you a lot

of good editorials." Gore attempts this by saying teachers "need tough new standards."

A close relative, also targeting opinion leaders, is the substance pander. Clinton, for example, wooed columnists by showing off his intricate knowledge of entitlement programs. Bush, needless to say, never attempts a substance pander. But he has proved adept recently at pandering to reporters with a technique used by one of his primary rivals: the access pander. Journalists, after all, care less about ideology than about rubbing elbows with the candidate. Call this one Pandarus mccainus.

Gore has two problems this spring. One is pandarus, the other is ponderous—being too much of an earnest egghead for people to like him.

He is, quite literally, playing the teacher's pet. In fact, following the rather alarming revelation may not be suitable for school-age children, not to mention Tipper Gore. But the truth must be told: The vice president has been sleeping around.

"I'm going to spend the night with a public school teacher in Michigan tonight," Al Gore told a crowd in Cincinnati not long ago, producing titters among the educators in the audience. A woman in the front row caught Gore's eye, pointed at herself and seductively mouthed a proposition: "Me?"

Gore tried to recover, making clear the teacher's husband would be home. But he hasn't changed his ways. Gore aims to sleep in the home of a teacher one night a week as part of his "School Days" tour. He's already done it in Michigan, Ohio, California and here in North Carolina. The man's a veritable Wilt Chamberlain on the campaign trail.

The George W. Bush campaign dismisses such "slumber parties" and insists its candidate sleeps with only one teacher—a former school librarian who happens to be his wife. The Republican, to be sure, is doing plenty to show how much he cares about education, even bragging recently that he has visited 100 schools. But it would be impossible to outdo Gore in his quest to be edu-wonk this spring.

Gore visited a school in North Carolina, then a Michigan school where he spoke gibberish in a drama class exercise. "Wub woo bub bub wub wub" is how the Associated Press transcribed it. Gore hosted a school safety forum in New Jersey and gave an education speech in Texas. He flew to a middle school in Tampa, a Montessori school in Cincinnati and a school in Columbus (where he ate cafeteria sausage and French toast). He sent out a release saying "Bush's education plans fail to make the grade" and called an education conference in West Virginia.

There is so much edu-campaigning going on in the 2000 presidential race that nobody seems to raise the obvious question: What are these guys doing? Education, after all, is largely out of the federal government's domain. The federal share of education spending is only 7 percent. Heck, the feds spend 50 percent more money on medical care for veterans than they do on schools. And states and localities call almost all the shots.

The presidential education duel is about as logical as two mayoral candidates running on missile defense. "You're right," Governor Bush says when asked about the paradox. The feds can give out some money and demand results, but "most of the power should be at the local level."

Campaign advisers know this well. "Honestly, I don't think anything you do at the federal level is something people will notice," says Nina Rees, a Bush education adviser with the Heritage Foundation. Elaine Kamarck, Gore's top domestic policy adviser, concurs: "There's no particular reason to take [education] over from the states."

The real importance of the edu-campaign is less policy than symbolism. A president can't do much about education, but isn't it fun to play school? In that spirit, then, pack your lunch box and grab a No. 2 pencil. We're going edu-campaigning in North Carolina with Al Gore.

Gore's school day starts the night before at Andrews Air Force Base. Our school bus says "United States of America," and it takes us to a similarly labeled jet. Gore climbs aboard in bluejeans, ready for his big date. Later this evening he enjoys the attentions of one Laurel Warfield, a sixth-grade teacher in Charlotte. The next morning, Warfield reports that she and her husband fed the vice president bacon and eggs. "It was like one big happy family," she says. "My son's going to have a new sign over his bed, 'Al Gore Slept Here.'" (Before a Michigan school visit, Gore slept beneath Britney Spears posters in a bed normally occupied by a six-year-old girl.)

Gore, escorted by Warfield, enters Marie G. Davis Middle School, "Home of the Dolphins." The schoolchildren are thrilled—and why not? "They told us not to bring our book bags, just be prepared to see Mr. Gore," says student Brandon Holmes. Gore works the school while men in dark suits speak into their sleeves ("Naylor—we're back in the art class.") Gore's questions are probing. "Is that a spectrum?" he asked art students. In typing class: "Do you like the iMacs?" In chemistry: "What are you making, H_2O?" And to the support staff: "You're gonna serve me lunch?" (He apparently hasn't seen the boys' room graffiti: "Flush twice—it's a long way to the cafeteria.") Later, Gore talks to a history class and shares a stage with North Carolina Governor Jim Hunt—"the education governor"—as a way to trash Bush's voucher plans as a "formula for disaster."

Gore would have reaped the same media coverage from a one-hour visit as he does from his numbing eight-hour day. And this stuff won't alter the state of the union. He learns, for instance, that a bus driver wants children to eat fewer Jolly Ranchers because they keep vomiting on his bus. A school nurse wants more positions for nurses. But enduring such long days allows Gore, as he put it, "to say, symbolically, that education is my number one priority." Then he vows to continue his "School Days" as president. You can almost see the reporters shudder.

This is not how you light a fire under the electorate.

Gore's other strategy this spring is to establish himself as a raging populist. On the one hand, this makes sense. It's his father's tradition and one Gore adopted easily in the Senate. On the other hand, Gore's ties to moneyed interests and his campaign finance abuses make this theme a bit tenuous. As a result, the two sometimes collide.

This is what happens when I follow Gore on a visit to Pennsylvania, Ohio and Illinois. Gore, at every opportunity, beats his populist drum while criticizing Bush's Medicare policies as a threat to the health of the nation's elderly.

Gore's answer to his Republican rival's plan, which the vice president delivered at a senior center in the Chicago suburb of Niles, is equal parts Ross Perot and Cesar Chavez, a mixture of charts and passion for the poor. Gore criticizes Bush for not proposing a prescription drug benefit under Medicare and for providing "not one dime" to extend the actuarial life of the program.

"I'm on your side," Gore tells the gray-haired crowd of about 200. "I want to fight for the people. The other side fights for the powerful."

The people and the powerful. The phrase is ringing in my brain, giving me nightmares. Gore says it to everyone, often more than once in a sentence. I sit in on a series of a dozen or so interviews Gore is giving to TV affiliates in Chicago, one after another, from the same seat in the same room (a janitor's equipment room, actually) at the convention center. He tells each and every one, repeatedly, that he's for the people, the other guy's for the powerful. After the session, I walk up to Gore. "Sir, I just need one clarification. I'm confused: Are you for the people, or the powerful?"

Gore, to his credit, takes the ribbing in stride. Without changing his dour expression, he replies: "This is complicated, and I can see how you might miss the distinction. I am for the people. He is for the powerful." I see him a couple of hours later on Air Force Two, and make sure I've got it right. "For the powerful?" I ask, pointing at him. "People," he corrects, patiently.

But the distinction is about to get further muddied—and this time no joke. One of my colleagues at the *Post*, Dan Balz, has found out that when Gore attacks Citizens for Better Medicare this week for "polluting the air-waves" with ads opposing the Democrats' prescription drug plan, he is leaving out one important fact: his own top message adviser once sought to run the pharmaceutical industry's ad campaign.

Carter Eskew, the same ad man who got Gore into trouble because of his ties to the tobacco companies, unsuccessfully made a pitch to the phar-maceutical industry in mid-1999 to handle the lucrative advertising and public relations account now being run through Citizens for Better Medicare, an industry-funded group.

In their memo to the industry, Eskew and his firm warned that "a lead-ing presidential aspirant" could turn prescription drugs into a central issue in the 2000 elections and give industry opponents an "enormous" forum. He proposed a public relations campaign "to chill support for legislative efforts to impose . . . price controls on prescription drug medicines by showing how those measures would stifle the innovation at the core of the positive image the industry has built since 1993."

Today, Eskew is the chief architect of Gore's new populist message attacking the drug industry, big oil and other corporate interests. This week Gore has relentlessly accused the pharmaceutical industry of "price gouging," called Citizens for Better Medicare "a phony coalition" and cast the difference between himself and Texas Governor George W. Bush as one of "Whose side are you on?"

The task falls to me to break the news to Chris Lehane, Gore's spokesman. He puts on a brave front on the plane. "Where's the hypocrisy?" he responds. "The guy wasn't working for us at the time, and we never changed our views." But by the end of the flight, Lehane has thought it over, and he is looking somber. "This is going to be bad," he says, walking across the tarmac at Andrews Air Force Base. The problem is if you're for the people, you've got to watch out for advisers who are for the powerful.

Still, all is not lost in Goreland. For one, there are signs that he has retained a sense of humor. Earlier this spring, he spoke to the annual din-ner of the Gridiron Club, and directed a number of one-liners at himself. On his Washington upbringing: "I have to admit I feel a little out of my element here, but I suppose it's good for me to get out of Nashville every now and then." On the fund-raising scandal at the Buddhist temple: "I only have two clear recollections. I remember wondering, 'Which one is Richard Gere?' and also admiring the majestic burnt-umber robes of the Buddhist monks and saying, 'Hmmm, earth tones.'"

Then he had some fun with his own propensity to exaggerate. He saluted the Gridiron Club's 115-year tradition, "one I invented," and talked about Senator John McCain's "Star Wars" campaign theme, noting that "Luke Skywalker was loosely based on me." Gore mentioned that his wife, Tipper, has been warning him against such tall tales: "She must have told me that 5 billion times—literally."

Another sign of hope for Gore comes in some recent personnel changes (no, not another pollster, though I believe he's on his seventh). He has replaced tyrannical campaign chairman Tony Coelho, who is ill, with a white-knight chairman, Bill Daley. And he has asked his friend and brother-in-law Frank Hunger, one of the few true Gore friends in the world, to be his traveling companion. Both seem to have Gore in better spirits as the conventions approach.

Daley is the sort of no-nonsense guy Gore needs to get his wayward campaign staff into high gear. I catch up with him early on the Sunday morning after he's named chairman.

A bald man in a gray pinstripe suit enters an office building on North Capitol Street and announces that he wants to go to the studios of Fox News.

The security guard is having none of it. "Do you have a photo ID?" she asks.

The man searches his pockets. "No, I don't," he says sheepishly. "I forgot my wallet."

"Well, I'll have to call upstairs," the guard rejoins.

Finally, a young woman from Fox emerges from the elevator. "Sorry about the mix-up, Mr. Secretary," she says.

Mr. Secretary? Yes, in the flesh. For William M. Daley, the U.S. commerce secretary and new chairman of the Gore presidential campaign, such invisibility is standard—and welcome. In a town of virtuoso publicity magnets, he is a practiced and expert second fiddle.

He's the Daley who's not the mayor of Chicago (that's his brother Richard), the Cabinet secretary who fainted from nerves at the announcement of his appointment. He's a regular at the Ground Zero of Ego, the Palm steakhouse, but warns that if they put his caricature on the wall, he'll never eat there again. He has declined the security detail offered to Cabinet members.

Daley, by his own admission, is a throwback. He wears a fedora in winter, sport coats on weekends. He instituted "casual Fridays" in the Commerce Department but still wears dark suits. He likes Sinatra and "easy listening." He doesn't use foul language or tell racy jokes. He opens doors for ladies. "He observes all the conventions," says Charlene Barshefsky, the U.S. trade representative.

Above all, Daley, 51, is retro in his love of doing politics in the shadows. "He's done that not only in politics but in life generally," says his brother John. "He's more back-room."

There are two types of power in Washington: the power wielded by the elected, who practice the art of self-glorification, and the power wielded by the unelected, who practice their art of power away from public view.

The latter has become, increasingly, a lost art in the capital, as even the behind-the-scenes guys demand the spotlight. Fundraisers such as Terry McAuliffe and lobbyists like Vernon Jordan take center stage on Washington's social scene, while lawyers like Greg Craig and Bob Bennett command greater name recognition than most pols. A former White House staffer like George Stephanopoulos aims for celebrity, while an ex-Cabinet member like Bob Reich publishes a kiss-and-tell book about the president.

Against that backdrop, a man such as Daley, who never held elected office and thrives on anonymity, is increasingly rare. He can be as vain as the next guy, as he readily admits. "I've got an ego, a healthy one, don't get me wrong," he says. "So far I've managed to keep it in check. In some of these jobs you tend to think you're the Second Coming."

To that end, he likes to play the fixer. He takes on embattled causes—NAFTA, the Commerce Department, trade relations with China. He fights doggedly for them, subjugating his own ego and usually engineering come-from-behind victories.

As Daley heads to Nashville this morning for his first visit to Gore headquarters, the question is: Can he do the same for the vice president?

They call it the Full Ginsburg. It is a feat so intricate in orchestration, so demanding in endurance, that only one man has ever done it. That was Bill Ginsburg, Monica Lewinsky's lawyer, who burst onto the sets of all five political chat shows one glorious Sunday in February 1998. Since then, Rudy Giuliani and Rick Lazio have imitated the feat, but from New York studios. On this third Sunday in June, says CNN producer Sam Feist, Daley is executing "the first Full Ginsburg in Washington since Bill Ginsburg."

Daley, quite obviously, is not at one with this role. He exhales deeply off camera to fight the jitters, and he shuffles his feet while answering questions. The campaign's spinmeisters told him they desperately needed a chairman to put his mug on the air, because Daley's predecessor, Tony Coelho, wouldn't. But Daley, as his friend Jim Johnson puts it, "does what has to be done." Along the way, Daley turns the Sunday TV marathon into an exercise in self-deprecation.

At Fox, the makeup woman sympathizes with him about the exertion of the campaign trail. "I don't know how you do it," she says.

"I don't know, either," he says.

Tony Snow, the Fox host, enters the makeup room. "The Full Ginsburg, huh?" he asks.

Daley isn't flattered. "Didn't Ginsburg get fired by his client?"

A few minutes later, he charges out of the Fox studio and to his car, through Rock Creek Park and up Massachusetts Avenue to NBC. Chris Lehane, the campaign press secretary, is trying to amuse Daley in the car with a tale about his days as a bellhop in Maine. "I'm just a different version of a bellhop now," Lehane says.

"We all are," Daley observes.

When Daley arrives at NBC, with a coffee stain on his shirt, he's hustled into the studio, where Tim Russert grills him on Gore's woes. "What's the problem?" he asks. But Daley is cool. "We have created an economy that's the envy of the world," he says. His Chicago accent makes the word come out *ecahnomy*. Why mess it up with a *myahssive* tax cut?

Within a minute, he's out the door and speeding toward the ABC studio downtown, this time with a network employee in the car shouting nervously into her cell phone. It's only ten minutes to air time. "We're passing the British Embassy!" she shouts. "We're at 22nd and Mass! We're passing the Westin Fairfax!"

"We should have a white Bronco," Daley observes dryly. He gets to ABC on time, but then has only a few minutes to linger before he's off to CBS.

By now, Daley is getting weary. He has a few testy lines on air, then faces a bank of cameras on the sidewalk. "Anything you plan to do differently right away?" one reporter asks.

"Stop doing so many TV shows," he says.

But not before the finale at CNN. Now he's so loose he makes a cross-eyed face at the camera before showtime. Wolf Blitzer, the host, flashes more bad poll numbers on the screen and fires off the same questions. "You've done a full Bill Ginsburg," Blitzer says. "Is this going to be a new policy of yours?"

"I hope not," Daley replies. It's hard to doubt his sincerity.

During Daley's long morning on the airwaves, one moment stands out as particularly revealing—perhaps inadvertently so. As he waits for his turn on ABC's *This Week*, he stands in the control room listening to Sam Donaldson talk about Gore's problems and about how the new chairman "has his work cut out for him."

"Why," Daley asks nobody in particular, "am I doing this?"

Why, indeed?

Daley, the youngest of seven children, learned from an early age that he liked living on the fringes of power. "When my dad was alive, everybody was in the shadows," he says. He got to visit JFK and LBJ and swim in the White House pool, he got to see the Democratic conventions of '64 and '68, he met the Queen of England. But he was a witness to history, never the center of attention. The senior Richard Daley, who ruled Chicago from the 1950s through 1976, preached to his children the Catholic virtue of humility. He lived in the same house his whole adult life, a half-block from where he was born, in the blue-collar neighborhood of Bridgeport.

"All his friends were policemen, mechanics, whatever," Bill Daley says. Today, he often cites the wisdom of his mother ("Keep your ears open and your mouth shut") and his father ("Take a small job. It'll last longer"). He also remembers his father's lesson that "there's nothing better than a dead politician" for measuring the ephemeral nature of political power. When his father died, the 28-year-old Bill found that to many supposed pals, "suddenly I wasn't quite their friend."

A decade later, he was devoting himself to another relative's glory, this time directing his brother's mayoral campaigns. "Bill is the political brains behind his brother," says Chicago Democratic consultant David Axelrod.

After managing his brother's losing bid for mayor in 1983, Daley scrapped the old campaign playbooks. He cobbled together a multiracial coalition that got his brother elected. Daley himself describes his role modestly: "I was able to live vicariously through my brother."

Daley loves political machinations, and he was the lord of Chicago's backroom deals in the 1980s. When Michael Whouley was collecting delegates for Michael Dukakis in 1988, Daley gave him a few names. One man, told that Whouley had been sent by Daley, filled out all the paperwork before even asking which candidate he had agreed to represent.

"It wasn't like meeting the pope, but it was like meeting a major cardinal," Whouley says of Daley. Even now, Daley's brother, the mayor, has a betting pool to see who can best predict the city's election results in each of the 50 wards. "Bill's walked away with the pot the last two elections even though he's not even in town," Axelrod says.

In promoting his brother, Bill Daley was also perpetuating the power of the Daley name, which has given him a good life so far. A graduate of Loyola University and John Marshall Law School in Chicago, Bill Daley practiced law with a brother; their father steered them business. Later, Daley landed on various boards, including Fannie Mae's, and after a stint in the early 1990s as a Chicago bank executive, he became a partner in 1993 at that city's elite Mayer, Brown & Platt law firm, where he was a powerful lobbyist.

When his mayor-brother helped Clinton in Illinois in 1992, Bill Daley became close to the campaign and expected a Cabinet post. He was passed over in the first term but finally was named commerce secretary at the end of 1996, an appointment his brother labeled an "early Christmas present" to the Daley family. Bill, unaccustomed to being the one onstage, collapsed while the president was announcing his appointment. He claimed he hadn't eaten that morning and was hot.

Naturally, the idea of vicarious celebrity, which had worked so well for Daley in Chicago, came with him to Washington. Grabbing the limelight is counterproductive, he says. "You just make enemies."

At Commerce, Daley had the dubious task of salvaging the reputation of the department, targeted by some in Congress for elimination. Commerce's critics on the Hill charged that the late Ron Brown had turned the agency into a Democratic fund-raising arm, using foreign trips to woo donors. Daley put a moratorium on trade missions and slashed Commerce's political appointees from 256 to 140. He made sure the department passed its financial audit for the first time, and he took care of each of the top ten problems cited by Commerce's inspector general.

"Nobody talks about dismantling us these days," says David Lane, Daley's staff chief and a likely candidate to join his boss in Nashville.

Daley buried himself in the humdrum tasks, such as working the phones to make sure Congress didn't let legislation against overseas bribery die, thus saving an international agreement. "He got no headlines as the man who saved anti-bribery legislation," says Andy Pincus, Commerce's general counsel.

It almost goes without saying, then, that Daley will demand that others adopt his love of anonymous toil at Gore headquarters. "There's only one face of the campaign and that's Al Gore's," he says. "I don't think there should be personalities around the campaign. Everyone's going to get their fifteen minutes of fame out of this."

How old-fashioned. But then, we're talking about Bill Daley, who is traditional to the point of cliché. He has been married to one woman, Loretta, for decades, and calls his siblings and 93-year-old mother almost daily. He owns one pair of bluejeans, purchased for gardening at his summer home in Michigan, which he never got around to doing. He vacations with family and keeps photos of his parents, his mayor-brother, and his four children, one deceased, in his office. He reads historical biographies. He plays golf. He likes the White Sox and big steaks. "I've known him for twelve years," says Whouley. "I don't know anything provocative about the guy."

Daley, asked about his archaic ways, offers a characteristic demurral. "It's the way I've always been," he says. "You are what you are. When you're 52 years old, you don't change."

Daley is that rare man in his fifties who rounds his age up a year. His birthday isn't until August 9.

Before Tony Coelho became chairman, Al Gore talked with Bill Daley about running his campaign. Ultimately, the vice president selected Coelho, the former House whip, as a turnaround artist who could shake up his lethargic campaign. Coelho bruised egos and made enemies, but he enforced discipline—and it worked. Gore won the AFL-CIO endorsement, cut his spending and whipped Bill Bradley. But after the primaries, Coelho's interest group–based politics lost its effectiveness, Gore advisers resumed squabbling and Coelho's intestinal illness flared up.

Daley now can play the enviable role of the white knight. He is well liked by staff: while Coelho was new to presidential politics and most Gore advisers, Daley knows Gore advisers Donna Brazile, Tad Devine and Whouley from his time on the Mondale and Dukakis campaigns.

Coelho didn't do TV appearances, and when he did answer questions, they tended to be about his own business dealings, not about Gore. Daley, too, has his p.r. troubles; labor doesn't forgive him for his free-trade advocacy, and there have been charges from his years as a lawyer and banker over conflicts of interest and "pinstripe patronage." But nothing has stuck.

Gore aides also expect the new chairman to loosen the operation. "Daley can serve more in a traditional chairman role," says Tom Nides, a friend who works at Fannie Mae. "He can focus on the big pieces, not worry about the size of the podium at the convention."

Daley seconds that analysis. "I do view my role differently, as chairman of a company instead of chief operating officer," he says. "Tony tried to meld two into one, and I think that's hard. A big part of the chairman's role is to be representing the campaign, not try to micromanage this thing."

Daley has the Chicago ward heeler's knack for demanding loyalty. His predecessor at Gore 2000 was a screamer, but Daley never raises his voice—except on the golf course, where he'll strike the occasional club on the ground.

Not that Daley avoids a fight. He defied a rebellion from congressional staffers and his own bureaucrats when he reassigned 10 percent of his senior executives at Commerce to break up what he saw as the agency's stale culture. "He got his doctorate in politics in Chicago," says Chuck Campion, a Democratic consultant and friend of Daley's. "Most politics is Cub Scouts. They're Hell's Angels." "We've already broken bread—well, bagels," Brazile reports after meeting Daley in Washington. She had cinnamon-raisin with cream cheese. And Daley? Plain, of course.

★ ☆ ★

While Daley rights the Gore staff, it falls to Frank Hunger to calm and soothe the candidate himself—something Hunger seems uniquely able to do.

Something strange is happening in the vice president's cabin as his jet flies from Chicago to Washington. Al Gore is uncharacteristically animated. One might even say, if such words can be used, that he is goofing around.

"Want to see what happens when you have a military contractor get you a VCR?" Gore asks a visitor, then leaps to his feet to demonstrate the custom-built Air Force Two machine. It is a baffling assortment of flashing colored buttons and mysterious commands. "Whichever one you press, it's the wrong one," Gore says, trying several buttons until a flashing airplane appears, but no movie. "It's perfectly logical," he says, chortling. "It's like that Simon Sez game without the music." Next, he demonstrates how he dislodges his TV screen from the ceiling—with a bent paper clip.

What's the source of this seldom-seen Gore mirth? Well, it appears to have something to do with the other gentleman sitting in the cabin with an impish grin, an aw-shucks manner, an Al Hunt hairdo and a Sam Adams beer in hand. The man is Frank Hunger, the husband of Gore's late sister.

Those watching Gore closely may notice a difference in the candidate's mood lately. This may have something to do with a rise in the polls. But you can't dismiss another recent change for Gore: his brother-in-law's decision to take a leave from the Washington office of the Long, Aldrich & Norman law firm to travel with Gore. Often wearing a rumpled blue blazer, khakis and incongruous wingtips, Hunger spends most every waking minute with Gore. He gets off the plane right after Gore at each stop and joins the candidate in his armored limo. Frank Hunger is, by all accounts, the number-one fan of the man from Tennessee.

"Frank's my closest friend, the closest thing I have to a brother," Gore says. "He's a voice of reason and calm." This relationship is one area of Gore's life absolutely immune from polls and calculations. He always wanted Hunger at his side down the stretch. "It was on page 362A of the plan," Gore jokes, "paragraph 3."

It is often said that Gore has few close friends, and many of those he does consider friends—Tom Downey, Roy Neel, Peter Knight and Jack Quinn—are Washington lobbyists or lawyers who, whether they seek it or not, stand to gain from their relationship with Gore. Hunger, like Tipper Gore, has only one loyalty. "There's no Frank Hunger agenda," says Jim Neal, the Watergate prosecutor, Gore lawyer and friend of both men.

"When he gives advice, it's his heartfelt belief, right or wrong." Adds Walter Dellinger, the former U.S. solicitor general, "Frank has absolutely no interest in gaining from his access."

Hunger, who at 64 is twelve years Gore's senior, met his late wife's brother forty years ago. In the sixteen years since Nancy Gore's death from lung cancer, Hunger, still a widower, has served Gore constantly. He has lived in the Gores' own private Virginia home for the seven years the Gores have lived at the Naval Observatory. He is a weekly fixture at the Gores' official residence, where he grows hot peppers and supplies beer for family cookouts.

Uncle Frank, as he is known, goes to his nephew Albert's football games and had a role in Karenna Gore Schiff's wedding ceremony. He took Albert and Karenna on a trip to Europe in 1996, spends holidays and watches movies with the Gores, and jogs with the vice president. "I love his children as though they were my own," says Hunger, who is childless.

When Karenna was younger, Uncle Frank gave her sips of beer and let her stay up late. She later confided in Hunger her doubts about finding the right man before she met her husband, and he's the guy who "always tracks down a bottle of red wine" on the campaign trail. And he's leak-proof. "He will never betray my father's confidence, so it allows my father to bat ideas or brainstorm or hypothesize without it showing up in the papers," she says.

Hunger, whose parents and wife are dead and who isn't very close to his only brother, sees the Gores as his family. "When Frank lost Nancy, I think the best way to still be connected to her was through her family," says Jay Stein, an old friend who runs the Stein Mart national retail chain. "That's what motivates him. More than anything else, he's saying to himself, 'Wouldn't my wife be proud?' Every time Al would win an election it was bittersweet because Nancy wasn't there to see it."

He keeps photos of Karenna and Kristin at their high school graduations, wearing a white dress of Nancy's, on the shelves of his Washington law office amid dozens of photos of the Gores. "I see some of her in every one of them," Hunger says with a tear on his cheek.

Hunger doesn't share information about the vice president even with close friends. "He doesn't talk to me about Gore," says Stephen Thomas, Hunger's longtime partner in the Lake Tindall law firm in Greenville, Mississippi, which Hunger left after 1992.

But Hunger is in on virtually every key Gore decision. He has advised Gore on top appointments to his campaign, combed through the line items in the campaign budget, recommended that Gore move his campaign to Tennessee and recently urged Gore to soften his attacks on Bush. He normally avoids offering strategic advice—Gore's advisers were nonplussed when he showed up for a recent political strategy session—saying he'd be "out of bounds" to do so.

But he doesn't hesitate to make occasional recommendations, with mixed results. He encouraged Gore to make a campaign issue of high gas prices, which worked out fairly well. But he also encouraged Gore to make his 1996 convention speech about Nancy's lung cancer death, which later came back to bite Gore. Still, Hunger sometimes is uncomfortable with this access to power. When Coelho called Gore to say he was too ill to continue as campaign chairman, Hunger, who was sitting with the vice president, decided to leave the room.

Gore is often accused of not knowing who he is, not being sure whether he grew up at St. Albans School for Boys or on a farm in Carthage, Tennessee. For Hunger, there can be no doubt about his roots. Frank Watson Hunger was born in Winona, Mississippi, population 3,000, the son of the local dry-cleaning proprietor. He keeps a thick Mississippi drawl and brings back tomatoes from Greenville for people in his Washington office. When in the Clinton-Gore administration he became an assistant attorney general, he drove a Toyota pickup truck to his job at the Justice Department. When in town, he dines nightly at the Calvert Grill, a fried-chicken joint in Alexandria, where he socializes with mechanics, insurance agents and telephone linemen. He keeps a toy pig in his office, a remnant of a lawsuit on hog cholera. He hunts dove and duck on his friend Billy Percy's farm.

Still, Hunger shows an eccentric streak. He keeps an old Jaguar and a Beechcraft 36 airplane in Greenville. He sends his neckties to a dry cleaner's in New York that unstitches them. On his sixtieth birthday, he jumped from a plane. "He has former roommates who are federal judges and U.S. senators on the one hand, and on the other hand good old boys whose Cadillacs have long horns on the hood," says Roy Campbell, a friend from Greenville. Indeed, Hunger has even been known to attend events for Republican Senator Thad Cochran, a law school roommate.

But it is Gore who gets Hunger's fiercest devotion. "I'll do anything for him," he says. "I've got no closer or better friend." If Hunger has a fault in his relationship with Gore, it's that he's so devoted to his brother-in-law that he can't even approach objectivity. In Hunger's eyes, Gore can do no wrong.

Did Gore have it easy in Vietnam? "That galls me. Give me a break."

Has Gore switched positions on abortion? "That's nonsense!"

Was Gore raised to run for office? "That's B.S."

Is Gore stiff? "[Expletive]!"

Was Gore insincere in his 1996 speech about his opposition to tobacco after Nancy's death? (The Gore farm continued to grow tobacco after her death.) "Jesus Christ—tobacco growing? Everybody in the world down there did. . . . He never thought about that more than flying to the moon. It's just nuts."

Hunger, fresh from the University of Mississippi, met Nancy Gore in 1959, when he visited Jane Dixon at Vanderbilt before leaving for Taiwan to be an Air Force personnel officer. He still remembers Nancy's outfit: plaid skirt, bobby socks, white blouse. "The most attractive woman I'd ever seen," he says. They married on the Gore farm in 1966, and she followed him to Greenville.

Hunger's interests, though, often turned to Tennessee. He got to know the teenage Al Gore and visited with the young Al and Tipper on the farm in Carthage. He encouraged Gore to go to law school, and when Gore first ran for Congress, Hunger flew up on weekends to drop leaflets. When Nancy Hunger was diagnosed with cancer in 1982, the beginning of a two-year illness, Hunger took time off from his law firm and flew her to Nashville for treatments. Hunger spent many hours with Nancy's only sibling as she died.

"He loved Nancy as much as I did," says an emotional Hunger. "He treated me like a brother, and his parents treated me like their child." When Ralph Thompson, a Hunger Air Force buddy and now a U.S. appellate judge, once dined with the senior Gores, Thompson remarked that they were lucky to have Hunger for a son-in-law. "Ralph," Pauline Gore replied, "Frank is our son."

Hunger piloted Gore around Tennessee in a single-engine plane for his '84 Senate race, and he appears in Gore's swearing-in photo, dedicated "to the world's greatest brother-in-law." Hunger keeps that on his office wall, alongside one of the two men embracing as the '92 election results were announced. Gore asked Hunger to join the administration in 1993, as head of the Justice Department's 700-lawyer civil division.

Throughout his ascent, though, Hunger has carried with him a palpable sorrow. When his law colleague Philip Bartz talked to him about Bartz's Labrador's death, "Frank couldn't talk about it—it got him choked up," Bartz says. Hunger keeps the 1972 Pontiac he and his wife used, even though it costs a fortune in upkeep. He preserves his Greenville home much as it was before she died, with pictures of the happy couple throughout.

Hunger also takes Nancy Gore's memory with him on her baby brother's campaign as he crisscrosses the country on little sleep. "I just know she would really want this," he says. "What success I've attained if any in life is in large measure from what she gave me as a person. She was always my champion and my best friend, the best thing that ever happened to me." With Nancy gone, the best Hunger can do now is repay the debt—to her brother. "I damn well am gonna be there for him," he says.

Part VI

★ ☆ ★

Summer 2000
Gore Takes the Conventions

25

★ ☆ ★

Candidates For Sale

Finally, the waiting is over. It's convention time. And we all know what that means. It means that the influence of corporate money, always the subtext in politics, becomes the actual text.

First, to Philadelphia, the first week in August. There are 15,000 reporters here for the Republican National Convention. Tom DeLay's goal is to avoid them all.

Dozens of politicians will take a turn at the podium this week, but DeLay, the usually garrulous House majority whip, won't be among them. Republicans are hosting hundreds of bashes and photo-ops, but the dozen events DeLay hosts or headlines will all be closed to the public and the press.

Not that this is surprising. As George W. Bush unveils a new and diverse Republican Party, the GOP convention is all sweetness and light, while DeLay, known as "the Hammer," is neither. He unapologetically packs cocktail parties and golf outings with cigar-smoking lobbyists, whose money provides perks to Republican congressmen and keeps them in power. "That's what politics is about," he says.

Problem is, in this post-McCain era, influence-peddling has become gauche. Just this week, Maryland's House speaker canceled a golf tournament for lobbyists, and this week Colin Powell blasted "affirmative action for lobbyists." In such a hostile environment, DeLay must protect his donors and members of Congress from those pesky reporters who tend to see him as an extortionist for conservative causes.

"Reporters are frustrated screenwriters," explains Jonathan Baron, DeLay's spokesman. "He fits a part." Specifically, the part calls for wearing a black hat and a painted-on mustache.

So far, DeLay has done a good job of avoiding 14,999 of the reporters here. But I am determined to watch him where he sleeps, where he eats, where he works, where he plays and, mostly, where he fund-raises.

If political conventions are all about money, this one looks like a tag sale. "Comcast / Proud Host / Republican Convention," says the sign on the convention arena, visible a mile away. Then there are the events: Representative J. C. Watts is brought to you by DaimlerChrysler, the New York delegation comes courtesy of Merrill Lynch, House Speaker Denny Hastert is provided by Morgan Stanley, Representative Bill Archer is sponsored by the Spirits Wholesalers of America, and the Commerce Committee is made possible by the American Chemistry Council.

DeLay outdoes them all. He has raised nearly $1 million from undisclosed sources to lavish on Republican members of Congress during the convention, allowing them to have chauffeured cars, concierge service, hospitality lounges and more.

I begin my effort to participate in such events on Sunday night at a downtown reception for the Texas delegation, at which DeLay is to be named Man of the Year by space contractors such as Boeing and Lockheed. A sign tells guests that the gathering is sponsored by Citigroup, Coastal Corp., Enron Corp., El Paso Energy and Reliant Energy—a bank and four energy companies. The event, like all DeLay events this week, is officially closed to the press. But a staffer allows me to enter, along with a few other journalists. It is a mistake that will not be repeated.

The spread is rich: cheeses, sandwiches, sweets and top-shelf booze. The banner on the stage is for DeLay's political action committee, ARMPAC: "Americans for a Republican Majority. Tom DeLay, chairman." Other PACs disguise their purposes with vague names like "American Renewal" or "Hope, Growth and Opportunity," but not DeLay. He wants money to elect Republicans.

When he enters the room, he is mobbed by admirers. Warily, he eyes the TV cameras closing in; they have ignored instructions to stay at the other end of the room. Within moments, an ABC reporter is in DeLay's face, demanding to know who paid for all the cars for members of Congress. "Can you name one or two?" the reporter challenges. "You'll never name them?"

"That's right," DeLay replies.

Don't you feel embarrassment at the excess? the reporter asks.

"None at all," DeLay says, and then walks away with a fixed grin.

An aide ushers DeLay to the podium, where he accepts the Boeing-Lockheed award with a big smile. The guests then depart with gift bags featuring lapel pins from the NRA and Citigroup, and a cigar from ARMPAC.

DeLay's staff tells me I can find him later that night at an event at the riverfront hosted by the National Republican Congressional Committee. But when I arrive, the woman at the entrance proclaims firmly, "No media." A big security guard pushes the gate closed, saying, "Step away from the gate. This is a private party." Instead, I try to see through the fence, past the blue fabric hung to deter prying glances. I can see candle lit tables, women in silk dresses and men in linen suits, and plenty of cocktails.

A Republican official sees me taking notes. "I'd like him escorted off the property," she says to the guard. "Will you please escort him off the property?" The guard does nothing, presumably because I am not on the property, which is, after all, a public park. Then another woman appears. "Sir, I have reports that you are harassing the staff," she says, and then asks two Philadelphia policemen to remove me.

Still pursuing DeLay, I try another entrance. Hundreds of Philadelphians, attracted by a planned fireworks show, have been similarly held back from much of the waterfront. The result is a scene that Bush's new Republican Party would be wise to avoid.

On one side of the fence is a largely white crowd, many lounging on the deck of a yacht (for another Republican event). On the other side of the fence is a diverse crowd of ordinary Philadelphians, in T-shirts, packed into an area too small to contain them. Various Philadelphians try to get into the event but are repelled. One of them is Osmand Taylor, an African American factory worker. "I was just trying to get to the bathroom," he says after GOP guards dismiss him from the premises.

Jim Wilkinson, a kindly Republican p.r. man, arrives at the gate to hear my grievance. I point to the wealth and race imbalance on either side of the gate. "You're way out of line, what you're insinuating," he tells me. It is no use arguing; I will not get in to see DeLay. Instead, I watch the event through an ABC camera's telephoto lens. We think we see DeLay, but we cannot tell for sure.

The hunt for DeLay continues Monday morning, when I visit the private Aronimink Golf Club in suburban Philadelphia, where DeLay is teeing off with about fifty lobbyists and congressmen. I drive up the club's driveway and see a big banner welcoming me to Tom DeLay's tournament. Then it lists the sponsors: America's Manufacturers, BlueCross BlueShield, American Insurance Association, and Qwest. Sneaking around the course, I notice that even the holes have sponsors. Citigroup has the first hole; the American Hospital Association has the tenth.

It is two hours and fifteen minutes before I finally spot DeLay on the ninth fairway. When DeLay realizes he is being watched, he points me out to his security guard, who approaches me to ask if I'm "with the tournament." I evade his question, then get a brief engagement with DeLay as he leaves the ninth green.

"Isn't anybody going to applaud?" he asks after sinking a long putt. I oblige. DeLay laments his declining game. "Since I've been deputy leader, my handicap's gone up," he says, but that's not important. It's about hanging out with lobbyists. "Getting to know these guys, that's what it's all about," he says.

With that, DeLay is gone. I realize I forgot to ask whether it costs more to sponsor a par-5 hole than a par-3.

The next chance for a DeLay sighting is at a Monday evening reception aboard the rail cars he has brought to the convention as a retreat for members of Congress and their donors. It is all off limits to the public and the press. A sign outside says, "ARMPAC and RoyB Fund's Celebration of America's Greatest Presidents."

Once again, a group of red-shirted Republican security men keeps me out, and once again I am peering through a chain-link fence for a glimpse of DeLay. Over the din of donors drinking cocktails, I can just make out what I believe to be the disembodied voice of DeLay railing about the ills of Democrats.

I spot Dani DeLay, the whip's daughter and a Republican official, and ask for her help. "Not now!" she shouts through the fence. "I have no authorization to talk." I ask when her father will come out. "When he wants to," she replies. Presently, a spokeswoman for DeLay named Emily approaches me at the fence. "You just going to stand out here?" she asks.

Unless I am allowed in, I reply.

"We've said from the beginning this is all going to be private," she says. "From what I know, he's not taking any interviews." In fact, "he may stay on the train" all night. I leave, without even getting one of the door prizes—a Microsoft seat cushion.

It is now midnight. There are multiple reports that DeLay is staying at the Philadelphia Navy Yard, a former military base, with 100 other lawmakers. The base is, naturally, closed to the public and guarded, but I wangle a ticket to a party for the California delegation at the base's "Congressional Village."

The party, if you're keeping score, is sponsored by United Airlines, General Dynamics and the American Chiropractors Association, among others. Women in bikini tops and straw skirts and two full-scale elephant sculptures greet us. Inside we feast on whole roasted pigs and sushi, listen to a reggae band and drink frozen cocktails from coconuts and pineapples. But there is no Tom DeLay.

I walk into the Congressional Village hotel (sponsors: Aramark, the U.S. Chamber of Commerce and about fifty others). I ask at the front desk for a Tom DeLay, as if I have a pressing appointment with him at 12:30 a.m. The clerk runs his finger down the guest list. "Deal, Diaz, Duncan . . . Nope, no DeLay." The Hammer has given me the slip again.

Clearly, it is time to negotiate. I arrange a Tuesday morning breakfast with Baron, DeLay's spokesman, and request a meeting with the congressman.

"I don't think it's gonna happen," Baron says. But soon after, he reconsiders. He invites me to Bookbinder's, a restaurant where DeLay is hosting a $120,000 fund-raiser for his charity, which helps neglected children. This sounds hopeful; the lunch is for a good cause, so perhaps DeLay will let me see him in action.

But it is not to be. "I wish I could invite you up to the lunch," Baron says when I meet him at the restaurant, "but I don't want to muck up the rules." There is, however, a consolation prize: If I wait 90 minutes, I can have a few minutes with him after he finishes the fund-raiser.

Finally, the clink of china and the applause end, and the Hammer is ready to see me. He acknowledges that he's keeping a low profile. DeLay's focus is singular.

"We're raising money left and right," he says, not yet sure of the total. "We'll leave this convention with a significant amount of resources."

And for that, DeLay says, he has nothing to be ashamed of. "It's cynical for the media to make it like it's bad," he says. "It's better to raise money than to have the government pay for elections."

DeLay sees himself as a champion of the First Amendment. "The Constitution gives you the right to assemble, the right to free speech without being harassed," he says. His donors "don't want Dan Rather calling up and saying, 'What are you getting for the money you're giving?'"

With that, our brief meeting is over. I still haven't seen DeLay in action with his lobbyists. But there is still hope. Tonight, DeLay is hosting a concert by the band Blues Traveler—officially closed to the press and public, naturally. But this time, I have procured a ticket. Tonight, just maybe, I will finally see DeLay in action. He will be brought to us by Coca-Cola and Continental Airlines, by the way.

The Democratic convention, in Los Angeles, is pretty much the same thing. The only difference is Staples has stamped its name on the arena, not First Union and Comcast. And just to remove any doubt about the real purpose of this convention, the chairman is Terry McAuliffe, the Democrats' top money man.

I first caught up with McAuliffe this spring, to get a peek at his art. There was a day, not long ago, when political fund-raising was done behind closed doors, and a guy who raised a lot of cash preferred to work in the shadows. But yesterday was not that day, and Terry McAuliffe is not that guy.

No, for I spent time with McAuliffe on the very day he was throwing the Democrats' $26.5 million fund-raising extravaganza on Seventh Street N.W.—the latest record-setting take of soft money. The Party partied at an MCI Center packed with upwards of 12,000 people, Stevie Wonder crooned for the likes of Ed Rendell, and Robin Williams told jokes for the likes of Al Gore.

Presiding over it all was the manic McAuliffe, the celebrated fund-raiser who put on the show to honor his pal, Bill Clinton. The president, swept up in the moment, joined hands to dance with rocker Lenny Kravitz, after which comic Williams remarked, "He opened a can of whup-ass, he did."

The event, like a similar (if slightly smaller) Republican bash a month earlier, was a milestone of sorts. Fund-raising, it made clear, is coming into the open. "I've never been shy about it," McAuliffe said. "I'm proud of it."

McAuliffe and the Democrats, in contrast to the stealthy Republicans, were so unapologetic about their fund-raising that they put it on C-SPAN, called in the news media and celebrated the party's image as champion of the little man—complete with LeAnn Rimes and Darius Rucker, the lead singer of Hootie & the Blowfish. There were checked picnic tablecloths, plastic plates piled with barbecued ribs, and buckets of beer. The president and vice president both wore bluejeans and cowboy boots (but while the president had a big belt buckle, the vice president opted for a Palm Pilot on his belt). Tipper Gore donned denim, too; only Hillary Clinton, the consummate New Yorker, opted for a black suit.

McAuliffe went to great lengths to juxtapose the Democrats' common touch with last month's black-tie Republican event. "How many people came to this event in a long black stretch limousine?" he asked. "Who here tonight is wearing a tuxedo?" He then flashed the Republicans' menu on the screen, featuring "creamy goat cheese medallion" and "orange meringue mirror cake."

"We're killing them on this bluejeans thing," McAuliffe told me earlier in the day as he prepared for the show. The workers-of-the-world moment was broken, briefly, by the ringing of his cell phone. It was Vernon Jordan, and I eavesdropped. "Vernon, I'm cookin' the barbecue," McAuliffe said. "You comin'? It's gonna be your kind of action. We've got ribs comin' up from Sims and Lindsey's and Rendezvous." But Jordan wasn't coming. "Anyway," McAuliffe said, "thanks for all your checks, man."

Right. The checks. It's so easy to forget about the money, amid the barbecue and the bands. True, some 12,000 people paid only $50 each for tickets, as the DNC was eager to point out. But that accounts for only

$600,000 of the $26.5 million raised. The rest came from those willing to pay $25,000 for a table, or to raise $250,000 or more (double that, in some cases) to get their names near the top of the program; these high rollers had a private dinner with the president and vice president Tuesday night at an MCI Center lounge. Also mentioned in the program were such grass-roots organizations as Anheuser-Busch, AT&T, Lockheed Martin and a gaggle of unions.

The bluejeans shtick seemed a bit self-conscious as the guests, many of whom had to change out of suits, filed into the arena. A small band of protesters was not fooled by the denim; they waved signs that said "Stop Selling Our Democracy" and "End Legalized Bribery." When President Clinton took the podium, a few hecklers chanted, "Stop corruption now!" Earlier in the day, as McAuliffe and I made the rounds of TV and radio interviews, he was stalked at many stops by Fred Wertheimer, the campaign finance crusader. Outside ABC's studio, Wertheimer teased McAuliffe about the price of tickets to the Democratic bash, but McAuliffe cut him off: "Remember, Fred—ban soft money! Get rid of the stuff! Get Bush to agree."

Terry McAuliffe calling for a soft-money ban? This is about as convincing as O. J. Simpson vowing to find his ex-wife's killer and John McCain promising to campaign "enthusiastically" for George W. Bush.

Touching on the awkward topic, Democratic National Committee Chairman Ed Rendell told the crowd, several of whose members had contributed tens of thousands in soft money, "When we win this election in November, we are committed to getting rid of soft money." Next time, he said, the top ticket would be $100. Gore, likewise, promised he would send a campaign finance bill to Congress first thing.

But let's not talk about money. This was, after all, a party. Clinton took the podium to "Simply the Best" and referred to himself as "an old gray-haired redneck." Gore took on Charlton Heston, joking that "the last time Moses listened to a bush, his people wandered in a desert for forty years." After that, the denim-clad hipsters—Dick Gephardt and Tom Daschle among them—rocked to the pounding beat of Kravitz's "American Woman" remake.

Before the show, McAuliffe escorted me into the rocker's dressing room. "You're hot—you're the man," McAuliffe told the star. Kravitz, who agreed to perform after getting a call at home from Clinton (the president promised to wear jeans to the show), seemed pleased, if nonplussed. "If you need me up on the mike, man, I'm ready," McAuliffe offered.

"I'll let you know," Kravitz replied.

Now, here at the Democratic convention, McAuliffe et al. are working their magic again. Even Barbra Streisand is hosting a fund-raiser. To get an inside view—or at least more inside than the one DeLay afforded me—I've decided to follow Simon Rosenberg around for a day.

In another age, Rosenberg would be fat. He would smoke a cigar. He would wear a watch chain on his vest and drink bourbon on the rocks.

But Rosenberg does none of those things. He's a short, bespectacled, hyperkinetic fellow given to saying things like "this is about 17 miles off the record, but . . ." He prefers Sierra Nevada beer, thank you very much.

He is the very model of the modern wheeler-dealer, a fund-raiser for the information age, a shepherd of Silicon Valley fatcats. As head of the New Democrat Network, a group founded by Joe Lieberman to raise money for pro-business Democratic candidates, Rosenberg's task is to tap into the lucre of the high-tech economy to elect centrist politicians.

"He's the digital version of the old hack," says Dave McCurdy, the former Democratic congressman turned lobbyist, and a friend of Rosenberg's. *Newsweek*'s Howard Fineman calls Rosenberg "the Kaiser Soze of the Democratic Party," a reference to the invisible but omnipotent (and criminal) mastermind played by Kevin Spacey in *The Usual Suspects*.

"I like that comparison," says Rosenberg, as we talk with Fineman outside the convention hall. The 36-year-old Rosenberg, who got his start with James Carville in the Clinton war room in 1992, created the New Democrat Network with Joe Lieberman and John Breaux in 1996. This year, the group expects to raise $5.5 million. It has a donor list that includes AOL, Microsoft and AT&T. It has a skybox at the convention—and it has its founder on the Democratic ticket.

Rosenberg sees himself as a Democratic Pete DuPont, the man who created GOPAC, the fund-raising machine that launched the Gingrich Republicans. But Rosenberg's is a revolution of raging moderates. "We've won the ideological war," he says. "What we need now is to grow in political strength." And that means raising cash. Lots of it.

That's why we find Rosenberg at this Democratic convention, taking place conveniently in California, home to the nation's high-tech and entertainment industries. Here, he is truly in his element: the precise nexus of new money and New Democrats.

For lunch Tuesday, he dined poolside at the Peninsula Hotel with Jonathan Tisch, high-tech executives Tim Newell (of e-Offering) and Chris Larsen (of e-Loan), and political strategist Morris Reid. All week long, he has been going to A-list parties in L.A., including an intimate gathering with President Clinton.

And the party Tuesday night that Rosenberg's group is throwing is at Hollywood mogul David Salzman's Beverley Hills home and is scheduled to include Quincy Jones, L. L. Cool J, Shaquille O'Neal, and the *X-Files'* Gillian Anderson, along with high-tech chieftains like David

Bohnett of Geo Cities, Stuart Wolff of homestore.com, John Zeglis of AT&T Wireless, Peter Chernin of News Corp., and a gaggle of politicos, including Mickey Kantor, the former commerce secretary, and senators John Kerry, Bob Kerrey, Evan Bayh, Bob Graham, Representative Harold Ford—and, of course, Lieberman. This party, and a larger New Democrat Network shindig tomorrow at the Garden of Eden restaurant, "will be seen as two of the hippest parties of the convention," Rosenberg predicts.

It's a sign of the times that a slightly nerdy guy like Rosenberg is not only on the A-list but the guy who makes the A-list. So when he offered to invite me to spend the day with him Tuesday, I couldn't possibly decline. This may be my only chance to see both Shaq and Lieberman in the same room.

4:00 p.m. Sitting in his skybox, high over the convention floor, Rosenberg is master of all he surveys. Jane Harman, the former congresswoman from California, is speaking. Yup, she's a member. Soon it's Evan Bayh, the Indiana senator. He's a member, too. Rosenberg's wife is home in Georgetown, due to have their child on Thursday, but he has business to conduct first.

He strolls down to the convention floor. Representative Dennis Moore, a new New Democrat from Kansas, greets him. "They're the ones who got me here," he says of the NDN. On the floor, Rosenberg embraces Gore aides and advisers such as Joe Kohlenberger, Nick Baldick, Karen Skelton and Don Fowler. Representative Shelly Berkley, another new New Democrat from Nevada, stops Rosenberg. "It's a great time to be a New Democratic Jew," she says.

Back upstairs, the skybox is buzzing with four executives from Enron Corp., Mickey Kantor's law partner and a variety of donors. They're munching cheese, fruit and asparagus while Jesse Jackson—decidedly not a New Democrat—talks on the floor. Jay Inslee, a congressman, watches Rosenberg work the room. "Ignore the man behind the curtain," Inslee says. "It's only Simon."

Soon, it's time to go. Rosenberg and I hop into the back of a black Lincoln Town Car. "Bob, we're going to David Salzman's house," he says. It must feel very good to say that. En route, Rosenberg writes his speech for the event and takes calls on his cell phone. "Five hundred people have RSVP'd," he's saying. "We were expecting 200." Lieberman's staff chief calls. "People are really fired up," he says of the party.

7:00 p.m. We arrive at the big event, at Salzman's huge Beverly Hills home, with a backyard tennis court, basketball court and pool. The inside is in the French style, with oil paintings throughout and "S" monogrammed toilet paper and a Renoir sketch in the bathroom. One hopes against hope that it's only a print. I take up a position in Salzman's wood-paneled study, to write this story atop his huge mahogany desk. Rosenberg ducks in to take me out to the party. "A lot of senators are starting to arrive," he says.

First, though, I have a chat with our host. "He's a true mensch, this guy," Salzman says of Rosenberg. "He's this cute guy who looks like he's in the first year of graduate school. He's a nonthreatening guy. I don't think of him as a money guy." And it's true: he certainly doesn't look like one. In this place, he looks like a rock star, as friends greet him with hugs and handshakes. "Man of the hour!" says one admirer, as Rosenberg introduces young high-tech execs to his political candidates.

The press leading up to tonight's party sought to paint a conflict between the righteous Hollywood scourge Lieberman and Salzman, the producer of Jenny Jones. (In fact, Salzman has produced just about every type of show, including *Dallas*, the Academy Awards, and two presidential inaugurals.) Lieberman, when he arrives and gives his speech, ignores the subject entirely. "Section VIII goes a long way," he says of his host.

The party, ultimately, is a disappointment for those hoping to do some stargazing. The highest wattage guests, other than Lieberman, are people like Delaware Governor Tom Carper and Democratic money man Steve Rattner. It's mostly a bunch of pols and the people who fund them. Next to the bar, a sign names a couple dozen corporate sponsors, among them Citigroup, Paine Webber and United Airlines. "This reminds me why I support public financing of elections," says one Democrat in the crowd.

O'Neal is a no-show, and there's no Cool J either, and no other celebrities. "No Shaq," Rosenberg says, a bit disappointed. "There was one actor I knew, but I couldn't remember his name."

Fortunately, the lack of star power is offset by a fabulous martini bar. Now that I have discovered it, I have concluded that any additional reporting would be unreliable.

26

★ ☆ ★

Nasty Is Nice

Has there ever been a more milquetoast meeting, a more treacly trade show, than the Republican National Convention of 2000?

Everybody is on excruciatingly good behavior here in the city of Brotherly Love. Colin Powell tells the crowd he's "in awe of the American dream," and Laura Bush informs us that "George will be a fabulous grandfather." The signs in the hall promote bland slogans like "Strength and Security." Even male delegates wear happy stickers declaring "W is for Women."

"Not much here," concludes political analyst Charlie Cook as he prowls the Philadelphia convention hall in search of red meat Tuesday evening, a time usually set aside at such gatherings as "attack night." But this is, he says, "a vegetarian night."

Fortunately, there is relief for those troubled by the tightly controlled, stubbornly saccharine convention. There's plenty of nastiness and partisanship to be found here. It has simply oozed to the outskirts of the convention after organizers banned slime on the inside. And that's where I'm headed.

Feeling down about the loss of attack night? Consider signing up for a "Bye Bye Clinton Cruise" being touted at a meeting of the conservative group Citizens United. (I've already put the request in to my editors.) "After eight years of scandal, lies and deceit, the Clintons will finally be leaving!" says the promo for the seven-night trip. For just $1,299, you can join Representatives Dan Burton and Bob Barr, former House investigator Dave Bossie "and many other fellow conservatives on a fun-filled cruise to the Caribbean." Need beach reading? The group offers Bossie's book, *Prince Albert: The Life and Lies of Al Gore.*

From the gathering of the Clinton-haters, I walk next door to the Politicalfest. At First Union Center, the convention's home, the souvenirs are fluffy elephants and innocuous T-shirts. Naughty items were banned. But here, everybody's free to be mean. "I can't understand it," vendor Jeanne McGowan says of the GOP convention's walk on the tame side. Blocked from the main event, she's at the Politicalfest gathering in central Philadelphia selling T-shirts that say "I love New York—it's Hillary I can't stand." Her favorite item is a pin that refers to the vice president's explanation that he missed a crucial campaign finance discussion when too much iced tea sent him to the men's room. It says: "Al: No iced tea here. Philadelphia 2000." A top customer for this one was the Bush campaign, McGowan says. "I think we sold twenty to W's people."

Nearby are booths with loads of tasteless stickers and buttons: "Nixon 2000—he's not as stiff as Gore," and "The road to hell is paved with liberals," and "Friends don't let friends vote Democrat," and "Republican women like men!" One T-shirt says "GOP—God's Own Party" on the front, and on the back is a message from Proverbs for Bill Clinton: "When a wicked man rules, the people groan." Regnery Publishing has a full line of anti-Clinton/Gore books and authors here, and there's a button featuring Hillary Clinton in a rainbow Dennis Rodman hairdo with the phrase "as bad as she wants to be."

Delegates, though restricted on the floor, are free to be bad at their meetings and parties. Here's Senator Sam Brownback of Kansas, speaking about Democrats to the Christian Coalition: "The values of the Playboy Mansion do not belong in the White House." Here's Senate candidate Rick Lazio at a New York delegation brunch: "We've been here one day, probably longer than Hillary Clinton has been in New York."

Convention organizers have gone to great lengths to keep the bad stuff out. Speeches are vetted, references to Gore removed. Everything is so strictly controlled, there's even a place designated as a "Guide Dog Relief Area."

"We like to keep it positive," explains Aileen Kishaba, who has been supervising volunteers who paint signs to be taken onto the convention floor. The toughest she has let through have been "Restore honor and integrity" and "Arkansas apologizes for Clinton." But then I ask her about the "recycle" pile nearby; that's where the good stuff is. "Make Gore gone," says one, and "No me gusta Gore," and "Democrats = Thieves," and "No more lies." One has Gore's name in red letters with hammers and sickles.

But officially, everything is nice and kind. Even McCain, never afraid to break with his party, and a man who gains much from a Bush defeat, has nothing but happy words about his former rival. McCain has decided to make Bush's case to the Shadow Convention, a group of good-government types led by the irrepressible Arianna Huffington.

This is not a pro-Bush crowd; it has managed to attract virtually every left-wing fringe interest in the United States, represented at the University of Pennsylvania by a sea of kids with nose rings, eyebrow rings and, we think, rings in other places. "God made marijuana. Man made alcohol. Who do you trust?" pronounced the sign from a group promoting legalized marijuana. A woman in a "Frankenfood" T-shirt circulated a petition against bioengineered food. There was the newsletter dedicated to "capping excessive income and wealth." And, of course, there was the group of what appeared to be spoiled rich kids who were very distressed about the Navajo-Hopi Relocation Act, passing out fliers titled "Hey, Cowboy John McCain, how many Indians you gonna kill today?"

When McCain speaks, things get ugly. Global-warming protesters wave red signs demanding "What's your plan?" And when McCain urges "all Americans to support my party's nominee, Governor George Bush," the place erupts in hisses and boos. One guy makes a big show of walking out, while another pounds a wooden pole on the floor to make noise. The Navajo-Hopi lobby chants about the murderous McCain. "If you'd like me to stop, I will," McCain says, as an aide moved to take him off the stage. Huffington scolds the crowd, which pipes down but can't help breaking out into isolated shouts ("Drug War!" and "Genocide!") as if this were the Tourette's Syndrome convention.

McCain heads to South Philly for a Pat's cheesesteak, where I find him unruffled (perhaps even pleased) by his failed promotion of Bush. "I had a feeling that part would rile them," he says, as I ride with him in his van. "If not, they'd probably be at the Republican convention."

McCain, as usual, acts as if he hasn't lost the nomination. He took four buses on a seven-hour ride from Washington to Philadelphia (a journey normally accomplished in a third of that time. He hosted a press conference, then went to the Ritz-Carlton to give a talk to AIPAC, the pro-Israel lobby. Then he hosted a meeting at his hotel with all his delegates. Later it's a dinner meeting at the trendy Tangerine restaurant with a group his staff has come to refer to as "the McCain caucus." This is McCain's most devoted constituency: the media. All three network anchors are planning to attend.

When I ask what he plans to do at this meeting of the McCain caucus, the senator replies, "I'm going to release them." When an aide points out that the question is not about the delegate meeting but the broadcaster meeting, McCain replies, "I'm going to release them, too."

Part of the reason the Republicans can tone down the nastiness is that they've already landed many a mean attack. "As you're seeing this convention, there's going to be very little criticism of Bill Clinton," says Floyd Brown, president of Citizens United, at a meeting of his group. "That criticism has already gotten through. One of the reasons George W. Bush can talk about an agenda is because Congressmen Dan Burton and Bob Barr ... have done such a good job of exposing the record of the Clinton administration and all the liberals in the White House."

"The only reason I'm at this reception," Barr said, "is because it's not completely nice."

Still, some negativity gets the party's stamp of approval. Downtown, at a stand set up to sell "Official Convention Merchandise," are $1 bumper stickers declaring "Gore would be the best president China ever had!" At an event on the convention grounds, a group passes out stickers declaring "No Gore taxes!" while Dick Armey, the House majority leader, proclaims that "big-government liberals" are responsible for "a corruption of the tax code."

On the convention floor itself, the few darts thrown are too soft to break the skin. Condoleezza Rice takes a pop at Clinton-Gore for using foreign policy for "partisan purposes." Laura Bush says her husband's principles "will not change with the winds of polls or politics." And when Arizona's Jim Kolbe, the only openly gay Republican in Congress, addresses the crowd, the Texas delegates bow their heads in protest. The Republican platform takes only a few gentle swipes at Clinton's "embarrassing presidential kowtow" to China and Gore's vision of "America as global social worker."

Such partisan pops are, to many delegates, welcome news. "I don't know why people are so sensitive. What's wrong with a debate?" asks Santa Mendoza, a Connecticut delegate and member of the platform committee, when I find her at a downtown restaurant. She's wearing a lapel pin that shows the painting *The Scream* and labels it *Clinton Health Care*.

Likewise, Kenneth Timmerman, in town to promote his self-published Clinton book, *Selling Out America*, quarrels with kindness. "I personally think Al Gore and Bill Clinton have a lot to answer for," he says as he hawks his book in a hotel here. "The American people need to know the full story."

And they will, in due course. For now, though, Bush has decided that the convention isn't the place for it. "We've changed the tone," says Bush spokesman Ari Fleischer, pointing to the Texas governor's rising poll ratings as vindication. In fact, Bush's post-convention train trip will be called the "Change the Tone Tour."

But lest the carnivores worry, Bush is sure to take out his sharp knives soon. Already this week, he has called Clinton "desperate." Bush "won't hesitate to vigorously defend himself when attacked," Fleischer vows.

Finally tonight, Dick Cheney takes up the cudgel, declaring that "we are all a little weary of the Clinton-Gore routine," mocking "the man from

Hope [who] goes home to New York" and demanding, "It is time for them to go." Now that's more like it.

Indeed, while Bush continues pious denunciations of smashmouth politics and negativity and talks about restoring decorum and civility, he dispatches his underlings to wage battle the old-fashioned—and more effective—way. With good old smashmouth politics.

Nobody practices that better than Republican National Committee Chairman Jim Nicholson; he's so good, in fact, that he takes his show on the road, to the Democratic convention. And so I find myself before sunrise on the Wednesday of the Democrats' convention, outside the arena in Los Angeles.

While the unsuspecting Democrats rest in their beds, four men in dark suits move purposefully toward the Staples Center, site of the Democratic convention. As political warfare goes, this is a guerrilla attack: coming down from the hills are Nicholson and three aides.

Their target this morning is Radio Row, the place in the press area next to Staples where morning talk show hosts are doing their thing. Using press passes obtained from sympathizers in the media, they've done this all three days of the convention so far, offering Nicholson up to any Podunk radio station that will have him on the air.

The Democrats, as usual this week, don't have anybody here. And the radio hosts are grumbling. "I've been having a tough time getting Democrats," says Gary Sutton of the Harrisburg station WSBA, echoing a common complaint in Radio Row. "I haven't gotten anyone national."

Nicholson, however, is happy to oblige. He sits down with Sutton for ten minutes. Talking points in hand, he unleashes a barrage against Gore and the Democrats. He talks of the "electricity" of the Republican convention and the "apathy" of the Democrats. He talks of the "flap over the Playboy mansion" and calls the Democrats "very hypocritical." He scolds Gore for saying "he invented the Internet and wrote Hubert Humphrey's acceptance speech." He blasts Gore's "tobacco flip flop" and calls him "a guy who will just do anything and say anything and . . . wear anything to get elected."

The Democratic response? Nothing. The only other partisan official making the rounds this morning is another Republican, an RNC co-chair.

If politics is war by other means, Nicholson, who battled the Viet Cong, is well prepared for such skirmishes. "It's like Vietnam," he says. "There's no front line and it's all enemy territory."

6 a.m. When Nicholson enters the press area in the convention center, in American-flag cuff links and a business suit, he parks at a booth next to *The Oliver North Radio Show* and goes through a stack of press clippings faxed from RNC headquarters in Washington. Aides put press

releases on reporters' desks, and also offer journalists a CD titled *More of the Best of Al Gore: Hits of the '80s, '90s and Today! Volume II.* Aides arm Nicholson with two cheat sheets, one titled "Talking Points for Chairman Jim Nicholson," and the other one the RNC's daily fax. The "key messages" in the talking points are the "shattered base" of the Democratic Party and the "leftover left" of old liberals who took to the podium the previous night.

If asked why he's here, it's recommended Nicholson respond, "I'm part of a team of Republicans who are filling in for a job the vice president has refused to fill: the Gore Campaign's fact checker." The points also cover Joe Lieberman's approaching speech: "Tonight, the 'Reinvention Convention' features Democratic Vice Presidential nominee Joe Lieberman—who was nominated for his core convictions, but has since given them up to follow Gore's far-left agenda."

Nicholson is remarkably on message in stop after stop. First it's KNRS of Salt Lake City. Gore, he says, has "trouble rallying his base," and "they have a pretty fractured base," and they're full of "old left leftovers." He moves on to KFIV of Modesto, California, where he's asked if there's "anything you want to talk about." Nicholson checks his talking points. "Well, Al Gore has had problems putting his base together," he says. On air, he cites a line from Jesse Jackson about the need to "hold our noses and take castor oil" to support the ticket, then he revisits the "leftovers of the left" and the "fractured party" lines, adding, "there's just kind of an apathy—there's a lot of empty seats." For good measure, he repeats the castor oil line.

Now he's up to WBAL of Baltimore, where he accuses Lieberman of "rank hypocrisy," and once more blasts the "leftovers of the left" and the Democrats' inability "to pull their base together." Metro One, a radio network, gets much the same message: "Here in Los Angeles things are apathetic at best—Al Gore has not been able to bring together his party—they paraded out what I call the leftovers of the left."

Get the point? Next, Harrisburg will get the point, then Colorado.

Nicholson's staffers, to keep up with their boss, are getting only about four hours of sleep a night. Chris Paulitz, who does radio p.r. for the RNC, takes out a packet labeled "Herbal Nitro" and swallows its contents. Nicholson himself admits only to taking Centrum one-a-days. When he sits down for an interview with KNRS, the host reports to him, "Sir, your staff has asked me to tell you to get up later."

But it's worth the punishment for the RNC. "We're the only show in town—I don't know why the Democrats haven't figured it out," says Mark Pfeifle, an RNC spokesman traveling with Nicholson through Radio Row in the morning. "The DNC has not brought anybody here until

10 a.m. That's 1 p.m. on the East Coast. The Democrats missed every East Coast drive-time show this morning."

One morning, Sisely says, a DNC aide who was either confused or desperate sent two or three interviewers to Nicholson for comment on the convention. The RNC is doing about 50 radio interviews a day here, a quarter of them by Nicholson, the rest by some 25 staffers and Republican officials in town, among them Representative Jennifer Dunn of Washington and New Jersey Governor Christie Whitman. Representative David Dreier of California set the record for interviews, doing 21 radio and 11 print interviews in one day. At one point on Tuesday, the RNC had five officials working the press hall; all the Democrats had was "some undersecretary of HUD," Sisely says.

Everywhere Nicholson goes in Democratic territory, he receives polite razzing. "Hey, Jim, you changing parties?" Virginia Senator Chuck Robb asks him. Nicholson bumps into New York Congressman Charlie Rangel, who taunts him: "Hey, good to see you here—like the diversity?"

10:15 a.m. After a conference call with the Bush campaign in Austin, Nicholson starts a press briefing in the RNC's "Victory Headquarters" across the street from the Democrats' convention. He is accompanied by a parade of GOP officials, including Virginia Governor Jim Gilmore, Representatives Henry Bonilla of Texas and Mark Sanford of South Carolina, and various "real people" to tell their stories: a Latino farmer to talk about the estate tax, a Korean American businessman to talk about the marriage penalty.

Most of the questions, though, are for Nicholson, who responds by (1) attacking the opposition and (2) criticizing the opposition for attacking. "They began the attacks eleven minutes into their convention," he says to one questioner. "They can't get their base solidified . . . I sense a great deal of apathy . . . he brought out those liberal leftovers."

Then he changes tack: "The American people are tired of the politics of personal destruction and of ridicule," he says. "I just don't think that kind of derision is right." Moments later, he switches back to Gore: "Al Gore has been through so many reinventions . . . Al Gore will say anything, do anything and wear anything to get elected."

6 p.m. Nicholson spends the afternoon visiting the Wiesenthal Center in Los Angeles before making appearances on CNN and Michael Reagan's talk show. As the convention starts, he's stuck in traffic.

Back at the RNC office, ten aides are planning a response to Lieberman's speech in a conference call with Bush spokesman Ari Fleischer. They have an advance copy of the speech and are figuring out their talking points. The consensus: The speech is tough but not thermonuclear. Therefore, a muted response is best—disappointed, but not angry.

Nicholson arrives in time for the speech itself, which he watches on television with arms folded or crossed behind his head, drinking water and occasionally remarking "they've been using that for forty years" and "that's a tired line." During the speech, an aide hands him the just-prepared talking points, which he quickly assimilates. Asked immediately after the speech what he thinks, Nicholson's first words are right on message: "It's disappointing."

8 p.m. "Time to go," an RNC official shouts. Nicholson heads to the men's room to prepare. On the way out, an aide hands Nicholson convention credentials as if passing him his rifle. We're going in! Back into the press room, that is, to do more radio interviews. The talking points, titled "Say It Ain't So, Joe," call for Nicholson to make two points: Lieberman is "being pressured to abandon [his] principles so Gore can continue his attacks against Governor Bush," and "The more time Joe Lieberman spends with Al Gore, the more partisan he becomes."

On the walk over to the convention center, I ask Nicholson what points he'd like to make about the speech. "I thought they'd hired a principled centrist," he says. "In two weeks they've morphed him into a left-sounding Democrat." That pretty much took care of point one, but left point two untouched.

I prod Nicholson. "Mr. Chairman, would you say that the more time Joe Lieberman spends with Al Gore, the more partisan he becomes?"

Nicholson smiles. "Yes," he says, "I would."

The Democratic convention, by contrast, is more self-consciously mean and nasty. The rules of smashmouth politics say a campaign will be rewarded for taking on the opposition and its policies in tough, harsh terms. But I am determined to look at the side the parties aren't showing. The Republicans were being nice, so I sought out the nasty. Here they are being nasty, so I am seeking out—blech—the nice. And that, alas, means a day with the Gore girls.

When it comes to Karenna Gore, it's impossible for a reporter to avoid a measure of jealousy. Just a few years ago, she was a junior member of the journalistic profession, an intern with an online magazine. But while the rest of us may have remained ink-stained wretches, she has found better things to do. She graduated from an Ivy League law school, landed a rich and good-looking doctor, got an enormous engagement ring, moved into a palace with high ceilings on Manhattan's Upper East Side and gave birth to a child on—gag me—the Fourth of July, just in time to make her papa a grandpa before his presidential campaign.

The serendipitous birthday matches everything else about Karenna's charmed life: annoyingly perfect. At 27, the oldest of the four Gore children is smart, pretty, eloquent, poised, telegenic—and perhaps the most effective spokesperson for her father's candidacy. It's enough to make you sick.

But if you're resenting Karenna Gore for being too perfect, imagine what the second-oldest of the Gore progeny, Kristin, must be feeling. I suspect it must be just what Jan Brady, of *Brady Bunch* fame, felt when watching her older sister, Marcia, get all the attention. "Marcia! Marcia! Marcia!" the aggrieved Jan screamed in a rage of sibling rivalry.

"I certainly don't want to invoke that image," the 23-year-old Kristin says when I ask her about the Jan and Marcia issue. "I'm incredibly proud of her." But surely she must feel some tension; I feel sibling rivalry with Karenna and I'm not even her sibling. "I'll let you guys work that out," Kristin says.

The interview, held in a supply closet in a food pantry Karenna and Kristin are visiting, is one of the first interviews Kristin Gore has ever given. She has some impressive accomplishments in her own right—like her father and big sister, she is a Harvard graduate and now works here in L.A. as a writer for the animated Fox comedy show *Futurama*—and this is the week of her political coming out. This Thursday, she'll give a prime-time speech at the Democratic convention, introducing her mother. Jan, it seems, is ready to share the stage with Marcia.

"It's an experiment," she says. "Hopefully, I won't be a big liability. We'll see Thursday night if I pass out and have to get carried off."

Today, her first day as a public figure, goes like this:

2:00 p.m. I arrive at the Los Angeles Regional Food Bank, in a dodgy part of town, for a Karenna and Kristin photo-op, Kristin's first-ever public event without her parents. Arriving early, I am waiting with Kristin's handler, Sean Crowley, for Kristin's arrival. Our wait is interrupted, though, when a photographer points out to us that Kristin is already here. Sure enough, she's been working on a food-sorting line for about twenty minutes—largely unnoticed by the press and audience, most of whom are waiting for Karenna.

Finally, after Karenna arrives at the food bank, the sisters come to face a huge wall of TV cameras. Karenna, naturally, takes the spot closest to the cameras. Kristin sorts groceries behind her sister for the photo-op, and though taller then Karenna, she is not as graceful before the cameras. When it's her turn to speak, she does so quietly. "Um, thank you, Steve," she begins. It's a quick speech about volunteering and civic participation, but its real purpose is to introduce Karenna, who gives a much longer talk, working the cameras expertly.

"I hope I didn't say anything stupid," Kristin says when away from the cameras. Told it was a credible performance, she replies, "They fell for it." So far, so good, for her first day on the stump. "I always wanted to help out," she says in our broom closet interview. But she wasn't ready until now.

"I was moving to a new city, a new job. It was important that I had a life of my own, that I didn't just feel like 'daughter of.'" Now she's established. "I realized I needed to be more public," she says. "It's not like I really wanted to go public, but it's something I can do."

6:30 p.m. After a stop at her hotel, Kristin pulls up for her first solo campaign appearance, a Handgun Control event at the trendy Eurochow restaurant in Westwood. She has switched from T-shirt and gray-olive jeans to a short black skirt, but she still has on the same Nike watch.

She gets out of a van accompanied by a small swarm of advance people and security agents in her motorcade. "I don't know *what's* going on," she says of her entourage. There is less fuss made about her inside, however. She gets a few curious glances, but virtually nobody recognizes her until a person from Handgun Control escorts her around the room. The event is billed as "open press," but I am the only press here. About ten minutes later, Kristin is out the door, without eating, drinking, or making a speech.

7:30 p.m. When we arrive at the Autry Museum of Western Heritage, where BP and Microsoft are fêting delegates from Oregon, Washington and Alaska, Kristin again encounters a recognition problem. When her advance man presents himself at the party sign-in desk and announces that Kristin has arrived, the woman at the desk shouts to a colleague, "Christine is here!"

Once inside, a delegate approaches and calls her Karenna. "Kristin," she corrects, without losing her smile. A woman offers her congratulations, something about her lovely little boy. "Thank you," Kristin says. "That's my sister, but thank you."

Yet another man talks to her for a couple of minutes, gives her a "No Son of Bush" sticker, then shakes her hand. "I'm sorry, what was your name again?" he asks her.

But anonymity aside, Kristin, because she's new at this game, has a certain authenticity her more polished father and sister can't always muster. She mixes, she mingles, she grips, she grins, she touches, she hugs, she flashes a shy smile. And she seems to like it. She cheerfully accepts a $2 bill from an eccentric woman who claims she gave one to Carter and Clinton before their victories. She seems most animated when somebody mentions her animated show. "You like it?!" she exclaims.

10:30 p.m. Kristin stops for a quick dinner in Hollywood with her boyfriend, then arrives at the Knitting Factory, a new Hollywood outpost of the NY nightclub, where people are six deep in line to get in. This time, it's Karenna who does the warm-up act for Kristin before the crowd of Young Democrats, introducing her as "my extremely talented little sister."

Kristin warms to her top billing. "Rather than doing a couple of numbers for you, which we considered, we're turning it over to the Goo Goo Dolls," she tells the cheering throng. As the band gets ready to play, the sisters work the rope line with hugs, kisses and handshakes, like rock stars themselves.

For Kristin, the night isn't done. She has at least one more party to hit before bed. Then tomorrow, she'll join her sister on Jay Leno. But she admits to no weariness. "This is so funny," she says of the crush of people around her. "I'm actually energized."

Uh-oh. Sounds like another Gore family pol in the making. "That's not likely," she reassures me. Good thing. Otherwise, we'd have to start resenting her, too.

Now, it's time for some fun. It's time to take to the streets with some women with hairy armpits and men with bad body odor, and together do battle with the L.A. police, the people brought us Rodney King.

The demonstrators at the Democratic convention this week call their headquarters the "Convergence Center," which is what you call a command center when your group includes anarchists who have problems with words like "command." Inside this decrepit former flea market in a rough section of town, I find a representative of just about every group—"Queers and Allies," "Transgender Menace" and "International Prostitutes Collective"—and somebody passionate over just about any issue: gay rights, immigrant rights, universal health care, police brutality, urban parklands, equal pay, welfare cuts, standardized tests, youth imprisonment, hate crimes, death penalty, breast cancer research, trade, missile defense, breast feeding, genetic engineering, Iraqi children, the U.S. military in Vieques, "heteronormative" thinking, U'Wa Indians, pollution and a man named Mumia.

Perhaps you are wondering just what the U'Wa have to do with missile defense, or whether Transgender Menace cares about urban parklands. If so, you are missing the point. "This is a real interesting movement because we don't all agree," says Lisa Fithian, one of two women who formed D2KLA, the umbrella group organizing the demonstrations. "You've got sectarians, leftists, liberals. We don't have to agree—who cares? But we have a common goal: we agree on nonviolence."

That, in short, is what the demonstrations are about this week: not a specific protest, but a celebration of the art of protesting itself. Fithian sees it as a cathartic exercise in democratic expression, making a ragtag group of kids feel as if they can get on the evening news and force bigshots to look at them. "It's about making people realize they have the power," Fithian tells me, as we begin our day together. "It's about people taking control of their lives, speaking in their own voice. Everything in this country is designed to prevent people from thinking they have power."

For this cause, Fithian is an ideal organizer. Fithian, a 39-year-old labor activist who calls herself unemployed, has been planning these demonstrations since she participated in the Seattle protests against the World Trade Organization. She shares the demonstrators' general anti-corporate sentiment, but unlike most marchers, she's not driven by a passion for a single issue; she just likes to see people demonstrate.

The former Skidmore College student government president, who orchestrated the Justice for Janitors campaign that shut down Washington's bridges a few years ago, doesn't wear the pins, stickers, tattoos, dyed hair, earrings, nose rings, lip rings and eyebrow rings that her minions do. She isn't marching to get big results. "I don't expect to see a revolution in my lifetime," she says. "I'm a pragmatist. This is the system I'm going to be living under."

Fithian's sole goal in L.A. is to allow her motley army of thousands to vent their spleen without letting the marches deteriorate into chaos and violence. As I follow her through a day of demonstrations here Monday, I discover just how difficult that is, not just because she's trying to herd thousands of angry punks, but because the L.A. police seem intent on provoking them with over-the-top shows of force. In her effort to keep the demonstrations calm, neither the demonstrators nor the police are her friend.

8:45 a.m. Fithian emerges from the Convergence Center with her bullhorn, wearing a purple tank top, old Reeboks and cargo pants. "It's not fun to be in jail in shorts," she explains. A cell phone, the protest leader's main organizing tool, is clipped to her waistband. She scribbles the number for her legal advisers and for the protest's media center on her hand in indelible ink, then we hop into her Saturn, which has a Buddha on the dash. Arriving near Pershing Square in downtown L.A., she leaves her identification in the car, to foil the police in case of arrest.

This is somewhat useless. The police know her well, and greet her as she walks a gauntlet of officers to the protest site. A police helicopter whirs overhead, and the number of police seems nearly equal to the couple hundred demonstrators in the park. She swaps phone numbers with the other march organizers and gets the troops—the drummers, the puppeteers—ready to march. The official cause of this morning's march is the U'Wa

Indians' battle against Occidental Petroleum, but that's just a technical-
ity; it's the same group that marched Sunday for Mumia Abu-Jamal, a
black activist in Philadelphia now on death row for killing a police officer,
and will march tomorrow for women.

10 a.m. All is calm as the parade starts. There's a ten-foot-tall Happy
Face, the Darth Vader corporate puppet, a twenty-foot-high democracy
puppet, and dozens of others, including one that says "More Homo, Less
Phobia." Fithian joins the chants of "Rise up," and "Ain't no power like
the power of the people," and "We are freedom bound." When the
marchers botch their lines, chanting "The people, united, will never be
divided," she instructs them in protest-march orthodoxy. "*Defeated*," she
yells, "it's *defeated*."

"This looks very good—we're kicking butt so far," she brags to me
between cell phone calls as we march down the street. "But we don't know
what's going to happen. It could get funky."

It does, of course, get funky. When the group reaches the Staples Center, site of the convention, she finds cement barriers blocking the way to
the court-ordered protest site, where Bonnie Raitt is waiting to sing.

"This is crazy!" she shouts, then commandeers my cell phone (her battery has died) to call her lawyer. "This is a dangerous situation. This is broken ankle–ville."

Once her lawyer arrives on the scene, they approach the police officer
in charge, who greets her with a familiar "How ya doin', Lisa?" Fithian
shakes the officer's hand warmly, then talks sweetly about the "safe and
easy flow" of people. "That's gonna create more tension," she says of the
barriers. She badgers and presses the officer for a couple more minutes,
until he promises to consider moving the barriers. "You're good, Lisa,"
the cop says with a smile.

Noon. But the other cops are not smiling. As the marchers prepare to
return to Pershing Square from the Staples Center, hundreds of police
arrive in full riot gear, tear gas grenades at the ready, with a long line of
police cars, sirens wailing. A helicopter circles low overhead. The police
action seems absurdly disproportionate to the threat from the demonstrators, who have been perfectly peaceful and orderly so far.

On the way back, a small group of demonstrators park themselves in
the middle of an intersection, where they expect to be arrested for their civil
disobedience. Fithian rushes to get the TV cameras to the intersection.

The police, to Fithian's dismay, respond by forming a line to push the
rest of the demonstrators down the street. At one point, the cops, batons
extended, lunge at the protesters, who retreat in a stampede.

"We've got a problem, Houston," Fithian says. "Time to deescalate."
She tries to get the demonstrators to sit down, but then another charge by

the police sends people running and falling. Officers with megaphones declare the march an "unlawful assembly" and threaten to arrest everybody on the street; they block off escape routes with ropes and call in baton-wielding riot police.

"Let's get out," Fithian shouts to the other leaders, who herd the demonstrators away. "We've got to get people out of here. We've got a whole week of actions ahead."

Fithian says she's been arrested more than a hundred times, but her goal this week is to stay out of the pokey, so she can keep order in the demonstrations. The only reason the protests turned ugly at the Republican convention in Philadelphia, she says, is because the demonstrators' communication broke down when the leaders got locked up.

And, in fact, Fithian seems to be devoting most of her time to keeping the crowd from turning violent. There's little sign of drug use, drinking or vandalism, and "security monitors" search for provocateurs in the crowd. The law-breaking, except for isolated cases, is of the civil disobedience variety. The only obvious crime is that many of the women are unshaven and many of the men have not felt a shower for quite some time.

2:45 p.m. Fithian has only a few minutes to recharge her cell phone and check in at the Convergence Center before returning to Pershing Square for the afternoon march. The marchers arrive in the thousands, and Fithian is getting nervous. Using a bullhorn, she assembles the security monitors and instructs them in how to "deescalate" and "keep people moving." She arms herself and the other march leaders with walkie-talkies.

Even before the march, as the demonstrators are doing nothing more than holding a puppet show in the park, the police circle with sirens, flashing lights, helicopters and an endless stream of officers in riot gear. As the demonstrators enter the street, Fithian barks commands: "Hold the line! Hold the line! . . . Stop, stop, stop! . . . Media, back up, back up!" Finally, the march underway, she allows herself a smile and dances down Broadway to the drums. "This is huge," she says. "We're gonna get 25,000 people."

5:30 p.m. Fithian walks back and forth through the march, looking for signs of trouble. She shoos away some anarchists harassing a cameraman. When she gets a call that people are throwing bottles in the protest area at the convention hall, she shouts commands into her walkie-talkie: "Put some music on! We're getting there! I'm gonna get a water truck to spray the crowd down and cool them off!"

The police have upped the ante now, greeting demonstrators at each intersection not just with batons and tear gas grenades but with guns that fire rubber pellets. At one point, they stop the march entirely, until Fithian reaches the front of the line and talks them back. "It's going real well so far," the presiding officer tells Fithian cheerfully.

But that changes a few minutes later, when the group arrives at the Staples Center to discover that the police haven't moved the cement barriers, causing a major backup and a crush of people trying to squeeze into the protest area. Fithian tries to herd the demonstrators in, but the anarchists, dressed in all-black, snarl at her commands and cause a bottleneck. A police commander approaches Fithian. "It was too late in the day to move these barriers," he explains.

7:00 p.m. Fithian by now has lost her earlier tact. "They should've been moved," she retorts. "It was a bad decision." And it soon becomes clear why. The police surround the protesters with some hundred motorcycles, in an absurd display of force more fitting for a May Day parade. Cops with tear gas grenades and rubber pellet guns stare into the protest area. And as the event proceeds—this time a concert by the band Rage Against the Machine—a couple of the demonstrators get rowdy and attempt to climb a fence to get into the convention center, while a few others throw objects over the fence at the police.

The police respond swiftly and severely, firing tear gas into the protest area. Some of the demonstrators retaliate by lighting their protest signs on fire, and the police move in. They shut the concert down and order everybody out of the protest area within fifteen minutes.

This, of course, is impossible—because of the cement barriers again. Fithian attempts to negotiate with police for a more feasible retreat from the area, but without success. After fifteen minutes, a line of police on horses charges the crowd inside the protest area. Those already outside the protest area are shot with rubber pellets. "It's a very ugly scene," Fithian shouts, after escaping from a horse's path. "They're inciting a riot."

9:15 p.m. It's now more than twelve hours since Fithian started demonstrating. She hasn't had much sleep all week, and she's not likely to get much tonight. "I've got to get back to the Convergence Center," she says, as things calm down. "We've got to get ready for tomorrow." And the next day, and the day after that.

After planning these demonstrations for the past nine months, Fithian isn't quite sure what she'll do when they end on Friday. "I think I'll travel for a while," she says. "I think I'm going to go to Prague."

A little European holiday? Actually, no. "For the demonstrations at the IMF meeting," she says.

27

★ ☆ ★

The English Patient

So the GOP went soft and fuzzy at its convention, and the Democrats went tough and mean. The results have been predictable. The Democrats earned larger audiences for their show, and Gore has received a much greater "bounce" in the polls. Before the conventions, Gore was down by anything up to 17 points; now, in the all-important Labor Day polls, he's pulled even or slightly ahead. And his staff claims for the first time he's on track to win an electoral-vote majority.

How did this happen? To me, it seems clear. Bush's "Change the Tone Tour" didn't work; people don't really have a problem with a negative tone, and in fact they rather seem to like it. Gore's toughness, meanwhile, steered the debate back to the issues, where he has a natural edge, and away from character, where the selection of Joe Lieberman as running mate (and perhaps Gore's embarrassing, seven-second convention kiss with Tipper) has helped to erase his deficit.

Let's track Bush's skid. Most people would point to his selection of Dick Cheney to join the ticket, at first seen as safe and now seen as dead weight. Three hours after Bush announced Cheney, I hopped a plane to Denver, then drove three hours to Cheyenne, Wyoming, slept at a roadside motel, and continued on to Casper.

I arrived just in time to see a modern-day cattle drive. In the 1870s and 1880s, Texas cowboys drove their cattle north onto the high plains and prairies, filling a vacuum left by the extermination of the buffalo. But now another Texan was on a cattle drive. George W. Bush herded his staff, security and press from Austin to Casper for a rally in the high school of alumnus Dick Cheney.

"Dick and I both have roots in the West," Bush told the crowd, to a roar of approval. "Dick was born in Nebraska and came to Wyoming as fast as he could. I grew up in Midland, Texas, a small town in the middle of a big desert."

Speaking in front of a flag with a buffalo on it, Bush extolled the virtues of the frontiersman. "The West is a place of straightforward people," he said. "People who say what they mean and mean what they say. The West is full of people who understand what the meaning of 'is' is."

Just in case anybody missed the point, the Bush people hung a hand-painted sign in the auditorium, "Cowboys for Bush & Cheney," and passed out fact sheets declaring that Cheney was the school's senior class president in 1959 and his wife, Lynne, was homecoming queen. But the folks in Casper, who lined up by the hundreds for the rally, knew all about that. This is the first all-Western ticket (unless you count the Reagan-Bush team, which included Dubya's migrant father). It is also the first time two men with oil ties joined a ticket. And the citizens of Casper, an oil town, couldn't have been more delighted.

"I think they'll fit right in," said Alonzo Rogers, a self-described "real cowboy," as he waited for the Bush-Cheney arrival in hat, jeans and clip-on suspenders. Rogers thinks Bush, who later promised the Wyoming Republicans that "help is on the way," will be the Westerners' avenger. "Those Eastern states think they own the whole White House," he said.

Bush's selection of Cheney has given the Republican ticket a heavily Western feel, reflecting what has become the party's utter dominance over the interior West: the mountain, desert and high plains states. It is a good symbol for Bush in that it conjures the romantic notion of cowboy movies with saloons and outlaws, country music, rugged individualism, open spaces and love of the land.

But the West, too, brings certain baggage that could hurt Bush in sub-urban America: militias and gun enthusiasts, big oil and mining, and deep conservatism—as reflected in the fuss over Cheney's voting record. The fact sheet passed out at Cheney's high school didn't mention another alumnus: Matthew Shepard, the gay man murdered down the road from here in 1998.

Above all, the interior West prizes a strain of libertarian, anti-government conservatism that is at odds with Bush's message of a new, active-government Republican Party. " 'Leave 'em alone' would be a basic Wyoming attitude," says Bruce Richardson, who heads the University of Wyoming's Casper campus.

The danger for Bush and Cheney is that the rest of the country may come to see the West less for the romance of its scenery and more for its rock-ribbed conservatism. The region finds itself increasingly isolated. The West Coast—California, Oregon and Washington—has parted

ways, electing Democratic governors. And despite efforts
New Economy to the high plains and mountains, most area
change.

This presents a dilemma for Bush and Cheney as they dec
use their Western roots in the campaign. Will the rest of Ameri
urban developments and office parks, still appreciate the small-town, indi-
vidualist image of the West? Or will it be frightened by the West's hostility to government? In the line waiting to get into the Bush event, the
near-unanimous complaints about the government sounded more like
Gingrich '94 than Bush '00.

"The government's just getting too intrusive," Paul Foster, an oil
worker, told me outside the Cheney event. "It's got a hand in everything,"
Jim Stevenson, another oil worker, agreed.

Their chief complaints: gun control and limits on offshore oil drilling—
things most other Americans favor. Their solution: two oil guys on the
Republican ticket. "I think it's wonderful," said Gerald Gay, another
Casper oil veteran. "It's a double bonus."

But a bonus to a couple of oil guys may not be such a prize for the swing
voters and soccer moms.

By contrast, Gore's choice of Lieberman, a couple of weeks later, has
been an unmitigated success so far. While Cheney tugs Bush back to Wild
West conservatism, Lieberman gives Gore the kind of moral politics he
needs to overcome Clinton.

Channel surfers who stumbled upon the Democratic National Convention last week could have been forgiven for thinking they had tuned in
to a meeting of the Promise Keepers. We heard about a "miraculous journey," about "private moments of prayer" and about how "Al Gore is a man
of family and a man of faith" whose wife "prayed for his safe return" every
night while he was in Vietnam.

It's not unlike Bush's efforts to bring out Republican compassion.
Both parties are now playing on each other's turf—for the first time since
the 1960s. Gore's Democrats are no longer allowing Republicans to
monopolize faith and family values; Bush's Republicans will no longer
grant Democrats the mantle of social justice. They are stealing shamelessly
from each other—and this is a good thing. The two parties have, in essence,
agreed on a new morality. (Even Pat Buchanan, who named a black woman
as his running mate on the Reform Party ticket, knows something has
changed—even if she is a John Bircher.)

If you doubt Americans' receptiveness to this new morality-based politics, consider the politicians who have best captured the public imagination this year: not Gore and Bush, whom many find uninspiring, but Senators John McCain and Joseph Lieberman. Lieberman is, to a surprising extent, the Democrats' version of McCain.

This new moral politics, as practiced by McCain and Lieberman, rejects both the harsh, absolute judgments of the right and the value-neutral, cultural relativism schemes of the left. Democrats, realizing they can't ride the economy to victory in 2000, have abandoned their resistance to religious programs and have begun to talk openly about faith. Republicans, in turn, have added "compassionate" to conservatism, "sucking away decades-old liberal presumptions of moral superiority," as a *Wall Street Journal* editorial put it.

It might seem odd to suggest that McCain, the gritty war hero, and Lieberman, the bookish lawyer, are strikingly similar. But both have created a moral authority that makes them seem almost unassailable. "We're talking about two individuals who can transcend party and ideology and appeal to the great center, and do it by appealing to something higher than banal, day-to-day politics," says Marshall Wittmann, the Heritage Foundation's political analyst.

Neither man's moral authority comes from the "family values" movement: though decent fellows, both have been divorced and have children from two marriages. Rather, their authority comes from a personal aura of service. McCain's comes from service to patria, from his years of enduring torture as a prisoner of war in Vietnam. Lieberman's comes from service to God, from his Orthodox Judaism, which causes him to avoid business on Saturdays.

Both Lieberman and McCain have cleverly bolstered their moral authority by loudly splitting with their parties on a few prominent issues— McCain by embracing campaign finance reform, and Lieberman by joining with the likes of Bill Bennett to oppose sex and violence in entertainment. In truth, both men are far more conventional ideologically than such stances suggest. McCain is deeply conservative and Lieberman surprisingly liberal. Americans for Democratic Action, the arbiter of liberalism, gave Lieberman a 95 percent rating in its most recent tally, tying him with Ted Kennedy and putting him ahead of Paul Wellstone.

Now Lieberman is using his moral authority to lift Gore above the fray. Lieberman famously denounced Clinton's sexual transgressions as "morally reprehensible" and "disgraceful." This seems to be sticking—and that deprives Bush of his best issue in the campaign. The folks in Austin are scrambling for a new plan.

★ ☆ ★

If you look closely, there were earlier signs of trouble to come for Bush, even before the Cheney flop and the Lieberman boost. I believe it all began when the Bush campaign hired Miami Air, a fly-by-night charter company with a green and purple palm tree logo, to be its campaign carrier. It started with two creaky old 727s. They drip oil out of the rear and onto passengers' clothing when we board and exit. There was a fire aboard one of them, when something overheated in the onboard oven. When we took off from Knoxville this spring, a section of the plane above one of the rows of seats, the part that holds the oxygen masks, fell out and dangled. Reporters have told the crew they saw loose rivets on the wing. And when we landed at LaGuardia once, we came close to missing the runway, bounced from one wheel to the other and up in the air again, leaving us all holding on for our lives.

Word of this, which I got into the *Washington Post*, turned up more allegations against Miami Air, including complaints that the company's chief frightened pilots over safety issues at a previous airline and that Miami Air planes have lost a window in flight, taken off with a cargo door open and nearly run out of gas. Recently, I heard that reporters had to abandon one of the Bush planes on the runway because a wing flap fell off.

But Bush has survived the Miami Air episode (and, more importantly, survived Miami Air). A tougher blow came in an event I witnessed in New Jersey. I call it the Garlic Press.

The Bush campaign had choreographed an event at a community center in Elizabeth, New Jersey, to show the governor going where no Republican has gone before, into poor minority communities with his compassionate conservative message. But today there was a wrinkle. Seated at Bush's right hand was the center's first director, an African American minister named the Reverend Joseph Garlic. Bush tried to season the discussion with Garlic. "How did you get the vision, Reverend Garlic?" the governor asked.

The wily Garlic, however, used his forum in front of the TV cameras to turn on Bush and ask a question he "may find a little sensitive." Garlic began by inquiring about Bush's recent visit to the NAACP, and Bush gave a stirring response. "People hear the word 'Republican' and think he doesn't care, particularly white-guy Republican," Bush said. But not the Texas governor. "I'll become the president of everybody." Bush must have thought he hit it out of the park; in fact, he had stepped into a trap.

Garlic roasted him with a question about the execution of Gary Graham, which Bush recently condoned in Texas. "You missed an opportunity to show some of this compassion and to show some of this new Republican spirit," Garlic lectured, as Bush aides stared at their toes and reporters began scribbling. "You trust the criminal justice system," Garlic said, even though it's "not always fair" to minorities.

Uh-oh. "I support the death penalty because I think it saves lives," Bush ventured. "This isn't a political decision to me, Reverend. If it costs me votes, so be it."

Garlic pounced. "With all due respect, sir, that is not a good enough answer," he said. "The issue was the doubt concerning the man's conviction. . . . While you may say to me this was not a political decision, this was definitely not a moral decision."

Bush cut his losses. "We just disagree," he said quietly.

When the event ended, I joined other giddy reporters in a thick scrum around Garlic the Conqueror. "They never told me I couldn't say anything I wanted to say," Garlic declared.

Whatever the cause, news coverage of Bush has definitely shifted. Once it was Gore who got all the tough questions, as the "Spice Girls," three women assigned to Gore from the AP, the *New York Times* and the *Washington Post*, led a hostile press corps, while Bush's press corps was seen as sycophantic. Now, everything seems to have shifted, in lockstep with the polls.

The swiftness and the severity of the change has surprised me. I wrote a lengthy article talking about the valuable experience Bush gained as owner of the Texas Rangers. It was a friendly piece (an editor even removed the bit about Bush getting scolded by his mother when she caught him on ESPN picking his nose at a ballgame), and even Bush's aides thought so. But even this flattering prose turned into grist for an attack on Bush's emphasis on marketing above substance, in a column by the *Times*'s Frank Rich.

"The salesmanship used to boost that struggling baseball franchise seems a blueprint for the campaign," Rich wrote. "To ensure favorable press coverage, Mr. Bush flattered reporters and gave them 'a great press box.' Though catering to the rich by adding a profusion of luxury boxes to his new stadium, he hired an architect to camouflage the class distinctions from the hoi polloi."

Odd. The piece, I thought, made a good case for why Bush would be a good president. It went, in part, like this:

Expectations were not high when George W. Bush bought the Texas Rangers baseball club in 1989.

"A total smartass who didn't have a clue about baseball," Randy Galloway, a sports columnist with the *Fort Worth Star-Telegram*, remembers thinking. "Snot-nosed kid" was the phrase that came to mind to Phil Rogers, then a Dallas baseball writer.

Hopes were no higher on the inside. Tom Grieve, then the team's general manager, thought he would soon be working with "a spoiled brat who thinks he runs the world because of his last name. Everyone felt that way."

The doubts were similar to those that greeted Bush's entry into politics, when he was dubbed "Shrub" because of his famous father. But in baseball, as in politics, the skeptics underestimated the man. And in baseball, as in politics, Bush disarmed them with a beguiling charm.

Soon after arriving, he gathered Rangers management to tell them about his time on the Yale baseball team. Yale was losing by ten runs late in one game, and Bush was warming up in the bullpen. When the manager came in to make a pitching change, he took one look at the bullpen and signaled the second baseman to come in to pitch, Bush told them. "And that was the end of my career."

"I can't tell you George is the smartest guy I ever met or the best business guy I ever met, but he's doggone good at what he does," says Jim Reeves, a sports columnist and a doubter who was won over, like most others, by Bush. "He's very good at making people around him feel good."

Baseball has been, arguably, the most important thing in Bush's life. It was his vehicle both for embracing a family tradition and for leaving his father's shadow. It made him a success after a series of business failures, it made him rich, and it launched his political career. Baseball also gave Bush a powerful, if intangible, asset: it made him a regular guy, not a president's son from Andover, Yale and Harvard but a guy who spit sunflower shells while hobnobbing with the on-deck batter.

Undoubtedly, baseball made Bush more of a man of the people. It's another issue entirely whether it gave him the skills needed to be president. His opponents say it didn't. John McCain imagined a Bush campaign ad based on his executive experience with the Rangers: "But when the scouting reports come in, there is only one lonely man in a dark office." Al Gore's spokesman, Chris Lehane, derides him similarly: "He says his experience is in the private sector. He was the front man for a baseball team where the greatest claim to fame was trading away Sammy Sosa."

But Bush's baseball career did give him the chance to demonstrate and develop his leadership skills. Though he may not have had the sharpest baseball or business mind, those who worked with him say, he had an uncanny ability to hire the right people and to create consensus and contentment among prickly peers and subordinates. He developed a management style that is not dogmatic or ideological in the least. And, to borrow a marketing phrase, he had a gift for p.r. that vastly improved the brand. It's no accident that those are the same traits Bush has exhibited as governor and candidate.

"I'm not so sure you can segue from baseball to a presidency, but there are some lessons about management, about developing a strategy," Bush said in a recent interview. "Baseball is a marketing business. It's a business of being able to relate to fans and convince fans to come out. This is a business about adding value." As for his management, Bush said: "I do build teams—that's what a president does. He builds an administration of people heading in the same direction with the same goal."

In his five years with the Rangers, Bush had significant success. He led a group that bought the team for $34 million and sold it a decade later for $250 million. He presided over construction of a $200 million ballpark—built mostly with government money—that boosted annual attendance by 50 percent. Top ticket prices soared from $8 to $60, as the Rangers boosted their payroll from $6 million to $70 million to lure the game's top athletes. The Rangers, who hadn't won a title since the team's move to Texas from Washington in the early 1970s, have now won three division titles in four years.

"When they came in, the Rangers were one of the low-end organizations," Rangers slugger Rafael Palmeiro says of Bush's management. "They changed that."

Any true baseball fan can tell you this without a hint of irony: baseball is a metaphor for life. "Baseball is not simply an essential part of this country; it is a living memory of what American Culture at its best wishes to be," wrote A. Bartlett Giamatti, the late Yale president and baseball commissioner.

If this seems a bit far-out, it doesn't seem at all strange to Mark McKinnon, the ad man who must sell Bush to the electorate. "When people look at a candidate, they're looking for cues, for threads," he says. "It goes way beyond issues to cultural DNA. Is this person like me? Does he share my values? It's much more likely somebody will pick that up through somebody's love of baseball than from his policy on prescription drugs." Just so nobody misses it, McKinnon promises to make baseball part of Bush's media campaign.

Bush himself doesn't much go for baseball metaphors. His wife, Laura, speaks in an interview about the "mystical way baseball fits in American life," about how watching a ballgame leaves "time to talk, time to daydream." But the governor? Well, he just likes the game.

"Baseball brings out your personality in a way," he says. "I'm a practical person. I understood the practical aspects of baseball." Then he trails off into a mundane discourse on ticket prices.

If Bush doesn't articulate the transcendence of baseball, he doesn't need to; it was bred into him. His father was the star Yale first baseman who met Babe Ruth and later coached his son's Little League team. "It was the one sport my dad shared with us as kids," says Marvin Bush, ten years younger than George.

Barbara Bush was the only Little League mother who could keep score at games, where her son was a mediocre player. "He had trouble," says Fay Vincent, the former baseball commissioner who as a Bush family friend spent a summer in Midland, Texas, in the 1950s. "I used to tease him about it. I remember him striking out a lot."

Today, Barbara Bush remembers her son as "the most enthusiastic player" who made the all-star team as a catcher. President Bush, in a contemporaneous letter to his father-in-law, described "Georgie" as "so eager. He tries so very hard."

Bush sent envelopes to the day's best ballplayers, with their baseball cards stapled to a stamped, self-addressed postcard. A decade later, he gave his brother Marvin a leather-bound collection of autographed cards. Bush has since tried to get them back, but Marvin told him they were lost, "just to get him off my back." In fact, Marvin still has them.

Told of "Big Marv's" admission, Bush guffaws. "This is a breakthrough story! I finally found my Willie McCovey autograph!"

The two brothers also played APBA baseball, a form of fantasy baseball with board, dice and a set of cards, updated annually. "One of the highlights of our year was getting the fresh pack of APBA cards," Marvin says. "On a rainy day, you could play for hours on end, arguing, rearranging the cards when the other guy went to the bathroom."

Herbert Walker, George's great-uncle, was then an original owner of the New York Mets and took George to see the team's first spring training. Uncle Herbie even named his dogs Metsie and Yogi—and George was smitten. "George always wanted to buy a baseball team, to be an owner like his Uncle Herbie," Laura Bush says.

After college, Bush coached a Midland Little League team through "quite the poor season," Laura Bush recalls. In the oil business, he became a partner of Bill DeWitt, son of the St. Louis Cardinals' owner; it was DeWitt who later alerted Bush that the Rangers were for sale.

Bush keeps 200 autographed baseballs in his office in the Texas capitol, including ones from Sandy Koufax, Stan Musial, Ted Williams and Joe DiMaggio. In an opposite corner of his office are three bats, one from the Rangers with his name engraved, and one from Mark McGwire wishing him luck in 2000. "He does have books, too," a Bush aide says as a reporter inspects the memorabilia.

Tom Schieffer, who as Bush's "ballpark czar" directed the construction of the Ballpark in Arlington, shows off his handiwork: the man-made lake outside, the corridor inside modeled after Chartres Cathedral, the lone stars in the railings, the longhorn cattle carving outside, the panels of Texas and baseball history near the portals, the local stone that makes the place look, just a bit, like the Texas capitol.

Fans throughout stop to praise Schieffer for the ballpark. "Just want to say thank you for making this happen," one stranger tells him.

The ballpark was Bush's signal achievement as a managing partner of the Rangers. The Rangers, he learned, would have been losing money in the old stadium even if they sold out every night, because of the preponderance of cheap seats in the former minor league ballpark. His solution was to get Arlington taxpayers to agree to pay for two-thirds of the stadium.

Local anti-tax activists howled about "corporate welfare." Bush figured that if the citizens agreed to it, there was nothing wrong with a tax hike. "George was not dogmatic," Schieffer says.

Bush also didn't mind squeezing Arlington a bit by flirting with Dallas and other cities that wanted to host the Rangers. He played a key role in selling the ballpark to the public, speaking at a rally and meetings and on television. He hired his father's pollster to help. In the end, the tax hike was approved 65 percent to 35 percent in a referendum. Richard Green, the former mayor, says Bush's name and effort swayed the referendum. "I'm not sure how else to explain the phenomenon."

Bush's ballpark-building experience was also central to his other triumph as a team owner: creating a desirable image for the lowly Rangers. It's an image-making skill Bush would duplicate as governor and presidential candidate.

One of Bush's priorities was to build plenty of lucrative luxury boxes, but without making it look that way. "We tried to downplay the distinctions in class," says David Schwartz, the architect. Bush wanted the stands built low (only 18 inches off the field) and tight, increasing the danger to fans but giving the place a cozy feel. Bush and his team also did the park on the cheap, taking advantage of a downturn in Texas construction to build the place for less than half the cost per square foot as Camden Yards.

Bush was the consummate fan, spreading an upbeat image of the team and seeing it as his obligation to sit in his front-row seat during the losing streaks, listening to the fans' abuse. During one rain-delayed game when a fan shouted continuous taunts, Bush got up and introduced himself to the man, a teacher. Bush apologized for the pitching, and the heckler apologized for the yelling. "Democracy works well because people can come and spew out their emotions and yell and scream and write letters," Bush says. "Being down there provided people an outlet."

Bush made sales calls to businesses to pitch season tickets and demanded more stroking of season ticket holders. He met regularly with the marketing staff and spoke at civic groups. "It's 81 games at home," Bush says, "81 times you've got to compete with movies and walks in the park."

Bush was also skilled at marketing another commodity: Bush. He handed out autographed photos of himself to fans; the photos were normally just for players, but "he wanted it so much," explains John Blake, the Rangers' p.r. man. Bush escorted the likes of Roger Staubach and Ben Crenshaw to games, getting his own mug on television. "He loved the trappings of being an owner," says T. R. Sullivan, a *Star-Telegram* sportswriter.

To win over the media, Bush insisted that his new ballpark have a fancy press box with skylights and an elevator straight to the clubhouse level. "We aren't going to get good reviews if we don't have a great press box," he said at the time. He took hostile reporters golfing to win their affections. He made himself available to reporters daily during batting practice, then often visited the press box and the radio booth during the game—even calling a few pitches on air.

The result: in a sports media world that has chewed up many owners (ask Marge Schott, Jerry Reinsdorf and George Steinbrenner), Bush thrived with his hail-fellow-well-met routine. When Bush was naming the new ballpark, he visited the "Einsteins" in the press box to get their suggestions. "Ann Richards Field," was Galloway's suggestion. Bush, who was already in the governor's race to beat Richards, led the laughter.

How hard is it to run a baseball team, anyway? Most young boys dream of doing it, and grown sports fans invariably insist they can do it better than whoever the bum is who owns a team at a given time. To them, it may seem as if all that's involved is putting up some cash and taking your seat in the owner's box, occasionally weighing in on trades as if swapping baseball cards. In reality, running a baseball team is like running most other businesses—but under intense public scrutiny.

"It's not world peace," says Wally Haas, who owned the Oakland Athletics and whose family's fortune is in Levi Strauss & Co. "But on the other hand, it's a very public business. What other business, other than running for president, is your business in the paper every day? It's really black and white: if you win, you're great, and if you lose, you're a bum."

Bush's style as a Rangers owner was equal parts childlike exuberance and Harvard Business School. He left the drudgery to colleagues and underlings, focusing only on those things he cared about. Bush left financial management to the other managing partner, Rusty Rose, operations to Schieffer, who became the president, and baseball judgments to Grieve, the general manager.

"Really, Rusty and Tom ran the thing," the sportswriter Galloway says. Mickey Herskowitz, a *Houston Chronicle* sports columnist who collaborated with Bush on his campaign biography, says, "He's probably retroactively gotten a lot more credit for running the Rangers than he really did. Bush was the front man, the p.r. man, the handshaker." Even for his main achievement, the ballpark, Bush "wasn't involved in the details," says Green, the former Arlington mayor.

But Bush didn't delegate blindly. He was careful to avoid allowing end runs, and he constantly grilled underlings to hold them accountable. "You hire general managers, and if the general manager isn't any good, you get a new one," Bush says.

When managers didn't perform, Bush could be fierce. "I'd seen him dress people down a few times," says John McMichael, the Rangers' controller. "I'm glad it wasn't me." In the fall of 1990, Bush fired Mike Stone, the club president, after Stone, in the owners' opinion, had tried to pit Bush against his partner, Rose. Stone's firing devastated Rangers morale.

Stone, who expected to resign quietly, instead saw Bush dash for the cameras. Stone complained to a columnist: "The bottom line is that George wants to run the club." A piqued Bush, according to reports at the time, then ordered Stone to clean out his desk and leave immediately. Bush was derided in the media as "strange" and "Scrooge Jr." and "head of complacency central." After word came out that Bush was looking to Disney for a marketing executive, one columnist noted that "Goofy is already in charge."

Bush learned his lesson. When he and his partners later fired manager Bobby Valentine and general manager Grieve, they kept on better terms. "If he asked me to campaign, I'd be the world's greatest salesman—and you're talking to someone who got fired," says Grieve, now a Rangers TV announcer.

As a managing partner, Bush also took on the care and feeding of the nearly twenty Rangers owners across the country. He was the main force behind assembling the ownership group, though it had as much to do with the Bush name as his abilities. Peter Ueberroth, then the baseball commissioner, convinced Richard Rainwater, an investor who had earlier rebuffed Bush, to join the effort. Then–Rangers owner Eddie Chiles, too, had a fondness for President Bush. Bush put up just $600,000 of his own funds, which turned into a $15 million fortune after he received additional shares for his management.

But Bush kept the ownership group together without benefit of his pedigree. He attended thrice-yearly meetings armed with jokes, organized a pickup game in the ballpark for owners, took them to Mexico for a retreat full of cigars, cards and fishing and had Valentine give them regular baseball briefings. Later, Bush hosted an owners' dinner at the governor's mansion. "He knew how to operate politically," Rose says.

Bush's Rangers didn't make much money; there were no profit distributions to owners, but no calls for capital either. His success was in keeping them together long enough to get a huge return on their investment.

Rose also ceded to Bush the role of maintaining relations with other teams' owners. Bush often found himself at odds with the others, as when they sought to replace Commissioner Vincent in 1992 with a weaker executive who would agree to break the players' union. Bush defended his family friend. "Trying to break the union, bomb it into submission, wasn't going to work," Vincent says. Bush lost, Vincent was sacked, and baseball suffered the devastating strike of 1994.

Throughout the Vincent battle, though, Bush kept on good terms with Bud Selig, who led the anti-Vincent forces and later became baseball commissioner. "It was a tinderbox, but we joked a lot, played baseball trivia, kept it very civilized," Selig says.

Bush kept his players happy the old-fashioned way: he agreed to spend money on them. One year, when Rangers scouting director Sandy Johnson was having trouble signing the team's top pick, shortstop Benji Gill, Bush told Johnson to "let a little more of the dough go," Johnson recalls. Other owners, Johnson says, "would say, 'He's not getting another penny.'"

Bush, with Schieffer and Rose, convinced the baseball executives to move away from the metrics and statistics of baseball to look at players' psychological profiles. They decided to weigh character, or "makeup," equally with talent; this meant exchanging prima donnas such as Ruben Sierra, Jose Canseco and Kevin Brown for lower-profile, easy-to-manage players. Of course, Bush signed off on at least one unwise—even rash—decision, trading future star Sammy Sosa and a top pitcher for fading slugger Harold Baines late one season. But overall, the philosophy reduced clubhouse scowling and whining—and coincided with a better record. "They want guys who want to be here," says Palmeiro, the first baseman. "They want everyone to fit in. I like that."

Bush, as owner, worked out in the team weight room, strutted into Valentine's office in his ostrich boots and held family picnics for the team and even a crab dinner before Opening Day in Baltimore in 1993. He went to player Julio Franco's wedding with his family, spoke Spanish with the Hispanic players (though most spoke better English than he did Spanish) and started a practice of explaining the team's financial books to players at the end of each season.

Bush became particularly close to Nolan Ryan, whom he'd met on the campaign trail for his father in 1980. He helped to convince the aging pitcher to stay five years, rather than the single season Ryan had planned—in part because Ryan liked what he saw. "He promoted the ballclub as much as anybody I'd seen," says Ryan, whom Bush, as governor, named to a wildlife commission in Texas.

During one extra-inning game Bush was watching with Vincent, Bush called to Palmeiro in the on-deck circle to ask him to hit a home run "so we can all go home." Palmeiro hit a round-tripper and tipped his cap to Bush after crossing the plate. "That'd be good to have somebody we know in the White House," Palmeiro says now. "Will he still remember us?"

No doubt he will.

I ask you: Was *that* a mean story? At this point in the campaign, even an effort to boost Bush seems to do the opposite.

The clearest of all signs that the press has turned on Bush comes from the revival of the Bushism. News reports are now full of Bush's malapropisms, including August 21's "We cannot let terrorists and rogue nations hold this nation hostile or hold our allies hostile," and August 18's "A leadership is someone who brings people together."

The Bushism, that malaprop uniquely suited to the Bush tongue, is a subject that has long intrigued me. But only recently does this seem to be getting a mass audience, and I feel qualified to comment on the subject because I have studied its scientific origins and consulted with experts.

Inside the human brain, a part of the frontal lobe called Broca's area directs the production of clear and intelligible speech. In the case of Bush, however, something between Broca's area and the tongue has an occasional tendency to go comically wrong.

When Bush endeavors to say "tariffs and barriers," it can come out "terriers and bariffs." "Handcuffs" mysteriously becomes "cuff links," and "tactical nuclear weapons" morphs into "tacular weapons." Once, Bush's brain cruelly caused its owner to pronounce "missile launches" as "mential losses."

The insensitive louts of the press generally respond to these examples of Bushspeak by making fun of their author. A network producer on the Bush bus nicknamed him "the English Patient." Garry Trudeau and

Maureen Dowd parody his gaffes. The online magazine *Slate* anthologizes the growing collection of "Bushisms." (This week's installment: "I hope we get to the bottom of the answer.")

Yuk, yuk. Very funny.

Surely we wouldn't make fun of a man suffering from diabetic attacks or epileptic seizures. And though Bush's affliction isn't so serious, there's the possibility that he can't control it. To examine this possibility, we asked the opinions of leading speech pathologists. They haven't examined the man, but they have a few ideas.

"It's a Verbal Goulash Syndrome," pronounces Sam Chwat, a New York speech therapist who has helped the likes of Julia Roberts and Robert De Niro say their lines. Lyn Goldberg, a George Washington University speech pathologist, pronounces the governor "motorically vulnerable." Ray Kent, a University of Wisconsin expert, says the governor suffers from "sequencing errors" and "lexical confusions."

Clearly. When Bush attended Perseverance Month at a New Hampshire school, he famously declared: "This is Preservation Month. I appreciate preservation. It's what you do when you run for president. You've got to preserve." Another time, he repeatedly insisted that "I denounce interracial dating," when he meant he denounced a policy against interracial dating.

Part of the problem is not of his making: it's the fault of snobbish Easterners who just can't understand his West Texas dialect. Sure, he talks about "nucular" warheads, but so do many Southerners, including Jimmy Carter. So what if "obfuscate" rolls off Bush's lips as "obscufate" and "obsfucate"? They understand him just fine in Midland. Yet he continues "getting pillared in the press and cartoons," as he puts it, grasping for "pilloried."

Bush's aides say the malapropisms are the by-product of an effervescent nature and an agile mind. Why the gobbledygook? "Because his brain works faster than his mouth does," jokes Mindy Tucker, the governor's spokeswoman.

It's true that Bush speaks far more freely than his Democratic rival, Al Gore, who gets panned for his slow and deliberate speaking style. Gore chooses his words carefully and corrects his own mistakes, but he orates like a somnambulist.

Some of Bush's errors could happen to any person under pressure and public scrutiny, particularly when their off-the-cuff remarks are transcribed for posterity. Surely, it was an honest mistake when he chanted, "If you're sick and tired of the politics of cynicism and polls and principles, come and join this campaign." Obviously, he knows it's not correct to say, as he has, "I understand small business growth—I was one," and "There is madmen in the world and there are terror," and "Rarely is the question asked: Is our children learning?"

Bush, however, unlike Ronald Reagan and the elder George Bush, doesn't get the benefit of the doubt after a linguistic lapse. Perhaps it's because of his history of related flubs: his juxtaposing Slovenia and Slovakia, and his East Timorians, Grecians and Kosovians.

Bush also has a rich tradition of verbal pratfalls. Bill Minutaglio, a *Dallas Morning News* reporter and Bush biographer, was the recipient of this Bush puzzler six years ago: "It was just inebriating what Midland was all about then." Presumably, Bush was reaching for "intoxicating."

Speech pathologist Chwat says the governor is probably modeling his speech after that of his famous father, consciously or unconsciously. It's simply the way he learned to talk, Chwat says.

Famous for coining phrases and words such as "hyporhetorical questions" and "hypothecate," Bush the elder constantly spouted Yogi Berraisms, once imploring: "Please don't look at part of the glass, the part that is only less than half full."

Indeed, some of the gaffes of Bush fils sound like his father's. The son launched this gem early in the campaign: "When I was coming up, it was a dangerous world and we knew exactly who the 'they' were. It was us versus them, and it was clear who 'them' was. Today, we're not so sure who the 'they' are, but we know they're there."

Tired clichés are given new life on the governor's tongue. "We ought to make the pie higher," he opines, and suggests that one "can't take the high horse and claim the low road." Particularly if he is one of those Internet millionaires "who have become rich beyond their means." Better call the credit bureau.

"He has a singular output channel, and he's jamming it with too many words," Chwat says. Some other errors, he adds, are evidence of an "incomplete education" (despite Bush's two Ivy League degrees). Among the flubs Chwat puts in this category: when Bush says, "I don't have to accept their tenants," instead of tenets, and when he talks about education being about more than "bricks and mortars," using the term for heavy artillery instead of the construction mixture.

But is Bush's problem simply a matter of nurture? Other scientists are convinced that nature has some role. Robert Shprintzen, an otolaryngologist and speech pathologist at the State University of New York's Upstate Medical University, says Bush's speech pattern, like everybody's, is influenced by genetics.

Much of the way people talk is biological, Shprintzen says, dictated by the physical structure of the brain, the number of brain cells and the level of neurotransmitters such as dopamine. Obviously, George W. would inherit characteristics from his old man. "Even children who have been separated from their parents at birth have been found to be astonishingly like their parents," Shprintzen says.

Still, Governor Bush's speech errors are arguably worse than his old man's: President Bush switched words and contorted sentences, but his son occasionally produces outright gibberish. That leads GWU's Goldberg to make a worrisome observation: he says Bush shares some traits with those suffering from a serious speech disorder known as apraxia, which at its worst leaves its victims unable to utter anything meaningful.

The disorder, often caused by a stroke, disrupts the neural programming of speech-related muscles, causing trouble selecting, timing and ordering sounds, and a tendency to shorten words.

But Goldberg hastens to add that she isn't diagnosing Bush with the disorder and, in fact, doubts he is apraxic. The symptoms are likely coincidental, in the same way someone with a winter cough shares certain symptoms with a lung cancer patient. Still, Goldberg says, "it's striking when you see these sound problems and timing errors in his speech."

Among the worrisome signs: in Bush's speech, "viable" has come out "vile," "subsidization" has posed as "subsidation," "balkanize" has masqueraded as "vulcanize," and "ascribe" has seen its duties replaced by "subscribe." Sentences, too, get condensed, to bizarre effect. "I know how hard it is for you to put food on your family," he told one perplexed audience.

Whatever the cause, the English Patient should survive this malady. Of greater concern is what's happening to the rest of us. "The problem is, it's catching," says Richard Wolffe, who has been following the governor for the *Financial Times*. "I can't even say 'tariffs' anymore. I say 'terriers.'"

Wolffe, who kept a log of Bush's verbal creations on his laptop computer, found his collection destroyed when the Bush campaign bus, suspiciously, ran over the laptop. Maybe that's what Bush meant by a mential loss.

With polls and reporters turning on him, Bush suddenly seems unable to do anything right. He tries to talk about foreign policy, and it's called ineffective. A judge hands him an embarrassing ruling about Texas not doing enough for poor children. Cheney embarrasses him over his lucrative pay package from Halliburton. The Republican National Committee makes a nasty ad about Gore and then cancels it because it's misleading, then gets panned for releasing a different nasty ad. And now, Bush has been caught on tape at a rally telling Cheney that *New York Times* reporter Adam Clymer is a "major-league asshole."

Clearly, the man can't catch a break—much as Gore could do no right for much of this spring. It is time for Bush to try something new. Actually, it's something he already did when threatened by McCain in the primaries. And it's something Gore has used against him to claw his way back. It's time for smashmouth politics.

Part VII

★ ☆ ★

Fall 2000
The Endless Campaign

28

★ ☆ ★

Smashmouth Triumphant

I've been covering the presidential race for nearly two years now, and it has been an utter failure: I'm no closer to knowing who will win the race than I was in 1998. On Labor Day, the polls say the race is a dead heat (although *Newsweek*, which is apparently polling only in Carthage, Tennessee, has Gore up by 10 points). And tensions are high. Gore declared that Bush ought to "put up or shut up" on the topic of prescription drugs for the elderly. Bush sniffed that Gore "didn't sound very presidential."

But it's the worried Bush who has renounced his Change the Tone Tour and is now playing the best type of smashmouth politics. The Republicans have just put out the meanest ad of the campaign, bringing up Gore's 1996 Buddhist temple episode. A narrator watching Gore on the tube declares sarcastically, "There's Al Gore, reinventing himself on television. Like I'm not going to notice." Bush is defending the ad. "This is a fellow that will say anything," he says. "He is willing to exaggerate in order to win."

It's good news for Bush that he's abandoned his prudish "change the tone" line. Now Gore is the one claiming the high road and pretending to be wounded by Bush's attacks. The Gore campaign has put out a "going negative fact sheet" and a timeline showing Bush going from "zero to negative in 24 hours." But sanctimony won't help Gore any more than it helped Bush. True, Bush has gotten tougher; just a week ago he pressured the Republican National Committee to withdraw an ad that used six-year-old footage of Gore to make it appear as if he were saying Clinton didn't lie during the Lewinsky scandal.

The Democrats would be much better off joining the Republicans in the smashmouth arena. But they seem more inclined to play victim. After the Bush campaign accused Gore of "reaching new levels of hypocrisy," the Gore side responded by grousing about "negative attacks." When Bush claimed Gore's prescription drug plan "forces seniors into a government-run HMO," Gore offered a "rebuttal to negative Bush address." After Bush's side said, "Gore Comes Up Short in Budget Document Battle," Gore sniffed about "misleading attacks." Finally, the Democrats gave up the piety and mocked Bush's new slogan, "Real Plans for Real People" as "Real Plans for Rich People."

Joe Lieberman holds promise as an attack dog. He has a knack for saying mean and nasty things, but in a mild way, prefacing them with "Sadly" or "Sorry to say." As the *New York Times* put it, he sounds like a "concerned neighbor leaning over a back fence, sharing a troubling bit of gossip."

Unfortunately, in the veep debate against Cheney in Kentucky, Lieberman came across as soft and philosophical, uttering not a word about Cheney's votes against Head Start, gun control, and Nelson Mandela. He neglected to mention even Cheney's status as an oil titan. The commentators all called the debate noble and uplifting for its high-minded tone. But in my scoring, Cheney won on eight questions, Lieberman on four, and the others were tied. The soporific debate, meanwhile, helped drive viewership to embarrassingly low levels.

Why, I find myself asking, couldn't the presidential race be more like the New York Senate race?

In need of some refreshing, hard-nosed politics, I take a break from the presidential campaign to fly to Buffalo, where Hillary Clinton and Rick Lazio are due to slug it out in their first debates. It's about time; the partisans on both sides are spoiling for a fight. For the Clinton antagonists, particularly, this is a rare chance to draw blood from a favorite demon. Years of anti-Clinton anger can finally be released.

Hillary-haters are not disappointed. Tonight, Lazio calls her "beyond shameless" and delivers a pledge banning soft money right to his flustered opponent's podium, as if serving a subpoena. Lazio even tags her with the worst epithet of all: he accuses Clinton of being "positively Clintonesque." Now that's low.

Supporters of both candidates, after hibernating through the campaign so far, arrive ninety minutes before the debate, armed with posters, air horns and strong lungs. Wayne Brown, a local salesman, carries a sign that says "Clinton for Change," with hammer-and-sickles standing for C's. Like many here, Brown, a Rush Limbaugh fan, isn't a Lazio guy per se. He would vote for a ham sandwich running against Clinton. "I know

I'm anti-Hillary, but I don't know enough to know whether I'm for Lazio," he says.

Nearby, Michael Powers is busy heckling a Clinton supporter: "Come on, did the union give you paid vacation for this? You got paid to come! They're from Arkansas." He surreptitiously places a Lazio sticker on a Clinton supporter's back. His wife, Sheila, waves a sign that says "Mrs. Clinton does not speak for me!" while Michael yells himself hoarse with a chant of "Hillary go home!" "I'm personally offended by her coming to New York," he explains. "Everything Hillary does is for Hillary."

Another man in the Hyatt Regency ballroom blasts his air horn and bellows "Whitewater!" and "Vince Foster!" It becomes immediately apparent that this crowd is less pro-Lazio than anti-Hillary. After all, they've hated her for eight years; they've known the New York congressman only a few months. "My vote's an anti-Hillary vote," says Brooks Jennings, as he watches the debate and drinks a beer.

But the enemy of Jennings's enemy is his friend, and Lazio wastes no time in cutting up Clinton. When she links his name with Newt Gingrich, Lazio turns on her fiercely. "You, of all people, shouldn't try to make guilt by association." The Hyatt ballroom erupts.

The Lazio fans in the ballroom don't seem to care much about the nitty-gritty of the debate. His response to a health care question gets no reaction at all. The room is silent as Clinton talks about hospital funding and tax credits. Lazio's discussion of the "dairy compact" and the Buffalo economy doesn't do much for them, either. But when Clinton talks about "my last eight years in the White House" as if she were the president, the crowd begins to murmur. When she utters the familiar line about "large, risky tax schemes," the Lazio fans give a contemptuous laugh. And when Lazio trumpets, "I don't think we need that Little Rock record in the Big Apple," the Buffalo Republicans, though they live closer to Cleveland than to the Big Apple, whoop and pump their fists.

And then, the Clinton-haters' Holy Grail: Debate moderator Tim Russert plays the old "vast right-wing conspiracy" interview in which she insisted that the allegations about White House intern Monica Lewinsky were "not going to be proven true." The crowd laughs. Hearing the conspiracy line, Joel Dombrowski, drinking a beer in the back, shouts, "Here I am, it was me, I did it!" When Clinton responds that it was "a very painful time for me," a woman in the audience pretends to play a violin, while Dombrowski shouts, "And your girlfriend!"

Clinton is clearly struggling now; someone in the audience makes the noise of a falling bomb. "I didn't mislead anyone," she is saying on the screen. "I didn't know the truth." Dombrowski screams as if he's ringside, "Oh, she's on the ropes!" Clinton talks about "using all my contacts" to help New York; the Lazio crowd howls.

After an hour of this blood and gore, Dombrowski is sated. True, Russert didn't ask the questions he sent in, including one about whether the First Lady wears "boxers or briefs." But Dombrowski's not complaining. "It was a watershed," he says, recalling the moment when Russert played the right-wing conspiracy interview. "Her face drained. You could see it physically. She really got shook."

Dombrowski and this crowd have been waiting a long time to shake up Hillary Clinton. "Hey," he says, sipping his beer. "Welcome to New York."

Lazio and his thuggish supporters, it appears, may have overdone the smashmouth thing. The Hillary haters have become something of a liability for Lazio. I join the candidate again a couple of weeks later, in East Rochester, where he is to address a Republican dinner. But before he speaks, Paul Fioravanti, a local GOP official, puts on a rubber mask of Hillary Rodham Clinton and declares that KFC now has a special Hillary package: "All thighs, no breasts, leaves a terrible taste in my mouth."

Patrick McCarthy, Lazio's spokesman, rushes around to disavow the man's routine. "We're only responsible for our part of the program," he says. Lazio, who makes no reference to the episode in his remarks, tells reporters on the way out that he "didn't approve."

Of course he didn't. The 42-year-old New York Republican Senate candidate, perpetually grinning and ingratiating himself, resembles nothing so much as an overage Boy Scout. But the episode underscores Lazio's central problem: his supporters tend to support him not because of who he is (a handsome, politically moderate Long Islander) but for who he isn't (Hillary Clinton). "You're carrying the torch against the princess of evil," a radio host tells him in Watertown—a typical greeting for Lazio.

Lazio accepts such remarks with ambivalence. He has learned that Hillary-haters alone can't get him to the Senate. "Mrs. Clinton elicits emotional, visceral responses in people," he says in an interview on his campaign bus. "My job is to turn that energy into positive energy. I want to win, obviously, but I want to be worthy of the win. I would not want to win with pure negative energy."

Nor can he. Once, Lazio and his strategists thought he could win New York's open Senate seat simply by making the race a referendum on Hillary Clinton's character. But it turns out Hillary-haters aren't a majority. And the hullabaloo around the First Lady has obscured Lazio. Twenty-eight percent of New Yorkers don't know who he is, according to one of the campaign's polls. Lazio has to tell his own story—quickly.

"I've got a confession to make," Lazio tells a luncheon meeting of a Buffalo Rotary Club. This raises tantalizing possibilities. Is he not wearing underwear? Does he cheat on his taxes? Well, not quite. "I've always been a supporter of tax relief," Lazio continues. A moment later, Lazio raises tension again when he declares, "In the interest of full disclosure, I have another confession to make." This stunning revelation? "I have two daughters of school age."

Lazio's speeches are full of such grand pronouncements. "We don't want to have any abuse of our seniors," he says at a nursing home. Other controversial stands include the belief that "we should put our children first" and "I love the idea of people owning their own homes" and "I'm a big believer in trusting the people." Raising issues, if they enter the campaign at all, tends to have ambiguous results. His crusade against Clinton's raising soft money lost its edge when it was reported that he had done the same thing.

The platitudes and ambiguity leave Lazio undefined. Sometimes he borrows from John McCain's maverick playbook: he quotes Teddy Roosevelt, travels on a bus called the *Mainstream Express* and employs a McCain consultant. But unlike McCain, who has a reputation as a straight-talking war hero, Lazio hasn't answered in voters' minds a fundamental question: Who is Rick Lazio?

"Let me tell you a little about myself," he is saying, warming up a crowd in Lowville. This sounds promising—but what follows is less than revelatory. "I've lived in New York my whole life. I have two daughters. Their names are Molly and Kelsey. I've been in public service 17 years."

Next comes a recitation of his resume, from assistant district attorney to county legislator to congressman. Yes, yes, we know the vital statistics, Rick. But who are you, really?

"Well," he says when the question is put to him. He pauses. Seven seconds pass. Finally, he speaks: "I think for people who have known me, people in my district, the image of me is of somebody who's a nice guy, good family guy, hard worker, brings a lot of energy to his work," he says. "I think I'm a big-hearted guy who really likes people."

That may be the real Lazio, but the candidate seems constantly to change the subject from himself to Clinton. At campaign rallies, his bus plays Ray Charles singing, "Tell your mama, tell your pa, I'm gonna send you back to Arkansas." His bus is adorned with lettering saying, "From New York, For New York" and "Save NY, Stop Hillary." Lazio bumper stickers pronounce "8 years is ENOUGH!" His stump speeches include complaints that New York taxpayers are "subsidizing Arkansas," that he is "the only candidate in the race who has paid New York state income taxes" and that "no one from Little Rock, Arkansas, or Washington, D.C., or Hollywood, California, is going to tell us as New Yorkers who should represent us."

But the carpetbagger theme doesn't work with those who don't already dislike Clinton. Perhaps that's because western New Yorkers don't all see Lazio as one of their own; the western part of the state is about as close to Hillary's hometown of Chicago—500 miles—as it is to Lazio's eastern Long Island. Sure, there's a woman greeting Lazio at a Utica factory tour with a homemade sign saying "A New Yorker For New York," and Lazio greets her warmly. But it turns out the woman, Judy Reusswig, is only in New York to visit her mother. "I come from Bethesda," she says.

The constant Clinton harping irks some of those who aren't automatically inclined to dislike her. At the end of Lazio's speech to the Rotary Club in Buffalo, local advertising executive Patrick Mills rises to complain about the "enormous amount of time spent disqualifying your opponent," and asks Lazio to name two things he would do as senator. Lazio offers a laundry list, emphasizing "bipartisanship"—but even this becomes an attack on Clinton. "I would ask everybody in this audience to point to one thing Mrs. Clinton has done in a bipartisan way." Mills pronounces himself unsatisfied.

Lazio, it seems, can't stop himself. Perhaps he really does, deep down, believe the race is a referendum on Clinton. Perhaps he really is just a vessel for forces greater than him. At stop after stop, Lazio describes the New York Senate race in hyperbolic terms: "This is the most important race in my generation. . . . It is a race that will determine whether character still counts, whether integrity matters, whether the rule of law applies to all or just to some.ellipsis This is a race over the heart and soul of our state and our country."

Why such lofty rhetoric? Asked this question on his bus, Lazio offers a rambling answer about societal change, science, moral judgments, artificial intelligence, robots, privacy, community and family. "This stuff is weighty stuff," he says. "It's very meaningful."

Okay, but the same could be said about any election. Lazio elaborates: "For a lot of people, and for me, you can either choose to discard trust, sincerity and integrity, or you can say these are timeless principles, that they're the foundation of who we are. . . . Disrespect and disregard and a lack of appreciation for the value of truth is contagious."

So that's what this election is about. Good thing he didn't mention Hillary Clinton.

The newly tough George W. has halted Gore's momentum. And Gore, as October approaches, seems to be getting back in fighting form.

When I catch up with him in St. Petersburg, Florida, his staff invites me to view a sneak attack it is planning to use against Bush.

Chris Lehane, Gore's spokesman, invites me to a back room at the event in St. Petersburg and plays a videotape for me. "Elderly people will not suffer as a result of this plan," Bush is saying, in reference to the House GOP's Medicare cuts. "It's gonna make the plan solvent. And Republicans will be heralded, not only for saving Medicare but at the same time for having the political courage to balance the budget."

The interview was broadcast on October 19, 1995, by KXAN in Austin, hours after the House passed the legislation by a vote of 231–201. After Gingrich made that infelicitous remark about how Medicare would "wither on the vine," President Clinton eventually forced the Republicans to back down, arguing that their Medicare plan would have increased costs and reduced medical services to the elderly.

A Democratic National Committee researcher dug up the old broadcast, and the campaign offered it to me, as the *Washington Post*'s representative, as well as to the *New York Times* and the networks.

Much has changed for Bush in the five years since he made the Medicare remarks. Clinton and Congress agreed to more limited cuts as part of the 1997 balanced budget agreement, and both Gore and Bush have called for partial restoration of those cuts. In his plan, Bush proposes increasing Medicare spending by an additional $198 billion over ten years, and like Gore, he would offer a new prescription drug benefit to Medicare recipients.

But that isn't stopping Gore. To drive the point home, his staff invited me to interview him aboard Air Force Two en route to Miami from St. Petersburg. "The effect of the Bush-Cheney plan would be to cause Medicare as we know it to wither on the vine," Gore says, as we talk outside his cabin. (Tipper is sleeping inside.) "He learned from Gingrich's rhetorical excesses, but the effect of his plan is the same."

The 1995 interview, Gore says of Bush, "revealed his truest feelings about Medicare." He argues that the Bush plan is "very similar" to the old House Republicans' plan, would result in "sharply increased premiums" and would put Medicare funds at risk of being siphoned off to pay for Bush's tax cut.

The Gore campaign's discovery of the Bush statement is part of a game of "gotcha" it has been waging against the Texas governor. Gore also used a visit by GOP vice presidential nominee Richard B. Cheney to review tornado damage in Xenia, Ohio, to highlight votes Cheney cast against the Federal Emergency Management Agency during the 1980s when he was the lone House member from Wyoming.

The Medicare gotcha is part of Gore's plan to devote this week to promoting his Medicare plan and undercutting Bush's proposals. Though he didn't mention the Bush interview during a speech on Medicare in St. Petersburg today, Gore sought to raise doubts about Republicans' attachment to the 35-year-old program. "The other side has called Medicare 'a government HMO,'" Gore tells 1,000 supporters here. "They never really have liked it. They've suggested that you shouldn't trust Medicare to provide prescription drug coverage."

Gore, to his credit, has dropped the wounded-victim routine and is hitting back. We see this at the first presidential debate, a few days later, in Boston. I fly up early in order to cover a Nader protest downtown. But when I arrive, there is nobody protesting. I call the Nader offices to inquire, and learn that the protest was the day before; the press release, true to form, didn't specify a date. I check with the Buchanan brigade as a Plan B, but he doesn't have any major events planned, either.

One reason for this is that both sides' partisans have been kept hundreds of yards away from the debate site at UMass-Boston. It takes me three I.D. checks just to get to the sign-in tent, where I pick up my credentials and go through two more checks, a metal detector and a thorough search of my luggage. The whole campus is closed—ostensibly to thwart terrorists, more likely to thwart Nader and Buchanan. Nader gets kicked out of the debate audience, even though he got himself a ticket from a student. He's threatening lawsuits. (How unusual for him!)

But I am not worried about such things. I am inside the debate area, and I am delighted to find an Anheuser Busch refreshment tent, where there is beer flowing, snacks, Budweiser girls in red sweater, the baseball playoffs on television, ping pong and fusbol. The Busch tent is far preferable to the ice rink next door, which is serving as the press center for some 600 journalists. Because I arrive early and there are not yet any A-list commentators in the hall, I am drafted to be interviewed on MSNBC; I offer some commentary on the Anheuser Busch tent.

The debate itself starts badly. Bush and Gore come out from opposite ends in—uh-oh—matching dark suits and red ties. Their similarities are such that the *Post*, in its story about the debate, labels them Gov. George W. Bush and Vice President Bush. But that's where the likeness ends. Gore launches immediately into an unrelenting attack on the subject of Medicare and taxes. Bush responds by ridiculing Gore's "phony numbers." "Not only did he invent the Internet, he invented fuzzy math," Bush says, repeating the phrase four times.

But Gore keeps up the attack. Bush seems halting and stammering on foreign policy questions, and perpetually on the defensive. Gore, as usual, is too theatrical, full of off-camera sighs and huffs. He sounds pedantic while lecturing Bush about policy details. But Bush seems weak in rebuttal, until the very end, when moderator Jim Lehrer practically begs him to attack Gore. Bush obliges, bringing up "controlling legal authority" and the Lincoln bedroom and the Buddhist temple. Now *that's* a lively debate.

Even before the last words are uttered, spinners for both sides flood the room, each preceded by an aide carrying a large sign with the spinner's name: Donna Shalala, Bill Daley, Stuart Stevens, Karl Rove. The whole thing has the look of a Mardi Gras parade. Among the punditry, the buzz is that Gore was best on the facts but that Bush won on style. This reminds me of the Gore-Bradley debates, in which Gore was invariably labeled too mean and Bradley much more likable. This time, too, the conventional wisdom favors Bush—until it is forced to shift 180 degrees when the first overnight polls come out showing that the public preferred Gore. (The public preferred Gore in the debates with Bradley, too.) An NBC poll even found that 55 percent thought Gore's performance mostly positive, while only 14 percent viewed it as mostly negative. The public, it seems, has more tolerance for smashmouth politics than the press gives it credit for.

Still, the truly nasty action unfolds outside the debate, a quarter of a mile away, where the protesters are fenced off. There is every manner of demonstrator here, from anti-abortion folks to "Roofers and Water-proofers For Gore" to four guys in orange robes and shaved heads imper-sonating Gore's Buddhist monks. But Nader's supporters take the prize. Angry that their man wasn't allowed to participate in the presidential debate, they attempt to prevent everyone else from getting out of the hall.

Waving "Ralph Nader For President" signs and chanting "Let Ralph debate" to a drumbeat, several hundred demonstrators amass along the road leaving the campus after the debate. Some hurl metal barricades at cars leaving the site, and about 100 demonstrators hold a sit-in to block the route. The demonstrators fail to block the exits of Bush and Gore, and they block others only temporarily, until police redirect them to another exit. The standoff lasts past midnight.

The police, in riot gear with shields raised, eventually charge the demonstrators. They also use dogs and horses to control the crowd; one horse makes the ultimate sacrifice, succumbing to an unknown cause, and is hauled off on a flatbed truck.

All in all, not a bad night. Two feisty candidates, a Budweiser tent and only one dead horse.

29

★ ☆ ★

Follow the Bouncing Polls

As we enter the homestretch of the election, the Bush campaign is rebounding (unless, of course, it still happens to be stumbling). Al Gore's operation, by contrast, is slipping into disarray (or perhaps it is becoming highly disciplined). Candidate Bush (or is it Gore?) is connecting with voters, while Candidate Gore's (or is it Bush's?) morale is falling.

In the real world, presidential campaigns progress slowly and steadily over many months. But this is considered boring in the alternate reality occupied by campaign staffs, party hacks and, particularly, journalists. Instead, they occupy themselves by hunting for subtle (and sometimes overnight) mood swings. They call this stuff "momentum."

"There are natural cycles of puff and collapse," says Paul Begala, the former Clinton hand and a Gore enthusiast. Bush adviser Ed Gillespie concurs: "Everything is just going swimmingly or everything is a misstep."

Recently, Bush has been in misstep mode. In front of a microphone he didn't know was on, he pointed out *New York Times* reporter Adam Clymer at a rally and told Dick Cheney the fellow was a "major league asshole." Replied Cheney: "Big time." Then came the word RATS exploding from the word BUREAUCRATS in a Bush ad for a fraction of a second. Bush, in front of the cameras, denied that the rodents were meant to be "subliminable" (rhymes with abominable).

Armed with such patterns of speech, Gail Sheehy, writing in *Vanity Fair*, diagnosed Bush with dyslexia. I had ruled out dyslexia when I accused Bush of having speech apraxia in the spring, but no matter: the story had legs. Bush, forced to respond, didn't appear to be joking when he uttered, "The woman who knew that I had dyslexia—I never interviewed her." The Bush malapropisms have since come fast and furious, the latest being about how he wants "wings to take dream."

Not long ago, though, the currently "focused" Gore was the one in the dumps. Remember the stiff and programmed Gore, the earth-toned, faux farm-working, pot-smoking, Fairfax Hotel–living, slumlord Gore? Don't worry—he'll be back, when the cycle turns again. We're due for a Bush recovery any day now.

Asked to forecast the campaign's boom-and-bust cycles over the next two months, Mindy Tucker, Bush's press secretary, drew a chart that "goes all over the place," as she put it, much like the Carter-Reagan race of 1980, when the two often traded leads in polls. Not surprisingly, her chart ends in an upswing for Bush.

The newly smug Gore campaign declined to provide an illustration. Instead, it volunteered Begala, who sees an equally volatile race ahead. Bush survives the first debate without throwing up, and Gore plunges; Cheney "does throw up" in the VP debate, and Gore surges; Bush holds his own in the third debate, and Gore plunges; analysts predict a Bush victory; Gore wins.

The smallest event can set the cycle in motion. It might start when an adviser to one of the candidates starts talking to the media about something that's "off message." The process, as one Bush adviser explains it, goes like this: "You get the stories that you're 'thrown off course.' . . . Then all the people who called a week before to say what a good job you're doing now have new ideas about how to fix things."

And then comes rock bottom: the dreaded panic. "There's nothing stupider than a campaign in panic," says Mark Fabiani, Gore's communications director. "You feel there's no way out of a downward cycle. It piles on. You get criticized. People get dispirited."

Predicting the cycles is rather like predicting the weather. There are underlying climate changes. There are seasonal changes. And then there are the usual cold fronts every few days, punctuated occasionally by a hurricane. "If a thunderstorm is on the way and you don't have an umbrella, you're in trouble," explains Tad Devine, a top Gore strategist.

Gore is hoping that the dominant cycle will be an overall warming pattern—his own political El Niño. Gore spokesman Chris Lehane prefers a different metaphor. He likens the Gore campaign to the Boston Celtics of the late 1960s: They would just barely make the playoffs, then grow steadily stronger and win the championship.

Bush, on the other hand, hopes that the recent troubles are just a passing storm. "There will be another twist," predicts Gillespie. "Maybe two or three before it's over." Each of the three scheduled presidential debates could cause a cycle reversal. So could a yet-unknown scandal or a major mistake by a candidate.

The feast-or-famine swings often have a kernel of reality. A candidate who is having trouble making his case is more likely to get knocked down by petty events (a Naomi Wolf scandal or a major-league expletive). Begala likens it to teaching his four-year-old daughter to ride a bicycle: "If you don't have forward momentum, anything can push you over."

The polls—now being done daily—are partly to blame for the swings. A jump in the polls sends political watchers searching for a sign—something in the candidate's message or demeanor—to explain the change. Usually there's no cause and effect. "It's like the way the old Incas worshiped: when the sun moved and something changed, they thought the sun did it," says Matt Dowd, Bush's polling director. "They want to attribute immediate cause and effect, and there are much longer-term patterns."

Reporters fuel the cycles with their constant desire to make the race competitive—knocking down the front-runner and building up the underdog. More insidiously, reporters also want to ingratiate themselves with the eventual winner. As soon as Gore pulled ahead in the polls, reporters traveling with Bush suddenly deluged Gore advisers with phone calls. When Gore was down, these same reporters wouldn't even return Gore advisers' calls.

For the campaigns, the trick is to be at a peak and have your opponent in a trough on Election Day. This is not easy. When a candidate finds himself in a trough, often the only way out is to "retool" or to have a shakeup, even if nobody feels one is warranted.

"You cannot get out of it until you admit something's wrong—whether or not it is," muses one Bush adviser. "It's like an intervention." The campaign must enroll itself in a 12-step recovery process, come up with the requisite staff change or a new slogan. The latest case is the rash of headlines about Bush's new plan to target the middle class. Who, pray tell, was he targeting before?

Before you know it, your campaign is back "on message," back to talking about Medicare or taxes or Social Security. Then it's time for the other guy to be off message or "on the defensive." Your candidate gets "traction," while the other guy concedes that his campaign is "tentative" and possibly "losing footing."

The game is easy. You don't need to be a political professional or a practicing journalist to play along at home. Simply select the words of your choice in the following sentences to construct your own cycle-turning news report—just as the pros do.

Thank you, (Tom/Peter/ Dan/Bernie). Tonight, the campaign of (Al Gore/George W. Bush) is (losing momentum/on a roll). The candidate had a (tentative/self-assured) day of campaigning, proving that he is (connecting with/struggling to connect with) the voters of (Michigan/ Florida/Missouri). In fact, Mr. (Bush/Gore) seems to be more (focused/ off message) than at any point I've seen him in the last few (weeks/ days/hours). At stop after stop, he is (rallying crowds/mangling syntax) to a degree unseen before. Clearly, this is a sign that the candidate is (stumbling/losing footing / cruising). With a few more days of (smooth sailing/fumbling) it is likely that he will encounter a (healthy bounce/bump in the road). On the other hand, we hear that Mr. (Bush's/Gore's) rival is (retooling/panicking/soaring in overnight polls), a development that has the potential to send the race into a period of heightened (tension/tension/tension), which should lead to (higher turnout/higher ratings). Reporting from (Austin/Nashville), I'm (your name here) for (ABC/CBS/NBC/CNN) news. Back to you, (Tom/Peter/ Dan/Bernie).

As if on cue, the Gore plunge has begun—within days of my prediction of a turn in the cycle. It came after Gore's first debate performance in Boston. Though his tough style won the debate, according to the polls, his theatrical sighing and his exaggerations began to sink him. He told the story of a Florida girl forced to stand during class for lack of desks—but the story was subsequently denied by the school's principal— and he falsely claimed that he traveled to Texas with the head of the Federal Emergency Management Agency. The bloopers weren't that much by themselves, but it reminded everybody of I-invented-the-Internet Al. Now Bush is effectively using Gore's trouble with the truth to discredit the v.p.'s entire program. Suddenly, Bush is on top again.

It's getting hard to keep track of the quick shifts in Big Mo. To get a better grip on who's ahead, I have come, of all places, to Utica, New York.

Genesee Street, running south from downtown, becomes Religion Row. There's the steeple of First Presbyterian Church and the yellow-brick Temple Beth El on your left. On the right, you'll pass Saviour Lutheran Church. Then, just before the Church of our Lady of Lourdes and the Church of the Nazarene, right next to the AMF Pin-O-Rama bowling alley, is a Cathedral of our Civic Religion.

This is the headquarters of Zogby International, pollsters.

In this election season, the operation is a frenzied factory of public opinion, tracking every hiccup and sigh in the presidential race. Callers begin at 9 a.m. and end at midnight, when number-crunchers figure out who's winning and release the Reuters/MSNBC/Zogby daily tracking poll to the breathless media.

In politics this year, polling is everything. The results of these surveys drive the candidates' moves and the press coverage, which may in turn influence the election's outcome. For this reason, I have made a pilgrimage here to worship at the altar of public opinion.

The dinner hour is approaching. I put on my headset and push the button that tells the computer to dial a number. I call Washington State—no answer. I call Colorado—answering machine. I call Kansas—no reply. I call Michigan, where a man shouts, "No!" and hangs up. I click "refusal—hostile" on my computer, and forge on.

My success doesn't improve much over the next hour. I get busy tones in Ohio and Kansas, disconnected numbers in Montana and Illinois, no answer in Virginia, Kentucky, Maine, Oklahoma and Massachusetts, a fax machine and a call-waiting "privacy manager" in Ohio, and a tree and shrub service in upstate New York. In New York City, a woman advises me, "Sweetheart, you're in the middle of our dinner," and another hangs up on me. A Virginia man, shouting over a crying baby, exclaims, "Excuse me? Nah!" Click. A California woman asks me, "No habla español?" A New Jersey woman informs me, "I'm one of Jehovah's Witnesses and there are certain things we don't do."

My hour of calling produces only one hit in 25 attempts: a 51-year-old woman in Cincinnati who is for Bush. The result of my piece of the tracking poll:

Bush: 100 percent
Everyone else: 0 percent
Margin of error: +/- 98 percent

Apparently, I'm not cut out for this. "You did a couple of things we would yell at our interviewers for," explains Steven McLaughlin, my tutor. "You've got to read your script word for word," he tells me.

But perhaps I shouldn't feel bad. With all the busy signals and disconnected numbers, it takes Zogby callers nearly 6,000 calls to get 400 complete responses. Only 35 percent of people reached by phone answer pollsters' questions, a number that has declined from 65 percent fifteen years ago. Answering machines, caller ID, and telemarketers poisoning the well have made poll-taking difficult. Even among those reached, it becomes immediately obvious that a large number of our compatriots have only the vaguest notion that there's an election happening.

But such cynicism is not necessarily warranted. Though large numbers of Americans are ill informed, ill mannered and ill prepared to choose a leader, when you add them up something magical happens. Individuals are transformed into a wise and noble creature: the American electorate. The polls, in their aggregate, invariably show a temperate and thoughtful nation. It would make Tocqueville smile.

"There's a collective wisdom that emerges," says John Zogby, who started the firm in the 1980s. "When it all adds up there's a clear message. The community is never stupid."

Still, Zogby is the first to acknowledge polling's shortcomings. The polls, particularly daily ones, are just snapshots. "We're not predicting," Zogby says. "You can't read too much into the day-to-day change or try to read causality into it."

But the press tends to look for some fault in the declining candidate to justify a poll drop. The explosion of cable and Internet news outlets, which commission polls and hype the results, exacerbates the problem. "Having it govern the way a campaign gets covered is dangerous," Zogby says. "It becomes a tremendous disservice."

Another caveat: While polls are good at measuring trends, the numbers tend to reflect the pollsters' hunches as much as the respondents' answers. The raw numbers in a poll are meaningless until "weighted" (certain categories of voters are over- or underemphasized) to mirror the population and to reflect the pollster's guess about who will vote. Most poll-watchers don't realize that a Bush lead in raw numbers can become a Gore lead in weighted numbers.

"Twenty percent of this business is art, 80 percent is science," Zogby says. "Ultimately, you have to make a call about who's going to turn out to vote." Pollsters adjust their responses by gender, race, religion, age, region and income. The time of day a call is made, the response rate, how the questions are phrased and ordered, the suggestiveness of the questioner, and how a pollster defines a "likely voter" and "undecided" can all alter the results. Zogby, controversially, also weighs party identification, which he gauges through a series of questions.

Some other pollsters think Zogby favors Republicans (he says he's a Democrat and works for both sides). But Zogby has a good record among the three major public tracking polls. In 1996, he got Clinton's eight-point victory exactly right. Lately, his tracking poll has had a smoother pattern than the Gallup tracking poll (which recently galloped 18 points in a couple of days) and has been more consistent with larger polls than the Voter.com/Battleground tracking poll.

Zogby's calling center is a collection of 94 cubicles in a decrepit, dank office building abandoned by the phone company. The callers, whose pay starts at $6.25 an hour, are a mixture of students, retirees, immigrants from Eastern Europe and part-timers with day jobs. The place smells of pizza or whatever else is in the break area, which also includes a snack machine that sells Chicken Cordon Bleu. One woman's lapdog naps on the floor of her cubicle as she makes calls.

"Hello, my name is Fanny and I'm doing a poll of U.S. voters for Reuters News Agency and Zogby International," says Fanny George, a retired nurse. She calls numbers that pop up on her screen courtesy of the "computer-aided telephone interview" or CATI system, pronounced "Katie." CATI sends Fanny plenty of duds: no answer, a law office, a couple of refusals. But George, an expert caller with a grandmother's gentle voice, completes interviews at the clip of three an hour. Each one requires her to give voters choices for president that most have never heard of: Harry Browne, John Hagelin, Howard Phillips and David McReynolds.

As night approaches, there are fifty callers in the room, and a round of "Very likely? Somewhat likely? Unlikely?" rises from the din. The callers struggle with a confounded electorate. Mark Carchedi interviews a woman who can't understand what he means when he asks how likely she is to vote. Later comes the man who agrees to offer his phone number in case a reporter wants to ask about the poll. "Your area code?" Carchedi asks. The respondent doesn't respond. "What's your area code?" Nothing. "Sir, do you have an area code? . . . Area code! . . . What's your area code? . . . If somebody's calling you long distance, what do they dial?" Carchedi finally procures the desired digits.

Callers here have heard it all. Many get obscenities and propositions, one polled Rodney Dangerfield, one respondent believed he was Jesus, another put her dog on the phone, and one woman described her status as "married, wanting to get divorced."

By 9 p.m., Frank Calaprice, a night supervisor, has begun to keep careful track of the tracking poll. He has met his quota of 93 responses from Zone 1 (Eastern) and must get 11 more in Zone 2 (Midwest) and 13 more in Zone 3 (South) by 10 p.m., when he turns his attentions to Zone 4 (California). He watches the tally on his computer, shifting callers from other Zogby polls as needed. He completes his last call in Zone 3 at 9:58, with two minutes to spare.

"It's very nerve-racking," Calaprice says. At 10 p.m., he begins to work on getting 26 more responses from the West Coast. By 11 p.m., he has ten to go. He could add callers and finish the whole thing in five minutes, but he's been instructed that this could skew results. "I know there's a logic to everything they do," he says. "I just don't personally know what it is."

"I'm going in," says Joe Mazloom.

It's midnight, and Mazloom, a wild-haired young man wearing blue-jeans and a T-shirt, enters the response database and commands his computer to "export off CATI system." After a brief scare before midnight—several West Coast respondents don't respond because of the baseball playoffs—Calaprice has reached his 400-call quota, and it's time to crunch numbers.

In his office, next to the Cordon Bleu snack machine, Mazloom hits a few buttons and pulls up the day's raw numbers: Bush leads Gore by 44.6 percent to 40.1 percent overall, and 49.1 percent to 42.9 percent in a hypothetical two-way matchup. That gives an unweighted three-day average of 44.2 for Bush and 42.8 for Gore, and a three-day average in the two-way race of 47.3 for Bush and 45.1 for Gore.

Now the fun begins. Mazloom begins to balance the day's sample so it conforms with Zogby's hunches (based on exit polls from previous elections) about which type of people will show up on election days. Republicans, men and Jews are overrepresented in the day's sample, while African Americans and young voters must be doubled. Mazloom whips through spreadsheets, hitting buttons, adjusting regions, typing incomprehensible numbers (1071 0.805, 499 0.483). After several runs, the sample is weighted: slightly more women and Democrats, a quarter Catholic, more than a quarter elderly, and four-fifths white.

The weighted results invert the findings: now Gore leads in the three-day average, 45.0 to 41.0; in the two-way race, Gore leads 47.5 to 44.5. The inversion, Mazloom says, comes mostly from the weighting for party identification.

Mazloom sends the results to a bleary-eyed Alan Crockett, Zogby's press man, who is waiting in his office to write the 2 a.m. press release. "The midnights are killing my social life," Crockett says. He slaps on the 3 percent margin of error and fields a call from Zogby, who dictates the day's headline and a quote. "Race Now Just a 4-Point Lead," the release says. "Make no mistake about it, this is a very tight race."

By daybreak, political reporters everywhere will be using the results to do just what Zogby warned against: to find a reason why one candidate is doing badly and the other is doing well.

For those who don't believe in the polls but still want to figure out who has the momentum, I've found a less scientific way of monitoring the election's progress. His name is Matthew Curry. Of all those employed by the conglomerate known as Campaign 2000 Inc.—consultants, staffs, party officials, journalists, think tanks, candidates—Curry undoubtedly has the best job.

Curry, a George Washington University junior, reports for work a little after noon at his L Street office, wearing jeans and Nike running shoes. He picks up videotapes of stand-up routines by Jay Leno, David Letterman, Conan O'Brien and Bill Maher, plunks one into a VCR and starts watching. While the TV plays, he scans the programs' transcripts for political one-liners.

I join Curry for an hour of toil, bringing with me the necessary tools of the trade: Doritos, M&Ms, and a Goo-Goo Cluster. Curry accepts the junk food and starts to hunt. He finds a Leno joke about Gore's propensity to make things up. "His favorite singer when he was a little boy: Eminem," Leno says. Curry calls up a "Joke Tracking" form on his computer and enters "Elections/Personal Issue/Honesty/Gore, Al." Curry types in the joke and clicks on the "New Joke" button.

This is hard work. "More M&M's?" he offers me.

Curry finds another Leno on Bush giving up drinking: "He said he used to drink to forget. Then he realized, 'Hey, I can forget without a drink.'" Curry enters "Elections/Personal Issue/Drinking/Bush, George W." He taps the New Joke button. Curry's labors have taken him across the landscape of political humor, from Gore's muted second debate—"He looked like a Great Dane who just got neutered," says Leno—to Bush's odd mannerisms—"Bush gets very, very excited whenever he starts talking about executing people," says Letterman—to how Ralph Nader could win— "Amend the Constitution so the candidate getting the fewest votes wins, like golf," Letterman proposes.

"I make $7 an hour to catalogue jokes," says Curry, who toils in this manner 17 hours a week. "I watch more TV on the job than when I'm at home." This work doesn't come without occupational hazards. "I feel bad if I laugh out loud," he says. And then there's Mother. "I tell my mom what I do and she says, 'What does this have to do with anything?'"

Don't worry, Mom. Curry works for the highbrow Center for Media and Public Affairs, a research group funded by the MacArthur, Ford and Pew foundations, among others. His project, generously titled the "Entertainment Study," aims to monitor the influence of late-night comics on the nation's political discourse.

And the center isn't the only organization convinced that jokes are playing a big role in the presidential campaign. At CBS News, Dan Rather has begun a weekly roundup of political jokes. The Associated Press puts out regular updates on late-night political jokes. The *New York Times* has a weekly tally. "A lot of people are counting and recounting jokes everywhere," says Howard Mortman, a stand-up comic and columnist for the Hotline, a political website that lists jokes, too. "There are tallies everywhere."

The candidates, if you judge by their frequent visits to the shows, seem to agree on late night's importance. "The road to the White House runs through me," Letterman boasted while hosting Bush this spring. "Even if I have a hundred bypasses."

Bush had a disastrous performance on *Letterman* during the primaries. (Letterman: "How do you look so youthful and rested?" Bush: "Fake it." Letterman: "And that's pretty much how you're going to run the country?") Bush, trying to improve on his routine, is due for another *Letterman* appearance now, in mid-October. Gore, for his part, has already done *Letterman* and *Leno* in recent weeks, while vice presidential nominee Joe Lieberman has done *O'Brien* (where he sang "My Way") and Jon Stewart's *Daily Show* on Comedy Central.

When Letterman called for a presidential debate on his show, Gore eagerly agreed—and Nader wrote a letter protesting that he wasn't invited. Even Nader has made the rounds of *Politically Incorrect* and *The Tonight Show*, where he pulled out a rubber chicken and got no reaction. "This comedy is not easy, is it, Ralph?" Leno remarked.

Bush and Gore are both looking at numbers showing a vast audience for these shows. A Pew Research Center poll in February found that 28 percent of Americans get some campaign news from late-night comedy (ranking the shows higher than, say, religious radio). For the under-thirty crowd, the number jumped to 47 percent.

But do the candidates' appearances on the shows do any good? Does a candidate's late-night performance reduce the number of jokes about him in the comedians' monologues? That's where Matthew Curry comes in. In August, when Bush was still riding high, Curry counted 78 jokes about Gore and 43 about Bush. In September, when Gore was strong, the count reversed: 94 about Bush and only 34 about Gore. Now that Gore is skidding, the October count so far has the two much closer: 78 for Bush, 67 for Gore.

Still, there's no evidence that this actually has any impact on the way people vote. For all its years of studying and counting late-night political jokes, the Center for Media and Public Affairs hasn't found any links between the jokes about a candidate and the candidate's electoral success. In 1988, Bush-Quayle got 96 jokes to Dukakis-Bentsen's 80. In 1992, Bush's 608 jokes exceeded Clinton's 423, not even counting Quayle's 357. In 1996, Bob Dole's 838 jokes topped Clinton's 655. This year, Bush has been more joked about (465) than Gore (322).

The only trends that emerge are that the Republicans, win or lose, tend to be the target of more jokes (another sign of liberal media bias?) and that there are far more jokes than a decade ago—a development it hardly takes a research grant to notice. The latter trend worries Bob Lichter, who runs the research group. "It's one small blip in the gradual decline of Western civilization," he laments. "There's no distinction anymore between news and popular culture."

Such worries, however, can be dispatched with a simple counterargument: Lighten up. Comedy Central's Stewart, for example, finds it absurd that "they'd even turn their attention to this."

This is comedy, not even pretending to be information, he says. "What news are they getting? We're not breaking any news," Stewart says. "We're a very reactive business." The comedians don't drive the national discourse—unless, perhaps, you think all the late-night jokes on the Lewinsky scandal turned the attention of Dan Rather, Tom Brokaw and Peter Jennings to an issue, he says, that "otherwise would've been ignored."

While the polls hop around like mad, and even the joke count shows alarming swings, the two campaigns are doing whatever they can to pretend that everything is stable and routine, that everything is going by plan. Key to this is an annoying strategy both campaigns have adopted to keep their candidates "on message," immune to the poll swings and the daily bloopers. I call it the Flavor of the Week. Join me for a trip with Gore to a community center in Altoona, Iowa, to see how it works.

In the end, it comes down to this: Winifred Skinner, or Whack-a-Mole?

In other words, will today's news about Al Gore be what the campaign wants it to be—in this case, Gore's Medicare prescription—drug plan—or a sexier story the press is chasing—say, whether or not Gore has a mole in the Bush campaign? Skinner, 79, gets up at a Gore event here to tell the cameras about how, because of prescription bills, she has to collect cans off the streets to make ends meet.

But can this compete with the intrigue surrounding the mole? Did a Bush staffer send stolen debate tapes to the Gore campaign, or was she merely returning trousers to the Gap? And what is it with all these rodents—first rats and now a mole? Stay tuned.

Campaigns are unwieldy instruments. To make them work, political strategists must break them down into bite-size elements: usually days, sometimes weeks. Put together a few good days, and soon enough you've had a good week; string together a few good weeks, and you win. From this philosophy springs a particularly irksome aspect of late-stage campaigns: the Flavor of the Week. Instead of pistachio or chocolate brownie, a campaign picks a theme—education, the economy, health care, etc.—and hammers away all week at nothing else. "Voters are busy," Bush spokesman Ari Fleischer says. "You want to repeat. Just because you said it on Monday doesn't mean voters heard it on Monday."

If you get through a week without the press knocking you off message—how Bush pronounces the word "subliminal" or how much arthritis medicine costs for Gore's dog Shiloh—you're having a good week. For Bush, this week was education. For Gore, alas for reporters, it was the nuances of Medicare policy. And both campaigns did just about everything to keep from straying from the Flavor of the Week. This is an account of this week's effort by Gore to keep the nation's eyes on Medicare.

The week begins, like most others, with a Saturday conference call between a Gore policy expert and reporters. This time it's Donna Shalala and a Gore spokesman. We learn that Gore will be opening a "new front" in the campaign by highlighting "big Medicare differences." But reporters aren't nibbling. Sunday's stories are not about Medicare but about questions like this: How could Gore's mother have sung him a lullaby that wasn't written until he was 27?

On Sunday, the Gore campaign escalates. The candidate himself holds a conference call with reporters, just to be sure they understand his "rock solid commitment" to Medicare. He describes the "iron-clad lock box" that he would put around Medicare, and how Bush would "push seniors into HMOs" and force them to "beg HMOs for coverage." We hear more than we need to know about Medicare actuaries. And yet, at the end of the phone session, a reporter pleads for one final question and asks Gore about the mole. Gore obliges with a brief answer—and that makes bigger news than Medicare.

On Monday, it's time to bring out the artillery. Gore flies down to Florida to outline his Medicare policy in a speech before 1,000 people in St. Petersburg. He comes armed with a 74-page booklet titled "Medicare at a Crossroads," detailing the Gore-Lieberman plan with plenty of charts and 28 footnotes. The accompanying press release is so detailed that it informs us that St. Petersburg uses 20 million gallons of recycled water each day to water its lawns. (Still, this is nothing compared to Economy Week, when this policy book was more than twice the size.)

Most of this is old news, but the sheer heft of the thing is impressive. It also includes a couple of new tidbits: that Gore would take special measures to stop HMOs from dropping Medicare recipients, and that he would increase Medicare's preventive-care benefits. Gore is executing a reverse Ponce de Leon: he is coming to Florida to deliver the Fountain of Youth.

Gore also tries to keep the focus on Medicare by launching a sneak attack. His aides give to the *Washington Post*, the *New York Times*, and the networks a TV interview from 1995, dug up by the DNC, in which Bush praises the congressional Republicans' Medicare cuts. This, they figure, is explosive stuff. Bush is proclaiming that "elderly people will not suffer" from the plan, and that the GOP would be "heralded" for its "political courage." Of course, the opposite happened: Clinton used the Medicare cuts to pillory and defeat the Republicans in the government shutdown of 1996, after Newt Gingrich allegedly said he wanted Medicare to "wither on the vine."

To drive the point home, Gore gives interviews to each of the news organizations that got the leak. "The effect of the Bush-Cheney plan would be to cause Medicare as we know it to wither on the vine," he tells this reporter aboard Air Force Two. "He learned from Gingrich's rhetorical excesses, but the effect of his plan is the same."

Ultimately, the bomb doesn't prove as thermonuclear as Gore had hoped. Neither paper puts the news on its front page, and ABC doesn't even play a clip of the interview on *Good Morning, America* Tuesday morning. Instead, Gore gets a question about how his lead vanished in the polls. About the Bush quote, Gore is asked, "Shouldn't he be judged on what he says today and not on what he said five years ago?"

Still, Gore has at least managed to keep the subject on Medicare, and the other two networks play the Bush clip on their shows. Gore aides claim that their tracking poll numbers are rising. The day is a success. And the week is just beginning. "Tomorrow, we've got the Lott-Hastert letter," Gore spokesman Chris Lehane says, cryptically.

While the candidates and their traveling staffs try to dish out their Flavor of the Week, the campaign headquarters and the parties in Washington are busily preparing their get-out-the-vote efforts. This, like the weekly flavor, gives operatives something to do other than watch the polls. Instead, they're focusing on curious aspects of technology and micro-marketing.

"There are fifty counties in America who may determine who's the next president," Joe Andrew, the DNC chairman, explains to me. By targeting individuals in each of those counties with coordinated, personalized mail, e-mail, calls, and visits, the Democrats will yet win the White House, he thinks.

Gore brought Andrew to the DNC to reproduce the Indiana experiment nationally. Gore has also hired some of the leading Democratic technologists, such as Hal Malchow, a direct-mail specialist.

Malchow, a sort of mad political scientist, pushes the boundaries of technology with Chi-Square Automatic Interaction Detection, or CHAID, analysis, which he believes improves on conventional polling. This software can use mounds of empirical data to predict the easiest voters to persuade, and the likeliest to vote. Malchow also talks about "neural nets," an artificial-intelligence software program, and "genetic algorithms," in which a computer finds the strongest links among a large number of variables by "breeding" variables to find the "fittest" combinations in a Darwinian game.

On the Republican side, Tom Cole, chief of staff to the Republican National Committee chairman, vows not to be outdone by the DNC. "We think this is akin to what television was in the 1950s," Cole says. Aristotle Publishing, a nonpartisan political technology company with strong ties to Republicans, has been working with America Online to create political banner ads that appear only on the screens of those computer users campaigns wish to reach.

Tuesday morning. Let it be said that Gore is on message in Medicare week. Flying on Air Force Two from Florida to Michigan, he comes to the back of the plane to listen as a staffer sings birthday greetings to an aide, Sam Myers, turning 50. Afterward, Gore offers to create "a Part C of Medicare for Sam."

Still, today presents some challenges to Gore. His first event is appearing on MTV's *Choose or Lose* show. Asked what this has to do with Medicare, an aide ventures that Gore might entice the youth by announcing that he would include tattooing and body piercing under Medicare. But this does not happen. Instead, Gore gets questions about education, abortion, gay marriage, Napster, marijuana, and other things not attractive to the over-65 set. Yet even here, the campaign tries to stay on message. It distributes two press releases, one highlighting the Bush 1995 tape—"Transcript Reveals: Bush Supported Gingrich Plan to Cut Medicare"—the other featuring a letter promised by Lehane from House Speaker Denny Hastert and Senate Majority Leader Trent Lott saying they favor a Medicare "lock box," which Gore proposes but Bush doesn't.

Gore's next event, at an Ann Arbor community center, is more conducive to the Flavor of the Week. He greets a couple hundred old folks seated around tables with apples and pumpkins and hay bales, while dueling signs on the wall announce, "Protecting, Improving, Strengthening Medicare" and "Protecting, Strengthening, Improving Medicare." (Well, which is it?) Gore talks about Gingrich's "wither on the vine" quote and crows that Bush supported that plan back in 1995. But it's not sticking as

well as it did yesterday. Downstairs, reporters are playing fusbol and soli-
taire, and eating donuts. The MTV event will be today's top story, particularly the bit about Gore preferring paper to plastic in the grocery
store.

"Yesterday we got the national story—we can't get the same story
two days in a row," explains Lehane, making the best of the situation.
"We're getting local coverage." And the campaign isn't surrendering its
Flavor of the Week. A new press release circulates in the press room: "Gore
Campaign Responds to Misleading Attacks on Medicare."

Stay the course.

Gore's Flavor of the Week strategy involves giving reporters little
news beyond the weekly topic. As a result, there is thin gruel for reporters
beyond Medicare this week, and they are getting ornery. The situation
worsens when the campaign assigns a group of journalists, including your
correspondent, not to Gore's luxury hotel but to a Holiday Inn in Des
Moines that apparently hasn't been renovated in thirty years. There are
stains on the carpet, walls, and sheets, rattling ventilation, freeway noise,
windows that don't shut, rusty water, and a sign in the rooms offering fans
and heaters because guests might "experience some discomfort." This puts
reporters in a particularly surly mood. We do not wish to hear more about
Medicare.

But we do. On Wednesday morning, we wake up to find a new press
release under our hotel doors, with a new logo proclaiming "Improving
Medicare" and featuring a picture of a glass and pills. The release trumpets: "Al Gore Will Provide Voluntary Prescription Drug Coverage for
Everyone on Medicare/Bush Raids Medicare Surplus; Leaves Millions
Without Drug Coverage." With that, we're off to Altoona, Iowa, outside
Des Moines, to hear another dreary Medicare session. Fortunately, this
one is enlivened by a walk-on, the 79-year-old Skinner, the retiree who
collects cans to supplement her $800 monthly income. The culprit: $230
to $250 a month in prescription bills—just the thing that Gore proposes
fixing.

For Gore, it is like an early Christmas present. He gives the woman a
hug. Later, Gore turns her toward the cameras and gives her a kiss on the
head. An aide rushes to get the spelling of her name, as reporters try to figure out whether the campaign planted her in the audience.

Gore follows up this triumph with the unlikeliest of events. Its description: "Al Gore Rallies Iowans for a Better Prescription Drug Plan."

A Medicare rally! This promises to be the most exciting event since the March for Fannie Mae or the Vigil for Glass-Steigel. There are flags fluttering and a band playing when Gore declares, "My friends, I came to Iowa today to talk about one of the most important issues in this election." But the candidate, perhaps thinking better of it, doesn't plunge into his prescription drug plan. Instead, he hits some favorite themes: farm issues, Bush's tax cuts for the wealthy and the like.

When Gore finally turns to the need for cheaper drugs for cholesterol and osteoporosis, the crowd is very quiet in downtown Des Moines. "People across America are being rocked by the burden of paying for prescription medicine," he declares. Ho hum, says the crowd. Gore, wisely, ventures on to other elements of his stump speech: class size, universal preschool, and Social Security. After a rousing finish, confetti explodes into the sky and the band cranks up. It's doubtful anybody in the crowd realizes they just attended a Medicare rally.

Then, Gore delivers a fatal blow to Medicare Week. His staff discloses that he talked to John McCain this morning about campaign finance reform, and they circulate a letter from Gore endorsing McCain's proposed ban on soft money in the campaign. The journalists begin to buzz. Forget Winifred Skinner. Forget the Medicare rally. *This* is news.

Finally, the mole returns. Gore wanders off to do some interviews with local TV stations, and one asks him about the mole story. Gore takes the bait. "Now they're trying to figure out who in the Bush campaign sent it," he says. Word of Gore's pronouncement is reported back to the press corps and added to the day's story. Once again, Gore will be waylaid by the mole, much as Bush was distracted a few weeks ago by the subliminal RATS that appeared in a Republican TV ad. What is it about these rodents?

Well, so much for Medicare Week. Back at Gore headquarters in Nashville, Mark Fabiani, the communications director, is declaring Medicare victory and changing the flavor midweek. "You may have picked the wrong week," he says. "We're going to do a big economic speech tomorrow." The weekly flavor, it seems, is turning into a stew.

30

★ ☆ ★

The End Is Near . . .

Ladies and gentlemen and children of voting age! Today's matinee performance of *Campaign 2000: The Musical* is about to begin.

Boarding the Gore campaign's press charter at Andrews Air Force Base in this, the homestretch of the 2000 campaign, I am surprised to be met by the sound of a cappella singing. The source: a 48-year-old man in shirt sleeves and gray curly hair. The man, Greg Simon, is Gore's technology adviser; at the moment, though, he is Gore's musical director.

He croons about the vagaries of the Zogby-Reuters tracking poll to the tune of "I'm Looking Over a Four-Leaf Clover":

I'm looking over a Zogby/Reuter
That I overlooked before
One week it says Gore is leading the race
Next week it says Bush is leading by eight
Who will be low in
The national pollin'?
Your guess is as good as mine
I'm looking over a Zogby/Reuter
That—wow—now has Gore up by nine!

After some applause, Simon launches into a ditty about Bush's economic plan, to the tune of "Heartbreak Hotel":

I thought my tax cut would be
A clever way to win
But Al Gore checked my numbers
Found I'm short a million
Tax cuts are so loaded baby

Tax cuts are so loaded
My cuts are so loaded I could cry

Simon continues, in his raspy baritone (or what he calls a "severely restrained tenor"), to the tune of "My Cherie Amour":

Our cherie press corps
Intrepid as the day is long
Our cherie press corps
We hope that you'll find nothing wrong
Our cherie press corps
You're the ones that we are spinning for
Hoping that like us you'll soon adore
Joe Lieberman and Albert Gore

The Gore campaign's one-man musical began on Labor Day, when Simon, a former rock-band drummer who joined the campaign in August as an all-purpose adviser, decided to write a song for the press corps. He's written and performed seventeen since then, collectively known as the Songs of Simon. He performed his version of Elton John's "Your Song" with Jan Wenner in the audience on Air Force Two ("that was *real* pressure") and told Sheryl Crow about his talents when he met her at a Gore fund-raiser. "She said, 'Let me know, maybe we'll do a CD,'" Simon reports. "Who knows?"

Along the way, Simon has found that singing works better than spinning. He's been able to unload many a barbed commentary in verse. Consider his version of "Johnny B. Goode":

Way out in Wyoming where the miners roam
Lived a man named Cheney who called Texas his home
People came from miles around in hopes that he
Would vet their resume and choose them for v.p.
Little did they know that he would be the one
That Papa Bush and Barbara would choose to run with son
Run Run
Run Cheney Run Run
Cheney's the one.

Way back in the Congress when he had to choose
Head Start and Clean Water voted he to lose
Miners and grazers he always voted to bail
But he said Mandela ought to stay in jail
Now he only votes his stock options galore
I wonder if he'll even vote for Bush over Gore
Run run run

Cheney run run
Cheney's the one

"If you just said it, it would be mean," Simon explains. "When you sing, it comes across much lighter and sweeter."

Gore himself has joined in Simon's act. On Air Force Two, en route to Michigan from Florida, Gore walked with Simon to the press section and got down on one knee as Simon belted out the day's ditty, to the tune of "Camelot." Gore laughed at the lyrics as Simon moved his hand from his heart to Gore's shoulder.

When I kissed my wife Tipper, I really had no notion
That one honest emotion could move the polls so
One kiss in a lifetime, it was well worth the chance
Thank god I chose to kiss her, not dance

The staff and press applauded, and Simon put away the lyrics. "Just kidding about the dancing, sir," he said to Gore.

"He really is quite a talent," Gore tells me when I ask about Simon, who served as his top domestic policy adviser for six years until starting his own firm in 1997. Still, Gore hastens to add, that talent is not immediately evident from listening to his voice.

Simon, an Arkansas native who lives in Bethesda, played drums and sang an Elvis impersonation in a rock group, The Great Zambini Brothers Band, which played on the bar and dance-club circuit in the 1970s. His latest musical inspiration comes from boredom. "This is a tedious job," he explains. "You've got a couple of hours of action and the rest is just waiting."

After his first week of song, Simon walked to the back of Air Force Two and announced that he was quitting his singing. "This is unbecoming," he explained. "For twelve years I've been a policy guy. Now people think I'm a balladeer." He started to walk back to the front of the plane, but then jumped, spun around and delivered his new ballad, to "Johnny B. Good." A few days later, on Day 56, Simon was in show-tune mode, borrowing from "Some Enchanted Evening":

Some enchanted meaning
We hope you'll be gleaning
We hope you'll be gleaning
In our next cr-r-r-owded room
'Cause if you're with us
We'll save the surplus
And health care we'll fix
Mark my words Day 56

The music and lyrics amount to a running commentary on the campaign. After Elton John performed at a Gore fund-raiser in Silicon Valley, Simon offered the following version of "Your Song" to the press corps, on the topic of Gore's avoidance of reporters:

We'll have a press conference
But then again, no
'Cause no one has a notion
Of where you might go
I know it's not news
But it's the best I can do
It's Day 48 and
This song's for you

Simon, who some days devotes an hour to his campaign music, tries out lyrics on his wife and children over the phone. One Friday, Gore, after listening to a few Simon creations, challenged Simon to pen one to the melody of "Louie Louie." By Monday, Simon had created the following:

The NBC poll . . . ohhh we got the mo'
The USA poll . . . ohhh we got the mo'
The ABC poll . . . ohhh we got the mo'

For a commentary on Bush's Medicare prescription drug plan, Simon turned to "Don't Cry for Me, Argentina":

What happened to Bush and Dick Cheney?
The last eight months they've squandered
Without a health plan
Their campaign floundered
Where is their drug plan?
The Nation wondered

The Songs of Simon give Gore's traveling entourage some esprit de corps—and perhaps some esprit de press corps as well. Perhaps it is no accident that Gore's once-hostile coverage has improved markedly since Simon began singing. Could it be? Simon only offers an angelic grin and looks heavenward. But surely this is what he had in mind when he wrote new words to "Sounds of Silence" for the press pool traveling with Gore:

Hello press pool my old friend
This long campaign week's at an end
We've been assaulted by a wet tarmac
We ate our way through a cheese-steak attack
But the memories that are planted in your brain
Still remain
They are the Songs of Simon

By the time I show up for the second presidential debate in Winston-Salem, North Carolina, Simon's giddiness (punch drunkenness?) seems to have spread to advisers to both candidates. Early in the afternoon before the debate, while stuffing myself with Krispy Kreme donuts, I witness the following rare show of bipartisan camaraderie:

Ari Fleischer, George W. Bush's spokesman, throws his arms around the shoulders of Gore adviser Paul Begala and Gore spokesman Doug Hattaway.

"Make sure you don't tell any reporters," Fleischer tells them, grinning at me, "but the governor's not going to do well. He's gonna get his clock cleaned. Gore's a master."

Begala follows this unusual confession with one of his own. "Your guy is awesome," he tells Fleischer. "He's a genius."

Both, I gather, are joking, but with an element of truth. For both sides know that one way to win a debate is to lower expectations for your guy and raise them for the other guy.

"This is what you're supposed to say," Begala explains. "Until 8:59:59"—one second before the debate's start—"George W. Bush is a genius, an idiot savant able to metamorphose into a great debater. At 9:01, he's back to being an idiot."

Whether a candidate is perceived to have won or lost a debate has a lot to do with what's said before and after. In Boston, the polls showed that Gore won the debate itself. But he lost the post-debate, when the Bush side successfully picked apart Gore's fibs. Bush also won the pre-debate spin in Boston by holding expectations low.

Today, Gore's team is determined not to let this happen again. "It's hard for me to describe the height of Bush's burden tonight," top Gore adviser Tad Devine says. Overhearing this, *New York Post* reporter Deborah Orin can't suppress a guffaw. "You gotta hear this!" she calls to a colleague.

"I'm telling the truth," Devine continues, unruffled. "I credit Bush with passing the basement expectations in the first debate. Now he has to face heightened expectations."

Nice try, retorts Bush adviser Ed Gillespie. "They've been saying [Bush] is a bumbling babbler, or a babbling bumbler, for the last 48 hours. To all of a sudden say he's really good in this format—not even they can do that with a straight face."

The whole thing resembles a playground taunt: Your Pa can lick my Pa.

And so the argument ensues, for about ten hours before the debate, in front of the hundreds of reporters who have come here to "cover" the debate. In this instance, that meant watching it on television in a different building from the actual debate, and then listening to the spin. Some 1,500 reporters received credentials and dine on free Starbucks coffee, sandwiches, cookies and Budweiser. The spinning began about 11 a.m., delayed somewhat by a problem at the gate to Wake Forest University, the debate's host. Security guards wouldn't allow people to enter without credentials, but the credentials could be picked up only inside the debate site.

As the debate approaches and the nightly newscasts began, the spinners take a breather. Then, at 7:30, the campaigns send the big guns out: Colin Powell and Pennsylvania Governor Tom Ridge for Bush, and a gaggle of officials for Gore. But the big shots are less willing to play the expectations game. "We've got to win tonight," said Tennessee Representative Harold Ford, here to speak for Gore. "We have no choice."

Begala, meanwhile, is preparing to throw himself into reverse after a day of low expectations. As the debate nears, he auditions his new line: "Some serious questions emerged tonight about George W. Bush's capacity to do the job," Begala deadpans. "The problem is I won't be able to say it to you with a straight face."

At this late stage, "covering" the campaign is something of a euphemism. Traveling with the candidates, never a rewarding affair, is now downright useless. A few weeks before the election, I decide to spend a couple of days on the road with Bush in Florida and Pennsyvlania. But four busloads of other journalists have the same idea. Not only can't I get a glimpse of the candidate, but even sightings of his advisers are rare. After 24 hours of this I abandon the effort in Pittsburgh and hop a plane to Michigan, so I can get a real front-row seat to view Campaign 2000: I am going to watch television.

Suppose you are an extraterrestrial who has just landed in front of a television set in the swinging city of Lansing in the swing state of Michigan. You would draw the following conclusions:

- Humans have a tendency to interrupt their political ads occasionally for news reports and sitcoms.
- The most important issue in the presidential race is yard-sign theft.
- George W. Bush doesn't know any white people.
- The average American is pushing 80.
- The highest office in the Free World is that of Michigan Supreme Court justice, and the most popular figure in Michigan is the mayor of Milwaukee, Wisconsin.
- Humans have the intelligence of common garden slugs.

These impressions come from watching a bank of televisions supplemented with videotape one evening for six grueling hours. It is Thursday, the largest viewership night, in which as many as half of Lansing's 238,000 households are expected to tune in to NBC's top-rated *Must See TV* and its rivals' equivalents. I'm sitting in the offices of WILX, Lansing's NBC affiliate, and watching its programming alongside that of CBS's WLNS, ABC's WLAJ and the Fox station, WSYM. The results: 196 political ads between 6:00 and 11:30 p.m.—not including those missed during bathroom breaks and trips to the vending machine for Pop-Tarts.

Watching this spectacle, the extraterrestrial would, above all, be overwhelmed by the sheer volume of political advertising. Ads for president contend with ads for candidates for the Senate, House, state legislature, local judgeships, for and against ballot measures, even an ad for one Sheriff Wriggelsworth. Lansing, which is between Democratic Detroit and Republican western Michigan, with a mixture of state employees, auto workers, lawyers, hunters and students, is highly contested. In addition to the candidates and parties, seemingly every interest group (the National Rifle Association, the Chamber of Commerce, teachers unions, the AFL-CIO and abortion rights foes and supporters) wants to air commercials.

For citizens of Lansing, changing the channel often finds the same ad on another station. The effect is a blurring of messages in which ads cancel one another out. "I'm so sick of TV I can't watch anymore," complains David Cederquist, a deliveryman lingering over coffee in the Flapjack Shack. "I've had so many points and counterpoints thrown at me—it's too much for an old guy." It's the same story at Bonnie's Place, a downtown hamburger joint. At the counter, painter Rob Orrin and his wife, Lori, say the ads have a perverse effect. "It makes me want to vote against them," she says.

The extraterrestrial viewing the ads and news coverage in Lansing would quickly understand the all-politics-is-local cliche. Sure, there are 36 spots for the presidential race, but there are 38 for the Senate race, 45 for the local House race and a whopping 77 for state and local offices and ballot propositions (including more than a dozen for a state Supreme Court candidate).

For all the chatter about attack ads and nasty politics, the ads, even the negative ones, are fairly tame. One glorious exception is a spot for Democratic Senate candidate Debbie Stabenow. "Tricia Lugar's daughter Jessica was dying," the announcer says. "Mrs. Lugar called Senator Abraham seeking help. Twelve times Abraham didn't call back."

Pink message slips fill the screen. "But official records show that during the same month Senator Abraham was ignoring Mrs. Lugar, it took him less than 48 hours to help a wealthy contributor seek early release of a convicted felon in California." The most delicious aspect of the spot is that this one airs on the same night another ad for Stabenow asks plaintively: "With so many negative ads, who can you trust?"

Otherwise, the campaigns stick with the usual good cop/bad cop routine, in which candidates run mushy ads about themselves while the parties run tough ads about their opponents. Phyllis Hunter, a black woman from Texas, praises Bush's education policies while he appears with black children and called reading "the new civil right." Another ad features Bush in schools with African American children, and shows other children, several black, running up a hill. Even an anti-Gore ad featured Bush speaking in front of a Social Security backdrop and—you guessed it—a black man.

Meanwhile, the GOP runs an ad asking, "Why does Al Gore say one thing when the truth is another?"

Gore, too, speaks over gentle music, about how "We have to make the right choices to make sure our prosperity continues and works for all Americans." Meanwhile, party ads obsessively attack Bush over Social Security as if it were the only issue in the campaign. With eerie piano music playing, eight gold medals filled the screen, and the Voice of Doom intoned: "Eight Nobel laureates, top economic experts of America, have reviewed George W. Bush's plan" and—surprise!—"the Bush plan does not add up."

If Lansing voters (not to mention the space alien) got a muddled message from this barrage, the evening news wasn't much help. At 6 p.m. the NBC affiliate begins with a report on yard-sign theft, while the CBS station did the same story and sent a reporter to the crime scene—live! By 6:04, all the stations have moved on to teen drinking, local crime and the like.

The 11 p.m. newscasts deliver political advertising's mother lode: 38 spots on three networks in half an hour. The CBS affiliate starts with a car accident, while the NBC station reports on a basketball coach who has a melanoma, and ABC's outlet goes right to the weather. The Fox station's late news, delayed because of the World Series, features a segment on inmates with HIV. Soon, it's to the dead baby in the trash, the gym shooting, the truck crash, the weather—and, naturally, more ads.

The ads are so overwhelming that it's unlikely any candidate is getting a coherent message out. The only winners, it seems, are the broadcasters. For the network affiliates in Philadelphia, for example, arguably the country's most important TV market in the 2000 campaign, the crush of ads has brought a bonanza. Ad rates have nearly doubled for some times in recent weeks, buyers report. With competitive Senate races in Delaware, New Jersey and Pennsylvania, a contested governor's race in Delaware, a couple of hard-fought House races in the area and a presidential battleground in Pennsylvania, the Philadelphia media market is, as Democratic media strategist Anita Dunn puts it, "really ground zero." The candidates, the two national parties and a host of interest groups have overwhelmed the airwaves.

"We're booked through the election," says Dave Davis, station manager for WPVI-TV in Philadelphia, as he and I watch the evening news on three televisions in his office. WPVI, the ABC affiliate, is by far the dominant station in this market, and therefore is at the epicenter of the ad wars. Flooded by demand, the station has turned away some 30 percent of political ads this year—leaving some candidates to gripe that they can't get much air time. "It's a unique situation," Davis says.

Actually, it's not all that unique this year. While Philadelphia may be the hottest market, similar rationing and price spikes have happened in Seattle, Orlando, St. Louis, Madison, parts of Montana, and the Michigan cities of Grand Rapids, Lansing and Flint. Ad rates have doubled and tripled, and some stations have stopped taking political ads altogether. Most ominously, free-spending interest groups have crowded out ads from the candidates themselves, who by law pay the lowest available rates but can get bumped by higher paying customers.

The flood of money from parties, interest groups and candidates has had the effect of saturating the market and diluting the impact of the ads; the spots in markets like Philadelphia are so ubiquitous that, as with nuclear proliferation, they have reached the point of overkill. The situation would be even worse if not for the broadcasters' bottleneck, which has caused the doubling and tripling of prices and refusals to run many ads. The system is so awash in funds that it's hard to place an ad—and even if you do, it's not likely to have as much impact.

The politicians blame the broadcasters. "Price gouging," is how New Jersey Senator Bob Torricelli, who's coordinating the Democrats' Senate campaigns, describes it. "The soaring cost of television advertising is fueling the increase in soft money. There's now a television dependency on political advertising." Torricelli notes that political spots, now more than 10 percent of advertising revenue, are the third largest source of funds for local stations after auto dealers and consumer goods. "Tens of thousands of dollars for 30-second ads on the public airwaves—it's outrageous," Torricelli says.

The broadcasters say the politicians are trying to blame others for their own inability to regulate soft money and independent expenditures. "It's out of our control," says Davis. "That's the politicians and the parties and the interest groups that want to get their message out." Davis is simply faced with a demand from advertisers that outpaces supply of airtime. "You're just kind of caught," he says. "If you don't sell them time, you get accused of cutting off access. If you do sell time, you get accused of taking in too much money."

As the broadcasters and the campaigns point fingers, the only thing they can agree on is that advertising is losing its clout. On second thought, maybe watching TV isn't any more useful than hanging around with four busloads of reporters on the Bush campaign.

So how to get a grip on the 2000 campaign? Following the candidates is pretty much useless, and the television advertising campaigns are a muddle. The polls, as we've seen, are a bit dubious. So, with the race is too close to call and the polls too erratic to predict the future, why not try the past?

The pols, pundits and the media are hauling out historical analogies of all types to support their guesses about what's going to happen come Election Day.

Karl Rove, Bush's strategist, started the game more than a year ago. With his candidate riding high, Rove conjured up the ghost of William McKinley, a Republican governor like Bush. McKinley's victory in 1896 unified and transformed the GOP into the party of the Industrial Age—much as Bush would like to do now for the Information Age. But if Bush wins, it won't be with the kind of mandate that McKinley claimed, and the issues Bush is running on are too conventional to transform his party.

Gore's team, when its candidate was down in the polls early in the race, preferred a different (if ironic) historical precedent: the elder Bush's come-from-behind victory in 1988, sprinkled with bits of Harry Truman's 1948 upset as well. When Gore caught up, the Bushies shed 1896 and tried 1980, the year Republican challenger Ronald Reagan caught the Democratic incumbent at the very end. But then Bush regained the lead, destroying both the GOP's 1980 model and the Democrats' 1988 model.

We're losing historical patterns left and right. Fortunately, strategists and journalists have suggested a dozen other possibilities, including 1824, 1836, 1876, 1888, 1908, 1920, 1928, 1932, 1944, 1952, 1968, 1984 and 1992. (The only limit, apparently, is the country has had only 53 presidential elections so far; it's a wonder nobody has dug up a precedent from the Virginia House of Burgesses.)

The proliferation of historical analogies resembles a parlor game, in which contestants try to impress each other with trivia. Are we headed for 1888, when Grover Cleveland (Bush) won the popular vote but lost the Electoral College count to Benjamin Harrison (Gore)? Or perhaps it's really 1844, when James Polk (Gore) won the White House but lost his home state of Tennessee.

Both sides like the 1960 comparison—Republicans because they see Bush as JFK to Gore's Richard Nixon, and Democrats because that was the last time they had held a convention in Los Angeles (and the last Republican convention in Philly was Thomas Dewey's in '48—now that settles it!).

There are so many historical models for the 2000 election, in fact, that they have only one thing in common: They're all useless. Though each comparison has a grain of truth, these historical patterns are proving as effective as a rear-view mirror in predicting this election.

This year, in the antithesis of philosopher George Santayana's oft-repeated saying, those who repeat the past are doomed. "The assumption that these historic indicators and the pocketbook issues hold sway has been blown away," says GOP pollster Frank Luntz, who hosted a St. Louis focus group for MSNBC.

For the third and final presidential debate, I try to put history to the test by watching the debate on television with a focus group in St. Louis, a couple of miles from the actual debate. This roomful of Missourians is staring history in the eye—and history is about to blink.

The assembled men and women— including a truck driver, two home-makers, a doctor, a lawyer, a loan officer and 30 others—have been invited to a TV studio here to participate in the tired rite known as a "focus group" because they are those most coveted of creatures this season: uncommitted voters in a swing state. But before they discussed the debate, I have a question for them: Why bother?

History says that the incumbent party always wins when the economy is growing. So I ask them: In this time of unprecedented prosperity, swing voters will inevitably side with Gore, right?

Only one man, auto-body worker John Kitchin, nibbles. "That's one of the reasons I'm going with Al Gore," he says.

The rest of the group quickly pounces on him. "The economic welfare of our country is bigger than any one man," argues bartender Jim Clauser. "The economy's doing well, but that's not going to last," says Cherie Bauman, a drug counselor. "The stock market's been down," protests software developer Greg Zavertrik. "Energy policy is a mess," complains Brent Cole, a Department of Defense employee. Businessman Kurt Walker hears no dissent when he said: "Typically Americans look at money issues, but I'm going to look for a president with greater moral values."

So much for history.

The voters are defying the political scientists this year. Instead of a Gore romp, the race is a dead heat, with neither candidate likely to win by much. "History argues this is a slam-dunk for Gore and it obviously isn't," says Charles Cook, who handicaps political races. The problem isn't just with political-economic history. Political-geographic history also is getting a rewrite this year.

Students of Electoral College history would say it dictates a Bush win as surely as the economy predicts a Gore victory. Before 1992, the GOP had won five of six presidential elections, and Bill Clinton won only with an assist from third-party candidate Ross Perot. This year's close race should have brought back Republican dominance, as many strategists and media outlets have noted. As recently as August, for example, a *Baltimore Sun* report cited the GOP's "electoral lock on the South and West."

But this lock was easy to break: It lasted barely a month. In September, the *Sun*'s sister publication, the *Los Angeles Times*, wrote that "there is no majority party anymore in Southern presidential politics." Gore has pulled even in Florida, thought to be safely Republican. California, New Jersey and Illinois, historically swing states, are safely Democratic. Bush, on the other hand, is on the hunt in states once considered solid for the Democrats, including Washington, Oregon, West Virginia, Clinton's Arkansas and Gore's Tennessee.

There are good reasons why history has lost its way this year. The state-by-state calculations of elections past have been reshaped by sprawling suburbs and Hispanic immigration. Though these are gradual changes, they seem to have reached critical mass this year: voters in rural areas—nervous about the Democrats' message on issues such as gun control, conservation, tobacco, school crowding and gay rights—have become more Republican than suburbanites. Just twelve years ago, Democrat presidential nominee Michael Dukakis did better among rural voters than suburban voters; now Democrat standard bearer Gore finds just the opposite.

Still, it's fun to pretend today is yesterday. "This is Kennedy-Nixon," GOP pollster Whit Ayres told *Los Angeles Times* political reporter Ron Brownstein. "This is 1960." Ayres was correct that this year's apparent dead heat repeats the drama of 1960.

And, like that year, the current election gives us an unloved incumbent vice president running against a charismatic but less experienced challenger. But Gore is a better campaigner than Nixon; Bush doesn't have the Kennedy mystique; Clinton doesn't bear the slightest resemblance to Eisenhower, and the economy in 1960 was weaker than it is now. Such reasoning caused no less an authority than conservative pundit Tony Blankley, who called himself "one of the early analogizers" between 1960 and 2000, to change his mind.

Okay, so 1960 is out. How about 1980? This model, popular in the Bush campaign, predicts that undecided voters will, in the late stages, favor the challenger once he proves his competence. This model ignores the fact that we're missing a few crucial elements this time, such as economic woes and an Iranian hostage crisis. Adopting the 1980 logic also contradicts the 1988 model, in which the incumbent party's candidate surges in the end.

Historic models of all sorts are meeting unpleasant fates this year. Consider the case of the George Washington University professors who developed a historical-statistical model to determine likely vice presidential candidates. Their Democratic list was topped by California Senator Dianne Feinstein (60.4 percent likelihood), Missouri Representative Richard Gephardt and Florida Senator Bob Graham; the Republicans were New York Governor George Pataki (64.3 percent chance), California Representative Christopher Cox and Michigan Governor John Engler. Oops. Better check the model.

As the campaign reaches its end, both sides are abandoning their promises to be "positive"—and that's a good thing. Mark Fabiani, Gore's communications director, says Bush is "bumbling and babbling." Karen Hughes, Bush's communications director, says Gore is a "serial exaggerator." The DNC says Bush needs a "simultaneous interpreter," while the RNC calls Gore the "whopper king." One of those sober academics at the University of Missouri has determined that as the campaign went into October, negative claims in ads increased from 68 percent to 75 percent for the Democrats and 45 percent to 50 percent for the Republicans. Gore has made an ad claiming Bush doesn't have enough brainpower to be president. Bush made an ad declaring: "Remember when Al Gore said his mother-in-law's prescription cost more than his dog's?" The ad then pivots to suggest that Gore's exaggerations have also caused him to make up his facts about Bush's Social Security plan.

Tough stuff—but fair game. True, as in the primary, some Smashmouth techniques may have crossed the line: Ed Asner warning in phone calls that Bush would cut current Social Security benefits; ads linking Bush to an elderly man's death in a nursing home and James Byrd's lynching; phony calls claiming the NAACP supports Bush; and a reprisal of LBJ's Daisy ad, suggesting Clinton and Gore gave away American nuclear secrets. But the unfavorable publicity surrounding these efforts has diminished their effect or forced them to be dropped. Once again, the voters know when an attack crosses the line to frivolous.

With a few exceptions, the increasingly nasty tone of the debate should be welcomed. The negative ads have been far more informative and truthful than the glossy positive spots. And though Americans claim not to like such ads in the same pious voices 98 percent of them use to claim that they will vote, they don't mean either one. Consider that after the final debate, a poll showed that by 56 percent to 25 percent voters thought Gore was more unfair in his criticism, but a majority also thought Gore won the debate.

Even the *New York Times* has joined the Smashmouth camp, with an editorial arguing that "sharp exchanges and rhetorical attacks about character and stands on issues" can be a "vital part of the process." In the second debate, when Gore heeded advisers and pundits and toned down his attacks, his performance was far worse. The neutered Gore still hasn't recovered on the eve of the election.

In fact, Gore's fear of Smashmouth tactics and Bush's ease with the technique may explain why Bush has recovered and now holds a small lead over Gore as balloting approaches—even as he continues to offer howlers, claiming that Social Security isn't a government program and talking about how "wings take dream." Bush's strategy is simple: Paint yourself as the candidate who will change the tone of our national discourse, while in the next breath using harsh words against your opponent. It's a political Jekyll and Hyde that Bush executes deftly.

Consider the "change-the-tone Bush." Early in most every stump speech he pronounces: "There's a better day ahead for America. Washington doesn't have to be a place of bitterness and acrimony and finger-pointing. There's a better way. Our administration will unite this country to serve the people, to get the people's business done, to solve some problems now before it's too late." His campaign gives out T-shirts and puts up banners proclaiming "Bringing America Together."

And how do we unite the country and remove the bitterness? Why, by savaging Al Gore. While listening to Bush in Florida, Illinois and Michigan, I jotted a few of his favorite lines in my notebook.

On Gore's claim to support smaller government: "I knew he was prone to exaggeration, but that one took the cake. This is a man who proposed more new spending than Michael Dukakis and Walter Mondale combined." On Gore's Social Security claims: "We're aware of your tricks. We're aware of your politics." On Gore's record: "My opponent's favorite slogan is 'you ain't seen nothing yet.' And he's right. We haven't seen anything yet." On Gore's energy policy: "They went to sleep at the switch."

My only complaint with Bush's Jekyll and Hyde strategy is the Jekyll part. He should give up the pious remarks about ending bitterness and partisanship and just enjoy the Smashmouth politics. By holding himself out as the man who would restore honor and dignity and decency, Bush puts himself in the unenviable glass-house situation.

The flaw becomes evident as I travel with Bush in Illinois just days before the election. Returning to O'Hare from a rally, the press bus begins to buzz: Fox has a report that Bush was arrested for drunk driving in 1976. The episode threatens to throw Bush "off-message" at this crucial stage, possibly erasing his small lead in the polls.

The problem for Bush immediately becomes clear: It's not the 24-year-old arrest, but the fact that Bush tried to hide it. A couple of hours later, after another rally in a cattle barn on the Wisconsin state fair grounds outside Milwaukee, Bush finds himself talking about his own truthfulness at a rare press conference. He acknowledges the arrest, saying, "I'm not proud of that," but then petulantly raises suspicions about the report's timing and origins.

Bush can't squelch the story. The next morning on the plane from Milwaukee to Michigan, reporters grill Hughes about why Bush allegedly said "no" about post-1968 arrests in an old conversation with *Dallas Morning News* reporter Wayne Slater. Hughes suggests that the conversation was off the record, a suggestion Slater, suddenly Bush's Linda Tripp, himself shoots down. "I think the implication Wayne was left with was that in fact the governor was acknowledging that he had in fact been arrested," Hughes ventures. Nobody buys that. "Truthfulness is answering a question yes or no," says one reporter. "That's not a direct answer," says another. The plane is in chaos. Journalists are piled on top of each other to get near Hughes.

One word keeps coming up as reporters talk about the story and question Hughes: Clintonesque. Bush, firing up a rally in Grand Rapids, breaks from his prepared speech to ad-lib about Al Gore. "I don't know if you remember when he said he was trying to escape from the shadow of the president," Bush roars. "Well, guess what? The shadow is back."

Bush is correct about the shadow. But this time, it's following Bush, not Gore. The Bush campaign dreads the comparison, because his entire campaign is based on the restoring honor and dignity principle. There can be no comparison between the offenses, of course. But the similarities exist: In both cases, the original offense proved less damning than the efforts the men made to cover their tracks. Both men, once discovered, say they concealed their actions to protect their families. Both men, while admitting culpability, spent most of their energy blaming political opponents. And both men parsed phrases, arguing what the meaning of "is" is.

Consider some of the phrases that have been used. "There is no sexual relationship." That's what Bill Clinton said when the Monica Lewinsky scandal broke. When questions were asked today about whether Bush honestly answered past questions about arrests, his campaign offered this 1996 remark: "I do not have a perfect record as a youth." In addition to the strange use of tenses, both phrases obscured the issue. The remark suggested that Bush was still "a youth" at age 30.

The following pairings juxtapose Clinton's address in 1998 after he confessed to Ken Starr, and remarks by Bush and his spokeswoman in the past day:

"I know that my public comments and my silence about this matter gave a false impression. While my answers were legally accurate, I did not volunteer information."—*Clinton*

"The governor does not believe he said 'no.' He does not recall saying that. He believes he has always been accurate. He has not addressed this issue directly."—*Karen Hughes, Bush communications director, responding to a reporter's claim that Bush said "no" when asked about post-1968 arrests*

"I can only tell you I was motivated by many factors. First, by a desire to protect myself from the embarrassment of my own conduct. I was also very concerned about protecting my family."—*Clinton*

"This arrest is something that he felt did not set a good example and is not something he discussed with his daughters. . . . The governor has twin daughters who were at a very impressionable age. He made a decision as a father that he did not want to set that bad example for his daughters."—*Hughes*

"The fact that these questions were being asked in a politically inspired lawsuit, which has since been dismissed, was a consideration, too. In addition, I had real and serious concerns about an independent counsel investigation that began with private business dealings 20 years ago."—*Clinton*

"I find interesting that four or five days before an election it's coming to the surface. . . . This happened 24 years ago. . . . A Democrat official in Maine has put this information out. . . . I believe most Americans are going to come to the conclusion that this is dirty politics."—*Bush, November 2 and 3*

"It is time to stop the pursuit of personal destruction and the prying into private lives and get on with our national life. . . . I ask you to turn away from the spectacle of the past seven months, to repair the fabric of our national discourse, and to return our attention to all the challenges and all the promise of the next American century." —*Clinton*

"Washington doesn't have to be a place of bitterness and acrimony and finger-pointing. There's a better way. Our administration will unite this country to serve the people, to get the people's business done."—*Bush*

At the rally in Grand Rapids, where a sign declaring "Honesty Works" floated before the cameras, Bush tries again to quiet the storm. "It's become clear to America over the course of this campaign that I've made mistakes in my life," he says. "But I'm proud to tell you that I've learned from those mistakes." The friendly crowd erupts in an extended cheer. If the rest of the country reacts the same way, Bush will share another trait in common with Clinton: survival.

31

★ ☆ ★

Hanging Chad

On Election Night, while George W. Bush was back in Austin and Al Gore returned to Nashville, I went to the National Press Club, the adopted home of Ralph Nader.

The event was billed as Nader's "Election Night Reception," complete with cash bar and Andean musicians playing New Age and Gypsy music. Calling it a victory party, after all, would have been a bit rich for a man hoping for 5 percent of the vote. The only question was whether Nader's bash would turn into Spoiler Central.

As midnight came to Nader's celebration and it appeared Bush had Gore on the ropes, James Williamson, a Nader volunteer from Massachusetts in beard and ponytail, joked to another Naderite: "It's all our fault."

"No, it's not," the other man replied seriously.

"I know," Williamson said quickly. When I asked about the exchange, Williamson elaborated. "Certainly there will be people who point the finger of blame. I don't believe it for a minute."

Well, believe it. Nader, who made a record three concession speeches on Election Night and gleefully danced from interview to interview, failed miserably in his bid for the 5 percent of the vote needed to make his Green Party viable in the future. But his 98,000 votes in Florida were more than enough to sink Gore.

Heck, forget about Nader's 98,000 votes. With Gore losing by only 537 votes in Florida, even the lesser third parties can claim spoiler status. Consider the showing of Socialist Party candidate David McReynolds, who netted 622 votes—84 more than Gore needed to win.

What does McReynolds have to say for himself? "You have reached the Socialist Party campaign office, where our motto is, 'It's not our fault

371

that Al Gore lost Florida,'" says the message tape in the party's New York office.

Also playing spoilers for Gore were Natural Law candidate John Hagelin, running on a transcendental meditation platform (2,281 votes), and the Socialist Workers Party's James Harris (562 votes). Greg McCarten, campaign director for Harris, who advocates a revolution of workers and farmers, tells me Harris's tally didn't "tip the scales" to Bush. And besides, he says, "other liberal Democrats like Ralph Nader got many more votes."

Williamson was right: everybody will blame Nader.

I rolled into the office just before noon on the day after the election, just in time for my editor to stroll by and suggest that I might like to be in Tallahassee right then. Out went the long-planned vacation to Argentina. Within two hours, I was on a flight to Florida.

The National Weather Service issued a tornado watch for the Tallahassee area on November 9—and with good reason. Under leaden skies and fierce rain and wind, a series of political twisters ripped through the grounds of the State Capitol.

Thirty TV cameras waited on the steps of the Old Capitol Building and fifty microphones crowded a lectern in the plaza while hundreds of reporters waited for news of the presidential vote recount in Florida. Hundreds of protesters held a sit-in inside the Capitol rotunda. Finally, the dignified form of James Baker emerged from the building to announce to the world the obvious: "The presidential election is on hold."

Just over an hour later, the Democrats retaliated with their own former secretary of state. Warren Christopher, in a natty double-breasted pinstripe suit with pocket hankie, approached reporters with a slow and grave gait that evoked judiciousness, or perhaps arthritis. "There are serious and substantial irregularities," he professed.

Along with Christopher came Bill Daley. A son of the man who many believe stole the presidency from Nixon in 1960, this Daley was concerned that Bush was stealing the 2000 election from the Democrats. Bush "blithely dismissed the disenfranchisement of thousands of Floridians," Gore's chairman said. As Republicans "presumptively crown themselves the victors," the aggrieved Democrats would back "legal action to demand some redress." Them's fightin' words.

Inside the New Capitol—actually, a skyscraper with barred windows that looks like a high-rise prison—toiled the frenetic and harassed Clay Roberts. As director of Florida's Elections Division, he is in the middle of the tornado. Chased by hundreds of reporters, he has been forced to put up a sign outside his office, next to pamphlets urging "Stamp Out Voter Fraud," that says, "No Media Beyond This Point." A cop stands guard. The officer estimates that some 700 reporters have come to the 18th-floor offices, "about 3,000 times each."

"No hablo ingles," said Roberts when I ambushed him as he left his office. Pursued into an elevator and down to a cafeteria where he purchased a very large Diet Coke, Roberts lamented that he was "getting mobbed." After two all-nighters, "I had to unplug the phone from the wall" to sleep last night, he said. Roberts said he had no idea his job would turn into this. Sure, he's had recounts before, but "usually we do it without satellite trucks outside."

At his press conference in the Capitol plaza, Baker was asked what foreigners would think of the American electoral confusion. "We cannot argue that it is good," he said.

Indeed, on Tuesday, November 7, Americans lived in the most stable democracy in the world. But by Wednesday, America had developed some embarrassing similarities to Yugoslavia. The election results are now in dispute. The candidate with fewer votes has declared himself the winner, while the other side levels allegations of miscounts and illegal ballots. The disputed vote is from a state governed by a brother of one of the candidates. Sounds like it's time to call in some international election observers.

"A state of 15 million people is in a position to decide the world?" asked Norio Yataka, correspondent for Japan's Kyodo News, who was trying to sort things out in the Capitol. "A national election is being controlled by counties? It's impossible. Why such confusion?"

On the Capitol grounds, Floridians watched the spectacle. An entrepreneurial paperboy sold copies of an early election edition of the *Tallahassee Democrat* declaring "It's President Bush"—for $5 each. "They're gonna be worth hundreds," he predicted. Inside the Capitol, David Morgan, a Vietnam veteran who joined the sit-in, was embarrassed for his state's "cock-up," as he put it. "Now we're the center of the world, for Chrissake."

Something very strange happened on Election Night to Deborah Tannenbaum, a Democratic Party official working in Florida's Volusia County. At 10 p.m., she called the county elections department and learned that Al Gore was leading George W. Bush, 83,000 votes to 62,000. So far, so good.

But when she checked the county's website for an update a half-hour later, she found a startling development: Gore's count had dropped by 16,000 votes, while an obscure Socialist candidate had picked up 10,000— all because of a single precinct with only 600 voters. The aberration Tannenbaum found was relayed to County Judge Michael McDermott, the election overseer. "We have a problem here," he said.

He sure did. It was the beginning of a week-long tragicomedy of errors in this central Florida county. Some breathtaking bungling has done much to put the validity of the American presidential election in serious, if not terminal, doubt. Volusia's mess is in some ways more damning than the mix-up in Palm Beach County, where 19,000 Gore voters mistakenly punched their ballots for Buchanan. While Palm Beach's problem involves a single confusing ballot design, Volusia's systemic woes undermine confidence in the whole Florida election process. The causes are not fraud or corruption but lax state oversight, low funding, obsolete technology and training problems—general ineptitude.

On Election Night, six precincts found they couldn't transmit their results, and the county's returns were delayed until 3 a.m. Then sheriff's deputies went on a 3 a.m. manhunt for an election worker who left with two uninspected bags. They found her an hour later and escorted her back to the office.

Wednesday, when county officials were attempting a recount in front of TV cameras, an elderly poll worker walked in with a bagful of ballots that had been left in his car the previous night. By Thursday, the elections office was surrounded by police tape, and a local Bush official had been thrown out of a meeting for getting too rowdy.

Friday, county workers found one ballot bag in their vault without a seal, another with a broken seal, and a third on a shelf with ballots spilling out of it. Meanwhile, dozens of black students from a local college complained that they had been turned away from polling stations even though they were registered to vote.

Saturday, 300 county workers and hundreds more party observers converged on county offices for an arduous manual recount of nearly 200,000 ballots. Volusia is one four Florida counties for which the Democrats requested such a hand count. It wasn't long into the recount when they realized—oops!—that they'd missed a couple hundred ballots in the first count.

"No wonder people in the North think we're a bunch of bumbling idiots—because we are," says James Clayton, a DeLand lawyer—and he represents Bush. "From a practical standpoint, nobody has any faith in the system." Douglas Daniels, a local lawyer for Gore, predicts there will be "television movies about how the election was stolen in Volusia County." He frets that Volusia will become conspiracists' new "Grassy Knoll gunman."

Florida's 67 counties have produced enough electoral bumbling to make both sides despair. There are, of course, the famous dimpled ballots of Miami-Dade, Broward and Palm Beach counties. There's Seminole County, where Republicans tampered with absentee ballot requests. One of my favorite examples is Nassau County, north of Jacksonville. After Bush lost 51 votes in a recount, the Bush-backers who run the local elections board decided to disregard the recount. When I visited John Cascone on Amelia Island the day after this outrage, he described the scene of deliberation: "People were getting very hostile," he told me. "They wanted to jump on me like I'm some villain."

The Republicans have reason to gripe, too. In Pensacola, the local Chamber of Commerce declared November to be Military Appreciation Month. There are flags aflutter downtown and banners declaring "Thank You, Military." Local schoolchildren compete in an essay contest titled "How the U.S. Military Has Affected My Life." The Democratic Party, though, found an ironic way to commemorate Military Appreciation Month. Its lawyers tried to disqualify as many absentee ballots sent in by overseas military personnel as possible.

The rationale was simple: in this whisker-close election, it pays to suppress votes likely to go to your opponent (and the county, Escambia, gave Bush 63 percent of the vote). But as a legal matter, the Democrats' effort in Pensacola was largely unsuccessful. And as a public relations matter, it was disastrous. By trying to void overseas military votes, the Democrats contradicted their professed desire to count every vote, and they opened themselves to charges that they're hostile to the American military.

At Rosie O'Grady's, a downtown bar where models of old planes hang from the ceilings and the obligatory shot of the Blue Angels sits amid the sports memorabilia, Tim Tellier, playing a game at the bar at lunchtime, says he and his father, both veterans, are "very upset" about the ballot issue. In fact, he says, the whole thing "sucks." And that's not Republican bluster: Tellier voted for Nader.

Both sides have plenty to be sore about in Florida. In the Democratic cosmos, the faithful see the Bush Republicans seeking to push through an incomplete count because a full tally would give Gore the presidency. They see Republicans working to suppress the votes of the elderly and minorities in south Florida. They see Republicans hypocritically trying to count military absentee ballots, even those that plainly didn't meet Florida's legal standards. They see Republicans tampering with absentee ballot requests in Seminole County, sending a mob to obstruct a recount in Miami-Dade and seeking to thwart "the will of the people" by using a partisan legislature to rewrite the law. And they believe Bush is only in contention because thousands of Gore voters in Palm Beach County accidentally cast ballots for Buchanan.

The Republicans, on the other hand, see Democrats repeatedly manipulating ballots, hunting for Gore votes that weren't actually cast. They see Democrats hypocritically demanding that every vote be counted while working hard to disqualify legitimate votes from military personnel. They see a partisan Florida Supreme Court engaging in judicial activism to rewrite the law to favor Gore. And they believe Gore is only a contender because the TV networks' premature call of Florida for Gore sent home hundreds, if not thousands, of Republican voters in the Panhandle, which is largely in the Central Time Zone and where the polls had not yet closed.

The solution to this is obvious: Have a hand recount throughout the state using the broadest standards on all ballots, whether absentee military ballots in north Florida or hanging chads in south Florida. This being Florida, though, and the two campaigns being what they are, we seem headed in the opposite direction: counting the fewest possible ballots.

The Democrats' effort to alter the course of history has an unlikely headquarters: two storefronts in a strip mall a couple of miles from the Capitol, in between a nail salon and a Mediterranean buffet. The Gore campaign's lease on its office space was about to end, so local staff moved in here with Democratic Party officials and national campaign aides, who have flown in from around the country. "I'm having clothes overnighted to me, so I feel much better," one woman told a colleague. The place has a few folding tables and chairs scattered about, along with a couple of computers, boxes of Dunkin' Donuts and cold pizza. Today, in the room where the lawyers hang out, the air conditioning was broken and toilet paper was on the bathroom floor because the holder was broken, as was the doorknob.

Presiding over the logistics is Democratic operative Jill Alper, who crouches in a fetal position in one corner talking into a telephone. Another man sits with a cell phone to one ear and a landline to the other. Alper and her workers keep in touch with lawyers and recount watchers in each of Florida's counties, making sure their numbers matched the official recount tally. Any sign of irregularities is passed on to the lawyers in the next room.

As the din of cell phones and shouting continues, Nick Baldick, Gore's Florida campaign chairman, walks into the makeshift office to survey the effort. I ask if he might just pull this off. "I think we might," he says. The Democrats, seeking to raise more doubts about Florida's results, have set up an 800 number to take reports (noted on "Election Day Problem and Complaint" forms) from citizens about abuses and irregularities in the vote. Among the findings: Doris from Boynton Beach may have voted for Buchanan by mistake, Martin from Boca Raton found the print on the ballot too small, and Joseph, also from Boca, had to jiggle the punch card to line up the right hole next to Gore's name.

So far, the Democrats airing their grievances in Tallahassee are more visible than the Republicans. Finally, at 7 p.m., a couple dozen young men arrive on the Capitol plaza to cheer for Bush. Four of them bare their chests to spell B-U-S-H, while others hold signs saying, "My Grand-mother Can Vote Correctly—Why Can't Yours?" and "Daley—Go Back to Cook County."

The Bush crew is going to heroic lengths to hide its post-campaign campaign war room, located here in Tallahassee. "I do apologize, but our office is closed," said the operator this morning at the Florida Republican Party, Bush's headquarters, where dozens of staffers were hard at work. How about an address? "Not at this time."

The phone book provided two addresses, one of which turned out to be the State Capitol and the other the Mason School of Music. Ray Sullivan, a local Bush spokesman, declined to divulge the location. Finally, a local Republican official spilled the beans: 420 East Jefferson. And sure enough, there was the three-story red-brick "George Bush Republican Center." Discarded campaign signs filled a trash barrel downstairs. But there were no tours. "You'll have to wait outside," said the person who answered when a reporter knocked on the "Staff Only" door.

Staking out the Tallahassee offices of Greenberg Traurig, which Bush's lawyers have been using as an overflow location, provided little more information. It could be learned that Barry Richard, who is leading Bush's efforts in Palm Beach County, was wearing jeans and a denim shirt and drove a Land Rover, but he had little time to talk.

Chaos reined in Tallahassee. A call to the state Republican Party to see when Baker would speak produced this response: "I have no idea. CNN and MSNBC are reporting that Baker will speak at 11:30." Sure enough, at 11:30 Baker emerged from the Capitol with Joe Allbaugh, Bush's campaign manager, acting as a blocker. As it began to spit rain, the diplomat spoke diplomatically, noting that the disputed ballot had been "approved by Democratic officials."

Three Nader supporters tried to get their signs in front of the cameras: "Fuzzy Voting" and "A Vote for Gore Is a Vote for Buchanan." All three voted for Nader, but, said Chris Busby, a student, "more people voted for Al Gore, so he should be the president." Soon after this protest, students from three local colleges began a sit-in in what passes for the New Capitol's atrium. They listed their complaints about the election on a pad. "We will sit here until our concerns are heard," their leader declared. Good thing they brought pillows.

Through the day, the two sides held dueling press briefings and conference calls while various numbers floated about from the recount. Gore was down 1,700, then 1,000, then back to 1,700, then 950. But it became clear that the recount itself wouldn't much matter. Bigger questions include the thousands of ballots in Palm Beach County that weren't counted and wouldn't be recounted. Those will be settled in court, another day. Or so the Democrats promise. At the Democrats' press conference, lawyer Kendall Coffey warned that the ballot "is completely illegal" and that the erratic returns "cry out for justice." Such "extraordinary confusion" would require legal remedies, including the possibility of a new election in Palm Beach County.

Inside the Capitol, the tornado had touched down. Outside, the rain was coming down hard.

Gore campaign spokesman Doug Hattaway had expected to be at a dinner party in Boston the Saturday after the election, and he was to have spent the week getting vaccinations for an upcoming trip to the Ecuadorian Amazon. Instead he finds himself in Florida, on the plaza of the State Capitol in Tallahassee, discussing hanging chad.

"I've heard of dimpled chad, pregnant chad and hanging chad," marvels Hattaway as we eat amberjack for lunch at Barnacle Bill's. He's referring to the bits of paper punched from ballots that have become a crucial part of the Florida presidential election recount. And he doesn't even mention swinging chad or bent chad.

While Hattaway haggles over chad, Florida Governor Jeb Bush, who happens to be George W.'s brother, is doing the people's business. Here he is, chairing a meeting of his Cabinet and discussing the intricacies of warrantee deeds in escrow. Then he's off to talk with citizens in Florida's Panhandle about schools and nursing homes. And there he is again, giving a technology address, meeting with his environmental protection chief and signing death warrants.

Whenever he is asked about the electoral mess in Florida, he talks of pain. "It breaks my heart to see passions overflow," he said today. "There's gonna be a lot of wounds that need to be healed." Not least of which are his own.

It's been a rough ten days for George W. Bush's younger brother. Some Republicans on the national scene grumble that he deserves some of the blame for W.'s failure to score a big win in Florida. One of his cousins is suspected of leaking media exit polls to the Bush campaign, and his state is being called a banana republic. As if that weren't enough, the *New York Post* reported this week that his 16-year-old son was caught in a naked romp in a car at a Tallahassee mall.

But Jeb Bush, who has recused himself from the elections debate, has sought to sail above it all. Before a Cabinet meeting, I wait with a gaggle of reporters at the bottom of the spiral staircase the governor takes from his office to the wood-paneled conference room in the Capitol basement. "A larger crowd than normal," Bush remarks with feigned surprise when he catches sight of the group.

Bush does his best to make the meeting business-as-usual. Drinking coffee from a mug decorated with flying geese, he sits in a dignified posture with reading glasses perched on his nose. He jokes with Bill Nelson, Florida's Democratic senator-elect, and playfully punches the state's agriculture commissioner when he's caught not paying attention to proceedings.

Two seats away is Katherine Harris, the secretary of state, who is overseeing the election. Beaming before the cameras, she drinks from a colorful mug and at one point shows a drawing to the other Cabinet members. "I just thought it was cool," she says. "See—you can see the Temple Mount."

Ah, yes, Katherine Harris. The same Katherine Harris who a few years ago had a nightclub act doing the chicken dance. Last winter, Harris, a former real estate broker from Sarasota, flew up to New Hampshire with other Floridians to campaign for George W. Bush, delivering oranges, strawberries and Bush fliers to state primary voters. In her zeal to elect Bush, she even kissed two lapdogs on the nose in one New Hampshire voter's home.

Now Harris, Florida's secretary of state, has announced that she would end the state's presidential vote recount a week after the election—a decision that would hand the presidency to Bush. Al Gore's spokesman, Chris

Lehane, doesn't like this: "Commissar Harris, who is a crony of the Bush brothers, a Republican hack and a lackey for the Bush campaign, is attempting to orchestrate an end run," he tells me.

The elaborately made-up Harris, 43, granddaughter of a cattle and citrus magnate, is now perhaps the most important person in determining who will be the next president of the United States. While even Republicans in Tallahassee have some doubts about her ability, there can be no doubt that she is keenly interested in the election of George W. Bush.

In addition to her work in New Hampshire for W., she was a co-chair of his Florida campaign and, with Jeb Bush, a delegate to the Republican National Convention. She recruited retired Army General Norman Schwartzkopf, a prominent Bush supporter who spoke to the GOP convention and taped phone messages for Bush in Florida, to do a taxpayer-funded get-out-the-vote commercial just before the election. This drew a rebuke from the watchdog group Common Cause.

Clearly, Jeb Bush, George W. Bush and Harris's people are on the same team, if not formally linked. Jeb's communications director and most of his legal staff have taken leaves to help W. The law firm Harris has hired to represent her office has ties to Jeb Bush. She is also using an adviser known as Mac the Knife, who ran Bush's 1994 campaign.

Behind the scenes, Jeb Bush is doing what he can for his brother—and that means not just participating in conference calls with W. and staff in Austin. On the evening of November 13, he received an e-mail from Dona Kay Hannagan, who complained that she was getting phone calls claiming that her vote and 19,000 others had been thrown out. "Are 'we' doing anything to counteract this?" Hannagan asked Bush.

Bush forwarded the note just before 11 p.m. to his communications director, Katie Baur, and his chief of staff, Sally Bradshaw. "This is a concerted effort to divide and destroy our state," he wrote.

Baur replied to Bush: "Ve have our vays also … I'm working on this." Bradshaw added: "This is obscene. I hope we are getting this to the press. Shouldn't we give them a list of all the scare tactics the Gore campaign is using?"

Baur answered Bradshaw: "Absolutely, and that is what I am gathering."

32

★ ☆ ★

No Surrender

There is a titanic struggle unfolding here in Florida's capital, a battle in which each side claims to represent the forces of good over evil, a fight with stakes so high it could alter the destiny of our nation and the future of humanity.

I speak, of course, of the Florida-Florida State game coming Saturday night, the 18th of November. What, you thought this was about politics?

Not so in Tallahassee, where the University of Florida Gators, ranked fourth in the nation, are coming to play the No. 3 Florida State Seminoles before more than 80,000 people. Forget about all the satellite trucks down at the Capitol—this is a nationally televised game. "That's more important around here than Wolf Blitzer and Bernard Shaw," says Eric Luallen, a former Florida State lineman who hosts a sports radio talk show. "Although Wolf Blitzer—that'd be a heck of a name for a linebacker."

Sure, Saturday is the day Florida is due, barring court intervention, to certify its election results, thus determining the president of the United States. But locally, the talk is about Saturday's football arch-rivalry. "Candidates will come and go, but your record against the opponent is written in stone and will be talked about in legend and song far longer than the election of candidates who just pass by," says Charlie Barnes, director of the Seminole Boosters.

Pity Florida Governor Jeb Bush, whom I find wandering rumpled and largely unnoticed through the capitol. Not only must he worry about his brother's election, he faces a no-win situation deciding which team to back on Saturday night. "That's even *more* controversial," he says when asked for his favorite.

The major concern locals have about the electoral standoff here is that the 500 or so reporters and political operatives in town will squat in the hotel rooms reserved months ago by football fans. Already, I've been kicked out of the Radisson and write this from a Victorian bed and breakfast. About forty CNN journalists at the Doubletree received eviction notices this morning; they'll stay at a Marriott until Friday, but after that "we're homeless again," says Mark Allen, who works for *Larry King Live*.

Last Saturday night, the closest room a travel agent could find for this week was in Cairo, Georgia. The *Chicago Tribune*'s Jill Zuckman, facing eviction ("parting is such sweet sorrow," the hotelier told her as she left), found a room on a plantation in Thomasville, Georgia. "I'm goin' to Georgia," says Zuckman, a Rockville native. "They told me to take Thomasville Road across the Georgia line, go eight miles and turn when I see the big ol' oak tree."

Now the right wingers have their own version of a Katherine Harris punching bag: the Florida Supreme Court. The court ruled on November 21 to allow the recounts to continue for several more days, a slap at Harris and an obvious win for Gore.

As they waited for the court's ruling, Gore's legal coordinator, Ron Klain, and his spokesman, Doug Hattaway, sat down to dinner with me and a couple of other reporters. It was a tense gathering from the start at Andrew's Second Act, a basement restaurant a block from the Supreme Court. Each of us had a cell phone in pocket, except for Hattaway, who had two phones on the table. Several false alarms sounded on Hattaway's phones before 9 p.m.—each asking if he knew anything yet. "No," Hattaway told one, "but each time I get a call my heart stops." Klain cautioned the reporters against a big buildup, suggesting the ruling could be ambiguous.

Then it happened, at about 9:15. Klain's phone rang first, followed by Hattaway's and a cacophany of the reporters' phones in rapid succession. The half-hour warning. What to do? Somebody canceled the second bottle of wine. The waiter said he could bring the entrees out, but they would be a bit rare. Klain, who had just tucked into his Caesar salad, paced a bit, then returned to the table, determined to eat his meal. After a few seconds, he reconsidered. "I have to go back," he apologized, and disappeared. Hattaway called for his bouillabaise and Klain's tuna to be brought out in styrofoam, to go.

Out on the steps and plaza in between the State Capitol and the Supreme Court building, the networks had erected blue and white tents against the unusual Florida chill, like so many arctic explorers. Most had installed propane burners with names like "Mr. Heater." The others shivered while they waited. The first level of the plaza hosted the tents of NBC,

MSNBC and ABC. The next level was home to Fox and CBS, the latter decorated with the sign "Welcome to Chadville." Towering high above it all was the CNN tent on a raised stage, where the *Larry King Live* crew, armed with a guest and with cell phones, stared down on the proceedings.

"Here we go!" somebody shouted, as the court spokesman walked to the podium erected on the court steps. A couple of tourists took each others' photos with the court as a backdrop. The spokesman's voice couldn't carry to Chadville, but the live broadcast of his announcement of the court's decision could be heard on television in each tent. Correspondents scribbled notes furiously. When the spokesman mentioned the November 27 deadline, two Gore fans in the area pumped their fists in the air. An NBC correspondent belted out the upshot to a colleague: "Gore wins—recount goes—in by next Sunday."

Soon reporters started running from the court to Chadville, the lucky ones with copies of the opinion in hand. The campaign spinmeisters, though not in evidence, were sure to follow. Surveying the scene, a CNN cameraman, his lens trained on the courthouse, offered his own analysis: "The torture continues."

Yes, the torture continues—at all hours of all days. It's Sunday morning, November 24, just after Thanksgiving. Taking a walk on the Capitol plaza in Tallahassee, I see three older gentlemen trying to get their anti-Gore signs on the cameras for the Sunday morning talk shows.

Before Election Day, the brothers Rodgers of southern Illinois and Indiana led quiet lives. Retired engineers and veterans all, they fished, golfed and gardened, doing nothing more political than planting campaign yard signs.

But when Fred, 60, saw on television that Democratic lawyers were trying to stop George W. Bush from being awarded a victory in Florida, he called his brother Ron, 65, in aggravation. "Let's go to Washington and protest this," he said.

Ron, ever the older brother, replied: "Nothing's happening in Washington. Let's go to Tallahassee. It's warmer." And so Fred, Ron and baby brother Jim, 58, hopped into Fred's Chrysler New Yorker the next day and drove 700 miles to Tallahassee, where they've remained pretty much ever since.

They share a $50-a-night motel room (with the AARP discount) and march on the Capitol plaza for twelve to fourteen hours a day—longer than any others, they say—armed with dozens of anti-Gore messages. The crudely lettered signs announce messages like "Al Gore: Commander-in-

Thief!" "Recount Rigged, Court Stacked" and "Gore Plan: Recount Until I Win."

The Florida recount has brought an unusual outpouring of Republican activism here from far-flung partisans such as the Rodgers brothers. This has fueled angry demonstrations that are encouraged, and in part orchestrated, by the Republican Party.

A Democratic official was chased by GOP protesters who suspected he was stealing a ballot (it was a sample), and a brick was thrown through the window of the Broward County Democratic offices. Demonstrators in Miami-Dade County were shouting and waving fists while rushing the offices of the elections supervisor the day before Thanksgiving. A Democratic spokesman, Luis Rosero, said he was shoved, punched and kicked by Republican demonstrators, while Democratic Congressman Peter Deutsch said he was manhandled by what he called an "illegal mob." Pickets have staked out Gore's residence in Washington.

Democrats here see the activism as organized and encouraged by the Republican Party, even as the Bush campaign and the Republicans portray themselves as above the fray. Among those photographed in demonstrations here were Tom Pyle, an aide to House Majority Whip Tom DeLay, and Doug Heye, a spokesman for Representative Richard W. Pombo (R-California). Many of the out-of-state GOP demonstrators told local reporters that the Republican National Committee paid for their travel, room and board, putting a number of them up at a Sheraton in Fort Lauderdale. Republican phone banks urged Bush voters to join the protest in Miami, and party activists joined the crowds, passing out signs and T-shirts.

The Rodgers brothers have nothing to do with any violence, but they share the passion. Each man carries a wooden stick with his name on it and a stack of signs held together by clips for easy message changes during the day. Among this morning's selection: "Katherine, Ignore Court. Certify First Count," "Gore Invented the Internet—Florida Court Invented Election Law!" and "Veterans for Bush-Cheney Say No More Gore!" Ron's favorite has a National Rifle Association bumper sticker on it and proclaims, "Butterfly Ballots Confuse Gorons." Whenever asked what a Goron is, Ron responds: "If you don't know, you must be one."

And that's not all. "We have a trunk full of signs," Fred says, leading a reporter a couple of blocks to the car. Naughty younger brother Jim calls out after him: "Look in the mirror and see if you can pop that pimple on your lip." In the trunk of the gold New Yorker are some of the Rodgers' classics: "Gore/Daley Fuzzy Math," "Gore/Daley/Boies: Liars, Cheaters and Thieves, Oh My," and "Katherine, Go Ahead and Certify."

Back on the Capitol plaza, Ron and Jim are moving around the roped-off media area, hoping one of their signs will appear on Fox or CNN. The cameramen, as usual, keep rearranging their shots to thwart the Rodgers. Yet the brothers are undeterred.

"I've got a lot of leaves in my yard that need to be mulched, so I'll have to raise my mulcher real high when I get back," Fred says. But that's a small sacrifice. "If Gore says I quit, we'll go home," he says. "If there's something going on tomorrow, we'll probably stay."

Yes, he probably will. The Tallahassee scene has come to resemble the movie *Groundhog Day*: each morning we realize we are no closer to a resolution than we were the day before.

So, three weeks after the election, here's the score: Gore has declared war on the Florida secretary of state. Bush has declared war on the Florida Supreme Court. And both have succeeded in putting into doubt the Florida electoral process and the legitimacy of the next president, whoever he is.

I've asked my editor to let me come home.

But I'm not going home before a trip to Panacea. Let the world mock Florida as a banana republic. Let partisans of George W. Bush and Al Gore talk about a disenfranchised electorate. In Panacea, Florida, all is well. "They're making jokes, I reckon, but it doesn't bother me," says Tammy Nichols, a fisherman's wife who is doing her shift as a waitress at Posey's Restaurant. "There's a lot of people think the election system is all messed up. I don't see what the problem is." Eating lunch in Posey's, Carlton Smith, 99, agrees. "There's a few things that could be changed," he says, but "it's not a problem for me." Nearby, on the shores of the Gulf of Mexico, Hank Agerton unloads mullet from a cooler on the back of his pickup truck and discusses the election. "I don't think they've messed up," he tells me. Just down Route 98, on the other end of Panacea, Bonnie Holub, an environmental consultant, thinks the critics have it wrong. "Outside Florida, people have little comments about 'who are these people who can't run an election,'" she says. "It doesn't feel that way here. It's stimulated interest in the political process." The Panglossian sentiment in Panacea is echoed in conversations with voters in other parts of this state. Yes, this process has been a hassle, and yes, it's a bit embarrassing to have Florida's electoral flaws exposed. But ordinary Floridians, unlike the political gladiators on television and the angry demonstrators (often from out-of-state), tend to view their home-state controversy with equanimity. Their silver-lining view is that this fierce and bitter contest has strengthened interest and participation in the political system. Holub, who voted for Gore—"at least I think I did," she jokes—believes Florida's controversy "points out how serious we are about choosing our leaders. It's tiresome and it's tedious, but that's what democracy is." That sounds right to me. Smashmouth politics, far from alienating the electorate, has brought a surge of interest in politics.

I continue my farewell trip by going south to Seminole County, scene of a legal dispute over absentee ballots that Democrats allege have been illegally handled by Republicans. The location is Barney's Bar-B-Q in the Orlando suburb of Altamonte Springs. I overhear Pat McKee, a fertilizer company worker, in a lengthy political conversation with his fourteen-year-old son, Daniel. "I think Gore's been a sore loser," Daniel is telling his father. "It's been recounted and recounted." The elder McKee, a Seminole resident, is amazed at how the controversy has gripped his son. "Until this happened, he didn't talk about politics—not at all," Pat says. "He'd talk about airplanes." Daniel, an eighth-grader, says all the kids are following the election mess. "Our social studies teacher, she keeps us up on it," says Daniel, who supported Bush in the school election. "In class, they're letting us watch the news, the recounts." His father sees good coming of this for Daniel—and for the rest of us. "I'd like to see it as a learning thing," he says. "I think we're a resilient country. We may not get it the first time, and we may not get it the second time, but eventually we'll get it straightened out."

That's the most sensible thing I've heard in three weeks in Florida.

As November stretches into December, Bush gains a larger aura of inevitability each day. Still, the Gore team continues to put up a brave front. On the very night Harris certifies the election results that give Bush a 537-vote victory, a Gore lawyer called me with some interesting news. "We win," he said, sketching out Gore's certain victory in the coming "contests" to the vote certification. An hour later, I found Greg Simon, the singing Gore aide, in the bar of the Doubletree Hotel, mapping out the same path to victory for me on a cocktail napkin.

The scene has become a familiar one: a Gore campaign that reads like an open book, particularly compared to a Bush campaign that keeps its own counsel. David Boies, Gore's top lawyer, could be found over the weekend sitting in Andrew's Second Act in his trademark rumpled attire, test-marketing his legal arguments on reporters while munching on chicken fingers and drinking orange juice.

At about the time Boies was holding forth, I placed a call to Mindy Tucker, Bush's spokeswoman in Tallahassee, following up on a phone call

Tucker hadn't yet returned from the morning. "She's gone for the day," an assistant said, adding that there was no way to reach her.

The campaigns have always been this way, to an extent. Last summer, Bush spokesman Ari Fleischer, who declined to give me his cell phone number, proudly displayed the easily obtained cell phone number of Gore spokesman Chris Lehane.

The Gore campaign's accessibility and the Bush side's remoteness have become more pronounced since Election Day. And this is no accident. "They have no choice but to spin like a top," Fleischer says of the other side. "One reason the Gore campaign is reaching so furiously to spin is they have a sense it's slipping away. We're able to handle this in a more gracious, dignified, leader-like manner."

The Gore people, of course, have a different view. "It's an approach that respects the American people," Lehane says. "The Bush campaign's strategy has been not to let the American people have information in front of them." Gore's aggressive PR posture, by contrast, "has allowed people to see that if every ballot is counted, Al Gore wins."

But in truth, Fleischer is correct. The Gore aides do see things slipping away. Privately, they are beginning to see their cause as a long shot. "We have to draw an inside straight, and they're holding all the cards," one of them tells me by phone a couple of days after the latest show of force.

Each passing day puts another, seemingly insurmountable obstacle in Gore's way. There's the small matter of W.'s brother, who happens to be the Florida governor. While reporters encircled the State Capitol on the night Harris finally was allowed to certify a Bush victory, three aides to Jeb Bush sneaked out under cover of darkness to hand over to the Florida governor the documents that would officially deliver the state to his brother.

The three aides drove the few blocks to the governor's mansion, carrying the "Certificate of Ascertainment," a list of electors to be sent to the national archivist. The certificate already had Harris's signature, but it required one more: Jeb Bush's.

So at 8:41 p.m., Bush, who had recused himself from the certification process, took a break from a relaxing Sunday night to sign the certificate giving Florida's 25 electoral votes to George W. Bush. But even the day after, the occasion was shrouded in secrecy. "I don't feel that I need to respond," said Baur.

Nor, presumably, does she feel a need to respond to Jeb's next bombshell: that, if appropriate, he would sign legislation naming a slate of George W. Bush electors if the courts came up with something different.

W. doesn't seem likely to need it, but his brother has brought out the safety net just in case democracy fails him.

The safety net, though, gets less necessary by the minute amid a blizzard of legal activity. The U.S. Supreme Court, in a case that has oddly become a sideshow, has concluded that the original recount should stand rather than the one Harris was forced to certify by the Florida Supreme Court. This gives W. a lead of nearly 1,000 votes.

Next, Gore lost his "contest" before Leon County Circuit Judge N. Sanders Sauls. The judge rejected every last challenge by Gore: no recount of the ballots in Palm Beach, no count of the uncounted ballots in Miami-Dade, not even an order to honor the recounted tally in Nassau County. Boies had said he'd give up the practice of law if he lost that one. Don't hold your breath.

Even as Gore quixotically presses on to the bitter end, his supporters and advisers are acquiescing in a Bush presidency. Al From, father of the New Democratic movement, tells me the election was a "tie." Sure, he thinks Gore won by a hair, but by definition, From says, you can't "steal" an election that was a tie. "It's petty theft as opposed to grand larceny," he says.

It's become fashionable to bemoan the damage the controversy is doing to our institutions: the presidency, the courts, democracy itself. The hand-wringers at the Harvard Kennedy School's "Vanishing Voter Project" have announced that Americans find the electoral dispute "depressing." Too bad. Buried in the poll results is the finding that an astounding 59 percent of the public is paying close attention to politics—a higher percentage even than during the campaign.

So much for vanishing voters. Let the K-School good-government types continue to talk about disenchantment. When the smoke clears, Americans will see their system vindicated: after the election ended in a statistical tie, our courts and elected leaders, though divided, were able to determine a winner, the presidency and the Constitution proved resilient—and everybody lived happily ever after.

Bill Schneider is on CNN warning, almost gleefully, of a "nightmare scenario." It's Friday night, December 8, and Gore has just won a surprise 4–3 victory in Florida's Supreme Court, which has ordered the statewide counting of "undervotes"—those ballots in which machines didn't pick up a presidential vote. Bush's lead is down below 200 and sure to shrink further. Schneider talks breathlessly of the election being decided in Congress now, after the court names Gore the winner and the state legislature names Bush the winner.

Crises like these tend to bring out the best of Bushisms. The last time the Florida court ruled against him, Bush complained, with a straight face, that "the court cloaked its ruling in legalistic language." (Was he expecting them to write their opinion in verse?) This time, though, he leaves it to Baker to return to his practice of trashing Florida's highest court.

The nightmare scenario, as it turns out, vanishes as rapidly as it appeared. One news cycle later, a conservative majority on the U.S. Supreme Court, temporarily shelving its love of states rights, decides to halt the recounts. Apparently, the justices agree with Bush that there would be "irreparable harm" to his presidency if it turned out his opponent actually won Florida. That would be embarrassing.

Unfortunately for Gore, Bush has too many insurance policies protecting his ascension. Justice Antonin Scalia. Dad's Justice Clarence Thomas. The Republican Florida legislature. The Republican U.S. House. For Bush, it's not a question of victory, but a question of how ugly the win will be.

On Sunday, December 10, I fly to Austin for the coronation, just in time to see Bush return to the governor's mansion from his ranch for some Christmas parties. In blue jeans and work shirt, he hops out of a mud-spattered Suburban and works the crowd outside. "I just want to come over here and shake these young gentlemen's hands," says Bush, as he greets Ryan Klimovitz, six years old, and Alex Morrow, five. Ryan's parents can hardly believe their luck. "Oh my—he kissed her cheek, too," gushes Wayne Klimovitz, holding up his eighteen-month-old daughter, Sarah, who is busy sucking on a Mickey Mouse toy. "She got kissed by the president!"

The president. It no longer sounds presumptuous.

I am in Sullivan's Steakhouse, a block from Bush headquarters in Austin, when it finally happens the night of December 12. The television in the bar, tuned to Fox News, reports that the United States Supreme Court, which already stopped the recount temporarily, has reached a final decision. The first headline, that the case is being sent back to Florida, sounds inconclusive. "Man, nobody wants to make a fuckin' decision!" groans one man at the bar. But then we get to the bottom line: there will be no recount. W. will become our 43rd president, installed by a divided Supreme Court to govern a public that gave more votes to the man he defeated. Should be an interesting four years.

The Bush advisers, true to form, have decided to mark the occasion by disappearing. A few reporters, our phone calls unanswered, get our steaks to go and dash over to Bush headquarters, but a security guard sends us away. I stop by the governor's mansion, where the president-elect has been holed up all day, but there is nothing: no celebration, no demonstrators, no spectators, just a few dozen cameramen puzzling over the ruling. After all the talk of triumphal rallies and victory parties, it has all ended on a cold and icy night in Austin, with barely a whisper.

Back in my hotel room, I get a call from Chris Lehane. "You calling to concede?" I ask. No, Lehane assures me. There will be no concession. Gore plans to turn his official residence at the Naval Observatory into a modern-day Alamo, refusing to surrender. While Gore plays Davey Crockett, "we'll all be there at the ramparts, in formation," Lehane says. I picture Gore manning the catapult and throwing hot oil on Cheney as he lays siege to the v.p.'s residence. Gore may have lost in legal and public opinion, but as long as he's at the observatory, he still has the high ground—topographically speaking.

Then again, maybe that won't work. Even smashmouth politics has its limits.

INDEX